Integrating Academic Units in the Elementary School Curriculum

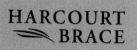

Integrating Academic Units in the Elementary School Curriculum

Cynthia Sunal

Deborah Powell

Inez Rovegno

Coralee Smith

Dennis Sunal
University of Alabama—Tuscaloosa

Susan McClelland
Tuscaloosa County Schools

Audrey Rule
Tuscaloosa City Schools

Harcourt College Publishers

Fort Worth   Philadelphia   San Diego   New York   Orlando
Austin   San Antonio   Toronto   Montreal   London
Sydney   Tokyo

Publisher	Earl McPeek
Acquisitions Editor	Carol Wada
Developmental Editor	Emma Gutler
Project Editor	Claudia Gravier, Michele Tomiak
Art Director	David A. Day
Production Manager	Andrea Archer

ISBN: 0-15-503953-9
Library of Congress Catalog Card Number: 99-64582

Address for Domestic Orders
Harcourt Inc., 6277 Sea Harbor Drive, Orlando, FL 32887-6777
800-782-4479

Address for International Orders
International Customer Service
Harcourt Inc., 6277 Sea Harbor Drive, Orlando, FL 32887-6777
407-345-3800
(fax) 407-345-4060
(e-mail) hbintl@harcourtcollege.com

Address for Editorial Correspondence
Harcourt College Publishers, 301 Commerce Street, Suite 3700, Fort Worth, TX 76102

Web Site Address
http://www.harcourtcollege.com

Harcourt College Publishers will provide complimentary supplements or supplement packages to those adopters qualified under our adoption policy. Please contact your sales representative to learn how you qualify. If as an adopter or potential user you receive supplements you do not need, please return them to your sales representative or send them to: Attn: Returns Department, Troy Warehouse, 465 South Lincoln Drive, Troy, MO 63379.

Printed in the United States of America

9 0 1 2 3 4 5 6 7 8 066 9 8 7 6 5 4 3 2 1

Harcourt College Publishers

To all the hardworking teachers who have contributed to this book through providing opportunities to observe and work with them as they practice the art and science of teaching. Your dedication to your students is evident as you integrate teaching, "putting it all together."

To Dennis, Alisa, Paul, and Michael, who provide the foundation to my life so that I can put it all together.

PREFACE

Integrating Academic Units in the Elementary School Curriculum demonstrates a firm conviction that children should experience learning as being of a whole piece throughout their schooling. We believe meaningful learning of content, skills, and values can be fostered through integrated teaching.

Drawing upon the combined experience of nearly 200 years of public school teaching and many years in higher education teaching, supervising, and reading and contributing to research literature, we have written a book designed to illustrate the following: 1) the process or strategies for integrated teaching, 2) the structure of the knowledge to be learned, and 3) the theory and research that explain meaningful learning. This book focuses on *meaningful learning,* recognizing that students construct knowledge in their own minds so that it has meaning for them. The research literature on constructivism has contributed heavily to the approach taken in this book. As we have worked with research literature, conducted our own research, and developed and taught lessons, we have practiced what we preach. We are convinced that the approach to structuring lessons described in this book provides teachers and learners with flexibility and assures the inclusion of the best aspects of the major theories describing how students learn.

This book is rich in examples and illustrations of integrated teaching. Examples of the different types of integrated units that are possible weave throughout the text and guide the user in planning and teaching successful integrated units and lessons. The book elaborates on the steps for teaching a variety of specific strategies and provides guidance in selecting appropriate content for integrated units. Recognizing that integration of content from many disciplines is a complex and challenging task, the book focuses on ideas that have worked in a wide range of classrooms.

Many thanks to Treva Joiner for her secretarial expertise, willing assistance, and patience. We also wish to thank our acquisitions editor, Carol Wada, for her encouragement and for keeping us on task.

The suggestions and comments of the reviewers were most helpful and challenged us to think in new directions. The extensive amount of time each devoted to reviewing the manuscript for this book is much appreciated. We would like to thank: Gillian Cook, University of Texas at San Antonio; Carol Cox, California State University—Long Beach; Phyllis Huff, University of Tennessee; Barbara Nilsen, Broome Community College; Dwayne Olsen, University of Wisconsin—Parkside; Beth Tulbert, University of Utah; Chuck Watson, James Madison University; Jim Zarrillo, California State University—Hayward.

CONTENTS

Chapter 4   97
Implementing and Reflecting on the Unit

Chapter 5   118
Assessing and Evaluating Integrated Thematic Units

Chapter 8   *222*
Integrating Mathematics Components

Chapter 9   *248*
Integrating the Language Arts

Chapter 10   271
Integrating Art and Creativity Into a Thematic Unit

Chapter 11   299
Integrating Physical Education and Dance Components

CHAPTER 1

INTEGRATED TEACHING:
AN INTRODUCTION

The integration of subject matter occurs naturally during the elementary school day. A teacher in a self-contained room integrates the disciplines, playing music of the period when students are studying colonial America, having them create a mobile representing the water cycle, investigating the local plants native Americans cultivated during the 1700s, and incorporating art as part of the culmination of a unit on fractions. Even in settings where groups of children move between specialist teachers, studying science with one individual and language arts with another, there is integration. The science teacher may help children use the writing process to prepare a report of an activity they carried out, the mathematics teacher may work with children trying to devise a way to estimate the height of nearby mountains for a social studies project, and the language arts teacher may assist children as they develop oral presentations about their experiences in mathematics. The foundations of an integrated curriculum exist in elementary classrooms. The problem is how to put it all together: subject matter, children's needs, and instructional strategies.

INTEGRATION OF SUBJECT MATTER

The integration of subject matter helps children perceive learning as a whole. It means that learning is no longer focused on working with separate ideas, issues, and skills. Instead, it's trying to figure out how various ideas, issues, and skills are all connected (Atwater, 1995). In this book, integrated teaching is defined as teaching that involves planning and organizing curriculum and instruction so the subject matter disciplines are related to one another in a design matching the developmental needs of the students and connecting their learning in meaningful ways to their experiences.

Integrated teaching means moving away from depending on one source for ideas, whether it is the textbook, a trade book, a guest speaker or a "hands-on" science lesson. Instead, the teacher recognizes that both the guest speaker and the "hands-on" science lesson offer pieces that can be put together into a whole picture. Neither is completely satisfactory by itself. Elements from the world outside the classroom are integrated into the curriculum to make it more meaningful (Atwater, 1995). Depending on what idea is being investigated, one source may have greater impact than another. Therefore, it is appropriate to use one more heavily than the other. The resources used will change as different ideas are investigated.

Integrated teaching uses a variety of resources to make connections between subject areas, ideas, skills, and perspectives. The diversity found in such teaching can help teachers better address the needs of students. Children with special needs, children for whom English is not their first language, children who are under great stress: Each of these children can contribute to learning in a classroom where integrated teaching occurs.

Integrated teaching can address the preferences children of different learning styles have for various conditions under which they like to learn (Dunn, Beaudry, & Klavas, 1989). Children differ in the ways in which they go about gathering and processing information. Their styles of learning are not better or worse, just different. Intelligence consists of a variety of quite different intellectual skills. There is thought to be not just one type of intelligence but multiple intelligences (Gardner, 1983) or multidimensional intelligence (Sternberg, 1990). Gardner presents a group of intelligences qualitatively different from each other that also work independently of each other. Intelligence is effected by the context and experiences in which it arises (Gardner, 1983; Baker & Piburn, 1997). Even if a child has an exceptional talent, that is not enough for expertise to develop. The child needs experiences that bring him or her into contact with the ideas and skills needed to foster expertise. Gardner (1985) gives the example of Srinivase Ramanujan, a mathematics prodigy born in rural India. He had no formal introduction into mathematics until late in life and never developed enough expertise to make a major contribution to mathematics. Gardner concludes that beyond natural gifts, a person must be in the right place at the right time having the right experiences. Seven major types of intelligences have been identified by Gardner. These are the following.

1. Linguistic: sensitive to forms, functions, and characteristics of language. Likes and is good at reading, speaking, reciting, memorizing, and telling stories.
2. Logical-mathematical: sensitive to logical and mathematical patterns and relationships. Likes and is good at experimenting, math and reasoning problems, categorizing and classifying, logic, abstract thinking, analyzing patterns and relationships.
3. Spatial: sensitive to visual patterns and their transformations. Likes and is good at drawing, visualizing, building, interpreting maps, graphs and charts, and solving hidden puzzles and mazes.
4. Musical: sensitive to musical aspects of sound including rhythm, pitch, and timbre. Likes and is good at singing, humming, recognizing and hearing sounds and melodies, playing an instrument, keeping time, and appreciating and responding to music.
5. Bodily kinesthetic: sensitive to one's own body in space and as related to other people and objects. Likes and is good at physical activities including sports, dance, body language, using space, learning through sensation, and manipulating objects.
6. Interpersonal: sensitive to others' moods, feelings, and emotions. Likes and is good at making friends, talking to people, joining, leading, sharing, organizing, conflict resolution, and cooperation in groups.
7. Intrapersonal: sensitive to one's own feelings, strengths, and weaknesses. Likes and is good at using self-knowledge to make affective and cognitive decisions, working alone, being original, pursuing personal goals, focusing inward, and following instincts.

The diversity inherent in integrated teaching makes a place for each child. The same outcomes are not expected from each child. Instead, the focus is on helping each child find meaning in the ideas, skills, and perspectives under investigation (Sunal, Sunal, McClelland, Powell, & Allen, 1994).

How learning is integrated within the curriculum varies depending on the teacher's own instructional and learning style, level of understanding of and comfort with various content areas, the structure of the school setting and school day, the time available for planning and implementing integrated curricula, levels of parental support and interest, and administrative support and interest (Atwater, 1995). These are some, but not all of the factors influencing each teacher's integration of content in the elementary school.

There are many ways and levels at which to integrate the curriculum. The curriculum can be integrated within a single discipline (Fogarty, 1991a). Language arts is an example of the effort to integrate components including spelling, grammar, listening, speaking, and writing. Traditional classrooms often do not accomplish within-subject integration (Atwater, 1995). Instead, facts, skills, and concepts are taught in a way far removed from the overviews and models that make them meaningful. Students don't perceive the whole picture because they seldom see it.

Integration can occur across several disciplines (Fogarty, 1991b). For example, students might study magnets in an integrated approach. They investigate polarity and other ideas studied by scientists. They examine the use of magnets by people at home and in industry, conducting an investigation of these uses as a social scientist might. They calculate the weights lifted by magnets of various sizes. They write about their experiences using magnets and draw machines that incorporate magnets.

A THEORETICAL BASIS FOR INTEGRATED TEACHING

Constructivism provides a theoretical basis for integrated teaching. There is a group of theories that hold that people are not recorders of information, but builders of knowledge structures that have come to be grouped under the heading of constructivism (Resnick & Klopfer, 1989). These theories share the view that children construct knowledge from their experiences. Because each child's experience in life differs, students come to school with varied ideas. Those ideas affect new information received. What a student learns, therefore, results from the interaction between what is brought to the learning situation and what is experienced while in it (Stofflett, 1994). Prior thoughts and understandings exert a strong influence on what we learn and how we interpret data we collect (Bransford & Vye, 1981; Driver, Leach, Millar, & Scott, 1996).

Learners create their own knowledge in a search for meaning and understanding. Knowledge without understanding is limited to the context in which it is learned and is easily forgotten. Constructivists stress the search for meaning in learning and focus on the process of learning, on learning to learn. Understanding is not acquired passively and can't be transferred from one person to another. The learner must actively construct meaning (Brooks, 1990). Traditional and constructivist classrooms have been compared by Brooks and Brooks (1993) (see Figure 1.1).

Learning must take place in a supportive environment in which it is safe to take risks in order for the learner to be able to construct new meaning

A Comparison of Traditional and Constructivist Classrooms   FIGURE 1.1

Classroom Comparisons	
Traditional	Constructivist
Curriculum presented part to whole	Curriculum presented whole to part
Emphasis on basic skills	Emphasis on big concepts
Strict adherence to fixed curriculum	Pursuit of student questions
Heavy reliance on textbooks and workbooks	Heavy use of primary sources and manipulatives
Teaching is disseminating information	Teaching is interactive, mediating the environment
Teacher seeks correct answers	Teacher seeks students' points of view
Teacher pretests knowledge	Teacher seeks to understand students' prior conceptions
Students mostly work alone	Students mostly work in groups

(Costa, 1992). Confusion and error can be acknowledged in such a setting and thus made meaningful (Sizer, 1991). The teacher provides a facilitative environment but cannot do the work of learning for the student because learning is a process of active construction by the learner (Schlechty, 1990; National Research Council, 1995).

Students construct meaning by having authentic experiences that involve and integrate all aspects of the idea or skill being learned. As students construct meaning, they build relationships between old and new knowledge. Learning in a subject area is enhanced when relationships can be built between that area and others (Cooper, 1993). People seek to understand how one idea is connected to other ideas. These connections make an idea meaningful. In building these connections, each person creates a knowledge structure in his mind. Gradually, different knowledge structures are created for sets of ideas. Connections are made between the different knowledge structures in the mind, and the complexity of our minds and our learning increases (Sunal, Sunal, & Haas, 1996). Such connections have been described by Holliday, Yore, and Alvermann (1994) in a discussion of reading and science learning. They describe both reading and science as interactive-constructive processes. Reading and science learning are described as interactions between prior knowledge, concurrent experience, and information accessed from print, science experiences, and other sources in a specific social context that is focused on constructing meaning.

Reading is an interactive and constructive process (Holliday, Yore, & Alvermann). Readers interactively process information by switching between selective perceptions of text-based information (print, charts, pictures) and concurrent experiences (concrete inquiries, discussions, thinking), and comparison of the information and experiences with their personal knowledge (topic, domain, scientific enterprise, textual, strategic).

The personal knowledge is retrieved from long-term memory to construct plausible interpretations (models) of the situation in short-term memory. Readers increase or change their understanding in two ways. They can either extract information from text, other people, and concurrent experiences and then assimilate this information into knowledge structures retrieved from their long-term memories. Or, they can accommodate discrepant information that doesn't fit with their existing knowledge structures by reorganizing the knowledge structures (Rivard & Yore, 1992). Thus, meaningful learning is an interactive-constructive process. Part of the process is metacognition, a conscious awareness and control resulting in verifying, structuring, and reconceptualizing information into meaningful networks of knowledge structures.

The reading process is a social event that involves internal regulation, is influenced by context, and utilizes higher order thinking (Bloome, 1990). Social constructivism focuses on the development of cognitive processes occurring within individuals as a result of their having interacted with each other. This means that the cognitive processes associated with reading are no longer viewed as residing solely in the individual; rather, they are seen as "being moved out of the privacy of one's head and into the interaction" (Mehan, 1981, p. 73). The interactive constructive view "emphasizes the active role of readers as they use print clues to 'construct' a model of the text's meaning." It de-emphasizes the notion that progress toward expert reading is the aggregation of component skills" (Valencia & Pearson, 1987, p. 727). Truly engaged readers of all abilities enjoy opportunities for open-forum type discussions where a free-flowing exchange of ideas among students and between students and teachers enriches and refines their understandings of the reading and heightens their motivation to read further (Alvermann, O'Brien, & Dillon, 1990). The interactive-constructive model of reading is compatible with views of science learning. This kinship makes it possible to build connections between reading and science through integrated teaching. Because constructivism provides a theoretical foundation for meaningful learning in all subject matter disciplines, connections can go beyond those suggested for reading and science learning. Connections can be built between all disciplines through integrated teaching.

An Example of a Knowledge Structure

Figure 1.2 gives an example of a knowledge structure for the idea of "car" as drawn by a 9-year-old girl. She probably has left out many details that exist in her knowledge structure but the complexity of the structure is evident. Also evident is her attempt to organize a hierarchy in the structure of her ideas.

A 9-Year-Old Girl's Knowledge Structure for the Idea "Car"   FIGURE 1.2

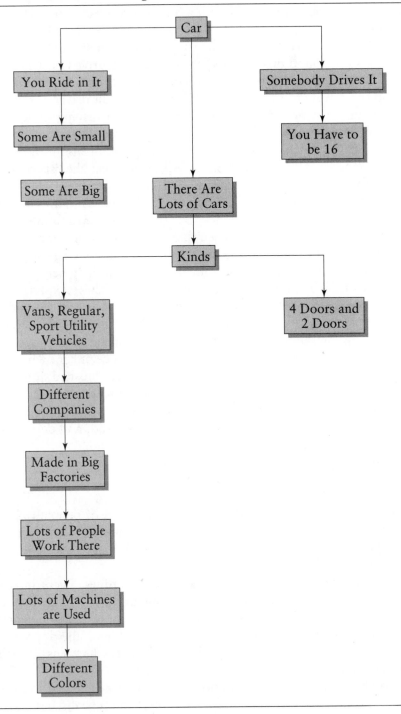

Her knowledge structure starts with two roles, rider and driver, and the generalization, "there are lots of cars." She has connected the size of a car and how many passengers it will hold to the role of rider. An adult driver also might connect the size of a car to the ease with which an appropriate parking space can be found or with how easily it can be driven down a narrow, crowded street. She has connected the age at which one can be licensed to drive and the drivers test to the role of driver. An adult driver also might include a description of the problems encountered in driving under various weather conditions and the need to look in all directions before making a turn. She has drawn more connections to the generalization about lots of cars than to the roles of rider and driver. All of the ideas she lists originate in her own experience. She has seen many different cars and probably ridden in several kinds of cars. She may have a parent who works in an auto factory or may have seen a factory in a video. She may have heard family members complain about "sticker shock" when they look at the price of a new car on the sticker in an auto dealership's showroom. Her knowledge structure reflects the range of her experiences. Someday she might help her sister put air in the tires of a car and change the spark plugs. These experiences will change her knowledge structure. A drawing of that structure made after these experiences might include a branch that identifies parts of a car and describes appropriate auto maintenance. She may connect this structure with the structure she has for personal care and maintenance of her own body and that of the family dog. A knowledge structure is never finished. It is changed constantly by the individual's experiences. The knowledge structure's connections to other knowledge structures form a network of structures. The network changes as new experiences help us revise, add, and delete connections between knowledge structures (Clarke, 1990).

MEANINGFUL LEARNING

Integrated teaching recognizes the interconnectedness of people's ideas and how such connections make our knowledge meaningful. It works to facilitate children's ability to make connections that represent the world as accurately as is possible.

We interact with parts of the world at various times. Every interaction is complex. If we are sitting at our kitchen table in the morning, we may listen to the radio or television news, hear the microwave beeping, smell coffee brewing, consider a question asked by our child, hear the dog scratch to be let out, and reach for a ringing phone. No event happens in isolation from other events.

In a highly separated subjects approach, learning is divided into slices, yet each slice is complex. Government, for example, cannot be discussed without touching on economics, social issues, natural resources, water supply, how many people are currently unemployed, and why people don't choose to vote.

In response to the complexity that exists in a slice of learning, a person can try to divide learning into an even smaller slice. But, that slice also will be complex. If it could be narrowed down to isolated individual slices there would be a new problem, how to find a way to connect them. If connections weren't made, the person's mind would be like that closet or drawer into which odds and ends are thrown. We don't really know what is in that closet because it has no organization. Maybe only outdoor things—boots, jackets, skis, a rake—are going to be found in the closet. If only outdoor things are thrown into the closet, the person won't look in it for an indoor item—such as a cookie sheet. By imposing this level of organization connections are being made—the closet is approached as a complex structure with outdoor items in it. So, the person has some idea of whether to look into it. If the closet is a real catch-all with no theme probably nobody looks for an item in it. The search is too intimidating because it holds all sorts of items with no relationship between them.

People have a tendency to impose order (Saunders, 1992). They want to know how things are organized and how they are connected to each other. It's only when they can see the relationship between things that an idea becomes meaningful. Otherwise ideas just sit there and are not learned because they do not fit with anything that is known. Without the fit they are useless.

Knowledge begins when the learner actively works with objects and events. The learner can take information coming in through the senses and construct a new idea. Or, the learner can take information and reconstruct an existing idea (Holliday, Yore, & Alvermann, 1994). Learning in the classroom occurs in several steps. First, the learner perceives a classroom experience. Then this perception is transformed in the learner's mind to fit the learner's current background knowledge. When the perception is fit in with what is already known, the learning experience is complete. The learner has given the experience meaning. Now that the experience has meaning it can be used in other situations that differ somewhat from the one in which it was learned (Sunal, Sunal, & Haas, 1996).

The teacher can never be sure what meaning an experience has to a student. It should be expected that the meaning each student gives an experience differs from that given to it by other students. Each of us has a different set of background prior knowledge into which a new experience is fit. This is why there is interest among so many teachers in approaching learning from many perspectives. It is the only way to ensure that most students give meaning to an experience.

Learning that goes beyond rote memory and recall is complex and requires experiences that involve the physical and social worlds of the learner

(Sunal, Sunal, & Haas, 1996). This is learning that results in the construction of concepts, generalizations, thinking skills, attitudes, dispositions, and values. In today's world, rote memory and recall serve limited purposes. Individuals need to have more complex learnings and to understand how they arrive at their ideas. For example, just being able to recite the amendments to the U.S. Constitution or repeat definitions of concepts such as independence and freedom of the press is not enough to live successfully and function as a contributing member of a democratic society. The amendments to the U.S. Constitution must have meaning to the individual when a candidate is given a vote in an election or a referendum question on a ballot is considered.

Some of our learning involves simple accommodation, adding more information to what we already know (Petrie, 1981). When an automaker comes out with a new model of car that is identified as a sport utility vehicle, for example, we add that model and the type of car to our knowledge about cars. We have extended our knowledge to include a new type of car.

Other learning involves either generalizing what we already know so it has greater application or refining our knowledge so it is narrower and more specific. A child may further generalize her knowledge when she decides that an ostrich is a bird. She may note its feathers and bill and decide these characteristics fit with her idea of a bird. She may narrow her knowledge when she encounters an animal, such as a rabbit, that hops a lot and decides that "not all four-legged animals run a lot; some hop a lot instead." Yet other learning represents a more major change is occurring within a person's knowledge structure or between knowledge structures (Rumelhart & Norman, 1981). It is called restructuring. Because children bring many ideas to school, much teaching time is spent helping them restructure their knowledge structures and create connections between various knowledge structures. Young children have some knowledge structures and over time develop many more in a complex network. In Figure 1.2 above, the child notes that "cars cost a lot because it takes a lot of people to make them." She probably is indicating connections between her knowledge structures for cars, jobs, and money. In order to facilitate meaningful learning teachers help children restructure individual ideas, relationships between the ideas in a knowledge structure, the types of experiences the knowledge structure can explain, and the relationship between one knowledge structure and other knowledge structures (Sunal & Sunal, in press).

INSTRUCTIONAL STRATEGIES

Integrated teaching involves many strategies but focuses on those that help children restructure their knowledge. It uses a wide variety of teaching strategies such as role playing, learning centers, and lesson summaries. Many learning strategies also are used. These are taught to students to help them learn. Examples of learning strategies are examining the main headings of a piece of informational writing before reading it and identifying one task you wish to accomplish before you begin anything else. A third set of strategies used in integrated teaching are metacognitive strategies, which teachers teach to children to monitor their own learning. For example, having students keep a journal in which they think and write about how they accomplished a task or describe to their partner the steps they plan to take to accomplish an assignment.

While some recall and rote memory learning is useful, it has a small part in integrated teaching that is concerned with helping children understand their complex world in a meaningful way. Integrated teaching can help children form new thinking processes, develop higher levels of thinking, and become aware of their own reasoning (Charbonneau & Reider, 1995). Integrated teaching enables teachers to address thought, attitudes, and values as interdependent with each other rather than as separate from each other.

Integrated teaching also enables teachers to use the ideas of those who describe and focus on either cognitive or affective/value processes. While there are many taxonomies for the cognitive and affective areas, Benjamin Bloom's (1956) often is used for the cognitive area while David Krathwohl's (1964) frequently is used for the affective/value area. Bloom's taxonomy identifies the following thinking levels beginning with recall at the lowest level and ending with evaluation at the highest level.

1. Recalling: naming, listing, locating, repeating, and describing.
2. Comprehending: telling meaning, interpreting, and giving examples.
3. Applying: explaining sequence or process, solving problems, and demonstrating.
4. Analyzing: outlining, categorizing, relating events or causes.
5. Synthesizing: revising, investigating, creating, and presenting.
6. Evaluating: ranking, judging, comparing, and using criteria.

Krathwohl's taxonomy is as follows.

1. Receiving: listening and observing.
2. Responding: participating and complying.
3. Valuing: initiating.

Before children have any formal teaching about an idea they are likely to have constructed their own version of the idea. Their version helps them satisfyingly explain and predict events. When they encounter the idea in school, they might have to modify and reconstruct it. This happens only if they are willing to change their idea and put in the effort changing an idea requires (Stofflett, 1994). Teachers help children construct, for themselves, ideas that are appropriate to the information available. The starting point of any lesson is the ideas the children bring to that lesson. The teacher acts as a diagnostician, trying to find out what ideas the children have, and then as a prescriber of appropriate learning activities.

Integrated teaching that aims to help children make learning meaningful uses a general structure often called the learning cycle (Karplus, 1979; Sunal & Haas, 1993). The teacher helps children become aware of their prior knowledge. Then the children compare the new alternatives being encountered to their prior knowledge. With experience they connect the new alternatives to what they already know, changing their idea to a lesser or greater extent. In this manner they construct their own new knowledge. Finally, they apply the new knowledge in ways that are different from the situation in which it was learned (see Figure 1.3).

In using such an approach, the teacher helps children become more aware of their own reasoning. Such awareness is called metacognition. The children are mentally and physically active. They come to recognize the shortcomings of the idea they brought to the lesson as they try out their idea in various classroom activities. The teacher helps them realize the integrated nature of knowledge as they apply an idea or process skill that worked well in one situation or discipline to another, different situation or discipline. They become better able to apply what they learn in a new setting. As they

FIGURE 1.3   The Learning Cycle

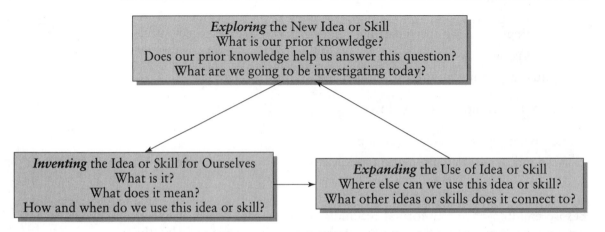

Exploring the New Idea or Skill
What is our prior knowledge?
Does our prior knowledge help us answer this question?
What are we going to be investigating today?

Inventing the Idea or Skill for Ourselves
What is it?
What does it mean?
How and when do we use this idea or skill?

Expanding the Use of Idea or Skill
Where else can we use this idea or skill?
What other ideas or skills does it connect to?

apply knowledge they also become better able to search for new patterns in the experiences they have (Lawson, Abraham & Renner, 1989).

In many ways, knowledge is finding patterns (Clarke, 1990). Once the learner realizes that some events or things fit together in a sequence or in some other pattern, those events or things are no longer separate, unrelated bits of knowledge. Finding a pattern whether it is a cause and an effect, a sequence, or a means by which items can be grouped is important. Patterns make sense out of what seems to be chaos. Integrated teaching creates opportunities for teachers to help children find patterns in information. Traditional teaching limits the possibilities of finding patterns that cross disciplines.

Integrated teaching leading to meaningful learning involves children in a sequence of activities. A typical lesson begins with an activity involving children in exploring the idea or process skill being taught. Their initial exploration is followed by one or more teacher-guided activities. Through these activities the idea or skill is explained to the children. The lesson ends with additional practice with the idea or process skill to expand its use to new situations. The teacher has a vast number of choices when deciding what teaching strategies to use in a lesson. These range from a cooperative group project through a short lecture to the use of a video, an historical document, an experiment, or a puzzle. The strategies that are used are chosen because they fit the type of idea or skill to be taught, the developmental level and specific learning needs of the children, and the part of the lesson with which the children are involved. The teacher makes many decisions as each of these is considered.

The learning cycle has three phases: exploration, invention, and expansion. The learning cycle will be used throughout this book when specific lessons and activities are described. Let's take a closer look at each phase.

Exploration

In the exploration, as the lesson begins, the teacher chooses one or more activities and strategies in order to accomplish three outcomes. The teacher needs to diagnose the starting point of the lesson. He needs to know what ideas or skills the children are bringing to the lesson. The teacher also needs to provide a focus for the children's attention. This is accomplished by asking a key question or involving the children in the solution of a key problem. The key question or problem stimulates the children's interest and helps them understand that their current idea or skill needs to be changed if they are to answer the question or solve the problem. The teacher also begins to relate the children's previous experiences to the idea or skill that is the focus of the lesson.

Invention

Next, the teacher guides the children into activities that help them work with the new idea or skill. When the new idea or skill becomes meaningful, invention has occurred. The children have invented the idea in their minds in such a way as to make it personally meaningful. Usually the invention phase of a lesson involves the children in some initial discussion of the exploration activity to build connections between it and the new idea or skill. The teacher provides an explanation of the new idea or skill. This can occur through the use of a trade book, a textbook, learning centers, a guest speaker, an experiment, a role play, or any of many other options. Then the teacher involves children in activities that provide them with clear examples or that model the new idea or skill. Finally, the teacher helps the children describe their new idea or skill or demonstrate it in an activity to provide closure (Sunal & Haas, 1993).

Expansion

Once children have formed the new idea or skill it is important for them to work with it further to expand their ability to use it. Applications help them store it in long term memory and access it when needed. Each new application helps them connect it to other ideas in their knowledge structure. The more connections, the more likelihood that an individual can access an idea when it is needed. So, the teacher provides practice activities with the new idea or skill. After the children can apply it easily in situations similar to that in which it was learned, they are given activities that have a new context. When they can apply it in new contexts the teacher and children summarize the lesson by reviewing the idea or skill, the activities through which they first worked with it, and the new contexts to which they expanded it.

The learning cycle is presented here as a three-phase process. It is a cycle. The expansion phase can be the lead-in to the exploration of the next lesson. Also, a teacher may return to an earlier phase of a lesson if it is evident that the children need more initial exploration of the key idea of the lesson, or need further activities that explain the idea so that they may invent it for themselves, or need additional opportunities to practice and apply the idea.

Integrated teaching involves the teacher in lots of decision making as instructional strategies and activities are chosen. The teacher makes decisions when deciding how to structure lessons. Units generally set the context for integrated teaching. These involve teachers in other decisions as a unit theme is chosen and the unit is developed, implemented, and evaluated.

UNIT TEACHING

The unit is an appropriate context for integrated teaching because focusing instruction around a theme is a complex task. This task is to investigate a topic or an issue in depth from a number of viewpoints. The task is accomplished only if it is structured in some manner (see Figure 1.4). The early part of the unit enables children to initially explore the unit theme. It allows the teacher to determine what the children know about the theme and what perspectives they are bringing to its study. It also challenges the children to investigate the theme. The main part of the unit involves the children in the deep investigation of the theme. The final part of the unit involves them in consolidating, summarizing, and applying their ideas.

An integrated unit has a beginning, a middle, and an end. It serves as a way of helping teacher and children organize their activities. It also ensures the exploration of a range of views. The integrated unit helps limit redundancy. Teachers know that an area has been addressed through a consideration of relevant ideas from a variety of disciplines.

The children may, for example, consider the theme of weather and investigate the science of weather (see Figure 1.5). Then, they can investigate how weather impacts people. During their integrated unit they lie in the grass and watch storm clouds building above them. They talk about their feelings when a field trip is canceled because of heavy rain, or when weather impacts an activity they looked forward to in some other way.

Unit Structure   FIGURE 1.4

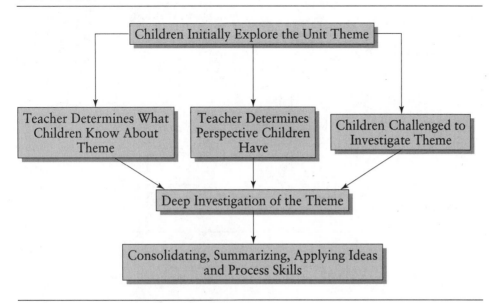

FIGURE 1.5   **An Integrated Investigation of Weather**

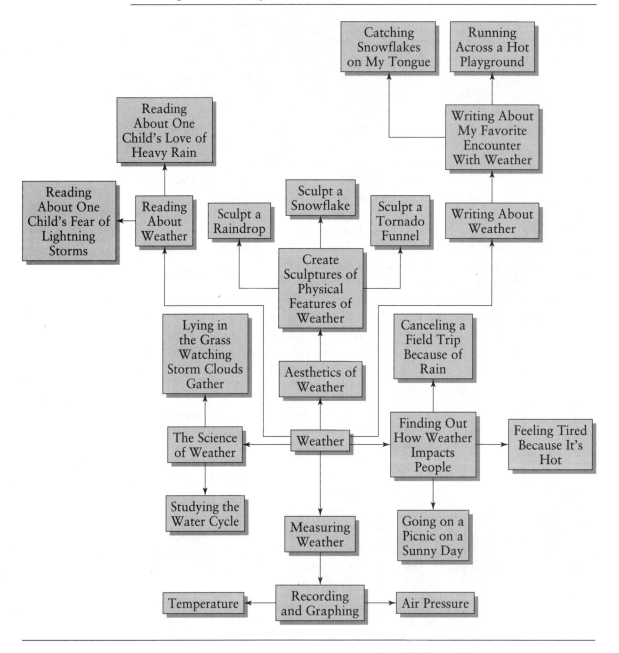

They talk about how very hot weather makes them feel tired or how warm, sunny weather is great for a picnic. They record and graph temperature, air pressure, and other statistics using weather recording devices. They read about one child's fear of lightning storms and another child's love of heavy rain. Sculptures of a raindrop, a tornado funnel, or a snowflake are created from clay. They write about their favorite encounter with weather—catching snowflakes on the tip of their tongue or running across the playground in the hot sun and enjoying its heat on their skin while their teacher seeks relief in the shade. A dance is created to demonstrate major weather events—a thunderstorm, a snowstorm, an extremely hot day. The children investigate weather from many perspectives while connecting those perspectives together. There is no separation between their graphing of air pressure and their reading of a story about a child and a big rainstorm. Units are a vehicle for organizing and implementing meaningful integration of subject matter.

AN EXAMPLE OF AN INTEGRATED THEMATIC UNIT

Constancy and Change Unit

An integrated thematic unit can take many forms. Each teacher puts a personal imprint on a unit. A concept-focused unit is the commonest type of unit (Sunal & Haas, 1993). An example of an integrated concept-based thematic unit is given below. This is a unit on "constancy and change." This unit has been taught more than 40 times in elementary classrooms by several different teachers. It has been changed numerous times in order to better satisfy children's needs. The example given below is the most recent version. This unit is presented as an example of an integrated unit that has had many changes made in it and that, no doubt, will change further as it is taught again. The process of developing and implementing this unit on constancy and change demonstrates the unit's topic in practice. Parts of the unit have remained constant while others have changed with use. Integrated units often are like this unit, they are in the process of being constructed as they are taught and are never truly a finished product.

Unit Introduction

Change is rapid in modern societies. This year's children's lunch box features cartoon figures that will be outdated next year, as may be the currently popular brand of athletic shoe and the favorite television show. Constancy also is an important feature of our lives. Some things rarely, if ever, change. A street usually keeps its name over decades. Boxes of salt have kept their cylinder shape and small pour spout over many years. Children need to develop an understanding of constancy and change. Examining the origins, forms, and effects of constancy and change builds such an understanding. As children become aware of changes occurring in their physical and social worlds, questions of causality become important (Piaget, 1960). The baby discovers causal connections as he physically interacts with objects. Later, the child begins to perceive the ways objects act on other objects. At first, the child attributes to the objects activities that are similar to his own actions. Later, the child recognizes that a network of related acts produce change. Observations of other children initiating change help construct a foundation of physical and social knowledge that builds the concept of change and the associated concept of constancy. Observations also help children construct an understanding of the factors influencing change and the values associated with change and with constancy. As these concepts are built, children acquire the tools that help them cope with change.

National standards in all disciplines address the concepts of change and constancy. Each discipline considers how and why some things change and some remain the same. These concepts are fundamental to our understanding of our physical, social, and aesthetic worlds.

Approach

Five basic focus questions structure the study of constancy and change:

1. Is something different?
2. What is changing?
3. What caused the change?
4. How much do we pay for this change?
5. Is the change worth what it costs? (Radford, 1977).

The study of constancy and change is best introduced informally, with children encouraged in the course of their work, to seek answers to these basic questions (Sunal, 1981).

Children's work with constancy and change arises from situations they meet in their world. Activities with potential for constructing an understanding of constancy and change are sequenced to provide starting points, encouragement, and careful questions.

The beginning point for a study of constancy and change with elementary school children is the recognition that changes occur. Encouraging children to look for differences is the first step in such recognition. Change cannot be recognized if differences are not observed.

Activities for the Study of Constancy and Change

There are many activities that can be part of a unit on constancy and change (see Figures 1.6, 1.7, and 1.8). These activities take place outdoors and in the classroom. Outdoor activities include mapping and noting seasonal changes in plants and weather. Classroom activities include comparing current events to historical events and comparing personal events such as the loss of baby teeth across individuals. Constancy and change can be examined through topics such as geography, transportation, and energy. The following are activities in an elementary unit on constancy and change that has been used in grades two through five.

Constancy and Change Unit Web   FIGURE 1.6

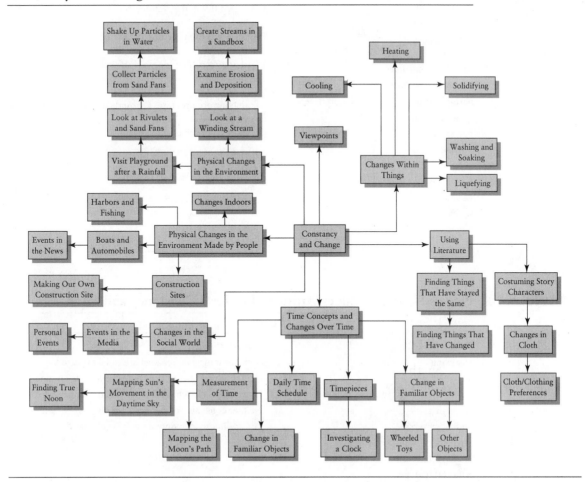

FIGURE 1.7   **Concepts and Generalizations List for a Constancy and Change Unit**

Constancy and Change Unit	
Major Concepts and Generalizations List	

Concepts	*Generalizations*
constancy/change	Natural processes continuously change the environment.
sand fan/river delta	People continuously change the environment.
erosion	People cause change in the population of other species in our environment.
deposition	
transportation patterns	Changes in our environment have a cost.
vehicle shape	Changes in the arrangement of the classroom affect how we like the classroom.
cooperation	
classroom layout	We can try to predict what will happen in the future with a public or a personal event.
current events	Timepieces have changed in recent decades.
personal events	Some familiar objects have changed in recent decades.
movement of the sun/moon	Features differ in the clothing for children of different ages.
solar/lunar calendars	
gears	Fabrics are chosen because of ease of care and their feel on skin.
gear-driven/digital clocks	
daily time schedule	Weather affects how long people voluntarily stay outdoors.
historical costumes	
natural cloth fibers/artificial cloth fibers	Heating, cooling, dissolving, washing, soaking, and liquefying are processes that indicate changes are occurring within things.
seasonal clothing	
bar graph	Our viewpoints change over time.
heating	
cooling	
dissolving	
washing	
soaking	
liquefying	

FIGURE 1.8   **Process Skills and Values/Attitudes List for a Constancy and Change Unit**

Major Process Skills and Values/Attitudes List	
Process Skills	*Values/Attitudes*
observing	Both constancy and change are to be expected.
questioning	I can find ways to cope with both constancy and change.
interpreting charts, graphs, maps	I need to decide what a change or no change will cost.
classifying	Neither constancy nor change are always the best choice.
finding patterns	I can't impose my control on some changes.
predicting	
finding relationships	
critical thinking	

Physical Changes in the Environment.   Outdoor activities related to physical changes in the environment provide a foundation for many skills, concepts, and generalizations. Children look for changes resulting from: digging in the ground, moisture, seasons, and different sizes of particles in the soil. They go to a playground before or after a rain and look around. Does the playground look any different after a rainfall? Is there any place where the rain has made a rivulet? If so, try to pick out the small sand fan it produces. Draw it. How is it built up? What can you say about the size of the particles? Look at the particles through a magnifying glass. What are they like? Collect some, shake them up with water in a bottle, and let them stand. What do you notice? Draw what you see. Look in a roadside ditch, a curbside gutter, at the mouth of a downspout. Are there any sand fans? Draw them. Compare them to those on the playground.

On a larger scale, a stream washes away sand and stone from one place and deposits them in another. Look at a winding stream or a winding rivulet on the playground. Note where water cuts away at a bank and where it builds up a spit. Draw it. The two processes of erosion and deposition occur together. This often is noticed on beaches along the ocean where beach front property may migrate a mile in a storm leaving the water lapping at the front porches of houses that once had a beach. Streams sort out material they carry along. Look for sorting and where it occurs. Visit the ditch, downspout, and gutter again. Are the same processes noticeable here? These activities provide examples of much larger processes studied later in geography. For example, a river delta is something like an overgrown sand fan. Next, create streams with water in a sand table or a sandbox. Draw the course followed by the water in the stream you made. When displayed, the drawings reveal differences in the streams they created. Discussion of the drawings explores the causes of those differences, for example, the amount of water used and the height from which it was dropped. After children become familiar with detecting natural changes, the examination of change can move to constructions made by people.

Physical Changes in the Environment Made by People.   Children consider common items such as boats or automobiles. Boats come and go. Where do they come from? Where do they go? What different shapes do you see? Why are those shapes used? Have the shapes changed over time? What do the boats carry? Are there always the same number around? If there is no harbor nearby, perhaps some event could start a related investigation. Often super tankers are mentioned in the news. How big are they? For what are they used? Why do people get angry when there is an oil spill? What does a beach look like before and after an oil spill? Do we need super tankers? Could we get the oil we need without them?

For classes with a nearby harbor, additional questions can be investigated related to those who work there. Do the fishermen fish all year long?

What do they catch? Do they change their fishing grounds or their type of catch at different times of the year? Which fish brings the most money? Have fishing boats always looked like they do now? What has changed? What would fishermen like to add to their boats? Why don't they add these items? Are the catches getting smaller, bigger, or staying the same? If they are changing, why are they changing? What might be done to improve catches if the catches are getting smaller? Should fishermen be helped by the federal government to get bigger catches?

Visits to a nearby construction site help children investigate changes in the physical environment. Such sites involve ditches or trenches in the process of being dug, foundations being laid, walls being built, or the construction of a larger structure. The children are encouraged to talk with the construction crew and, if possible, to handle some of their tools. Visits are frequent enough to allow children to become aware of a series of changes at the site. Photographs or drawings by the children are used to record the changes.

When visiting a ditch, children consider questions such as: How does a worker use a shovel? How does a steamshovel dig a ditch? How does the worker know where the ditch is supposed to go? Why is it being dug? Could it be filled in again? What if it isn't dug? Visits to a wall under construction often present an opportunity to watch a bricklayer at work. How many bricks are laid in an hour? How are the bricks arranged? How many different kinds of bricks are used? How is the wall kept straight? What pattern is being used in the brickwork? Can the children find other patterns? Maybe the children can be allowed to take one brick of each kind back to school. The children can build their own wall from wooden blocks, shoe boxes, or real bricks and cement. They will find they need to work together to build the wall. What sorts of large-scale changes require cooperative effort if the task is to be completed? This question plus the five major questions relating to constancy and change are used during these activities.

After visiting the site of the construction of a house, the children make their own mock construction site. Large boxes placed together create different levels. Construction materials such as wooden blocks can be placed in a wheelbarrow and wheeled up a plank to the site. How do the children decide to place their blocks? Can they make a roof? How do they decide who does what? This project involves children in recognizing the creation of a change as a complex matter. With children at the second- or third-grade levels, construction materials can be purchased from supply stores set up in the classroom. Wages could be paid to the workers. The question "How much do we pay for this change?" is addressed in a concrete manner.

Investigation of changes in the physical environment also occurs indoors. Rearrange the furnishings of the classroom. What are the children's reactions to it? Can they suggest further rearrangement? Do they like this change? Remove some major item(s) of classroom furniture; for example, the art table. Discuss: "What can we use instead?" "How do you like this change?" As a concluding activity, the children are asked to decide on a change in classroom space arrangement that could be implemented for Friday. Each Friday the process is repeated with a different change implemented by group consensus. Evaluation of the change should occur at the end of the day. Changes that facilitate activities and are deemed worthwhile are retained and continued.

Changes in the Social World.   Change occurs in the social world as well as in the physical world. Children follow an event as it is reported over several days on television, radio, the Internet, and in newspapers. Comparisons are made between the amount of information given by different media. An event chart follows developments as they are reported. The children make predictions regarding "What will happen next?" They develop a log of the event recording each day's news, their predictions, the extent to which their predictions are confirmed, and the evidence available confirming or disconfirming their predictions.With younger children change is studied in relation to personal events such as changes in hairstyle, teeth, clothing, holidays, and the arrangement of space in the classroom. Instant photographs are used to record the loss of a front tooth, a new haircut, or a new space arrangement in the classroom. Or, children draw a picture of the personal event.

Time Concepts and Changes Over Time.   Changes over long periods of time are difficult for children to follow. The study of constancy and change requires some consideration of concepts of time. Children can study the measurement of time and the use of timepieces.

This begins by mapping the sun's movement in the sky during the school day. An "x" is made with masking tape or chalk on the school playground. A child or an item such as a bottle is placed on the "x." The child's shadow is traced with chalk on the playground once each hour, e.g., at 9 A.M., 10 A.M., 11 A.M., and so on. The shadow will shorten in the morning hours then lengthen during the afternoon hours. The time of shortest shadow is true noon. The shadow also will move in a semicircle so the shadows at 9 A.M. and 3 P.M. point in opposite directions although they are the same length. These activities are used to explain how the sun is used to determine time of day. Children locate the moon in the daytime sky, make observations every hour, and mark its location with an "x." The "x's" are connected with a line to show the moon's path across the daytime sky. Children make similar observations at home to identify the moon's path during the early evening hours. These activities emphasize change occurring around us in the natural world although we do nothing to initiate it. Carried out over a few weeks, the activities help students understand lunar calendars.

Activities involving "telling time" and studying timepieces can be combined. Perhaps some discarded clocks can be taken apart. What keeps a clock moving? How is a digital clock different from a gear-driven one? With which kind are the children familiar? Which kind existed when the children's grandparents were children? Drawings can be made of clock parts and graphs record the kinds of timepieces with which children are familiar. A visit from a watch repairer who brings along an eyepiece and samples of the often tiny parts found in a watch may be of great interest to the children.

Children examine other familiar objects to determine whether they have changed over time. A tricycle can be examined. Your legs go up and down during pedaling. How does this pedaling make it go? How do you stop it? How have tricycles and bicycles changed in the last 100 years? Did their grandparents play with a Big Wheel or other such plastic riding toy? If not, what sort of wheeled toys did they have? Children might draw a series of pictures depicting a favorite wheeled toy, a wheeled toy they would like to have, and a wheeled toy they no longer use.

The children's daily time schedule serves as another source for the study of constancy and change. It is altered in a major way once a week for a few weeks. Discuss the children's feelings about this change. How did it affect them? Ask them if they would like to have more time to spend on an activity. If they would like more time, give them additional time the next day. At the end of the day, debrief by asking: How do you feel about this change? Was the change worth the effort it took? What if tomorrow you had more time for another, different activity? Try it and see how they feel about it. A final product is a preferred daily time schedule made up by each child. These are compared. The rationale for personal preferences is discussed.

Using Literature.   Literature supports children's study of time and the concepts of constancy and change. Children's literature is examined for elements that are the same over time and those that change. For example, the love family members have for one another always has been present in families as has the need to help each other, comfort each other, and share the work that must be done. People's housing, however, has changed. People today more often live in metropolitan areas than in rural areas. Occupations have changed. Transportation and communication systems are different. Children's literature reflects both the constancy and the changes in people's lives. Children's books are used to stimulate discussion. Two appropriate books for young children are *The Growing Time* (S. Warburg, NY: Harper & Row,

1969) and *Annie and the Old One* (M. Miles, NY: Little, Brown, 1971). Both books lead to a discussion of change in people over long periods of time—change that eventually leads to death. This is an instance of a change that is necessary and inevitable and is compared to changes that are neither necessary nor inevitable—such as changes in hairstyle.

After reading literature dealing with historical events, children dress pipe-cleaner dolls in historical costumes they have made. Changes in fashion are traced. Work might diverge into a consideration of changes that have occurred in the way cloth is made and how threads are spun and dyed. Children discuss such questions as, "Do you like a piece of cloth better after it has been dyed a certain color?"

Children are asked to bring in samples of clothing they have outgrown. These are compared to the clothing they now wear and to samples of adult clothing. What parts of the child have changed? How? What will have to change to enable the child to fit into adult clothing? Why does the very young child's clothing have some features not found in the school-aged child's clothing (e.g., snaps along the inside length of pant legs)? The children are encouraged to ask grandparents what sort of clothing they wore to school, for play, or on special days when they were the child's age. Has there been a change over the years in the type of clothing worn by children for these activities? What do the sizes of clothing mean? Does a 5-year-old wear size-five pants and size-five shoes? Photographs, video, and magazine pictures extend the discussion beyond the concrete items with which it began. Children conclude by creating a display of clothing ranging from the infant's to the adult's clothing. Each item is accompanied by a photograph of an appropriate individual wearing it.

The fabrics used in children's clothing have changed greatly during the past fifty years. Wool and cotton have been replaced by polyesters and other artificial fibers. Children explore this change and inquire into the reasons for the rapid spread of the use of artificial fibers. Possible questions for exploration include: Do any of the children's clothes have to be dry cleaned or ironed? How much does it cost to dry clean clothes? How long does it take to iron a shirt? How does wool feel against the skin? Could the answers to these questions tell us why the spread of artificial fibers was so rapid a change? A collection of cloth swatches are sorted into those that feel good when touched to the skin and those that do not. Glued down, they represent a record of the child's likes and dislikes.

Effects of Climate.   The effect of climate on people's movements also is examined. Once a month, the children keep a day-long diary of their activities. Why does it take so long to actually get outside when it is very cold? How long does it take to put on boots, coat, mittens, muffler, and cap?

Compare this to a rainy day or a sunny day. Does the weather make a difference in how long the children voluntarily stay outside? Make a bar graph showing the daily weather and how long the children stayed outside that day. Is there any relationship?

Chemical Change—Changes Within Things.   The kitchen is an ideal place to begin a sequence of experiences investigating chemical changes or "changes within things." Much science goes on when something is cooking. There are seven specific processes that yield experiences teachers can use to build an awareness of change. These are: heating, cooling, dissolving, washing, soaking, solidifying, and liquefying.

Heating. Have children put a piece of candle wax in a cup. Add hot water. What happens? What is causing this change? How do things get to be hot? Repeat the questions when the water and wax cool and the wax begins to harden. Children see a sequence of rapid changes. Try putting margarine or egg white on plates above cups of hot water. Children touch the cups as they are heated by the hot water inside. What changes do they notice?

Cooling. Cool hot water in glasses insulated by different materials—fur, wool, cotton, polyester, paper. Have children help measure equal amounts of hot water into plastic glasses. Use thermometers to make sure the water is hot but not scalding to the touch. Help the children concentrate on the water temperature by keeping the colors of the wrapping materials similar. Let children test the temperature of the water throughout the day. Rearrange the glasses in order from hottest to coolest after each testing. Does the water temperature differ? What is changing? What causes the change? If you wanted to keep warm, which material would you choose to wear?

Washing and Soaking. Hand washing can build concepts of washing and soaking. Introduce variables such as water temperature, soap, or lack of soap. Discuss results. Give children dehydrated prunes, apricots, peas, and soups to examine and taste before and after soaking the foods in water. Try soaking non-dehydrated foods. Use the five basic questions to focus discussion.

Solidifying. Making butter is a good way to study solidifying. Pour a small amount of whipping cream into baby food jars. Cap tightly and take turns shaking 50 times. A clump of butter will form and float on a watery liquid that is natural buttermilk. Let children taste both. Salt a portion of the butter and taste.

Liquefying. Offer children a variety of liquids to name, touch, and taste. Pour them into ice cube trays and freeze overnight. Observe the trays the next day. Feel first the frozen form, then the melting substances. Changes in rate of melting, shape, color, and texture can be discussed. Ask the children to match the frozen substances with samples in their liquid state. Arrange the melting substances according to rate of melting, from most to least melted. Some substances, such as cooking oil, will melt rapidly.

Viewpoints

At equally spaced points throughout the year, ask children to declare their views on items of interest by using a questioning technique, such as asking: "How many of you . . . would like to live on a farm? to change your first name? to have a special place to go to be alone? Children's responses are charted and compared. Is there a difference? Why have some items stayed the same? Why has a particular item shown change?

Organization, sequencing, and questioning allow the activities suggested above to be used in building awareness of change. When children notice snow melting or holes forming in the tips of athletic shoes, changes are occurring. Teachers guide children to an awareness of these changes and their causes.

A snowfall provides a good opportunity to study changes within things.

Instructional Strategies and Unit Conclusions

In all activities exploring constancy and change four processes are emphasized: observing, participating, discussing, and recording. Children are primarily concerned with gathering experience—observing. Natural curiosity about their surroundings motivates exploration (Piaget, 1960). Exploration results in meaningful learning. A study of change and constancy and an attempt to build awareness of changes builds on children's natural motivations and centers on experiences that invite observation and participation.

Children record their observations. They decide which elements of the experience are important enough to be recorded. Recording observations allows teachers to assess the effects of the children's experience. Rearranging objects such as jars of warm water cooling at different rates enables children to produce a three-dimensional record of their experiences. Boxes in which samples of dehydrated and soaked forms of food are glued side-by-side also produce a three-dimensional recording of experience. Records include graphs, stories, maps, drawings, a dance, a musical performance, and other products that are an integral part of the experience.

Discussion best occurs in heterogeneous, cooperative groups in which peer interaction is encouraged. Teachers encourage discussion by calling attention to discrepant events or by creating them as necessary. Ask children to explain or justify conclusions, predictions, and inferences using questions such as "Why do you think this will not change back to the way it was?" When children have described a change they observed, ask for a way to reverse the change. "We've put these rocks into this rivulet on our playground. Now the water is flowing over here instead of where it was flowing before. How can we get it to flow where it was flowing before?"

At a learning center children were interviewed before and after a unit on constancy and change using the activities described above. In one part of the interview before the unit, children predicted that both sugar and pepper would dissolve in a glass of water. Slowness in dissolving could, they felt, be overcome by "mixing it up real fast." They were surprised to see no change in the pepper no matter how fast they stirred. They tasted the solutions and decided that, yes, the sugar was in the water. They also thought the sugar couldn't be made to come back out of the water. No child could name other things that change, nor any process producing change, although they had observed change produced by stirring sugar into water. After experiencing the unit activities the children were interviewed again. They defined change and gave many examples.

In discussing examples of change and processes causing change during the post-interview, the children correctly predicted whether the various changes were reversible. Athletic shoes with holes cannot be returned to their original condition. A melting, soft popsicle is hardened by being placed in a freezer. After working with the unit activities, the children could name instances of change, identify processes causing change, and predict reversibility of changes.

During the unit, children began to call teachers' attention to instances of changes, discussing changes in objects other than those used to demonstrate the concept. Several months later, teachers reported that children talked about changes they saw in the environment in the classroom and among each other.

Using the five basic questions throughout the process of studying constancy and change ties children's experiences into a coherent whole. This is the beginning of a conceptual framework that gives greater meaning to future experiences.

Constancy and Change Unit References

Piaget, J. (1960). *The child's conception of physical causality.* Totowa, NJ: Littlefield, Adams & Co.

Radford, D. (1977). *Changes: Stages 1 and 2 and background.* Milwaukee, WI: Raintree.

Sunal, C. (1981). The child and the concept of change. *Social Education, 45*(8), 438–441.

SUMMARY

Integrated teaching works because people live in a world where all events are integrated. Every event is related to what came before it and to what follows it. The natural and social worlds interact with each other. Humans and their environment are integrated with each other. Learning best occurs when those connections existing in the real world also exist in learning experiences. Children use their experiences to construct their understanding of the world. This construction is built piece by piece and integrated with pieces of what we already know. Once the decision is made to move toward integrated teaching, teachers usually use integrated thematic units. Units help organize the experiences students have.

REFERENCES

Alvermann, D., O'Brien, D., & Dillon, D. (1990). What teachers do when they say they're having discussions of content reading assignments: A qualitative analysis. *Reading Research Quarterly, 25,* 296–322.

Atwater, M. (1995). The cross-curricular classroom. *Science Scope, 19*(2), 42–45.

Baker, D. R., & Piburn, M. D. (1997). *Constructing science in middle and secondary school classrooms.* Needham Heights, MA.: Allyn & Bacon.

Bloom, B. (1956). *Taxonomy of educational objectives, the classification of educational goals. Handbook I: The cognitive domain*. New York, NY: David McKay.

Bloome, D. (1990). Anthropology and research on teaching the English language arts. In J. Flood, J. Jenson, D. Lapp, & J. Squire (Eds.), *Handbook of research on teaching the English language arts* (pp. 46–56). New York, NY: Macmillan.

Bransford, J., & Vye, N. (1981). Programs for teaching thinking. *Educational Leadership, 39*(1), 26–28.

Brooks, J. (1990). Teachers and students: Constructivists forging new connections. *Educational Leadership, 47*(5), 68–71.

Brooks, J., & Brooks, M. (1993). *In search of understanding, the case for constructivist classrooms*. Alexandria, VA: Association for Supervision and Curriculum Development.

Charbonneau, M., & Reider, B. (1995). *The integrated elementary classroom*. Boston, MA: Allyn & Bacon.

Clarke, J. H. (1990). *Patterns of thinking, integrating skills in content teaching*. Boston: Allyn & Bacon.

Cooper, P. (1993). Paradigm shifts in designed instruction: From behaviorism to cognitivism to constructivism. *Educational Technology, 33*(5), 12–19.

Costa, A. (1992). *Developing minds*. Reston, VA: Association for Supervision and Curriculum Development.

Driver, R., Leach, J., Millar, R., & Scott, P. (1996). *Young people's images of science*. Philadelphia: Open University Press.

Dunn, R., Beaudry, J., & Klavas, A. (1989). Survey of research on learning styles. *Educational Leadership, 46*(1), 50–58.

Fogarty, R. (1991a, Oct.). Ten ways to integrate curriculum. *Educational Leadership, 49*(2), 61–65.

Fogarty, R. (1991b). *The mindful school: How to integrate the curricula*. Palatine, IL: Skylight Publishing.

Gardner, H. (1983). *Frames of mind: The theory of multiple intelligences*. New York, NY: Basic Books.

Gardner, H. (1985). *The mind's new science: a history of the cognitive revolution*. New York: Basic Books.

Krathwohl, D. R. (Ed.). (1964). *Taxonomy of educational objectives: The classification of goals, Handbook II—Affective domain*. New York, NY: David McKay.

Lawson, A. E., Abraham, M. R., & Renner, J. W. (1989). *A theory of instruction: Using the learning cycle to teach concepts and thinking skills*. Atlanta: National Association for Research in Science Teaching, Monograph #1.

Mehan, H. (1981). Social constructivism in psychology and sociology. *Quarterly Newsletter of the Laboratory of Comparative Human Cognition, 3*(4), 71–77.

National Research Council. (1995). *National science education standards*. Washington, D.C.: National Academy Press.

Petrie, H. (1981). *The dilemma of inquiry and learning*. Chicago: University of Chicago Press.

Resnick, L., & Klopfer, L. (1989). *Toward the thinking curriculum: Current cognitive research*. Alexandria, VA: Association for Supervision and Curriculum Development.

Rivard, L., & Yore, L. (1992). Review of reading comprehension instruction: 1985–1991. *Resources in Education*. (ERIC Document Reproduction Service No. ED 354–144).

Rumelhart, D., & Norman, D. (1981). Accretion, tuning, and restructuring: Three modes of learning. In J. Cotton & R. Klatzky (Eds.), *Semantic factors in cognition* (pp. 37–60). Hillsdale, NJ: Erlbaum.

Saunders, W. (1992, March). The constructivist perspective: Implications for teaching strategies for science. *School Science and Mathematics,* 69–78.

Schlechty, P. (1990). *Schools for the twenty-first century: Leadership imperatives for educational reform.* San Francisco: Jossey Bass.

Sizer, T. (1991). No pain, no gain. *Educational Leadership, 48*(8), 32–34.

Sternberg, R. (1990). *Metaphors of mind: Conceptions of the nature of intelligence.* Cambridge, England: Cambridge University Press.

Stofflett, R. (1994). The accommodation of science pedagogical knowledge: The application of conceptual change constructs to teacher education. *Journal of Research in Science Teaching. 31*(8), 787–810.

Sunal, C., & Haas, M. (1993). *Social studies for the elementary/middle school student.* Ft. Worth, TX: Harcourt Brace Jovanovich.

Sunal, D., & Sunal, C. (in press). *Early childhood and elementary school science.* Ft. Worth, TX: Harcourt Brace Jovanovich.

Sunal, C., Sunal, D., & Haas, M. (1996). Meaningful learning in social studies through conceptual reconstruction: A strategy for secondary students. *Inquiry in Social Studies, 32*(1), 1–16.

Sunal, C., Sunal, D., McClelland, S., Powell, D., & Allen, B. (1994). Integrated teaching units: Preservice teachers' experiences. *Journal of Social Studies Research, 18*(2), 10–18.

Valencia, S., & Pearson, P. (1987). Reading assessment: Time for a change. *Reading Teacher, 40,* 726–732.

Yager, R. (1990). The constructivist learning model. *The Science Teacher, 58*(1), 52–57.

Yore, L., & Shymanski, J. (1991). Reading in science: Developing an operational conception to guide instruction. *Journal of Science Teacher Education, 2,* 29–36.

CHAPTER 2

CHOOSING A FOCUS
FOR AN INTEGRATED UNIT

LET'S LOOK AT AN EXAMPLE OF A UNIT

Choosing a focus for an integrated unit is a process that involves teachers in a complex decision. One way to start thinking about choosing a focus for an integrated unit is to consider and critique an example of an integrated thematic unit. A first-grade unit is described below. The unit's theme was a common one, Thanksgiving. Language arts, reading, mathematics, social studies, and science were to be connected in the unit. The teacher's pre-unit planning, unit implementation, and post-unit reflection are described. After the unit, the teacher was uneasy with the unit. As you read about this unit, you are encouraged to identify elements that may be sources of the teacher's uneasiness.

The teacher had started the planning with some concerns about integrated thematic units. She thought there was something important missing from many integrated units. Analyzing her outline and organization, she concluded that an emphasis on process skills, on helping students improve their thinking skills, was a good organizational theme. However, she felt uneasy about the content of the unit. She noted that her unit outline identified no process skills, yet she had started out by listing the process skills such a unit might teach. After teaching the unit, she analyzed the lessons actually taught and decided that she had addressed all of the process skills she identified.

A First-Grade Integrated Thematic Unit on Thanksgiving

The teacher began planning the unit by considering process-skill objectives appropriate for young children. These included observing, mapping, comparing, classifying, finding relationships, predicting, finding patterns, and problem solving. A number of concepts to be taught were identified: voyages across the Atlantic, local Native Americans' homes, celebration, local Native American symbols, local Native American and Pilgrim clothing, germination, seed parts, patterns, addition, recipes, and thank-you notes. Two generalizations would be taught: "Thanksgiving has a special meaning" and "Thanksgiving is celebrated around the world." Finally, attitudes and values would be a part of the unit as students shared ideas, materials, and food. They would demonstrate an appreciation for what it means to be thankful by illustrating that for which they are thankful in many different ways throughout the unit.

Next, the teacher identified the unit's objectives indicating the students would:

a) actively participate in Thanksgiving customs, activities, and crafts,
b) recognize and describe some characteristics and clothing of the Pilgrims and the local Native Americans,
c) create a menu resembling what the Pilgrims and local Native Americans had at the first Thanksgiving, and
d) describe what it means to be thankful by illustrating that for which they are thankful.

Then, a unit outline was prepared.

I. First Thanksgiving
   A. Historical facts
   B. Present facts
II. Pilgrims
   A. Voyage to America
   B. Relations with the Native Americans (local)
   C. Customs
   D. Clothing
   E. Survival and Food
III. Native Americans (local)
   A. Relationship to Thanksgiving
   B. Customs
   C. Homes
   D. Symbols
   E. Clothing
   F. Survival and Food
IV. Why We Celebrate Thanksgiving
   A. Tradition
   B. Customs
V. Thanksgiving Feast in the Class like the First Thanksgiving.

The unit began with students sitting inside a shape of the ship, the Mayflower, outlined with masking

(continued)

(continued)

tape on the floor while an audiotape of waves breaking on a shoreline played. Once inside the boat, they were told they would be taking a trip. They used a globe to show their starting and ending points and the path the ship would take. Next, the children heard a story of the trip that described the difficulties faced by the Pilgrims during the voyage. The lesson ended with a worksheet onto which the students colored a line indicating the path across the ocean taken by the Pilgrims and then colored the land yellow and the water blue.

Lessons that followed involved the students in comparing and classifying the foods typically eaten by the Pilgrims and the local Native Americans. Typical homes for both groups were compared. Students sorted and classified plant seeds by their physical appearance. They examined fruits and vegetables that had been cut in half and observed their characteristics. Then, they predicted the number of seeds likely to be found in various fruits or vegetables. The seeds were planted and their germination period was predicted. They eventually created the generalization that the characteristics of a seed—its color, shape and texture, do not predict what the adult fruit or vegetable will look and feel like. This generalization had not originally been planned by the teacher but developed during the lesson.

The students focused for a while on celebrations, finding relationships between how peoples in various nations celebrate holidays. They talked about harvest festivals in various nations.

Pictures of Pilgrim clothing and those of Native Americans living in the area of what would later be the state of Massachusetts were examined. Symbols used on clothing and in face painting by Native Americans were discussed. The children used face paint to mark their own faces.

Turkey feathers were examined to find patterns. Then the children used them as manipulatives to solve problems with addition and with subtraction.

They designed and wrote a book about wild things and another book of Thanksgiving-related words. Learning centers had books related to the theme and involved the children in craft activities.

As a culminating activity, a Thanksgiving feast was planned. The children created, with some help, their recipes for the feast and wrote these in a Thanksgiving cookbook. They wrote invitations to family members to attend their feast. Afterwards they wrote thank-you notes to those who had attended and to those who had contributed items for the feast.

She was concerned with her integration of mathematics into the unit. Using turkey feathers as math manipulatives had tied into the unit well. The children had examined the feathers and found patterns in them. But what other mathematics had been included? There had been some measurement and some sorting. There was some problem solving. However, next year she would consider how to incorporate mathematics more deeply into the unit.

This teacher appropriately felt that process skills are an important part of an early childhood thematic unit. Process skills are recommended as an organizing focus for any grade level, but especially in the early childhood years (Sunal & Haas, 1993). Younger children need to improve their ability to use process skills. These skills are necessary if learning is to occur. In the later elementary and middle-school years, both process skill and content-focused units are needed (Sunal, Sunal, & Haas, 1996). Examples suggested by the American Association for the Advancement of Science (1993), the National Council for the Social Studies (1994), and the National Council for the Teaching of Mathematics (1989) include interdisciplinary themes such as patterns of change, interaction, systems, and models.

AN ALTERNATIVE APPROACH TO DESIGNING THE SAMPLE THANKSGIVING UNIT

To address the uneasiness the teacher felt about the Thanksgiving unit, an alternative approach might have been to work with an *underlying content organizing theme* such as "interdependence." As a theme around which to integrate a unit, Thanksgiving can easily become a recitation of information conveying stereotyped images. Many Thanksgiving resource books and materials for teachers, for example, focus on children making Indian headbands with a paper feather in them, or on making square white "Pilgrim" collars to wear. These are stereotypes in the process of transmission to a new generation. Native Americans in Massachusetts did not routinely wear feathers sticking up from a headband. Pilgrims rarely wore black clothes with white square collars. Black dye and white cloth were very expensive. Most Pilgrims could not afford them and wore everyday homespun collarless clothes dyed with local plant dyes. Their clothes were brown, purple, yellow-gold, and gray.

An organizing theme such as interdependence, instead, allows the teacher to focus on how the Pilgrims used the sea in their survival. The first Thanksgiving had more seafood entrees than food from the land. The Pilgrims ate lobster, clams, eels, and cod. This theme also encourages the exploration of the Pilgrim's growth of interdependence with the land itself. Then, the unit could study the Pilgrims' interdependence with the Native Americans and with their British homeland. Eventually their interdependence with both the Native Americans and their British homeland led to problems. The descendants of the

Pilgrims survived these problems well while those of the Native Americans did not. Both land and sea have suffered from the onslaughts of the Pilgrims and their descendants and now the relationship, the interdependence, between both is becoming more and more evident as solutions are sought to the problems created in recent centuries. A major problem with the Thanksgiving unit described may be the theme upon which it is based. Using a different theme, such as interdependence, with Thanksgiving celebration–related content could produce a stronger, more meaningful unit (see Figure 2.1).

The process skills should be a major focus of an early childhood unit (Sunal & Sunal, 1991). However, a unit cannot be content-free. If the theme of interdependence were chosen to underlie the unit, Pilgrims and Native Americans can serve as a catalyst for studies of interdependence. The focus can be on "Pilgrims and Native Americans needed each other." This can be supported by ideas such as:

"The Native Americans taught the Pilgrims ways to live in this new place."
"The Pilgrims traded to the Native Americans knives and blankets and other things they could not make."

FIGURE 2.1 **Interdependence Web**

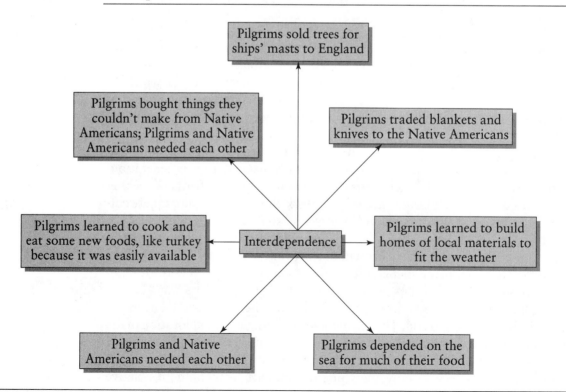

"The Pilgrims bought things they could not make from England and sold to the English things they did not have."

"The Pilgrims sold trees to England to use for ship's masts because wood was scarce in England since the land had been cleared for sheep herding and farming."

"The Pilgrims learned to cook and eat some new foods, like turkey, because they easily got it around where they lived."

"At first, the Pilgrims tried to build homes like those they had left behind in England. After a while the Pilgrims used what they found around them and built homes that fitted the materials and the weather in their colony."

"We can classify the foods they ate."

"We can investigate and predict how soil conditions, light conditions, and moisture are interdependent and effect the germination of seeds and the growth of plants."

"We can compare the homes of the Native Americans with those the Pilgrims built and investigate how they used local materials and responded to the climate."

"We can compare the dress of the Native Americans and the Pilgrims and investigate the culture that resulted in the dress of each group."

The long-term *goal* for this unit would be *to investigate the development of interdependence among people and their ecosystem*. This goal is dealt with time and again in units in future grades.

Other problems with the unit develop from the fact that the overall theme of Thanksgiving suggests neither *a sequence* nor an *organization* for the development of process skills, nor basic concepts and generalizations in support of the theme. For instance, why is it important to classify seeds, types of homes, forms of dress? How does such classification fit with the theme of Thanksgiving? When in the unit should this occur? The same can be said for many of the activities suggested earlier in the Thanksgiving unit. What is the place of:

- questions and ideas centered around describing and classifying Pilgrims and Native Americans in a variety of ways?
- the concept of giving thanks?
- the events that occurred in the Pilgrim's voyage and early years in their colony?
- the nature of asking questions and gathering evidence involved in an investigation?
- the nature of a scientific way of thinking? and
- the nature of historical thinking?

The lack of an appropriate theme leads to inappropriate planning and trivial learning. A unit designed around "turkeys" traditionally has been used in some early elementary classrooms around the Thanksgiving Day holiday. In such a unit, for example, students are given name tags in the shape of a turkey, they read stories about turkeys, make turkey drawings after tracing their hands, write stories about turkeys, make observations of a turkey egg and turkey feather, and visit a turkey farm. Thoughtful decisions about appropriate knowledge themes, interconnections between concepts and generalizations, and the process skills used are supplanted by considerations of how well the activity fits the theme of Thanksgiving. Themes should be considered on the basis of whether they will help students construct knowledge that has meaning to them and whether they will help produce a cohesive and complex knowledge structure. An integrated unit should result in learning that is meaningful to the students' present needs and future success.

While the focus in the discussion above was on teacher planning, students have an important role. Their interests and questions guide day-to-day lesson planning and development. They also guide the choice of a unit theme. Students can be deeply involved in inquiry learning. Upper elementary students are able to develop and test out hypotheses. Younger children can carry out guided investigations. Heavy involvement of students in identifying a theme and in planning and implementing the unit's activities and focus means that the teacher must be well-organized and do a lot of planning if all the parts of the unit are to come together into an effective and challenging whole.

FOCUSING AND ORGANIZING AN INTEGRATED THEMATIC UNIT

Selection of a theme is an important step in the development of a unit, because a lot of time and effort is invested in its development. There are an infinite number of themes and many ways of categorizing themes. Six types of themes have emerged from our experience with developing and teaching integrated thematic units. These are useful ways of categorizing themes and are helpful in selecting a theme to develop and teach. These are themes that result in:

- concept-based units,
- skills-based units,
- content and skills-based units,
- issue-focused units,
- project-focused units, and
- case study–oriented units (Table 2.1).

Concept-Focused Integrated Units

Concept-focused units are probably the most commonly found form of unit (Sunal & Haas, 1993). In these units, the further development of students'

Types of Integrated Unit Themes	**TABLE 2.1**

Concept-Focused Integrated Unit
Example: Constancy and Change
Process Skills–Focused Integrated Unit
Example: Communication Skills
Integrated Unit Mixing Concepts and Skills Almost Evenly
Example: Diversity
Issue-Focused Integrated Unit
Example: Conflict Resolution and Peace
Project-Focused Integrated Unit
Example: Air Quality
Case Study–Oriented Integrated Unit
Example: The Talladega National Forest Manager

Note: The last three types of integrated units usually encompass the first three types.

process skills plays a lesser role than does the acquisition and understanding of concepts. An example of a major concept around which such a unit can be built is "interdependence." Another example is the pair of concepts "constancy and change." Many courses of study focus upon concepts with a lesser focus on process skills. So, generally the sources a teacher uses to choose a theme lead to concept-focused units (Chaille & Britain, 1991).

In such units a typical structure begins with an exploration of students' prior knowledge about the concept(s) on which the unit is focused. During this early part of the unit, students are motivated to learn more about the major concept. This is done by involving them in activities that explore the concept. These activities challenge or puzzle them but do not overwhelm. Then, they begin actively investigating the concept. The last part of the unit involves students in examining the concept in other settings or situations so that they can expand its use. While the focus of this unit is on one or more concepts, a few lessons may focus on process skills that need further development if students are to fully investigate the concept.

Skills-Focused Integrated Units

In these units process skills are the major focus and content plays a lesser role (Johnson & Louis, 1989). There are many potential skills for such a unit. Table 2.2 lists process skills used to focus a unit. Five categories of process skills are identified.

1. The first, *data gathering,* involves those process skills that enable us to recognize and gather information from our natural and social environment. Perhaps the most basic skill of all is observing. Through our five

TABLE 2.2   **Process Skills**

Data Gathering	Data Organizing	Data Processing	Communicating	Overall Thinking Skills
observing	classifying	finding patterns	reporting	critical thinking
reading skills	ordering observation	predicting	writing	
library or research skills	interpreting observations	finding relationships	formal	reflective
questioning		inferring	informal discussing	decision making
interviewing and surveying		hypothesizing		
Reading charts, graphs, and maps		raising questions		

senses we make observations of the world around us and initially gather information we will use in many ways.

2. The second category of skills, *data organizing,* identifies those we use to organize or arrange the information we gathered.

3. Once we have organized our data or information *data processing* occurs. In some way, we process the data or information and arrive at an understanding of it.

4. Then we communicate our understanding of the data or information. This involves the fourth category of process skills, *data communicating.* Communication always is important because people are social by nature.

5. Finally, the fifth category includes a set of three *overall thinking skills* that depend upon all the other process skills and, in turn, influence our use of the others. These are critical thinking, reflective thinking, and decision making.

A unit might work on one skill such as classifying or decision making (see Table 2.3). Or, it might work on a set of skills such as communication skills. The structure of the unit is similar to that of the concept-focused unit. Most of the lessons focus on further process skill development rather than on concept development. Some lessons in the unit may focus on a concept to provide students with content to which they can apply a process skill. Students learn content in this unit but it is not a primary goal. For example, in a unit built around communication skills, students may build their ability to do informational writing. Their writing is about information of personal interest. So, one student writes about trucks and transportation, another writes about pecan farming, another writes about birds, and another writes about soccer. Each student investigates an interest and learns a

An Outline of a Process Skills–Focused Unit	TABLE 2.3

Decision Making

1. Ask students to read a story about Sir Henry Creswicke Rawlinson's efforts to copy inscriptions off a cliff face in Iran in order to "crack the code" of cuneiform writing. Ask them to identify the decision Rawlinson had to make and the choices from which he had to choose.

2. Discuss students' ideas. Then, have them examine pages showing a picture of Rawlinson and the cliff-face carvings in *Sumer: Cities of Eden* (1993, Alexandria, VA: Time-Life Books). Pass around a reproduction or a personally made copy of a cuneiform tablet and discuss the clay and writing stick used by the Sumerians and Akkadians to create such tablets.

3. Talk about the possible long- and short-term effects of the different ways Rawlinson could have used to copy the cuneiform that was 300 feet high off the ground on the cliff face.

4. Outline Rawlinson's steps from identifying a goal through choosing the best alternative. Have the students apply these steps to choosing a birthday gift for one's friend when there is a limited amount of money available.

5. Ask the students to define "decision making."

6. Show the students how to assign an importance score to each alternative they are considering. Use importance scoring to determine which of three alternatives would make the best choice of a site for an upcoming field trip.

7. Talk about where decision making is used in their daily lives. Help each student plan a decision making activity using importance scores that has meaning in their life and that can be used in making a decision during the following day (when to do their homework, what choice to make from the lunch menu). Implement and discuss afterwards.

8. Show graphic formats for decision making (such as a Venn diagram). Discuss and apply to the problem of how to rearrange the cubbyhole assignment to give everyone easy access. Implement the choice made and discuss the results.

lot more about it. The unit encourages their investigation as well as their writing. However, the focus is on informational writing that communicates information not on a specific common set of information.

Content and Skills Integrated Units

In some units content and skills are mixed almost evenly. Some examples are the themes of diversity, sinking and floating, or identifying causes of a situation. In studying each of these three themes students work with content from a variety of sources. In studying diversity, they might note diversity in the physical appearances of people, in the growth rates of plants, in weather patterns across the nation, or in attitudes toward a political candidate.

In the process skill focused unit in Table 2.3 students use content about cuneiform writing and its initial translation, so this unit is not content-free. However, the unit then moves on to examples from daily life, field trips, and other unrelated content. It is the process skill focus that holds the unit together whether or not the content topic is consistent throughout the unit. In a content and skills focused integrated unit, the theme is constant—diversity, for example. A wide range of examples are used but the content theme does not change as it did in the process skill focused unit example in Table 2.3.

The teacher also helps students further develop their skills in a content and skills focused unit. Often, one or a few process skills are part of the focus of the unit. In a unit on diversity, for example, students' ability to utilize the process skills of observation and making inferences is further developed.

Issue-Focused Integrated Units

Issue-focused units arise from current events or from an issue the students recognize as ongoing and troublesome (see Figures 2.2 and 2.3). The purpose of an issue-focused unit is to investigate impartially an issue through research and data collection. Students are investigating the issue on a local level *and* more broadly through research.

Some curricula are built upon the investigation of issues. More often, however, the students express concern about an issue and follow up on

FIGURE 2.2   **Type of Integrated Unit, Purpose, and Domain**

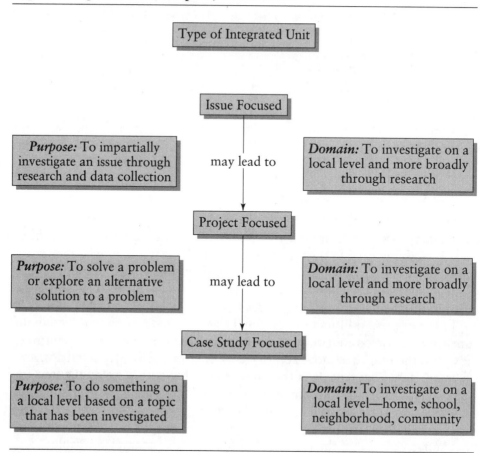

Example of Three Related Issue/Problem/Case Study Related Units FIGURE 2.3

One type of unit can develop from another.

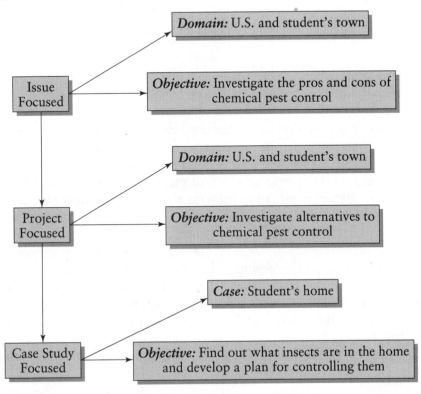

their concerns. Sometimes, teachers bring an issue to the notice of the students and an investigation of it begins. Some examples of issues that can be investigated are pollution, flood control, or endangered species. Issues of local interest and for which there are ample means of investigation often are the most productive. Some nonlocal issues, such as the international decline of rainforests also may be studied. These issues may not appear to have immediate local application but their investigation often indicates local applications. Rainforests, for example, affect the totality of life on our planet. Their reduction mirrors the reduction of the forests once found in the United States. The management of local biomes in the United States— forests, grasslands, deserts, and swamps—all present the same major problems as those presented by rainforest management.

Table 2.4 outlines the structure of an issue-focused unit. Students acquire information for the analysis of the issue in several ways, depending on the issue. They are likely to do library research and to use the Internet.

TABLE 2.4   **An Outline for an Issue-Focused Unit**

Step 1: Identification of the issue

Step 2: Students acquire information about the issue

Step 3: Information acquired is analyzed

Step 4: Students present findings of their analysis to each other

Step 5: Students decide whether they have a better understanding of the issue and of the arguments presented by those advocating for different sides of the issue

They may use a survey, conduct interviews, and carry out experiments. The teacher helps students identify possible means of data collection. Teachers encourage students to suggest several alternative data collection procedures and sources that seem promising. Each of these are considered to determine which is most likely to yield the information needed. Sometimes students find that a procedure has many limitations and is frustrating to use. Teachers guide students toward the use of procedures likely to be useful but do not strongly discourage them from trying out those the teacher judges to be less promising. Trial and error and reflection by students on their efforts are important parts of the learning experience. However, the teacher ensures that the classroom is a risk-free environment supportive of students when they are dealing with failure and limited success as well as when they have significant success.

The analysis of the data collected is an important part of the project. Methods of analysis vary depending on the problem investigated and the students' level of development. Students may, for example, use graphs, spreadsheets, webs, or maps. The teacher guides the students stressing the importance of kinds of analysis that can be clearly communicated to others.

Once the data collected are analyzed, students present their findings to each other. They decide whether they have an improved understanding of the issue and the arguments given by those who are expressing their views on the various sides of the issue.

Project-Focused Integrated Units

Project-focused integrated units work with a specific issue, concern, or interest. The issue, concern, or interest is investigated with an intent to find a solution, alternative, or explanation. An explanation tries to identify cause and effect. The *purpose* of a project-focused unit is to solve a problem or explore an alternative to a problem. The *domain* of the project-focused unit is investigation on a local level and more broadly through research (see Figures 2.2, 2.3). Examples are projects that try to identify useful strategies for earthquake survival, analyze the impact of underground mining operations on water quality, examine the effects of automobiles on air quality, or attempt to identify the causes of the explosion of interest in Greek and Roman art that occurred during the Renaissance in Europe.

The project generally examines a problem on a large scale. For example, how have automobiles affected air quality in:

large cities?

rural areas?

my community?

cities that have mountains around them?

cities located on plains?

areas where cars are 5 years old on average in comparison to cities where cars average fewer years?

The project tries to *answer a key question* or *resolve a key problem*. It may follow an issue-focused unit. In this instance the students have identified the various perspectives related to an issue and the arguments used by those who support each perspective. The students are at a point where they are framing the issue as a question or a problem. They want to find an appropriate solution.

The students follow a set of procedures in their project similar to those used in an issue-focused investigation. They collect and process data, analyze their data, and communicate it. Once they have obtained and worked with their data they decide which solutions, alternatives, or causes and effects are supported and which are rejected. They may find their results are unclear and more investigation is needed.

Case Study–Focused Integrated Units

Case study-focused integrated units are the *most specific* units. They study problems such as:

- management of household insects like cockroaches and ants in a community or by the people who live in households in the community,
- effects of and solutions to local noise pollution such as that caused by factories, traffic, or some residents in an apartment building,
- management of a local national forest, or
- money management by children their age.

The case study unit often follows a project and takes the problem to the *local level*. The local level can be the community, the school, the neighborhood, or even the students' individual homes. The case study is undertaken because the students are interested in trying to do something about a problem they investigated. They might try to find out what household insects are found in their homes and what can be done to control them. They might visit a nearby national forest as they try to determine why some adults they know are glad to have it and some wish it had never been started. They may find out how many people it employs, what products are taken from it, how it is protected, and what problems local residents have with its existence.

The case study uses the same methodology found in the issue- and project-focused units. Communication of its findings is important because the students usually are trying to *resolve a local problem*. So, students need to describe clearly the steps they took to acquire information, process it, and analyze it. They also need to describe how they tried to be objective and let the information speak for itself.

Relationships Between the Types of Units

The last three types of units typically incorporate much of the first three units. They may be concept or skills focused, or an almost even combination of both. They often build upon an earlier concept- or skills-focused unit. A project-focused unit is probably focusing on one or more specific concepts imbedded within the problem that is being studied. Or, it may follow up on an important skill or combination of concepts and skills.

Often these units are found in the upper elementary grades. However, younger children may be involved in one of them in a problem area with which they have some experience.

The broadest based of the last three types of units is the issue-focused integrated unit (see Figures 2.2, 2.3). The next, the project-based integrated unit is narrower and can follow up on an issue-based unit or any of the first three types of units. The narrowest type of unit is the case study. It can follow up on the project-based unit or any one of the others.

CHOOSING AN APPROPRIATE THEME

Within each of the six types of units, there are many possible themes around which the unit can be developed. Six questions can be asked when the selection of a theme is under way.

1. What are the important *central concepts* and/or *central issues* for this theme?
2. What are the *guiding questions?*
3. What *activities* can be used?
4. How will these activities engage the students in *thinking?*
5. Will the students be able to make *significant connections* between the disciplines? and most important of all,
6. Will the theme be of *interest* and *relevant* to the students?

These are important questions because the teacher wants to avoid a less effective theme. When a less effective theme is chosen the teacher makes forced choices compromising the quality of student learning outcomes and the teacher's own beliefs in the worthwhileness of the unit. As each of these questions is addressed students are participants in decision making. Student input into the decisions made is a critical component.

What Are the Important Central Concepts and/or Central Issues?

Themes usually have many concepts and sometimes many issues associated with them. The teacher determines which are central to the theme. Teachers are curriculum decision makers. The real teaching time available is small in most classrooms. So, teachers want to make the best use of the limited time available. This means that depth is more important than breadth (Driver, 1990). The stress on depth rather than breadth of coverage is supported by recently developed national standards in the disciplines, for example those of the National Research Council adopted by the National Science Teachers Association (1995). The teacher uses students' levels of development, background experiences, prior knowledge, and personal interests to determine those concepts and issues with which they can to work successfully (Sunal, Sunal, McClelland, Powell, & Allen, 1994). If the students can work with central concepts and central issues, related ideas are added to the student's knowledge structure when they are encountered. This happens because they are added to the student's solid foundation of understanding of the central concepts and issues (Aubrey, 1994).

The students use their foundation to decide what is central or essential to the theme. They are less likely to give too much weight to a side issue or to jump to a conclusion that is based on just a few relevant pieces of information (Harlen, 1992).

As an example, consider the concept-based theme of constancy and change described in chapter one. The two major concepts are constancy and change. Other important concepts might be: then and now, cause and effect, the likelihood of change, adaptation to change, social change, personal change, and environmental change. Some central issues are:

- Is change always for the best?
- How do we convince people to change their ideas about something when there is evidence to contradict their old ideas but they still hang on to them?
- Is society changing too fast today for most people?
- Constancy lends society a feeling of stability, so should our society act to limit change?

These issues are phrased in adult terms, but variations of them are developed for consideration by elementary school children. Using this theme, by the end of the second grade children could have considered questions related to the following generalizations (American Association for the Advancement of Science, 1993).

- Things change in some ways and stay the same in some ways.
- People can keep track of some things, seeing where they come from and where they go.
- Things can change in different ways such as in size, weight, color, and movement.
- Some small changes can be detected by taking measurements.
- Some changes are so slow or so fast that they are hard to see.

As they consider related questions students have the opportunity to form these generalizations. These become the learning outcomes toward which the unit is directed.

The national guidelines developed by professional organizations such as the National Council of Teachers of Mathematics, the National Council for the Social Studies, and the American Association for the Advancement of Science will be useful in determining central ideas and issues related to a theme. Teachers also refer to their state courses of study. Many school districts have developed local courses of study that are a fine guide to identifying central ideas and issues. Textbooks from college-level courses in a discipline and elementary-school textbooks also may be of help.

What Are the Guiding Questions?

As central concepts and/or issues are identified, teachers begin to develop guiding questions. Some of these questions come from the children, expressing their interests and concerns. These are used to organize the teacher's background reading and collection of materials. They also help determine which disciplines contribute to the unit and the extent of their contribution. Later, they are used to sequence lessons and activities in the unit. Finally, they are used to evaluate the unit.

In the unit on constancy and change there are many potential guiding questions. Some examples of these are shown in Figure 2.4.

What Activities Can Be Used?

Once a set of guiding questions is selected, activities and materials are identified to support and explore each question. As this process occurs new questions may be added to the list. Some questions may be emphasized and some de-emphasized.

Sample Guiding Questions FIGURE 2.4

Possible Guiding Questions for a Unit on *Constancy and Change*

For younger elementary students:

What changes do you notice in the world around us?

What changes have you noticed in yourself, in your size, in what you like to do, in what you like to eat since you were very little?

What are some things that always seem to stay the same?

Do you like to do the same things in the same way every day?

Can you sing a song where you think the music changes a lot and one where the music is mostly the same?

For older elementary students:

What is meant by constancy and change?

Do Americans place a high value on change, on constancy?

What are examples of technological change, social change, and environmental change within the last decade?

What effects can you determine from the rapid political change in what was once the USSR?

Can there be too much change, too little change?

What cycles of change can you identify in the natural and physical world?

How do we use mathematics to show constancy, to show change?

What characteristics of constancy and change should be incorporated into a dance that demonstrates a struggle between constancy and change?

There is always a large range of activities that can be used even when materials are limited. The choice between possible activities is decided by the guiding questions. The activities selected relate to those questions. The guiding questions indicate which disciplines contribute to the unit and how extensive is the contribution of each.

Will These Activities Engage the Students in Thinking?

Because teaching time is limited, activities that are really just time-fillers, or fun but with little purpose to them are rejected. Other activities are available that are fun yet address one or more of the guiding questions.

For example, children investigating the westward movement in the United States might be asked to make a covered wagon out of pretzel logs and pasta wheels. The activity might be fun, and surely would involve some eating of pretzel logs but it probably won't contribute much to learning unless more is done with it.

If the children do some research and find out the typical measurements of a covered wagon (for example, most were just 3 feet wide) then they could build a model covered wagon to scale. Groups of children might be involved in building the scale wagon. Additional learning occurs if they built the wagon out of real materials such as wood and cloth. To do this the children research how wheels were put together, how the wagon's boards were attached to the axle, and how draft animals were hitched to the wagon. Now the model covered wagon activity takes more time but it involves the children in studying the covered wagon and the technology it represented. Their activity has depth and offers them many more opportunities to learn than did the initial pretzel stick wagon activity.

The teacher identifies thinking or process skills fostered by various activities. Then, the teacher considers which skills the students need to further develop at this time. For example, to study constancy and change, a primary-grades teacher may decide children need to further develop their ability to sequence events and classify them. An upper-grades teacher may decide students need to work with prediction and inference skills. Activities that are more likely to develop the targeted skills are chosen.

Decisions occur regarding content. Those activities specifically addressing the central concepts and issues of the unit help the students reflect on those concepts and issues. The activities give the students the information needed for reflection and the tools or skills with which to reflect.

Will the Students Be Able to Make Significant Connections Between the Disciplines?

Most themes can interconnect subjects. But, some provide limited opportunities for learning. Some examples of themes that have proven difficult to appropriately address in a thematic unit are: rabbits, zoo animals, farm animals, dinosaurs, the Constitutional Convention, Thanksgiving, and the American Revolution (Sunal et al., 1994). Each of these has interconnections between social studies, science, mathematics, literacy, and the arts. Each also requires some stretches that have the potential to trivialize one or more of these. Teachers need to decide whether significant connections between disciplines can be made.

The American Revolution is an example of a theme that may have to stretch to include all the major disciplines in the elementary curriculum. This theme certainly addresses important social studies concepts and issues. However, science may be more difficult to interconnect. Some teachers have included a history of science component, talking about science during the late 1700s and the role of science in the social and political upheavals that occurred in the 1700s and early 1800s in Europe and the Americas. Others investigated static electricity, because Benjamin Franklin is well-known for his work with it. These are both worthwhile interconnections with science for this theme. The unit is strengthened by this investigation into the science of the period. The investigation gives students a better understanding of the society and culture of the period and, in Benjamin Franklin's case, of a complex individual who had an important role in the American Revolution. However, if this theme was part of a social studies course of study that focused on American history throughout the year, students might develop some understanding of the history of science but may not get enough study of the ideas with which professional and amateur scientists of different periods were engaged. The students might not really better understand electricity, or bacteria, or vaccinations.

In mathematics the students could determine the distance each of the signers of the Declaration of Independence traveled to Philadelphia. They might read about travel in the American colonies during this period of time. Using their information they could determine how long a journey each of the signers had. They also would develop some ideas about the many difficulties faced by the signers. Even transportation was a burden. This can be compared with the ease of transportation today. For example, how long would it take the signers to make this journey today by road and by air? The students would have to consider the question of why the signers would make such a journey and why they considered it worthwhile to do so. During the unit they might calculate the ratio of exports and imports between England and the American colonies. They might create graphs comparing the populations of major cities in England and in the American colonies. Each of these is an excellent mathematics-related activity. However, studies of graphing, ratios, and measurement are unlikely to be all a strong focus in this unit. So, one or more has to occur elsewhere if students are to construct a useful knowledge structure for understanding them.

Art activities can support this unit. Students might study portraits of George Washington and of him with his family. They could create portraits of people important to the Revolution. They might examine drawings of events in the American Revolution. They might investigate styles of painting of the period. These add to the richness of the unit. However, an understanding of portraiture needs a greater range of experiences than those found in this unit. Guidance in understanding portraits done in the past and in creating one's own portraits needs some intensive experience.

As another example, dinosaurs is a theme that does not lend itself well to integration with social studies. The social world is the focus of social studies and people and their societies were not to be found during the Mesozoic Era. Students could explore the lives and work of the scientists important in the study of dinosaurs. They might begin with reports of a recent "find" in the media. They could talk about laws preserving important dinosaur sites and controlling access to specimens. Each of these social studies-related considerations informs the study of dinosaurs. But, these social studies concepts

*This student has found her integrated unit on
plants to have a most relevant theme.*

need an in-depth study of the process of developing and passing a law and of
the pressure groups that influence the passage of a law. In the case of themes
such as dinosaurs and laws, mathematics content is a forced choice. Mathematics is involved in each case, for example, understanding the relative sizes
of various dinosaurs or the determination of a majority vote in the passage
of a law. The point is made that mathematics is found everywhere. However,
if mathematics always is viewed in these terms, basic mathematical concepts
may not be constructed by children.

Activities should be used from a variety of disciplines in an integrated
unit as appropriate to the central concepts and/or issues addressed by the
unit. There must be an effort to ensure that many of the activities create significant connections between disciplines. These connections enable students
to understand that the central concepts and/or issues of the unit are complex
and arise from information and events that represent several disciplines.

Will the Theme Be of Interest and Relevant to the Students?

As the outline of the unit emerges, teachers need to consider whether the theme will be of interest to the students and relevant to them. No matter how well put together nor how clear the learning outcomes are, if students have little interest in a theme, they are not active learners and construct limited knowledge from the study of that theme. Students are likely to have little interest in a theme that does not match their developmental abilities or one for which they lack the basic skills needed to study the theme. A theme incorporating knowledge with which they are quite familiar holds little challenge and interest for them. For example, some students and teachers have reported units year after year at each grade level that deal with George Washington and Abraham Lincoln or with Martin Luther King Jr. (Sunal & Haas, 1993). Students go over the same basic information regarding these individuals every year. After a couple of years, the information loses interest because of its familiarity. Student interest could be revived if Washington and Lincoln are incorporated into a thematic unit investigation of the development of the American presidency and Martin Luther King Jr. become a part of a thematic unit investigating the civil rights movement.

A theme that is too challenging because students have too little prior knowledge also is of little interest to them. Their base of prior knowledge is too limited to build upon. They can't make connections with what they know and reconstruct their current ideas to a more complex level. So, they give up and display a lack of interest.

Interest and relevance are related. Students usually are interested in ideas and process skills they view as relevant. Developmental abilities relate to students' views of relevance. A theme that is overly challenging or too easy is viewed as less relevant than one matching their abilities and challenging them at a level to which they can respond and build upon. Relevance also comes from the national and regional culture, students' home backgrounds and cultures, the neighborhood in which students live, and personal interests and hobbies. Thus, a student in an urban school may find a unit on the parts of an effective farm of less relevance than a unit on the parts of a city neighborhood. The rural student may be more interested in a unit on outdoor and rural occupations such as fisheries manager, state police officer, extension agent, and feed store operator than on city occupations such as parking meter readers, bicycle messengers, pizza delivery persons, and specialists such as orthopedic surgeons and computer programmers. Both rural and urban students, however, may find relevance in studying a wide range of holidays from the Day of the Dead, associated with Hispanic culture, to Kwanzaa, associated with African American culture, to Eid-al-Fitr in Muslim culture. Such a study is relevant if these holidays are incorporated into a unit examining why people have holidays, the similarities between how people celebrate holidays (eating a lot of food, celebrating with family members, and so on), similarities found among holidays around the world (celebration of the harvest, independence day celebrations, and so on), and the effects of modern media on traditional celebration of holidays.

PROBLEMS WITH LESS EFFECTIVE THEMES

If thematic units are used exclusively basic understandings of concepts such as photosynthesis and the development of laws may be lost. Thematic units are best interspersed with disciplinary units, such as one on plants. Or, a thematic unit may be in progress while a separate topic unit such as one in science on plants also is under way.

A less effective theme leads to understanding the ideas related to the theme at a low level. Students may be able to describe objects related to the ideas somewhat, but cannot go beyond them to explain interactions between those objects. Knowing the names of Pilgrim leaders and describing their clothes and homes is meaningless unless one also can explain interactions among the leaders and the people, why they wore specific types of clothing, where their clothing was obtained, and the dependence of all people on their natural environment.

Studying Thanksgiving without an accompanying study of the conditions that made survival difficult in the new colony, of why the Pilgrims undertook their dangerous and difficult enterprise, of why they were so thankful for the harvest, of their relationships with native Americans, and of why any of this has relevance to Americans today also is a less effective approach. In particular, it is important to wonder why there are Thanksgiving Day parades, why the "horn of plenty" symbol is used, why certain colors are associated with the holiday, and why people accept stereotyped cute pictures of Pilgrims and Native Americans and turkeys with few questions. In the Thanksgiving unit described earlier in this chapter, several concepts, some process skills, and generalizations are identified but not well connected to each other. There are several activities that help children develop process skills, particularly observation and classification, and some concepts. There are some weak activities that result in little learning. For example, it is not important for children to know how to add with turkey feathers. It is important for children to develop a way of thinking that involves problem solving, the gathering of evidence, and developing conclusions from that evidence. It may be that Thanksgiving is not a productive and meaningful theme for organizing an integrated unit.

Less effective themes usually lead to a unit that teaches one subject well at the expense of others. When selecting a theme, one must ask a question such as, "If students followed through on the activities, what important science, social studies, art, literacy, physical education, music, and mathematics ideas will have been learned?" These ideas must be part of the curriculum design for the school program. Thematic units should be taught because they more fully inform students. But, they should not supplant all units because thematic units generally cannot teach all of the major concepts and generalizations that need to be addressed if students are to become truly educated.

SUMMARY

Teachers are curriculum decision makers. Many choices are made when a focus for an integrated unit is chosen. The major consideration is "Which theme is best taught through an integrated thematic unit?" Consideration always is given to whether a theme might be best taught initially in a stand-alone manner and later applied more widely. As these considerations occur, teachers focus on the central concepts and/or issues to be investigated in the unit. They determine whether these are of interest and relevance to the students. When these are identified, questions are formed to guide the unit. Activities are selected to address the guiding questions. Each activity is chosen because it engages students in thinking. Finally, the unit as a whole and the activities within it are evaluated to determine whether significant connections between the disciplines are made. Students needs, abilities, and interests are considered during the planning process. Most importantly, students participate in the planning process and their input is a critical component of the decision making that occurs.

REFERENCES

American Association for the Advancement of Science. (1993). *Benchmarks for science literacy.* New York, NY: Oxford University Press.

Aubrey, C. (1994). *The role of subject knowledge in the early years of schooling.* Washington, DC: Falmer Press.

Chaille, C., & Britain, L. (1991). *The young child as scientist.* New York, NY: Harper-Collins.

Driver, R. (1990). Assessing the progress of children's understanding in science: A developmental perspective. In G. E. Hein (Ed.), *The assessment of hands-on elementary science programs.* Grand Forks, ND: University of North Dakota, Center for Teaching and Learning, 204–216.

Harlen, W. (1992). *The teaching of science.* London: Fulton.

Johnson, T., & Louis, D. (1989). *Bringing it all together.* New York, NY: Collins.

National Council for the Social Studies. (1994). *Expectations of excellence: Curriculum standards for the social studies.* Washington, DC: National Council for the Social Studies.

National Council of Teachers of Mathematics. (1989). *Curriculum and evaluation standards for school mathematics.* Reston, VA: Author.

National Research Council. (1995). *National standards for science education.*

Sunal, C., & Haas, M. (1993). *Social studies for the elementary/middle school student.* Ft. Worth, TX: Harcourt Brace Jovanovich.

Sunal, D., & Sunal, C. (1991). Balance in the forest. *Day Care and Early Education 18*(3), 22–25.

Sunal, C., Sunal, D. & Haas, M. (1996). Meaningful learning in social studies through conceptual reconstruction: A strategy for secondary students. *Inquiry in Social Studies, 32*(1), 1–17.

Sunal, C., Sunal, D., McClelland, S., Powell, D., & Allen, B. (1994). Integrated teaching units: Preservice teachers' experiences. *Journal of Social Studies Research, 18*(2), 10–18.

3

THE PLANNING PROCESS

The planning process varies greatly among teachers. It can be cooperative occurring between several teachers or it may be highly individualized. Each teacher's planning process develops over time (Carlson, 1991). This personalized process becomes so much a part of a teacher that often individuals can't easily explain what they do, how they do it, and why they choose various options (Carlson). The planning process develops in new teachers through a time-consuming struggle (Sunal, Sunal, McClelland, Powell, & Allen, 1994). Because it is such an individualized process it is hard to prescribe a specific means of accomplishing it. This chapter presents planning strategies found useful by teachers in order to help readers identify a process helpful to them.

PLANNING THE YEAR'S CURRICULUM

Many elementary teachers outline the year's curriculum before the first day of school. As this planning is occurring, themes for integrated units are tentatively identified.

Teachers who have not used integrated thematic units may want to plan just one in their first year. Once they have had the experience of planning and implementing an integrated thematic unit, one or two more can be added in the following year and the first unit can be improved if it is taught again (Sunal et al., 1994). By adding one or two integrated units each year, soon the teacher has units to use throughout the school year.

There are many ways to outline the year's curriculum (Yager, Hidayat, & Penick, 1988). Table 3.1 identifies three common formats. The divisions used in the school calendar are frequently used to determine the sections into which the curriculum is divided. These usually are the grading periods established in the school. Yearly planning can be divided into the periods defined by such reports even though reporting systems vary widely across schools and include letter grades, pass/fails, anecdotal reports, and conferencing. Teachers provide an assessment of the progress of each student at the stipulated times. Units and other ways of structuring the curriculum are scheduled to finish before the report is due, so that their results are included in student assessment. These periods may occur every six weeks, quarterly, halfway through the school year, or may follow some other schedule. Teachers of very young children may find the divisions of the school year are too long. Integrated thematic units one to three weeks in length often are appropriate for very young children.

Another means of dividing up the school year into manageable parts is to use the divisions of a course of study. In many states school systems are able to establish their own reporting periods. With no standardization, a statewide course of study or curriculum guide cannot follow a set formula of weeks per topic. Instead, the topics in the state course of study are identified and outlined in terms of the content and thinking skills appropriate to the topic and to the developmental level of the students who will be investigating that topic. The period over which a topic is studied varies. In those school systems where a local course of study is used, there is a better fit between the topics studied and the reporting periods over which they are studied. Courses of study usually are designed by disciplinary area. In this instance, teachers take the major topics of the course of study in a discipline and use them to divide up the school year. That discipline becomes the focus of the integrated units. In our experience social studies or science are the disciplines most often used for such a focus.

TABLE 3.1   **Planning the Year's Curriculum**

Typical Planning Choices
1. Using Existing School Calendar Divisions—often grading periods
2. Utilizing the Divisions of a Course of Study
3. Matching a Course of Study to Reporting Periods

A third means of dividing up the school year into manageable parts is to take the expected reporting period for the school and match a course of study to it. The result is that one reporting period may have one integrated thematic unit while another may cover two or more shorter integrated units. The topics and the depth to which they are studied determine how many fit into the reporting period. Other disciplines then are fit into the major topics.

Examples of Yearly Planning Formats

Wheel Design

Figure 3.1 is an example of a wheel design for planning the year's curriculum from Martha Lockard and Edith Merritt, teachers in Tuscaloosa, Alabama. The state course of study in social studies was used as the basis for yearly planning. It is divided into six sections. These form the center sections of the wheel. Section one deals with Beginnings, from prehistory to 1607. Sections two through five deal with the period from 1607 to 1919. Section six deals with Modern America: 1920 to the present.

The second ring of the wheel describes the topic further. In section one the second ring addresses two parts: early civilizations and Indian culture. The early civilizations component focuses on ancient Greece. It covers science, mathematics, architecture, democracy, myths, and fables. The Indian culture component covers Native American myths and relates to the ancient Greek component through the study of myths.

A third ring identifies one or more overarching themes. For section one these are patterns and community. Added into rings two and three is the science component of the theme. In section one it is classification of organisms and the human body. Greek efforts at understanding the human body and classifying life forms are related to modern science. The process skill of classification plays an important role in this integrated thematic unit. Mathematics enters into the study of ancient Greece and also into the consideration of patterns. Language arts and reading are woven throughout the theme.

Column Design

At another school teachers have used a chart with columns to do yearly planning. A second-grade teacher noted that the theme of communities was important in both social studies and science. She listed the major ideas in both courses of study. When she placed the lists side by side she found the concept of communities represented frequently in both lists. In social studies the course of study identified communities as a major concept. The science course of study identified plants and animals as major concepts. The teacher decided that any investigation of plants always examined communities of

FIGURE 3.1   **Yearly Planning With a Wheel Design**

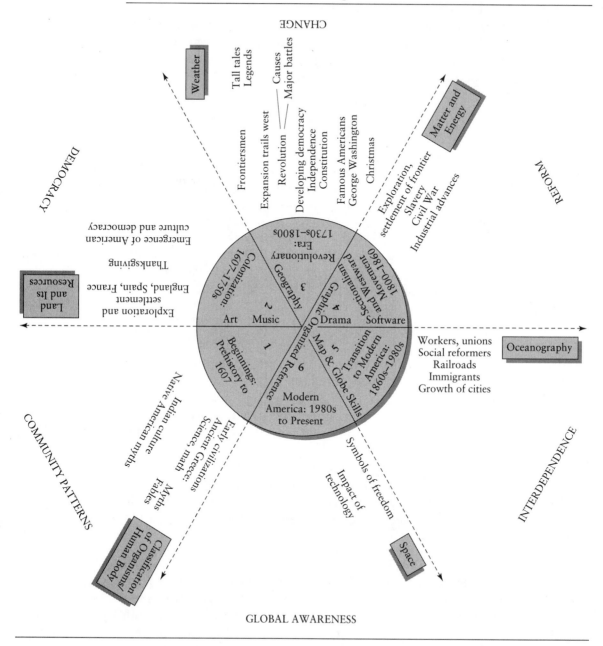

plants. These might be the community of lima bean sprouts in cups along the classroom window or it might be the community of plants in a rainforest, in the field just beyond the school parking lot, or growing up in the cracks in sidewalks. But, they are all plant communities. Animal communities are diverse because animals generally live in mixed-animal communities and may also live in same-animal communities.

Mathematics became important because the study of communities required the use of graphs and charts to represent numbers and comparisons. Addition, subtraction, and multiplication were important and problem solving was necessary. The columns labeled social studies, science, and mathematics were filled in quickly. Next, the teacher added language arts/reading, noting that many of the stories the children read during the year dealt with communities. Music, art, and physical education then were added.

At this point there were a lot of items in each column. In listing the items, the teacher noted that communities was a frequent theme. But, since she mostly had listed topics in the order found in the curriculum, the relationships between the content in each area was not obvious. Therefore, she reorganized the contents of each column so related ideas appeared in the same row. Lines were drawn across the columns to form rows. Finally, each row was dated to indicate the tentative time period when it would be taught. Figure 3.2 shows part of the yearly planning chart developed.

Sample of a Partial Yearly Planning Chart With Columns　　　　FIGURE 3.2

Second Grade

Tentative Date	Social Studies	Science	Mathematics	Language Arts/Reading
	human communities	animal communities	numbers	stories about communities
		plant communities	addition subtraction multiplication	
	map/globe skills	weather		stories about places/weather
	friendship			reading/writing about friends
	graphing	graphing	graphing	interpreting graphs
	observing	observing		recording observations
		finding patterns	finding patterns	finding literary patterns
	reporting	reporting	reporting	reporting
	problem solving	problem solving	problem solving	problem solving

Bubble Design

Another group of teachers use bubbles to connect the pieces to be taught in a curriculum (Figure 3.3). The central bubble contains the focus concept, skill, attitude, or issue to be investigated. In the example in Figure 3.3 the process skill of classification is the focus. Related skills and ideas from other disciplines are added in. Then a second bubble set is constructed. Generally there is an overlap between two bubbles in the first and second set to provide continuity and a transition. Then, a third bubble set is constructed. Again, there is an overlap with the second set. The third bubble set constructed overlaps with one or two bubbles from the first set. Bubble sets are added until planning is completed. Figure 3.3 shows a partial bubble set. The teacher is using classification as a major yearly planning theme. A bubble set is attached focusing on communities. Students will be classifying communities as human, plant, or animal. They will be using addition to help them process material as they classify it. A second bubble set is attached focusing on map/globe skills. It has a subtheme of places. The content is being classified as stories about places, weather in places, or drawing places. More bubble sets will be added to the bubble planning map and more detail may be added to each set.

Whichever format is used to plan the yearly curriculum, it is important to compare the topics between the disciplines. Where potential for integration occurs, initial planning can occur. See also Figure 3.9 given later in this chapter. Finally, a tentative timeline is developed to show when integrated units are taught. The timeline also can indicate when stand-alone units representing just one discipline are taught if these are to be part of the curriculum.

FIGURE 3.3   Sample of a Partial Bubble Yearly Planning Map

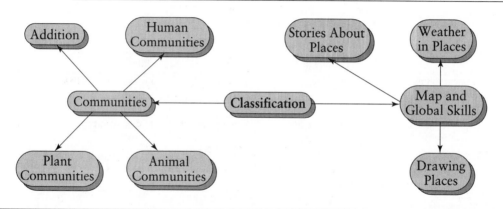

Planning With Other Teachers

Integrated thematic units frequently are planned by teams of teachers. These can be grade level teams or they can cross grade levels. The team may include other teachers such as the physical education teacher.

In cases where a team of teachers is doing the planning, coordination and consensus become very important. The team meets to develop a structure for the yearly plan. A teamed unit shares the work among teachers but also creates new work. Coordination among teachers is time-consuming (Sunal et al., 1994).

Several possibilities for structuring the yearly plan are described above. An option is to select one theme that will be investigated all year long. Examples of such a theme are written communication, observing the world, rivers, storytellers, patterns, and global interdependence. Other themes are taught in smaller integrated units or in stand-alone disciplinary units. But students continue to come back to the yearlong theme.

One annual theme used in a school was "nations around the world." Each classroom investigated a different nation using categories shared across the teaching team. The categories included physical geography, ecology, national literature, and language(s). The results of the investigations were shared at various points throughout the school year. As an alternative, each class could have investigated the same set of nations using common categories or through devising their own categories of investigation. Their results may or may not have been shared. Choosing a yearlong theme is difficult because it gets boring if the students quickly exhaust the resources available or run out of avenues for investigation. However, if a theme seems to have potential and the teachers are willing to try it, the effort usually is worthwhile. If the theme proves to be too limited, it is ended whenever there is a consensus that it is time to put it aside. The experience will have provided opportunities for integration that otherwise would not have occurred. It also helps teachers determine what sort of theme works best with their students.

Coordinating an integrated thematic unit among two or more teachers is time-consuming and takes good negotiation skills. A lead teacher should be designated for each unit. This is best done through volunteering. The lead teacher spends a lot of time coordinating the effort. Because of the commitment required, the job of lead teacher should rotate through the units. A workshop or inservice program on consensus-building is helpful to all members of the team.

Beginning Points

Identifying the theme of a unit is the real beginning point for planning. The theme is sometimes suggested by resources available, an assessment carried

TABLE 3.2   **Steps in Planning an Integrated Thematic Unit**

Brainstorming
Using a K-W-L
Listing Unit Objectives
Acquiring Background Information
Identifying the Focus Questions
Writing the Rationale
Identifying Intended Learning Outcomes
Naming the Integrated Unit
Considering Special Needs Among the Students
Categorizing Intended Learning Outcomes
Selecting Resources for Learning
Developing a Web
Developing the Lesson Plans
Developing an Assessment Plan
Developing the Integrated Teaching Unit Tentative Outline
Implementing the Unit

out with a group of children, a political event, or any number of other situations. So, the unit may begin with a step that usually is found late in the planning process, such as assessment. Whatever the starting point, unit planning is a circular process. Teachers return to earlier steps, changing an idea, activity, outcome, or focus question. Even when the unit is completed and the class has moved on to a new unit, teachers and students find resources that can be added to the unit the next time it is taught, or think about changes in activities. The unit planning process continues.

Steps in planning an integrated thematic unit are described below and in Table 3.2. The teacher can begin the process at any step and return to a step at any time. Previous work even can be completely discarded. The steps described below are one way of planning a unit from the initial idea for the unit through plans for its assessment. Teachers may add or skip steps. This is a plan we have found works well, but it is not a cookbook recipe and must be adapted by the teacher to the students and the classroom in which the unit is taught.

BRAINSTORMING THE THEME

Once a theme for the integrated unit is identified, brainstorm terms, words, and phrases related to the theme. This is an initial list of ideas and process skills. It will be revised and changed as the process is continued. Let the ideas flow and don't try to limit them. It can be webbed. The web serves as a "thumbnail sketch" of the total unit. This initial web probably differs from the unit that is actually taught as input is received from students, peers, and the resources that are chosen. An example of initial thematic brainstorming for an integrated unit is given in Figure 3.4.

The theme, conflict resolution and peace, is identified in the center of this brainstormed web. Four major subthemes branch off the main theme: the adult world, classroom behaviors, training strategies, and good and bad examples. Three subdivisions then are identified for each subtheme.

Initial brainstorming can be done by a teacher or by a team. The chalkboard, a big piece of newsprint, or a computer webbing program is used. The theme is put in the center. In the case of a team, each member uses a different colored marker or different symbol on a computer webbing program, particularly if each team member is responsible for teaching a different discipline,

An Example of Initial Thematic Brainstorming **FIGURE 3.4**

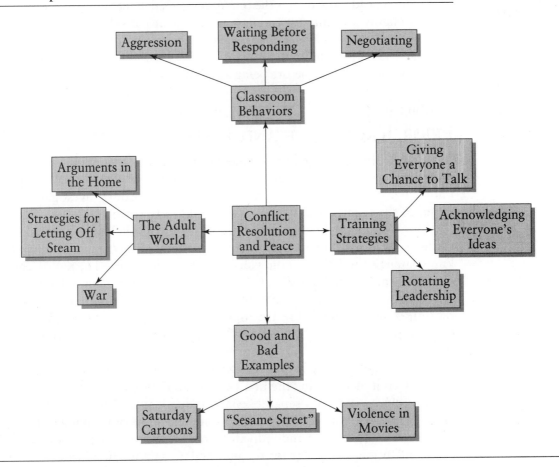

strongly prefers teaching particular disciplines, or demonstrates a quite different teaching style. The web items can be identified with an individual when different colors or symbols are used so this teacher later can be asked to describe why the item should be part of the unit. Depending on the personalities of the teachers involved or the size of the team, the teachers may decide they do not need to identify who generated each item.

Team members may ask one teacher to start off the web with others following. Or, a team may ask a teacher to serve as the recorder, writing others' ideas on the web. This can be time consuming because the recorder has to identify where the speaker wants items to be recorded on the web. In either situation, flexibility is important. A teacher may see a connection that wasn't obvious earlier or may want to add something after noting additions by someone else. Taking turns is important in making sure each person gets a chance to be involved and has some idea when their turn will come. The leadoff teacher can be the person who takes responsibility for coordinating the unit. Or, the coordinator can be identified after the unit is developed, depending on the individual's strengths and interests. Unless some means of releasing a teacher to coordinate the unit is available, care should be taken not to give one teacher too many units to coordinate. Novice teachers with little experience should work with several units before being asked to coordinate one.

USING A K-W-L PROCEDURE TO IDENTIFY PRIOR KNOWLEDGE AND INTERESTS

If the initial brainstormed web suggests there is a good opportunity for an integrated thematic unit, it is important to identify the students' prior knowledge about the theme and their interests regarding investigations relating to the theme. A K-W-L can be helpful in this process.

The K-W-L is a three-step procedure (Ogle, 1986). The teacher asks the students: 1) What do you *know* about the theme? 2) What do you *want* to know about it? and 3) What did you *learn* about this topic? The K-W-L can be done through group discussion. Or, each student can record his or her ideas on paper. Group discussion is preferable since sometimes it stimulates students to recall information related to the topic after they have heard someone else's contributions. Students' "K" and "W" comments are recorded on a chart with three columns. The last "L" column is used after the unit.

Following the group responses, two or more students in each class can be interviewed in depth using the first two of the K-W-L questions. Their comments are recorded on a separate chart. Individual student interviews offer an opportunity for a teacher to follow a student's line of thinking as far as it can be taken. The group and individual interview comments are analyzed to determine beginning points for the unit and areas it might address.

After the unit has been completed, the "L" portion of the K-W-L is done. The class discusses the third question, "What did you *learn* about this topic?" The teacher records students' comments in the third column of the chart that was begun before the unit was taught. Those students interviewed for the "K" and "W" portions of the unit are interviewed again and their comments are added to the "L" column of the interviewees' chart. The pre and post comments made in the discussion and interviews are analyzed as part of the unit evaluation.

Develop Unit Objectives

Various sources are used to create a list of unit objectives for the theme that correlate with student interests. These include sources that were used earlier to identify the theme. Among them are courses of study, national standards, local curriculum guides, and textbooks. Some unit objectives also may be derived from the results of a K-W-L process. The objectives structure background reading. Generally unit objectives are broader than are lesson objectives.

There are many ways to write learning objectives. All objectives, whatever their specific format, focus on what the students learn, communicate clearly the teacher's intentions, and indicate how success is achieved. Unit objectives, because they are more general in nature, do not always indicate how success is achieved. As objectives are developed for specific lessons, indicators of success are typically added to the objectives.

The objectives include ideas, process skills, and affects—attitudes and values. With some topics there also may be psychomotor skills, particularly in measurement, in science laboratory experiences, in map and globe activities in social studies, and in the fine arts.

The process of writing objectives helps the teacher consider what the important things are that students should do and learn. Each objective is weighed carefully to determine whether it must be included to help students learn important content knowledge, skills, or attitudes (Sunal & Haas, 1993, p. 108).

When first writing objectives, novice teachers may worry most about how to properly word them. The wording is important and must communicate to the reader. Some educators say that objectives should clearly state what a student will be able to do after instruction that he or she could not do before being involved in instruction. This view of an objective sees the student as an "empty vessel" that is "filled up" during instruction. Students do acquire content knowledge and learn to perform new skills during instruction. However, meaningful learning often requires students to use skills they already have to reorganize their knowledge. This means there are times when what the learners are doing during the instructional process is more important than new knowledge. This view places a greater emphasis on the development of skills (Sunal & Haas, p. 108).

A unit objective can be written as follows:

> "Students will graph population changes in the USA and in the world over a specified period of time."

A lesson objective, by contrast, usually is more specific. If it is written behaviorally the lesson objective will include three parts: 1) under what conditions (specific sources of information), 2) the action of the student (action verb) and 3) the degree of acceptable accomplishment (minimum performance level) (Mager, 1962). An example of such an objective is:

> "Given accurate USA and world census figures totaled every minute and spanning the same 10-minute period each day for three days, students will graph population changes in the USA and in the world on the same graph with 90% accuracy."

This objective illustrates all three parts. It is most appropriate for a lesson objective because it identified the materials that are used. This form of objective is helpful when the student is practicing a skill that has several rules to apply when performing each task.

Many lessons, however, do not include tasks that follow a systematic series of steps. There is a middle ground in the wording of objectives for lessons and units (Jarolimek, 1991). The key to writing such objectives is to use a verb that describes what is done by the learner during the lesson. Among the verbs that accomplish this are: name, list, describe, role play, tell why, and graph (Sunal & Haas, 1993, p. 109). Examples of these types of middle ground objectives are given below in three categories, those that describe ideas, process skills, and attitudes or values. These have enough specificity to be lesson objectives. Note how the descriptive verb suggests what the learner will do during the lesson.

Some examples of objectives indicating *ideas* (a concept or a generalization) students will construct are:

Students will give examples of how the climate influences the lives of people.

Given a list of famous people and their accomplishments, students will make a list of the personal characteristics that have contributed to making people famous.

Students will give examples of pollution they have personally read about or observed.

Students will define a want as something a person would like to have.

Students will give examples of wants they have.

Objectives indicating *process skills* with which students will work are:

Students will gather data by conducting a survey.

Students will organize data into charts.

Students will list their criteria and decision options in a chart form when making an economic decision.

Students will conclude that the price of their wants is greater than the amount of money they have.

Objectives indicating *attitudes or values* with which students will work are:

Students will share their knowledge about Native Americans with other people.

Students will stop using prejudicial language.

Students will demonstrate respect for the elderly.

Students will state that they respect the elderly because of the efforts they put into their work.

The more experience a teacher has writing objectives and evaluating the objectives others have written, the easier it becomes to master the mechanics of writing objectives. Lists of objectives play an important role in planning and evaluation of units and of lessons. Unit objectives set the stage for the eventual development of the lesson plans.

Mastering the mechanics of objective writing does not address the concern about whether the objectives are appropriate. This is a concern that requires an understanding of children's needs and of the curriculum as well as decision-making ability on the part of teachers. Teachers make important decisions as they review the objectives to determine whether they will result in meaningful learning by students.

ACQUIRE BACKGROUND INFORMATION

Researching the theme is critically important. It enables the teacher to assess his or her prior knowledge, add to a personal knowledge base, identify misconceptions held by the teacher or students, and plan ways to reduce misconceptions.

A background information handout is prepared for a theme when a team thinks it needs information in more depth and/or breadth on the theme. Each teacher contributes a section or the unit's coordinator can prepare the handout. Adult resources rather than sources written for children are used for background reading. Some children's books overgeneralize ideas leading to stereotyping or misconceptions.

IDENTIFY FOCUS QUESTIONS

Next, the main points or focus questions for the integrated unit are identified. This is an important step particularly when the ideas have been planned for teachers, as in a textbook chapter or in a detailed local course of study. Textbook chapters typically contain more information than students can construct into ideas. Without focus or central questions it is difficult to help students see the main points of a textbook chapter or of a unit. Focus questions help students make a link between their prior knowledge and the ideas they are encountering in the unit. They also help establish a rationale for studying the unit. Some examples of focus questions for a unit on conflict resolution and peace are:

> How can knowledge about conflict resolution affect my responses to comments people make about my clothes, looks, or ideas?
>
> How should people act when someone seems to be making fun of them or threatening them?
>
> What can families do to prepare children to respond to bullies?
>
> What are the major types of strategies used to resolve conflicts?
>
> What strategies demonstrate appreciation of the contributions of each member of the class, of a group?
>
> Has the most likely way of dealing with an angry situation changed in this century? If so, how has it changed?
>
> Why is conflict resolution an essential element of our society?

Once focus questions are generated they should be analyzed using the following: Which of the focus questions really get at the heart of the unit? What kinds of questions are being asked? Are they mostly "where" or "when" questions? Are there any "how" or "why" questions? To what extent do these questions relate to the students? If the unit is a team effort, all the teachers should analyze the focus questions. The varied teaching and learning styles represented by the team members will result in differing viewpoints. An analysis carried out by all the team members results in a richer and stronger unit.

WRITE A RATIONALE

Now that some time has been invested in thinking about the initial ideas of the unit, a rationale is written describing why this unit is being taught and how it will be communicated to the students. In writing the rationale for the unit these questions are considered:

- How does the unit affect the future of the students as well as their individual needs and interests?

- How does the unit contribute to an understanding of societal issues and help students deal responsibly with them?
- How is the unit developmentally appropriate for the students?
- How does the unit reflect the spirit and character of inquiry and the nature of the learning enterprise?

A rationale statement reflects the values that influence the teacher's perception and conception of students and the relationship of what they learn to society and to the subject matter. Unit rationales are influenced by current trends and directions in education. For example, since the 1970s there has been a shift toward a more student-centered (hands-on and minds-on) approach to the learner (Hendry, 1996).

The unit rationale includes a statement of goals. This is a broad statement of intent reflecting the integration of ideas concerning students, society, and the nature of subject matter. For example, a rationale for a unit on "the earth's past" might contain a goal statement such as, "This unit is designed to give sixth grade students insight into and an appreciation of life as it existed in the past, and ideas concerning how life has developed on earth." As the unit rationale is written, the teacher:

- examines the unit objectives,
- considers the students' characteristics and how the content relates to them,
- formulates the relationship between the content in the unit and potential social issues it brings up, and
- considers how the nature of subject matter is approached in the unit.

IDENTIFY INTENDED LEARNING OUTCOMES OR OBJECTIVES FOR LESSONS

Intended learning outcomes or objectives are statements of what the students should learn at a minimum. These statements can include skills, concepts, generalizations, attitudes, and values. The process of identifying learning outcomes or objectives begins with a consideration of the initial list of ideas from the brainstorming session. These are not activities or things the students will do. When the teacher identifies an interesting activity or field trip, what the students learn from the experience is considered in order to derive an intended learning outcome.

Teachers may derive many of their intended learning outcomes from a course of study. Integrated thematic unit teaching is compatible with state or locally mandated minimum outcomes. The unit is planned around the minimum learning outcomes and then moves beyond those minimums as the student's interests and the resources and time available allow.

The following is an initial list of ideas for a unit on conflict resolution and peace. Those with an "X" best represent potential intended learning outcomes. Those without an "X" are activities, not intended learning outcomes. These activities may have appropriate intended learning outcomes but those have not been identified.

X Strategies for conflict resolution

X Defining aggression

X Learning to count to 10 before reacting to a negative comment from someone else is a usually successful technique for reducing conflict

X Putting oneself in someone else's shoes is difficult to do

X Birds at a bird feeder often demonstrate aggression and conflict

Tallying how often conflict occurs at the author study center

X Finding out how to determine the ratio of economic cost to months of war

X Finding out the cost of property damage caused by riots in U.S. cities in the past two decades

X Measuring the distance children keep between themselves and someone in front of them versus someone in back of them from photographs taken at a learning center

X Giving each person a turn during an informal discussion

Field trip to a drug rehabilitation center

Taking a group picture of the children all shaking hands

X Finding patterns in time(s) of day when arguments tend to break out

NAME THE INTEGRATED UNIT

By this time, the integrated unit has probably already been given a name. This is the time to take a few moments and consider its name as a way of emphasizing the focus the unit is taking on. Does the name capture the importance or value of the unit, as well as its content? Does the name indicate the initial ideas are logically connected to each other? The following are the names of some integrated thematic units developed by teachers.

Native Americans Are Us

Atoms, Molecules, and You

Australia Is a Unique Habitat

Chemical Reactions and Food

Mexico: A Land of Many Cultures

Living Things and How They Adapt

Rules—For People and in Nature

Transportation Is How We Move People and Things

Properties of Matter

The Global Economy Is Interdependent

Conserving Our Environment

Involving Children in Social Action

Sounds of Music

Using the Skies

Unit titles can communicate the essential meaning of a unit. An alternative way of naming the unit is to use a question. The unit serves to answer the question. For example,

What Are the Properties of Matter?

What Are the Characteristics of a Global Economy?

What Steps Can Be Taken to Conserve Our Environment?

How Can Children Be Effectively Involved in Social Action?

How Do People and Things Move From Place to Place in Our Country?

Why Should We Consider Space Travel?

What Have Been the Critical Events in Space Travel?

How Do We See Colors?

CONSIDER SPECIAL NEEDS AMONG THE STUDENTS

The individual teacher developing an integrated thematic unit is aware of the special needs of students within the class. Early in the school year, however, the teacher may need to list out these needs as a new unit is developed or a unit from a previous year is considered for use this year. When a team of teachers is planning an integrated thematic unit, discussion of the needs of students in each of the classes to be involved occurs. The discussion covers those needs identified through the special education program. It also covers needs which do not fall within the purview of the special education program. The discussion includes children: 1) who are having difficulties academically, 2) who are gifted and talented, 3) whose native language is not English and who are not yet fluent in English, 4) who have physical and emotional difficulties, and 5) who are experiencing severe stress in their families resulting from divorce, death, a move from another state, or major illness. Each of these children requires adaptation of the unit.

CATEGORIZE INTENDED LEARNING OUTCOMES

After special needs among the students are considered, the intended learning outcomes are grouped into categories. Grouping them into two categories, ideas and process skills, is useful. When the "idea" category is completed, each is identified as a generalization, concept, attitude, or value. The two categories are analyzed to determine whether all the ideas and process skills important to the unit are included. The proportions of the ideas and skills also are examined to determine whether they are appropriate for this unit.

SELECT RESOURCES FOR LEARNING

The selection of resources is a collaborative process involving students, teachers, and media specialists. All appropriate materials are listed. The list is as specific and as complete as possible. A brief synopsis of each book and other resource is helpful in a teamed unit. It also is helpful to individual teachers who intend to use the unit again in the following school year.

DEVELOP A WEB

At this point a web is developed as a means of analyzing the important ideas and skills the students should learn in the unit (see Figures 3.5, 3.6, and 3.7).

The list of ideas and skills is used to develop this web. Additional ideas or skills are added as needed to support the unit theme. The web can have a hierarchical format or it can take a schematic components format (Figures 3.5, 3.6, and 3.7). The format should fit the theme.

A Hierarchical Web

To create a web using a hierarchical format, the following steps take place.

1. Select the main idea or process skill.
2. Add ideas and skills to the list if needed.
3. Write the ideas and/or skills on index cards or use a word-processed list.
4. Rank the ideas and/or skills from the most general to the most specific.
5. Group the ideas and/or skills into clusters. Add more specific ideas and/or skills if necessary.
6. Arrange the index cards of ideas and process skills in a two-dimensional array or use a computer webbing or drawing program.
7. If using index cards, write the ideas and skills on a sheet of paper as they appear in the two-dimensional array.
8. Link the ideas and skills on the paper or computer web and label each link.

A Sample Hierarchical Web   **FIGURE 3.5**

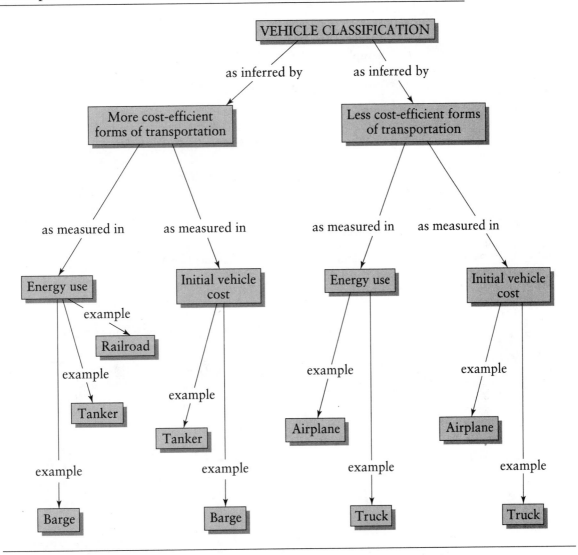

An example of a list of some ideas for a unit on the theme of classification, a process skill, follows. In this example, the skill is studied through content related to vehicles. The list is ordered from most general to most specific.

Vehicle Classification	Initial Vehicle Cost
More Cost-Efficient Forms of Transportation	Helicopter
Less Cost-Efficient Forms of Transportation	Railroad
Energy Use	Automobile

FIGURE 3.6   **Partial Example of a Schematic Components Web**

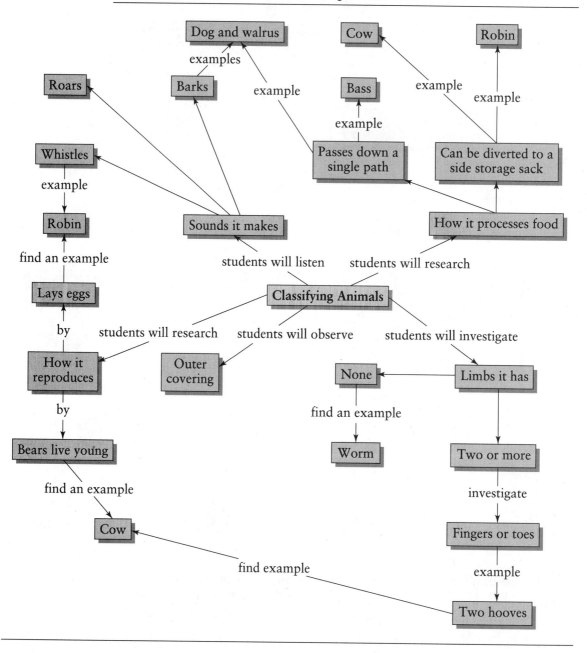

A Sample Lesson Plan

FIGURE 3.7

Sample Lesson Plan on Folk Tales and the Natural World*

Key Idea: To examine the role nature plays in culture as described in folklore.

Goal: To describe ways in which natural elements are portrayed in some Native American folk tales and the evidence given for their importance to the society described.

Exploration Phase

Objective: Students will make observations of a kachina doll and note details suggesting a relationship to natural elements.

Materials: Colored pictures of five different kachina dolls (one set per group), writing materials

Procedures:

1. With class, identify elements of natural world and list on board: sun, moon, weather, plants, etc.

2. Place students in small groups. Have group materials manager give each student a kachina doll picture. Ask, "Can you identify anything on this doll that looks like it is suggesting an element of the natural world?" Make a chart with a row for each doll and the element(s) it suggests. Share ideas and make a class chart.

Evaluation: Examine class chart noting which natural elements have been identified.

Invention Phase

Objective: Students will explain the importance of natural elements to the Hopi, particularly in regard to their major crop, corn.

Materials: One kachina doll picture set for each group, Hopi folk tales on selected natural elements related to raising corn

Procedures:

1. Talk about the Hopi using a U.S. map. Use video, *Hopi* (1982, produced by Tellens, Inc. Flagstaff, AZ: Museum of Northern Arizona). Ask students to note: the main crop, the way weather determines farming practices, and where corn is used as more than just a meal item. Write each as a category on a chart on board.

2. Fill in chart. Discuss natural elements corn needs if a good crop is to be produced. Which seems most important to the Hopi and most worrisome?

3. Talk about kachina dolls as representations of the spirits of the natural world especially rain, crops, sun, and people. Talk about how kachinas today help the Hopi as they try to get rain for their crops.

4. Talk about how folk tales are passed down through the years and explain how the Hopi understand the kachinas and their part in the natural world. Talk about how the folk tales tell us about the ideas of people of long ago.

5. Assign each group an element from the natural world including sun, rain, crops, and people and a folk tale focusing on that element. Ask each group to present to the class an analysis of how their element is depicted in the folk tale using evidence from the story. Does the story tell how the Hopi think that element came about? Does it tell why the Hopi think that element is so important? Does the folk tale mention an element that the Hopi think is important but which none of the groups is investigating? If so, what is the evidence for this in the folk tale?

6. Review information on the water cycle and on photosynthesis. Ask students to review the role water plays in plant growth.

7. Closure: Ask the class to construct a web to show what natural elements the Hopi would think are important in raising a corn crop and how they are connected. Draw the web on large newsprint, put it on a bulletin board, and ask each group to put a kachina that suggests that element next to the element on the web.

Evaluation: Ask the students to examine a color transparency of a new kachina, identify its relationship to a natural element, and determine whether it would fit into the web and if so, where.

(continued)

FIGURE 3.7   *(continued)*

Expansion Phase

Objectives: 1) Students will make a kachina doll that represents a natural element not previously investigated and describe how the doll creates that representation. 2) Students will determine whether, and if so, where, the new element would fit into the web constructed earlier to identify elements important in raising a corn crop.

Materials: Three empty spools for each student, cardboard, glue, feathers, paint, paintbrushes

Procedures:

1. Present students with a list of natural elements not investigated previously (for example: lightning, thunder, wind). Ask them to research the characteristic(s) the element they have identified would have in a kachina.

2. Have students make a kachina doll replica. The three spools will be glued together end to end to create the body. Arms will be painted on the middle spool and legs on the bottom spool. Next, the top spool will be painted to resemble the spirit's head. Decorated cardboard will be added to the head. Feathers and cardboard symbols will be added to help show the element with which the kachina is associated.

3. Each student will describe how the kachina creates a representation of the natural element and will tell whether it might fit into the "raising a corn crop" web constructed earlier and if so, why. Ask them to consider information they have from previous lessons on the role water plays in plant growth.

4. The students will briefly summarize the lesson's activities and key idea.

Evaluation: Ask students to fill in a note card giving evidence for: 1) his/her doll's representation of a natural element and 2) whether or not the element the doll represents belongs in the "raising a corn crop" web. Examine the note cards to determine appropriateness of the evidence cited.

*Adapted from: Sunal, C. S., & Sunal, D. W. (1996). Interdisciplinary social studies and science lessons with a native American theme. *The Social Studies 87*(2), 72–77.

In the hierarchical web, Figure 3.5, the more general ideas are located at the top of the web (vehicle classification, more cost-efficient forms of transportation) and are followed by more specific ideas down the web.

A Schematic Components Web

Many of the procedures listed above for the hierarchical web can be followed in creating a schematic components web (for example, using index cards or a computer webbing program). In the schematic components web in Figure 3.6 the unit topic is located in the center of the web. Note that one component of this web has been filled out fully—the component on atmosphere and space. The other components could be filled out in greater detail as well. Also, note that this web contains a generalization—"transportation has changed through time."

The Technique of Webbing

Both types of webs connect the main ideas and process skills with defining terms such as "has," "depends on," "as measured in," and "as inferred in." These terms are defining the processes used in learning this content—inferring, measuring, etc.

Using a webbing technique helps the teacher analyze the nature of the unit at this stage. Questions to be asked include the following.

Does the web show ideas and process skills?

Are there too many abstract ideas?

What concrete ideas could be added to help the students understand the abstract ideas?

Are there any values or attitudes included?

Webbing When Using a Textbook

A textbook may be the source of the theme, or its major support. Sometimes a story in a reading book is used or a chapter in a social studies or a science textbook. When a textbook chapter is used as the focus of the theme, a list is made of the important ideas, process skills, values, and attitudes contained in the chapter. The web is created from this list. The teacher may modify the web by adding concrete ideas or process skills that were missing from the textbook's approach to the topic, or the teacher may have to de-emphasize and eliminate some concepts. Typically, social studies and science textbooks contain a large number of concepts. Teachers need to sift through these to decide which are the major concepts providing the foundation for the theme.

DEVELOP THE LESSON PLANS

The initial learning outcomes are revised and written as objectives, and grouped into practical categories for teaching. These objectives typically are more specific than are the unit objectives.

As lesson plans are developed, the topic, objectives, and methods of presentation are identified. Writing the lesson plan helps the teacher:

1. organize its presentation,
2. anticipate student responses and problems that may arise in students' understanding, and
3. plan management procedures such as passing out materials or moving into groups (Clark & Yinger, 1979).

Careful planning directs students' attention during instruction toward the behaviors needed to accomplish the objectives (Smith & Sendelbach, 1979).

This is the meaning of the phrase "time on task." Interesting tasks, particularly student-generated ones, and clearly given directions and procedures eliminate distractions and many discipline problems.

Lesson planning involves applying theory about effectively helping students learn. This assures that students' attention is gained and directed and that thinking skills are practiced, used appropriately, and assessed for accomplishment (Sunal & Haas, 1993, p. 113).

Lesson Plan Structure

In the beginning of the lesson, the teacher focuses students' attention and creatively directs it toward the content of the lesson. This brings the students' prior knowledge and experiences into their working memory. It is an open-ended part of the lesson. It uses concrete and manipulative materials where possible. The purpose of this first part of the lesson is to confront or challenge what students know and motivate them to want to learn something new or to restructure what they know (see Table 3.3 and Figure 3.7). In the sample lesson given in Figure 3.7 the teacher challenges students to identify natural elements (such as rain) in traditional Hopi kachina dolls. The teacher notes elements students are able to identify.

Next, the lesson becomes more teacher directed as the teacher provides some information for the students to examine. Materials and activities are used to help students invent the skill or idea that is the focus of the lesson. Teachers explain the idea or skill, model it, and have students try it out. The teacher may deliver this information in the form of an oral presentation, or the teacher may select another form of stimulus such as a set

---

TABLE 3.3   Lesson Outline Summary

First,
    Focus students' attention on topic in an open-ended manner,
    Assessing their prior knowledge, and
    Challenging what they currently know.
Second,
    Explain the new idea or skill,
    Model the new idea or skill, and
    Have students **try it out.**
    Find out whether students have invented the new idea or skill for themselves.
Third,
    Students **use** the idea or skill just invented, then
    Summarize what they've done in the lesson and
    Identify what idea or skill they've invented.

of pictures, story, poem, recording, chart, map, or artifact to present knowledge. The information challenges students' existing content knowledge, skills, or attitudes. After the students and teacher examine the information, the class interacts with the data. Often questions are asked to accomplish this. Sometimes the teacher directs the students to perform a task such as ordering the data from largest to smallest, after which they are asked to make an interpretation or to form a conclusion. During the class interaction the teacher observes to see if most of the students have constructed the knowledge or skills represented. At the end of this portion of the lesson, the students and teacher are involved in a closure that wraps it up and indicates whether students have invented the idea or skill for themselves. If not, the teacher reteaches the portion where errors occurred. Then another task is provided in which groups or individuals again practice with the data.

In the sample lesson in Figure 3.7, the teacher uses a video, folk tales, and a review of the role water plays in plant growth to help students investigate the role natural elements play in the life of the Hopi, particularly in relation to their primary food crop, corn. The ability of folk tales to tell us about the culture of a group of people and of their understanding of elements of the natural world is explained. The teacher brings closure to this part of the lesson by involving students in an activity, the construction of a web. The web focuses on Hopi viewpoints and brings closure to the idea that the Hopi have identified and interconnected natural elements impacting their ability to grow their main crop, corn.

In the last part of the lesson, the teacher involves students in using the idea or skill just invented so it sticks with them as part of their long-term memory. After working with the idea or skill, the class summarizes what they have done in the lesson and identifies the idea or skill invented. At this time the teacher observes more closely and may collect students' work to evaluate accomplishment of the lesson objectives. If all or some of the students do not accomplish the objectives, the teacher reviews, reteaches, and reevaluates those portions of the lesson where problems have been found before proceeding on to the next lesson.

In the sample lesson in Figure 3.7, students are asked to investigate how a kachina doll represents a natural element previously not investigated. Then they are asked to determine whether this new element is important to raising a successful corn crop. These activities apply and expand on the ideas the students constructed for themselves under teacher guidance in the middle portion of the lesson.

As the lesson is taught, the teacher observes and interacts with the students. The teacher also interacts with the materials and equipment used. This combination is not easy. Many teachers express the wish to be more than one person. Planning the lesson and the management of students and materials in advance are important to successful teaching.

Researchers tell us that most teachers usually stick close to their lesson plans (McCutcheon, 1981). That is why the lesson plan is thoroughly prepared. Teachers seem to plan more thoroughly when they are teaching new material because of their lack of experience in this particular situation. Beginning teachers need more detailed lesson plans because they have limited experience in teaching students various content areas.

IDENTIFYING ACTIVITIES AND RESOURCES AND PLANNING LESSONS

Potential activities emerge from the list of learning outcomes. One way to look at the activities is to consider the resources available and resource strategies possible. Among these are: textbooks, field trips, games, guest speakers, computer software, laboratory equipment, videos, manipulatives, case studies, debates, and role playing or simulations. Each of these can serve as a focal point for a type of experience designed to facilitate the accomplishment of an objective. For example, in a unit on scarcity, one objective might be: "Students will give examples of wants they have." Possible resources and resource strategies for this objective are:

A field trip to a store

A video clip of the "shopping channel"

Advertising supplements from newspapers

Pages 11 and 12 in the social studies textbook

Each of these resources and resource strategies has an integrity of its own. Each can be used to achieve one or more different outcomes. Bibliographies of teacher books and materials and of student books and materials are part of the resources used.

Most teachers have severely limited money available for the purchase of resources. Schools in large cities have access to libraries, museums, dance troupes, and a wide variety of other resources. The cost of field trips may limit the use of some of these resources. However, there usually are many options for the loan of materials and access to materials. Rural teachers often have more limited options in regard to the social world although they have many more options around them in terms of the natural world. Rural teachers may find a wealth of resources in even the smallest community (Sunal, Christensen, & Sunal, 1997). Many rural areas have historical societies whose members come to the classroom and bring or lend artifacts for study in the classroom. Rural teachers can use county records for information regarding how property has been handed down in families, who the streets in small towns are named after, and the birth dates of ancestors of the children in the class. The state forestry and fisheries departments, farmers' cooperatives, local bank employees, postal carriers, local government officials, and the state office of the national geological survey are all resources that provide material for classroom use.

Technology as a Resource

Internet

Technology serves as a wonderful resource when it is available. The Internet is a resource utilizing current technology. Information is available on virtually any topic that might be taught. It can be accessed in a number of ways. Many areas have freenets that allow users access to the Internet for a specified number of hours a week or a month in return for a low or no fee. Local libraries usually have information on whether a local freenet is available. Web sites on the Internet change rapidly. When material is located that is appropriate for the unit the best policy is to print off a copy or to save it on a disk because it may change, move to another web site address, or disappear from the Internet. Students can access the Internet to search for materials supporting the unit with appropriate supervision from teachers.

The Internet offers a huge range of materials on many topics. In one recent integrated unit on simple machines, for example, a search of the Internet yielded the home pages of over 50 companies that make pulleys, a simple machine. Further examination of their Internet pages indicated that some make pulleys for clotheslines and other devices familiar to most people. However, many of the companies make pulleys for robotic arms and other forms of robots. Pulleys today still are simple machines. But, they are used widely in the most complex of modern machines. These sometimes miniaturized pulleys serve the same function that a clothesline pulley serves, but are made of different materials and result in a machine that is complicated yet may be still serving a simple function—such as inserting a bolt into a car's framework. The teachers had not realized the extensive role simple machines play in today's complex industries. Their unit was made more meaningful by their greater ability to move from the science and technology of the past to the science and technology of the 20th century and then into the science and technology of the 21st century.

The Internet includes collections of lesson plans sponsored by professional organizations such as the National Science Teachers Association and the National Council for the Social Studies. These lessons plans often include materials that are useful in a unit or they indicate where materials for a specific lesson might be obtained. It also includes chat groups such as

K12.CHAT.ELEMENTARY. This is a place where children in grades K–5 can talk with peers.

K12.CHAT.TEACHER is a casual conversation group for teachers in grades K–12.

There are many sites which offer various services for teachers. Examples are

K12PALS@SUVM.SYR.EDU. This site is a list for teachers to help students seeking pen pals.

NETSRCH@IUBVM.UCS.INDIANA.EDU. This site helps teachers find workshops on topics of interest to them.

Newsgroups present ideas relating to curriculum and instruction. An example is K12.LANG.ARTS. This is devoted to language arts instruction.

Listserves are groups of people discussing a common interest. One such group is FLAC-L@BROWNVM.BROWN.EDU. This is the Foreign Language Across Curriculum list.

There are many sites just for children. These include sites offering a newsletter such as the KIDlink Newsletter at KIDNEWS@VM1.NODAK. EDU. Children also are interested in sites such as those offered by the tourist bureaus of many nations. These include maps, pictures of historical sites, travel information, and weather updates. Museums and zoos have web sites, as do theaters. Many classrooms create their own site and encourage other classes to visit them.

The Internet is accessed with a modem from a home, school, or university computer. There are a number of services available such as America Online, CompuServe, and Prodigy, through which teachers can access the Internet. All of these services can be contacted via a toll-free telephone number. These services charge a monthly fee for access. School systems and universities often purchase software such as Netscape or Mosaic that allows users to browse the Internet. Telephone companies usually offer low school rates for phone lines used to access the Internet. Because they are used frequently in school and university settings, phone lines often are dedicated just to Internet access.

There is so much information on Internet that a checklist for evaluating it is useful. Five categories are suggested by Ryder and Hughes (1997, pp. 185–186): purpose and audience, authority, scope, format, and acceptance of material. A section on purpose and audience considers whether the material is designed for your student audience, the site's goal, and who supports the site and their goal. Authority involves considering the credentials of the site's originators. This is done by sending them an electronic mail requesting information about their credentials if they are not obvious from the information given at the site. Scope involves considering the breadth and depth of the information at the site. It is important to skim the information to determine whether the time spent on a careful reading of the site will be worthwhile. Format involves the presentation of information in the site. Is it easily interpreted and can it be easily printed off? Acceptance of the materials involves others' opinions of the information. Is the site from a widely recognized source? Teachers should acquaint students with materials from good sites and talk about the five categories of characteristics. Students can learn to evaluate a site's usefulness.

Schools need to develop an acceptable use policy if one does not currently exist. Samples of such policies are available at gopher://riceinfo.rice.edu:1170/11/More/Acceptable. A policy describes the limits that are put on the use of Internet by the school, the conditions under which Internet may be accessed and used, any exceptions, and the results that can be expected to occur if the conditions for use are not met. There is a range of protection programs used with Internet. Typically, these refuse student access to specific sites or to sites with certain characteristics, or to sites with specific words in their name.

Compact Video Laser Discs and Compact Audio Discs

Compact video laser discs and compact audio discs often are interactive and can be manipulated by teachers and students. These offer a wealth of visual and auditory resources for the classroom. The choices grow daily (Falk & Carlson, 1992). Some contain a huge amount of information. Examples are Grolier's American Electronic Encyclopedia (Grolier) and Microsoft Bookshelf (Microsoft). Such multimedia resources can include full-motion video clips, photographs, and sound recordings of speeches. They often have searching capabilities making it easy to locate one topic out of the many available and to set up one's own catalog of topics of interest.

Specialized discs are available on many topics. Examples are Time: Man of the Year (Time), A House Divided (Grafica), Eyewitness Photo Gallery: 3—Wild Animals (DK Miultimedia), and The Ultimate 3D Skeleton (DK Multimedia). Some offer reenactments of events such as Struggles for Justice II (Scholastic Software). Even specialized discs may be multipurpose. For example, Struggles for Justice I and II (Scholastic Software) detail the experiences of Native, Latino, and African Americans, women, labor, and immigrants in the United States.

Audio discs make available music from every region of the world. They also make available speeches, old radio shows, poets reading their poetry, and oral storytelling.

These discs give students access to information they can use to conduct research and for a variety of creative endeavors. Many such resources are located in a central area in a school where anyone who needs information has access to it. But, many classrooms now are acquiring discs for immediate use by students as the need and interest arises.

Hypercard Stacks

The creation of a hypercard stack by students is a unit activity that produces a resource that can be used by other students now and in the future. The stack can include material from many visual and auditory resources. Information is shared on nested screens called "stacks." Each screen is like an index card. The developer writes and/or draws information on a card then puts it somewhere in a stack of cards. The stack can be shuffled in different ways. Buttons are put on the screen to give the user the option to go on to new information. With a simple stack the user progresses from card 1 to card 2 to card 3, and so on. By using buttons, the user can branch out and go from card 1 to card 40, back to card 1, etc. Another user may go from card 1 to card 2 to card 3 and then to card 25 and back to card 3. Software packages are available for use in developing stacks. These include Guide, HyperCard, LinkWay, and SuperCard. Internet sites often have colored words that serve as buttons to take the user to another place. As an example of a hypercard stack, the first screen of a stack may show a map of Egypt. With a keystroke or the click of a mouse, a second screen comes up identifying the map as Egypt. Another keystroke returns the user to the map or brings up any one of a number of other screens showing locations or features. The user might go to a screen showing Cairo. This screen may offer the user several choices:

- a map of Cairo
- information on Cairo's major industries
- information on Cairo's form of government
- information on Cairo's oldest building

Students are able to move back and forth in these programs, review earlier information, and explore additional information in areas that they do not completely understand. Pieces can be added to the program to enrich it or to address areas of need identified among students.

Video, Tape Recordings, and Older Technologies

There is a huge amount of resource material available for older technologies ranging from tape recordings to filmstrips to film to video. Most school systems or schools have catalogs of these materials indicating which are available within the school system to teachers and students. Video stores often carry materials of interest to schools that can be rented for use.

Acquiring Simple Materials

Many simple materials can be acquired from parents. These include throw-away items such as plastic containers, empty milk cartons, discarded clothing, old material, yarn and thread, paper towel rolls, magazines, and boxes. They also include simple items parents will want to part with: cookie cutters, ingredients for cooking, recipes, old tools, old small appliances (both in working order and broken), and greeting cards (Charbonneau & Reider, p. 165).

Other items may be obtained from local businesses, professionals, frame shops, print shops, restaurants, tailors, florists, packing houses, travel agencies, pet stores, and lumber yards. These include: boxes, cardboard box inserts, matte board, newspapers, old restaurant menus, old stethoscopes, shoe boxes, buttons, milk crates, carpet and tile samples, wallpaper samples, calendars, and blueprints. These materials are donated or provided at a minimal cost. Since acquiring materials is time-consuming, students help by writing letters of request and collecting materials with their parents (Charbonneau & Reider, p. 165).

Resource People

Guest speakers and other resource people are identified by the teacher or the team members and by students. Resource people are available in all communities even in small, rural ones. They are found among Geological Survey personnel, political party personnel, tribal leaders, soil conservation managers, county surveyors, local historical society members, antique collectors, justices of the peace, legal counsel for industries, and union representatives (Sunal, Christensen, & Sunal, 1997). Students discover interesting hobbies, talents, and memories of community residents once contact with an individual is established. For example, in an informal discussion with the game warden, students in a rural school learned that she is the great-granddaughter of early pioneers in the area, and that she possesses actual cooking utensils used by her great-grandmother and photographs of early local homesteads (Sunal et al. 1994). Resource people are contacted either by students or by a teacher. Scheduling and a list of speakers and resource people is organized by the lead teacher.

Other Resources

There are many other resources for integrated thematic units. These include: articles from magazines, newspapers, journals, and periodicals; assessment items; sources of computer software and compact discs; game sources; mathematics manipulatives; media catalogs; multimedia program sources; motivational ideas; and supply catalogs. Free and inexpensive materials are identified in several publications. Libraries often carry one or more such publications. Among them are annual guides including *A guide to print and nonprint materials available from organizations, industry, governmental agencies and specialized publishers,* New York: Neal Schuman, and *Educator's guide to free materials,* Randolph, Wisconsin: Educators Progress Service. Because the publication of these materials is subsidized, they focus on a viewpoint desired by the individual or agency who is paying for their development and distribution. Teachers need to identify the focus of the materials and the views that are promoted. If these are appropriate to the unit, they can be used. In some units, such as those investigating issues, carrying out a project or creating a case study, materials with a strong view or even obvious bias may be used. In such cases the students are studying the views of different sides and need to find out what are these views and what reasons are given to support them. Many commercially produced resource materials also are available. These are evaluated by teachers as are free materials.

The ERIC System

The Educational Resources Information Center (ERIC) system provides lots of curriculum ideas and research results. University libraries generally have copies of ERIC materials on microfiche. They also provide addresses for specialized ERIC clearinghouses dealing with the various disciplines taught in the elementary school. For example, there is a clearinghouse for science, mathematics, and environmental education, another one for social studies education, and one for reading and communication skills.

Professional Periodicals

Professional periodicals are another superb source of ideas and resources. There are many. Some useful ones are: *Science and Children, The Early Childhood Journal, Social Studies and the Young Learner, Instructor, Science Activities, The Arithmetic Teacher, Young Children, Social Studies, The Computing Teacher, Language Arts, Childhood Education, Learning, School Arts, The Reading Teacher,* and *School Science and Mathematics.*

DEVELOP AN ASSESSMENT PLAN

There are two elements of assessment important at this stage in planning a unit. First, the assessment answers questions and provides feedback with regard to student learning and second, it provides data with respect to the effectiveness of the lesson plans. Chapter 5 discusses assessment in greater detail.

The most common or traditional approach to this step is to prepare a post evaluation instrument (a quiz or test) administered when the students complete the unit. The instrument provides feedback on student learning and information from the students about the effectiveness of the unit.

Other forms of assessment are possible and lend themselves well to integrated unit teaching. Among these are a student writing project, artwork, a map, an interview, a dance interpreting a major idea or process skill, or a group/individual project. Teachers should be wary of identifying "observation" as an assessment strategy. Observation and recording of data on more than one or two students often cannot be successfully carried out in the limited amount of time available to a teacher who is actively involved in a lesson. Assessment can include other items and approaches. Informal and semiformal methods, as well as having students develop portfolios of their work, can be incorporated into an assessment plan.

Assessment instruments are designed to evaluate each type of learning outcome included in the unit. Measures are developed to assess ideas, process skills, and affects.

DEVELOP AN INTEGRATED TEACHING UNIT TENTATIVE OUTLINE

Finally, it is time to implement the unit! Develop an outline indicating when the lessons tentatively will be taught. The outline should be organized by days with lessons indicated in the order in which they will taught. This is an important step in a teamed approach where all members develop the tentative outline together.

The daily schedule may remain the same but where teachers have some flexibility in scheduling, an integrated thematic unit usually results in a schedule that varies across days. For example, students may need some language arts-focused lessons on the writing process before they undertake a research paper in science. Then, they may need some science-focused lessons before they consider an idea in social studies. A mathematics-focused lesson on ratios may be a prerequisite to reading a story that has several references to ratios. So, Monday, Tuesday, and Wednesday may begin with a focus on the writing process and then move on to mathematics. On Thursday and Friday the day may begin with science followed by more writing process activities. The schedule of lessons and activities always is tentative and expected to change as the unit progresses. The initial tentative schedule helps teachers make sure that students have the prerequisite process skills and ideas needed for each lesson and learning experience.

MULTIAGE PROGRAMS

Multiage programs require additional planning. These often are team-taught. They require teachers to analyze and find the relationships between the courses of study for more than one grade level. Mary Calhoun, teacher in Tuscaloosa, Alabama, suggests that themes be staggered. Since the teacher works with the students over more than one year, all the material for each of the grade levels combined in the multiage classroom does not have to be covered in a year. The courses of study for each grade level should be examined. Themes identified involve all the students and are appropriate for their needs. Broader themes may be best, such as "patterns" rather than "ancient Egypt." A tentative two- or three-year plan can be structured by the teacher(s). An example of a tentative plan developed by Terri Phillips, a K–1 multiage teacher at Central Elementary School in Tuscaloosa, Alabama, is given in Figures 3.8 and 3.9. This ensures the coverage of the major topics in the courses of study at all of the grade levels in the multiage classroom. Ms. Phillips tentatively has identified the content areas, major process skills, and mini-units to be taught during the first year in support of a yearly theme, "Everything Has a Story." These are shown in Figures 3.8 and 3.9. A list of literature and related activities tentatively identified to support the yearly theme is given in Figure 3.10. Teachers expect to

FIGURE 3.8   **Sample of a K–1 Multiage Classroom Tentative Two-Year Plan by Terri Phillips, Central Elementary School, Tuscaloosa, Alabama**

Theme Plan

1996–1997 Yearly Theme: "Everything Has a Story"

1997–1998 Yearly Theme: to be identified

Topics	Year 1 1996–1997	Year 2 1997–1998
Community "What's Your Story?"	Family/self Communication	Tuscaloosa/self Transportation
Health "Stories That Make Sense"	Five Senses Human body	Nutrition Dental health
Customs & Holidays "Once Upon a Time"	Long ago USA	Far away Other cultures
Physical world "The Story of Machines"	Matter Magnets	Energy Machines
Universe "Stories From Out of This World"	Space	Earth Air, weather, etc.
Other cultures "Tales from Other Lands"	Various countries	Various countries
Plants & Animals "Wild Animal Tails"	Forest/rainforest Wild	Farm Domestic

Tentative Plan Identifying Content Areas, Process Skills, and Mini-Units to Be Used to Support a Yearly Theme in a K–1 Multiage Classroom, by Terri Phillips, Central Elementary School, Tuscaloosa, Alabama   FIGURE 3.9

Theme Plan 1996–1997

"Everything Has a Story"

Content Areas supported by and integrated into the theme:

Language arts/reading:

Children will explore stories in quality children's literature all year long. Stories will have a diverse range of topics. Included will be a study of folk tales from the United States as well as folk tales from other countries. Children will be read to for enjoyment daily. Children will use various extending activities to extend stories such as webbing, sequencing events, predicting, illustrating, and verbalizing the main idea. Students will also be asked to describe characters, compare and contrast characters, use letter writing skills, and role-playing.

Mathematics:

Children often will be involved with story extending activities related to mathematical concepts. For example, after reading *Strega Nona,* students might count and group pasta into tens. Other math activities with literature connections will include graphs, story addition and subtraction, weighing, telling time, measuring, comparing, ordering, odd/even numbers, and ordinal numbers.

Science:

Children will practice using the scientific method in exploring various topics related to theme literature. Children will be encouraged to conduct research related to topics such as space, matter, and magnets.

Social Studies:

Children will learn of similarities and differences in children's literature and stories across several cultures. Children will use analysis skills and map skills in order to locate different countries studied on world maps and globes. (See attached list of literature to be used for the study of Italy, Russia, Mexico, China, and Japan.) As well as learning about differences in cultures, children also will have the opportunity to research things that are similar in every culture.

Art:

Art will be integrated through the study of different art forms represented by each country studied. For example, we will make origami objects while learning about Japan. Children also will have the opportunity to artistically respond to each topic studied in the medium of their choice.

Cooking:

The study of stories from other countries also allows us to explore the foods that are common in the different countries. Field trips will be planned to restaurants such as those that serve one particular kind of food, for example a Chinese or Mexican restaurant. Chefs at local restaurants will be invited into the classroom to demonstrate food preparation from the various countries to be studied.

Process Skills supported by and integrated into the theme:

Listening:

Since the theme itself is storytelling, students will be actively involved in listening daily for critical information.

Questioning:

Children will conduct a cluster-wide survey to find out the favorite story of first-graders and kindergarteners. Children will be answering comprehension questions after each story such as who? What happened then? How did that happen?

Required curriculum:

The state of Alabama curriculum guide for kindergarten and first grade will be used to incorporate the required content for all kindergarten and first graders. All readiness and level skills will be taught individually and in some small groups.

Class products:

The children will write and publish their own "class story" to be displayed in the classroom or the library. Students also will publish and write individual stories to share with classmates or other classes.

FIGURE 3.10   **Tentative Literature List and Related Activities to Support Yearly Theme in a K–1 Multiage Classroom, "Everything Has a Story" by Terri Phillips, Central Elementary School, Tuscaloosa, Alabama**

Yearly Theme Tentative Literature List and Activities

Theme: "Everything Has a Story"

Listed by Major Country Studied

Italy:

The Legend of Old Befana by Tomie DePaola

Activities: cook a cake, sort and graph candies

Opinions: Was Befana really a witch?

Strega Nona by Tomie DePaola

Activities: sorting and grouping pasta into tens, visiting chef, pasta collage

Cenerntiola (Cinderella)

Activities: Venn diagram with other Cinderella stories

Grandfather's Rock by Joel Strangis

Activity: write letters to grandparents

Pinocchio by Carlo Collodi

Activity: make puppets

Others: *Petrosinella* by Dianne Stanely (Rapunzel) and *The Mysterious Giant of Barletta* by Tomie DePaola

Russia:

Bearhead by Eric Kimmel

Activity: make make-believe creatures—human bodies with animal heads

Bony-Legs by Joanna Cole

Activity: sequencing events

Baba Yaga by Ernest Small

Activities: weighing and measuring fresh turnips

The Mitten by Jan Brett

Activities: sequencing characters in the story, each child make a mitten from favorite color of paper, graph mittens by color. Ask, "How can you keep your hands warm on a cold day?" List student responses.

The Fool and the Fish by Alexander Nikolayevich

Activities: Ask "What would you wish for?"; make a magic fish

Others: *Babushka* by Charles Mikolaycak, *The Fool of the World and the Flying Ship* by Arthur Ransome

China:

The Empty Pot by Demi

Activities: decorate clay pots, plant seeds, learn about plant care—what they need to grow

Liang and the Magic Paintbrush by Demi

Activity: children paint their own pictures

(continued)

(continued) **FIGURE 3.10**

The Magic Boat by Demi

Activities: pausing in the middle of the story to ask students how they would solve the predicament of Chang. Discuss answer, find out what happens.

Yeh-Shen by Ai-Ling Louie

Activities: Venn diagram, compare with Italian Cinderella

The Seven Chinese Brothers by Margaret May

Activities: using ordinal numbers

The Fourth Question by Rosalind C. Wang

Activity: lesson on odd and even numbers

Momotaro the Peach Boy by Linda Shute

Activities: Ask "What would have happened if Momotaro had been selfish?" Plant a peach tree. Cook Kibi Dango.

Tikki Tikki Tembo by Arlene Mosel

Activities: patterning children's by clapping, look up children's names to see what they mean

Others: *The Luminous Pearl* by Betty Torre

Mexico:

Borreguita and the Coyote by Petra Mathers

Activity: making lambs

Abuela by Arthur Dorros

Activity: paint construction paper houses

Too Many Tamales by G. Soto

Activity: eat tamales

The Legend of the Poinsettia by Tomie DePaola

Activity: examine a poinsettia

The Witches Fancy by E. Kimmel

Activities: celebrating Cinco de Mayo, making pinatas, making tortilla cookies

Japan:

The Tale of the Mandarin Ducks by Loe and Diane Dillon

Activities: talk about kindness, care of pets, graph pets

The Badger and the Magic Fan by Tomie DePaola

Activity: making fans—paper Uchiwa

The Paper Crane by Mbang

Activity: making simple origami—paper hats or boats

Grandfather Tang's Story by Ann Tompert

Activity: make tangram pictures

Others: *Three Strong Women* by Claus Stamm, *The Greatest of All* by Eric Kimmel, *The Tongue-cut Sparrow* by Momoko Ishii, *Grandfather's Journey* by Allen Say

FIGURE 3.11   **Sample Unit Planning Form**

Unit Planning Form

Item

Choose Theme	Brainstorm Theme	Schedule Time for Teaching/Planning	Use K-W-L

Person(s) Responsible

Date(s)

Item

List Unit Objectives	Background Information	Focus Questions	Write Rationale	Identify Objectives	Name Unit

Person(s) Responsible

Date(s)

Consider Speical Needs	Categorize Outcomes	Select Resources	Identify Materials Manager	Develop Web

Person(s) Responsible

Date(s)

Item

Develop Plans	Develop Assessment Plan	Involve Parents	Develop Tentative Outline	Assign Special Activities/Responsibilities

Person(s) Responsible

Date(s)

revise the tentative plan but can continue to use its major topics as a guide. A sample unit planning form useful in a situation where more than one teacher is planning a unit for a single grade or a multiage setting is given in Figure 3.11.

SUMMARY

The planning process for an integrated unit begins with an examination of the yearly curriculum outline. Integrated thematic units are included in the yearly plan. They are identified initially by determining where topics from different disciplines are related. There are several ways of displaying these relationships. An integrated thematic unit may be planned by an individual teacher or by a team of teachers. Teaming requires a lot of coordination and consensus building. Usually, it works best when one teacher takes on the role of lead teacher for a unit and oversees its coordination between the various teachers involved.

There are a number of steps to planning a unit. Teachers often return to a step they worked with earlier. Unit planning is circular with no real beginning nor ending point. Even when a unit is over, teachers think about how to add to it or change it the next time it is taught. This chapter outlines steps in unit planning beginning with the theme. However, unit planning can start almost anywhere. The steps described above for unit planning can be followed step-by-step or can be adapted to the individual classroom.

REFERENCES

Carlson, E. (1991, April). Teaching with technology: "It's just a tool." Paper presented at the annual meeting of the American Educational Research Association. Chicago, IL.

Clark, C., & Yinger, R. (1979). Three studies of teacher planning (Research Series No. 55). East Lansing, MI: Institute for Research on Teaching, Michigan State University.

Hendry, A. (1996). Math in the social studies curriculum. In D. Schifter (Ed.), *What's happening in math class? Volume 1: Envisioning new practices through teacher narratives.* NY: Teachers College Press.

Jarolimek, J. (1991). *Social studies in the elementary school* (8th. ed.). NY: Macmillan.

Mager, R. (1962). *Preparing instructional objectives.* Belmont, CA: Fearon Publishers.

McCutcheon, G. (1981). Elementary school teachers' planning for social studies and other subjects. *Theory and Research in Social Education, 9*(1), 45–66.

Ogle, D. (1986). K-W-L: A teaching model that develops active reading of expository text. *The Reading Teacher, 39,* 564–570.

Smith, E., & Sendelbach, N. (1979). Teacher intentions for science interaction and their antecedents to program materials. Paper presented at the annual meeting of the American Educational Research Association, San Francisco.

Sunal, C., Christensen, L., & Sunal, D. (1997). Learning opportunities in communities with limited resources. In B. Hatcher (Ed.), *Learning opportunities beyond the school* (2nd. ed.), Wheaton, MD: Association for Childhood Education International.

Sunal, C., & Haas, M. (1993). *Social studies and the elementary/middle school student.* Ft. Worth, TX: Harcourt Brace.

Sunal, C., Sunal, D., McClelland, S., Powell, D., & Allen, B. (1994). Integrated teaching units: Preservice teachers' experiences. *Journal of Social Studies Research, 18*(2), 10–18.

Yager, R. E., Hidayat, E. M., & Penick, J. E. (1988). Features which separate least effective from most effective science teachers. *Journal of Research in Science Teaching, 25*(3), 165–177.

C H A P T E R 4

IMPLEMENTING AND REFLECTING ON THE UNIT

Implementation is where it all comes together, and where it sometimes all seems to fall apart. Teaching is a fascinating and challenging profession because it has such high points and sometimes, low points. Thoughtful planning and careful implementation increase the number of high points and reduce the low points. Integrated thematic units are complex entities whose effective implementation is influenced by several factors. These include: time, identifying a scope and sequence, identifying and allocating materials and resource people, involving parents, helping students keep the theme in focus, utilizing cooperative learning, considering culminating activities, and reflecting on the unit. Each of these factors is discussed below.

IDENTIFYING A SCOPE AND SEQUENCE

Integrated thematic units are more than a sampling of several disciplines put together (Jacobs, 1989). The scope and sequence of the original disciplines is maintained in the integrated unit. If it is not maintained the unit lacks connectedness because the pieces that make it up are not internally connected. A lack of scope and sequence also makes the content of the unit more difficult to understand and ultimately leads to a lack of depth. Chapter three discusses webbing and other means of identifying connections between disciplines. As connections are identified and the unit is planned and implemented, it is important for teachers to keep in mind the scope and sequence of the disciplines being integrated.

IDENTIFYING AND ALLOCATING MATERIALS AND RESOURCE PEOPLE

Materials and resource people are the starting points for many units. Without available materials and resource people, some themes cannot be taught in a meaningful way. An advantage of a teamed approach is that there are more teachers who can find materials and identify resource people. A greater range and depth of resources are likely to be available for the unit.

As materials are identified and gathered it is important to use some guidelines in their selection:

1. the materials should be educationally significant and
2. the materials should foster, rather than disrupt or nullify, goals within subject areas (Brophy & Alleman, 1993, 1991).

Chapter three discusses the resources for units and gives information on how to identify and collect resources for an integrated thematic unit.

MANAGING MATERIALS

In a teamed situation, teachers meet to identify needed materials several weeks prior to the beginning of a unit. In all settings, notes requesting materials are sent home two weeks prior to the unit and letters soliciting materials from other sources such as a photo shop, are written three weeks prior to the unit. Starting early allows time for follow-up contact if needed and for collecting, inventorying, and organizing materials.

Collected materials need to be inventoried and stored for easy use. The school library often is a good place to store materials for checkout. Even consumables such as boxes are stored there if room is available. In a teamed situation, various members of the team store different materials and maintain a running inventory of them. Inventories are updated on a weekly basis and placed in a visible spot for easy checking by a teacher in need of materials. Inventory information can be stored in a computer to which all teachers have access. It also can be kept as part of an electronic mail system.

Students in upper grades can maintain the inventory. An inventory area, whether it is in the school library or in an individual classroom, is maintained in an organized manner. Organizing materials and inventorying them

Some materials are difficult to keep as part of an inventory!

is time-consuming. This task is taken on by volunteers or by upper-grade students. A teacher is assigned to supervise. This may be the lead teacher for an integrated unit.

INVOLVING FAMILIES

Informing Families

Families are part of the unit in the classroom and through activities carried out at home. Family members can be guest speakers, identify resource people, and collect and provide materials. In the classroom, they can help carry out activities preparing and organizing materials for use in activities. When family members help in the classroom, they need to be supportive of the "less is more" philosophy of effective integrated thematic units. They also need to support a problem-solving focus among the students, rather than telling them in detail how to accomplish a task. Family members can be asked to specialize in one type of activity or one discipline at first (Charbonneau & Rider, 1995). This helps them conceptualize the "less is more" and problem-solving approaches being used in the unit. Family members are thanked immediately after volunteering their time, as they are about to leave the school. Some teachers use a software program to make certificates to give to family volunteers at the end of an integrated unit. The certificates can differ for each major integrated thematic unit, or the same design can be kept throughout the year. Giving family members certificates for volunteering their time at the end of the unit is an immediate reward encouraging further volunteerism throughout the year. It is a reward taking on more importance if the children are involved in producing the certificates and if they present them to their family members during the classroom day.

Parents support the use of family members in the classroom. Sunal, Strong, Wilmoth, and Fassig (1983) used interviews to examine the perceptions of parents of elementary school students in regard to the use of family volunteers in schools. They found parents believe the use of volunteers influences positively student achievement and student attitudes. They approve of family members making classroom materials at home, constructing learning centers, tutoring in the classroom, reading to students, making bulletin boards, and assisting with class projects and field trips. Parents like to be involved in demonstrating their hobbies and heritage to children, be interviewed by students, and respond to students' surveys.

Because of the demands on the time of many adults, a unit is not based on the participation of family members in classroom activities. Many family members are able to work with children at home but not during the school day. During the planning phase of the unit, teachers should consider activities that can be expanded into the home. These generally should follow up and expand on ideas and process skills the students have already invented for themselves in class. The home can provide an opportunity to apply these to another setting, thus expanding their usefulness for students.

Having Family Members Help at Home

Family members can work with children in several ways at home (Sunal, Christensen, & Sunal, 1997). They are involved in their children's reading, listening to them read, and/or discussing the material afterward. They watch a television program with their children then discuss it together. Family members are involved in informal learning activities. This includes the construction and use of a game or other activity. An activity might involve examining whether generic or brand name products are purchased by the family, looking at clothing labels to determine the countries in which clothing was made, calculating the approximate amount of fat grams in the family dinner, or determining the favorite radio stations of different family members and identifying the type of music each plays.

Family members also are involved through formal contracts. In the contract, a family member agrees to be responsible for specified readings, study sessions, library visits, or other activities. These are identified as a required part of the unit, the home-based portion. Students have input into activities that involve family members. The use of a formal contract requires a thorough knowledge of the community served by the school and of the individual family situations of the students. The contract must be acceptable and appropriate to the students and their families.

Some families avoid contact with teachers. There can be many reasons for this behavior. Family members may have had bad school experiences. The family member may think he or she doesn't know much and has little to contribute. Personal problems with health, finances, family members, or a job may be overwhelming. Parents have reported not being involved in their children's school work because of fears for their personal safety at evening events in inner city neighborhood schools, late notice of meetings, and not understanding what they should do to help students with school-related work at home (Tangri & Leitch, 1982). In the early grades, particularly, there are some very young parents who are adolescents. Some families have cultural backgrounds that instill great respect for teachers and view school involvement as parent interference (Krogh, 1995). The teacher maintains an understanding perspective realizing that family members' behaviors have a cause. Building bridges between families and the school is an important part of the planning and implementation of an integrated unit.

Meeting With Family Members

There are many ways to build bridges between family members and the school. A first step is finding a way to meet the family member in person. Some suggestions for first steps follow.

Home Visits

Family members are informed and made a part of the unit through opportunities to talk with a teacher. Home visits are one way to build a bridge between the family and the teacher. These often are scheduled early in the school year, or just before it begins. An appointment is made for the visit. The teacher brings an activity or a toy with which the child can play or has a form the child fills in at the beginning of the visit. This gives the child something to do and relieves the stress children often feel with a first visit by a teacher. The family member and child can be asked to fill out a student information form together with information about the child's favorite television shows, books, games etc. The form is discussed to provide a beginning point for the informal meeting. The idea of integrated units is introduced at this time with a discussion of the first unit to be taught. Home visits should be scheduled for 30 to 40 minutes. Ample time is allowed between visits so that a teacher can stay longer if the family member and child are comfortable and want to talk further with the teacher.

Neighborhood Coffees

A neighborhood coffee or tea session is another effective idea. In cities, several families may live in the same apartment building or on the same block. If the coffee is held at the home of a student or in the commons room of an apartment building, the teacher comes to the children and conveys the importance of the child's home in learning and the teacher's respect for the children's families. Integrated units, their purpose, and potential benefits are discussed at this time. If the neighborhood is one where English is not the home language and the teacher is not reasonably fluent in the home language, a bilingual speaker is recruited to come with the teacher. This conveys respect for the family. In rural areas, neighborhood coffees are scheduled at a home, in a church's meeting room, at the extension agent's office, at a campground, or at the feed store.

Before-School Breakfasts

Before-school breakfasts held at a school, or at a local breakfast spot, are another effective means of involving family members. Working parents often are willing to get an early start on the day but are tired and less willing to go to a meeting with a teacher in the evening. Family members can bring their children along if the meeting is at the school. The school provides babysitting during the meeting and an inexpensive or free breakfast for everyone. As with the other forms of initiating and maintaining contact with family members, the breakfast meeting can offer a forum for introducing and discussing integrated unit teaching.

Family Nights and Unit Fairs

A unit fair or family night can be considered as a culminating activity for an integrated unit. Children develop and prepare games, posters, demonstrations, debates, readings of favorite literature, or other activities relating to the unit. Family members can be involved in a mystery, a scavenger hunt, dancing, board games, or even a version of karaoke. Refreshments are served (Frazee & Rudnitski, 1994). The family night or unit fair also is an opportunity to gather family members' views on the unit and to share plans for the next unit.

Involving Families in Decision Making

Families can be involved in the unit as decision-makers. An advisory group of family members or one or more open meetings with family members is initiated. Family members share their ideas about the direction of the unit and resources and possible activities for it. This often is a difficult route to follow. It involves a lot of preplanning well before a unit is initiated.

Teachers can involve family members during earlier months of the school year in planning for a unit to be implemented much later in the school year. Family members need to understand the purpose and goals of integrated thematic units and the relationship of the unit under development to the course of study and to the scope and sequence of the disciplines involved.

A clear understanding is needed regarding how differences of opinion and philosophy between family members and between family members and teacher will be resolved. When several people are involved in making decisions some conflict is to be expected, and give-and-take will be necessary. Teachers embarking on family members' decision making in relation to the integrated unit should seek training to develop their consensus-building skills. The rewards from giving family members decision-making ability in regard to an integrated unit are many. They include support and a connection between home and school that provides a strong and multifaceted foundation for meaningful learning.

HELPING STUDENTS KEEP THE THEME IN FOCUS

Students are better able to keep the theme in focus when teachers identify the scope and sequence for the unit and are faithful to the scope and sequences within the disciplines involved in the unit. Meaningful learning activities and resources help keep the theme in focus as does sharing responsibility for the unit with students.

Students are involved in identifying the specific content of the unit. Conducting a K-W-L (see chapter three) with students is one means of identifying what they would like to know about a theme.

The students should have choices of activities. There may be some activities that all share. But, choice allows for students to follow their individual interests and use their strengths. The teacher needs to plan the diversity of activities carefully. No student is allowed to engage in trivial or meaningless activities or to have such a narrow focus that the sense of the theme is lost. Activities challenge students' existing knowledge and skill levels but are not be too difficult to achieve.

Because each student and each group of students is different, there is no formula for what sorts of choices to provide in an integrated unit. Each teacher and group of students finds the mix that best produces meaningful learning in the participants. However, some examples of choices in activities follow in order to demonstrate how individual teachers work to provide choices.

A fourth-grade unit on weather had a heavy social studies focus as well as a science focus. One section of the unit worked with "wild weather."

Among the science concepts addressed were weather, climate, clouds, and tornadoes. Social studies concepts incorporated included regions of the United States, continents, similarities and differences among places, and states in which tornadoes occur frequently. One set of activities in this portion of the unit is described below. The students chose to work on one of three activities.

Students could choose to label state names on a map of the 50 states in the United States. Atlases were available as needed. This activity could be done individually, in pairs, or in small groups. Small group discussion followed initial labeling of the states. The students discussed which regions of the country were most familiar, which were least familiar, which seemed confusing and why. The students listed their ideas on charts. Next, the discussion moved to the role of physical shape, rivers, and other geographical features in identifying states. Students working on other activities were surveyed to determine with which states they were most familiar and which states they identified with a highly recognizable shape. The survey results were reported using bar graphs.

Other students examined maps of the United States and tried to decide into which regions they might divide the nation. Atlases were available. Then, these students examined weather reports in newspapers saved over a two-week period. They addressed the question, "Could the United States be divided into regions based on weather?" They began to do reading in a variety of reference sources. Eventually, they decided to divide the United States into five regions using weather as the criterion. Later, these students worked with the students who had chosen the first activity, map labeling, sharing their ideas and rationale.

Another group of students looked through magazines and books to find pictures of various places in the United States. These students classified the pictures by the type of weather shown in the picture. They created a bar graph indicating how many times each type of weather was depicted, finding sunny days the most common. Then, they tried to identify the state in which the place depicted might be found. They used maps constructed by the first group and used students from the first group to help them find states on the map. They also used reference sources to read about the range and type of weather found at various times of year in each state. Deciding weather patterns might be considered in a regional rather than specific state framework, they met with members of the second group to identify regions. After some discussion, they adopted the regional classification system developed by the second group and classified their pictures using that system.

All three groups shared their work with each other. The discussion involved everyone and required groups two and three to create a rationale for their decisions. Activity one proved to be the easiest. The students choosing it, however, became experts sought out by others. They became involved in the discussions of the other groups and quickly became participants. The third group had the most difficult task. They found it was complex and needed simplification. The regional approach to weather classification did simplify the task in comparison to identifying fifty different weather patterns, one per state. Yet, it also meant that variables had to be combined and some differences needed to be ignored. So, the task became one requiring higher-order thinking, and took on a new complexity. Eventually, all students worked on all three activities in some manner.

These three activities accommodated the needs and abilities of all the students. In another situation, the teacher might encourage individual students to work on their own, or might have a larger number of groups. The important aspect is the full and meaningful involvement of each student in such a way that each is learning and each is contributing to everyone's learning. Student involvement was maintained and increased because each group was able to generate and carry out new relevant activities. Among these were the first group's surveys of other students, the bar graphs made by both the first and second groups, and each group's involvement of members of other groups.

The students involved in the activities above were experienced in working in cooperative groups. They soon shared out jobs in the activities. One person became the materials manager, keeping track of atlases, pictures, crayons etc. Another took notes during discussions of important points on which decisions had been made. A third person queried the teacher on various points and reported back to the group. A fourth person visited students working on other activities asking questions and eventually bringing members of other groups into the discussion. Students filled other roles as needed. While the teacher had not asked the students to work as a cooperative group, because they had formed the appropriate skills, they did so without being asked. Cooperative strategies worked well and enabled them to pool ideas and accomplish goals that otherwise would have been too difficult to manage.

Many strategies help students keep the theme in focus. The use of cooperative groups, discussed below, is one such strategy. Another is scheduling. Students have input into the tentative unit schedule as it is initially developed. Teachers work with them to revise the tentative schedule for the unit while it is in progress so that it allows enough time to complete the activities students have undertaken (Krogh, 1995). As problems are encountered, students are encouraged to solve them by themselves in ways that are satisfactory to all. Formative evaluation throughout the unit involves students in critiquing how things are going and whether the theme is being adequately and effectively addressed.

Frazee and Rudnitski (1994, pp. 217–218) suggest the following instructional strategies as ways to foster student learning during integrated thematic units:

- use active learning;
- set a purpose;
- make connections;
- incorporate student interests;
- use a variety of materials and activities;
- state concise instructions for activities;
- take risks;
- be prepared;
- provide multicultural components;
- show enthusiasm;
- know your students;
- provide feedback;
- create outlines, agendas, and study guides; and
- summarize and review learning.

UTILIZING COOPERATIVE LEARNING

Cooperative learning lends itself well to teaching integrated thematic units. The notion of cooperation fits well with the idea of connections between: disciplines; students; family members and teachers; and students and family members and teachers. Learning and the creation of knowledge is fundamentally a cooperative enterprise.

In many activities in the weather unit described above students worked in cooperative groups. In one science-focused activity, students spend time outdoors examining and drawing clouds in the sky. They return to class and share their observations and drawings. Next, they make a cloud in a bottle. The materials manager partially fills a bottle with hot water, then quickly places several ice cubes at the jar's mouth. Two other students then shine flashlights on the jar so that all group members observe what is happening. Two recorders write down observations in weather logs. A group manager makes sure the group follows the directions for the experiment. After some discussion of what is observed, the students read about the three main types of clouds and the context in which they form. They divide themselves into three research sub groups. Each group presents its results to the whole group. The drawings students make of clouds outdoors are considered and the group decides what type of cloud they observed and drew. The group then goes outside daily over a two-week period, observes and draws clouds, and classifies them by type. The materials manager makes sure all drawings are kept in file folders designated by cloud type. The group's reporter presents their observations and conclusions to the rest of the class. Each student in this cooperative group makes an important contribution to the group's work.

Cooperative learning research indicates students achieve higher scores on academic tests, have a higher proficiency in critical reasoning abilities and strategies, have higher levels of intrinsic motivation to learn, and engage in more and higher quality on-task, academic, and group interaction behaviors (Stahl, 1994).

The essential elements of cooperative learning include:

- a clear set of specific student learning outcome objectives,
- common acceptance of the student outcome objectives,
- positive interdependence,
- face-to-face interaction,
- individual accountability,
- public recognition and rewards for group academic success,
- heterogeneous groups,
- positive social interaction behaviors and attitudes,
- postgroup reflection (debriefing) over group processes, and
- sufficient time for learning (Stahl, 1994).

The goals for the use of cooperative grouping overlap with those for the use of integrated thematic units. In the cooperative group, students work with others to learn. The integrated unit takes a holistic view of learning incorporating the view of learners as a community. Cooperative groups support the view of a community of learners. Students in cooperative groups listen to each other as well as to the teachers, enhancing the community of learners. In so doing, they learn from their peers within the group. To make listening productive the talk within the group is focused on the theme. Students make decisions about what they are doing and what they will do, and reflect on what they have done. They are active learners sharing the goals of integrated thematic teaching.

Teachers structure heterogeneous groups and group tasks specifically. They don't just tell a group to work together. Instead, the specific steps and procedures that group members are to follow are outlined. Teachers provide experiences helping students learn about each other. Initial activities help students recognize their similarities. As groups learn to work together, teachers facilitate students' acquisition and refinement of skills needed in group work. Teachers help group members develop strategies for coping with behaviors that are unacceptable while maintaining each student's individuality. Teachers teach skills such as listening actively, perspective taking, and paraphrasing. As group skills develop, teachers help students maintain their group skills making sure they continue to reflect and debrief. They are facilitators and consultants to groups (Stahl, 1994).

FIGURE 4.1   **Group Skills**

Cooperative Group Skills

Group Formation Skills

Move into the group location quickly

Stay with the group while it is working

Speak in quiet voices

Let each person have a chance to share his or her ideas

Listen with interest

Keep your hands and feet to yourself

Share materials

Group Achievement Skills

Review what to do before starting

Offer ideas about what would be the best way to get the task done

Make a plan for what you are going to do

If you don't understand what someone says, ask him or her to explain it

Ask questions

Ask for help

Offer help and to explain ideas or what to do

Pay attention to how much time you have to carry out your plan

Say what you think someone else has said to find out if you have got it right

When you are trying to solve a problem, say out loud what you are thinking

Say why you think this is the best idea and give your evidence for it

Ask for, or give, other answers to the problem or task

Check your group's conclusion to decide whether you carried out your plan and did what you we supposed to do

When you are done, make a summary of what you have learned and say it out loud

Group Interaction Skills

When two other students don't agree, compare and contrast what they are saying

When two other students don't agree, try to put together parts of their ideas to come up with a compromise idea

Make sure everyone is part of the plan and gets a chance to do their part

Make sure everyone has a chance to say what they think before someone gets a second chance

At least once, give each person in your group a compliment about something they are doing or said

Give your compliment aloud or in a silent way (like with a smile)

Show everyone in your group that you like them and are friendly to them

Don't say things to others in your group that you wouldn't want them to say to you (don't be mean)

Tell the others whether you do or do not like something, but do it in a nice way

Talk about each person's idea and why it might not work but don't criticize the person

Show that you are interested in what you are doing so others will stay interested

When things get tough, joke a little so that everyone relaxes

Listen to everybody's ideas before you decide together on the group's conclusion

Students need training in expected working behaviors Cohen (1986). Figure 4.1 identifies skills involved in group formation, group achievement, and group interaction. These are social skills students learn through cooperative groups. They are skills cooperative group members must develop if the group is to function effectively. Teachers teach these skills systematically. There are five major steps in teaching cooperative skills (Johnson, Johnson, & Holubec, 1992).

Step 1: Help students see the need for the skill, thereby motivating them to learn the skill.

Step 2: Make sure students understand the skill, how to use it, and when to use it. Model the skill and have students role play it.

Step 3: Provide practice situations so students can master the skill.

Step 4: Help students process and evaluate their ability to use the skill through discussion and reflection.

Step 5: Encourage students to continue practicing the skill until it is a part of their behavior.

Students evaluate their cooperative group's products and the process of cooperation. A simple student evaluation of group process used in a third grade classroom is given in Figure 4.2. The contents of the evaluation vary so that all the group skills identified in Figure 4.1 eventually are evaluated. Teachers incorporate opportunities for students to discuss ways to improve their skills.

Specific strategies for cooperative grouping and cooperative learning and its theory are available from a number of sources. Among these are:

Johnson, D. W., & Johnson, F. (1991). *Cooperative learning lesson structures.* Edina, MN: Interaction Book Company;

Johnson, D. W., & Johnson, F. (1989). *Cooperation and competition: Theory and research.* Edina, MN: Interaction Book Company; and

Johnson, D. W., Johnson, R. T., & Holubec, E. (1992). *Circles of learning: Cooperation in the classroom,* 3rd. ed. Edina, MN: Interaction Book Company.

A Group Skills Evaluation Form   FIGURE 4.2

How Did We Do?

Write down what you think about each question. Use the key to tell what you think.

Key: E = Excellent   A = Average   N = Needs improvement

_____ Did each person in the group participate?

_____ Did each person contribute ideas to the activity?

_____ Was everyone able to work together and cooperate?

A DAY IN THE LIFE OF AN INTEGRATED THEMATIC UNIT

Each integrated thematic unit varies in its day-to-day activities. Although there is no formula for organizing the day's activities, the examples below present a day from one integrated thematic unit. These examples are presented in order to give the reader a feeling for a real-world classroom day in such a unit.

The first day of a sixth-grade integrated thematic unit built around the topic of India had three major objectives:

1. Students will list interesting facts from a pretend trip to India during which they will view slides and transparencies about India.
2. Students will make predictions about the biomes depicted in pictures of India.
3. Students will generate a biome web.

The day began with the regularly scheduled physical education period during which the students were introduced to a game from India. After a restroom break, the students gathered together in the front of the room. Each went by a table where the teacher issued them a passport. Then they went to another table where a volunteer issued them a boarding pass with a seat assignment for a flight to India and a second volunteer stamped their passport, giving them a pretend-visa stamp so they could visit India.

Next, each student found a seat using the boarding pass's seat assignment. Rows of chairs that had been arranged inside a large masking tape outline representing an airplane. The teacher and one volunteer acted as flight attendants during the process. While the students were in their physical education class the teacher and volunteer had set up the classroom for the first day of the unit. The school principal came on the intercom with announcements for the departure, telling the students he would be their flight captain.

After taking off, the students were served their in-flight snack. The students talked with the teacher about an overhead transparency depicting their flight path from the United States to India. Then, they watched a slide show about India. The slides showed landmarks such as the Taj Mahal, Indian families, street scenes, and scenes of the countryside. Soon after the slide show, the plane arrived in India and landed.

The students moved their chairs outside the airplane outline, and pulled up the masking tape outline. They rearranged the chairs into small groups of three. They would be sharing their hotel room with two other students. The teacher now transformed into a tour guide. The group examined an overhead transparency of India with major cities identified. Then, it examined another transparency that identified land regions in India.

Next, each student settled down at a table with their two roommates and each wrote about their experiences thus far on their trip to India. The trip diaries would become part of an India notebook.

The teacher became a tour guide again getting the whole group together and introducing them to the major biomes found in India. This was done by placing the students in cooperative groups of five and giving them a set of pictures representing one biome in India. The cooperative group would be their "traveling group." Each group would visit one biome region in India. The group examined the pictures and made inferences about them. The group's recorder wrote down everyone's responses. The group chose a reporter to list the inferences as the teacher wrote down each group's ideas on chart paper. Then the whole group created a web of their ideas about the biomes of India.

The teacher read the students a "Just So" story by Rudyard Kipling. Then, they went to lunch.

After lunch the cooperative groups began research on their biome. They examined recent weather data from the biome and made lists of common plant and animal species from resource materials such as *Encarta* and encyclopedias available in the classroom. Each group decided they wanted to know the relative frequency of the common plants and animals in the biome. After talking with the teacher, it was decided that the class would need to work on understanding and using percentages. They returned to their cooperative groups to finish up the group's work for the day. They began to identify information they wanted to find. They chose two group members who would visit a local plant store to find out whether any of their biome's common plants were sold locally. This plant store was willing to let teachers borrow plants for a few days in the classroom. A list would be made of any appropriate plants and the teacher would make arrangements to borrow them for a few days.

The teacher worked with the group on an initial review of percentage. Plans were made to use information gathered on frequencies of plants and animals in Indian biomes in lessons over the next few days that focused on using this information to derive percentages.

Then, they reviewed the writing process because each group would be producing a research paper on their biome to share with the other groups. They made a list of new words they had encountered. Several were selected for the week's spelling list. These were: biome, Hinduism, caste system, Himalayan Mountains, and Indus Valley. Students returned to their individual table places and added to the class spelling list creating a personalized spelling list. They chose new words they thought they needed to be able to spell and those that were interesting to them even if they were not thought to be of major import at this time. A few of the words chosen were: Buddha, curry, rupee, Taj Mahal, topi, sari, Brahmin, Kshatriaya, monsoon, and peasant.

The whole group came together again, reviewed the day, and made some plans for the next day. The teacher wrapped up the day by reading an Indian folk tale about reincarnation to the students. Then, they cleaned up the classroom and got ready to go home.

Over four weeks the students continued to explore biomes: desert, tropical rain forest, grassland, and tundra. Week two introduced a study of weather-related concepts and the climates found in the biomes of India. They also studied animals and their relation to Indian culture (weeks two and three) including Indian elephants, cows, cobras, and camels. They focused on animals used for transportation and war (such as the Indian elephant and camel); animals associated with religion (such as the cow); animals that are often feared and have many folk tales associated with them (such as the cobra); and animals that work with and for people (such as the water buffalo). The biomes in which the animals are naturally found and into which people have imported them were part of this study. Weeks three and four focused on culture and religion considering concepts such as the caste system and reincarnation. An overview of major points in Indian history was constructed as part of the process of studying the culture and religion. Week four and five also considered modern India and recent pre-Independence colonial history. The future of the caste system was discussed.

On the last day students reboarded their plane and flew back to the United States. Prior to their departure, they packed up "souvenirs" they had collected and made to take home. After arriving back in the United States they spent two days preparing a videotape. The videotape was their culminating product and was intended to give an overview of India that could be used by other students. Parents were invited to an evening showing of the videotape.

CULMINATING ACTIVITIES

Integrated thematic units often have a culminating activity. The activity usually is a natural outgrowth of the unit. Student projects may be presented—as games, a play, a role-play, etc. Or, students may have worked toward the culminating activity as the project in which all participate. In teamed units, a culminating activity often is planned to draw together the work being done by the team members. A culminating activity, however, is not a necessary part of the unit.

A culminating activity can involve students in creating a long-term resource for other students at the school. For example, a heritage trunk can be developed for a unit focusing on an historical theme. The trunk can be a large box containing items representing the time period that have been duplicated by the students. It also contains a discussion of the items and their relationship to the topic studied. If the time period is recent enough, these include items from the student's household that a parent was willing to contribute such as old postcards, records, clothing, or photographs. Interviews with local residents can be part of the trunk's contents. These could describe memories of the time period or family stories related to it (Sunal, Christensen, & Sunal, 1997).

A today trunk can focus on a current issue or on popular culture. This trunk can contain newspaper clippings, recordings, posters, and other items related to the topic (Sunal, Christensen, & Sunal).

A community profile is another example of a culminating project. The profile is a compilation of accurate, interesting, and informational material portraying people, places, and events that have shaped the identity and personality of an area. It can have a chronological format or it can focus on case studies highlighting life stories, major events, or experiences of community residents (Weible, 1984).

A hypercard stack is yet another product having long-term use as a resource for the school's students. Hypercard stacks may include sound as well as visual information. They are adaptable and can be a product related to most themes.

Culminating products such as the heritage trunk and community profile serve as the focus of a culminating activity. The students present the product and explain its components to other groups of students and/or to family members and teachers.

Culminating activities do not necessarily have a culminating product. Students might participate in a Community Days activity with traditional food and games. Or, they might have a travel fair to introduce others to a country they studied or to the national park system in the United States. They might have a panel presentation on ways of reducing conflict in the school. The culminating activity might be a field trip to a site that ties in well with the unit's theme. The culminating activity should highlight and expand student learning in the unit. There are many choices for such an activity.

REFLECTING ON THE UNIT

Involving Students

Student feedback is important in reflecting on an integrated thematic unit. A student feedback form such as that in Figure 4.3 is a means of encouraging

FIGURE 4.3   Sample Student Feedback Form

What Do You Think?

1. During the unit, how satisfied were you as a learner?

   _____ very satisfied _____ satisfied _____ unsatisfied

2. What could the teacher have done to increase your satisfaction?

3. What were your favorite activities? Why?

4. What were your least favorite activities? Why?

5. Is there something else you wanted to know about, but we didn't get to it?

   Yes   No

   Is so, what was it?

students to reflect on the unit. Opportunities for reflection by students on a whole unit give teachers feedback on the impact of the unit has had on students. Students have to think about a long period of time filled with many activities. This is difficult for very young children. However, through practice, they become better able to reflect. Teachers assist students by

A student can reflect on a unit outdoors as well as indoors.

encouraging them to compare and contrast their ideas at the beginning of the unit with their ideas at the end of the unit by using an opener such as "Think back to what you knew about _____ when we first started our unit on _____. How are you different now?" They also ask students whether they are more able to perform some skills than they were at the beginning of the unit, such as using a microscope or mixing paints to create a desired color.

Reflecting by the Teacher

Curriculum development and instructional planning are part of a large cycle. One of the most important parts of the cycle is a period of time for gathering feedback on the unit and reflecting on its effectiveness. Some questions to consider are:

1. What evidence of motivation to learn about the topic did you find?
2. What evidence of learning about the topic did you see?
3. To what extent did students attain the learning objectives?
4. Did the lessons flow together well?
5. What did the students remember and not remember from day to day?
6. Which lesson was the best? Why? Would you have predicted this?
7. Was the scope and sequence of each discipline maintained?
8. Was the whole unit tied together well and in significant ways?
9. Would you use this unit again in its present form? If not, how would you change it? What modifications would you make?

Sharing Reflections Between Teachers

An informal debriefing session is helpful in stimulating reflection among a team of teachers. The discussion reviews each teacher's thinking in regard to the personal reflection questions stated above. The team reflects first of all, on whether the students were involved in meaningful learning. Was the integrated unit compelling, powerful, and meaningful for the students? Did one discipline become subservient to another—or to the theme—and thus get misrepresented or diminished? Did we give up anything important here? (Roth, 1994). Then they consider their efforts as a team. These include the team's strengths and areas that need more attention in the future. How is the team evolving? Where would you like to be in the future? Questions can be asked such as those in Figure 4.4 (Pickler, 1987). Both individual teachers and teams consider how efficiency can be increased because time is limited for both planning and teaching.

FIGURE 4.4   **Specific Questions for Team Reflection**

Questions to Help Our Team Evolve

- How can we cooperate with and support each other more thoroughly?
- Have we established a team identity our students recognize?
- Do we bring all our students together for occasional activities?
- Are our team meetings regularly scheduled with an agenda?
- Do we follow up on decisions that are made at our meetings?
- Do we divide up the work that is to be done?
- Do we have a team calendar to coordinate our assessments, projects, homework, etc.?
- Do students have access to the team calendar?
- Do we share student information and concerns and look for team solutions to problems?
- Do we share information for the purpose of recognizing those students who are doing well?
- Have we established some team goals for the year?
- Do we reinforce basic skills as a team effort?
- Do we meet with students as a team to discuss problems or provide positive reinforcement?
- Are our parent conferences well planned, productive, and positive?
- Do we plan some "off the wall" activities for our students?
- Do we often eat together at school?

SUMMARY

The implementation of a unit varies in length, structure, and effectiveness between teachers and teams of teachers. There is no sure formula for implementation because each teacher, student, and community has its own history, culture, and perspectives. There are some commonalities between individuals and settings that are considered as a unit is implemented. These include: time, identifying a scope and sequence, identifying and allocating materials and resource people, involving parents, helping students keep the theme in focus, utilizing cooperative learning, considering culminating activities, and reflecting on the unit. Each of these factors impacts the unit. Considering each in advance increases the likelihood that the unit is effective in helping students create meaningful learning. Reflection by teacher and students during and after the unit increases its effectiveness and strengthen the connections being built by an integrated thematic unit.

REFERENCES

Ackerman, D. B. (1989). Intellectual and practical criteria for successful curriculum integration. In H. H. Jacobs (Ed.), *Interdisciplinary curriculum: Design and implementation*, 25–38. Alexandria, VA: Association for Supervision and Curriculum Development.

Brophy, J., & Alleman, J. (1993). Is curriculum integration a boon or a threat to social studies? *Social Education, 57*(6), 287–291.

Brophy, J., & Alleman, J. (1991). A caveat: Curriculum integration isn't always a good idea. *Educational Leadership, 49*(2), 7–12.

Charbonneau, M. P., & Rider, B. E. (1995). *The integrated elementary classroom.* Needham Heights, MA: Allyn & Bacon.

Cohen, E. (1986). *Designing groupwork: Strategies for the heterogeneous classroom.* New York: Teachers College Press.

Falk, D. R., & Carlson, H. L. (1992, September). Learning to teach with multimedia. *Technical Horizons in Education Journal 20*(2), 96–101.

Frazee, B., & Rudnitski, R. A. (1994). *Integrated teaching methods.* New York: Delmar.

Jacobs, H. H. (1989). *Interdisciplinary curriculum: Design and implementation.* Alexandria, VA: Association for Supervision and Curriculum Development.

Johnson, D. W., Johnson, R. T., & Holubec, E. (1992). *Circles of learning: Cooperation in the classroom* (3rd. ed.). Edina, MN: Interaction Book Company.

Krogh, S. (1995). *The integrated early childhood curriculum* (2nd. ed.). New York: McGraw Hill.

Pickler, G. (1987, February). The evolutionary development of interdisciplinary teams. *Middle School Journal,* 6–7.

Roth, K. J. (1994, Spring). Second thoughts about interdisciplinary studies. *American Educator 49*(2), 44–48.

Ryder, J., & Hughes, T. (1997). *Internet for educators.* Columbus, OH: Merrill.

Stahl, R. (1994). *Cooperative learning in social studies.* Menlo Park, CA: Addison-Wesley.

Sunal, C. S. (1986). Parent involvement in social studies programs. In *Elementary school social studies: Research as a guide to practice* (pp. 146–164). Washington, DC: National Council for the Social Studies.

Sunal, C. S., Christensen, L. M, & Sunal, D. W. (1997). Learning in communities with limited resources. In B. Hatcher (Ed.) *Learning opportunities beyond the school* (2nd. ed.). Washington, DC: Association for Childhood Education International.

Sunal, C. S., Strong, M., Wilmoth, E., & Fassig, B. (1983). Improving school-family relations. Paper presented at the annual meeting of the National Association of Elementary School Principals, St. Louis.

Tangri, S., & Leitch, (1982). *Barriers to home-school collaboration: Two case studies in junior high schools* (Final report, the National Institute of Education). Washington, DC: The Urban Institute.

Weible, T. (1984). Using community resources to enhance the rural school curriculum. *Small School Forum 5,* 13–14.

C H A P T E R 5

ASSESSING AND EVALUATING
INTEGRATED THEMATIC UNITS

Assessing and evaluating the integrated thematic unit is an integral part of its development and implementation. The process enables teacher and students to obtain information needed to decide whether to make changes in their unit activities. It identifies process skills, concepts, generalizations, and affects to be included within the unit.

Using a wide diversity of tools and methods to address different purposes for evaluation is important in an integrated thematic unit. Such a unit is diverse because of its incorporation of material from more than one discipline. Its assessment and evaluation are correspondingly diverse. Appropriate assessment and evaluation help teachers plan an integrated unit that promotes meaningful learning and measures progress for a wide range of students' development.

Assessing and testing are not the same thing (Ary, Jacobs, & Razavieh, 1990). Assessing is gathering information for specific purposes. Testing is the use of a tool or instrument in assessing. Assessment involves documenting observations, student verbal exchanges, and student products. Evaluation occurs when the information gathered during the assessment is interpreted and used to make judgments and decisions (Ary, Jacobs, & Razavieh).

The purpose of the assessment suggests the type of information to be gathered, how it will be gathered, and what kind of evaluation will result from the assessment. Assessment and evaluation involve a purpose, criteria, methods and tools, evidence, people, and consequences.

AUTHENTIC ASSESSMENT—ASSESSING FOR MEANINGFUL LEARNING

Many teachers and students have had little experience with assessment of areas beyond the memorization or recall level because these are areas traditional assessment often tests (Borko, Flory, & Cumbo, 1993). Teaching and assessing for meaningful learning involve considering higher-level outcomes and reducing emphasis on recall or comprehension.

Authentic assessment in integrated thematic unit teaching refers to assessing those capacities and products deemed essential to the unit and to the context in which they are learned and used. Authentic assessment is the involvement of the student in an activity requiring him or her to integrate various skills and levels of understanding in order to solve a problem. In authentic assessment teachers consider: "What performances are expected from our students?" and "What challenges should be met?" Teachers do not view assessment as the use of formal tests nor as an after-the-event way of finding out what students learned. They view assessment as instructional. It is a way of clarifying, providing feedback, and setting goals toward which to direct student activity (Herman, Aschbacher, & Winters, 1992). Reflection (see chapter 4) is an important part of such assessment. Authentic assessment involves students in demonstrating performance during a unit activity, simulation, project, experiment, game, play, debate, recital, or in everyday problems.

Turning a goal into an authentic assessment requires a different kind of work than many teachers typically carry out when planning traditional assessment. For example, in a unit on conflict resolution, a traditional assessment might ask students to:

- define aggression,
- list strategies for reducing impulsive responses to negative comments (such as "count to 10 before reacting"), or
- draw a picture of Martin Luther King, Jr., and write a paragraph describing nonviolent means of promoting change in society.

In authentic assessment the teacher may set up situations where supplies for a project are scarce and decisions are made regarding how to share them. For example,

> the teacher may involve the students in making valentines at a learning station during the early part of February. However, only a few lacy red hearts are available, there is a shortage of pink construction paper, and not enough scissors. The students quickly discover the shortages. Do they argue about, trade, steal, or negotiate desired items?

Some choices promote conflict while others resolve what could become a conflict. Or, in another example, the teacher pairs students who in the past, usually have not gotten along well together for an activity. He can make observations and keep anecdotal records noting whether conflict arises and whether it is resolved positively.

USES OF ASSESSMENT

The teacher needs to identify the use of an assessment. What is it that is going to be evaluated through the assessment? In an integrated thematic unit, assessment considers students' prior knowledge, hands-on performance (how they get their answers), cooperative group work, problem solving through higher-order thinking, attitudes, values, and dispositions. Each of these typically utilize specific types of assessment tools. However, some assessment tools are useful in several areas.

First, teachers decide what needs to be assessed. Then they choose a type of assessment that fits the purpose. To decide what needs to be assessed, teachers identify the goal of a unit, a lesson, or an activity. Clear goals allow effective assessment. An effective *unit evaluation* assesses:

- prior knowledge;
- hands-on, minds-on performance;
- collaborative and cooperative learning;
- higher-order thinking;
- affects;
- depth of understanding and/or thinking skills; and
- memory.

Finally, teacher's evaluation of the unit examines the closeness of the match between the assessment and the developmental abilities of the students. It also examines the match between the assessment and the instructional methods. The assessment is part of the instructional process not a special event.

Assessment of Prior Knowledge

Assessment before or at the beginning of the unit occurs during the exploration phase. It is part of the exploration task. It focuses on what the students bring to the lesson. It assesses those beliefs and experiences related to the unit's theme. The assessment of prior knowledge often is accomplished by using tools such as student observation, interviews, a K-W-L, and problem-solving tasks. An example of an assessment using prior knowledge appears in Figure 5.1. This figure also gives the responses of two students in interviews on the same topic.

Assessment of Hands-on Performance

Hands-on performance is a widely used term describing physical actions students perform during a lesson. Assessment addresses student actions relating to how they have met the lesson's goal. Throughout the lesson, hands-on involvement engages students' minds. Assessment occurs throughout the lesson to determine whether students are engaged in hands-on performance. Their minds are engaged when they are discussing, writing, reporting, charting, or working cooperatively with others. Authentic assessment of hands-on learning requires involvement of body and mind in the learning. Such learning is assessed by observation, interviews, work samples, portfolios, diaries/logs, and group discussion. In assessing a unit on plants, for example, one teacher examined students' ability to observe and record the physical changes in corn plants during their growth process. Groups of students set corn kernels in dishes of water. Each group's materials manager made certain that each seed was in one inch of water all of the time. Every three days, each group's recorder drew the plants and recorded the changes described by the group's observer. The group members examined the observations and drawings to make sure no important details were overlooked. At the end of the unit the group's reporter described the changes observed. Prior to the report, the group members met and discussed the contents of the report. In this example the teacher assessed the students' ability to make and report accurate observations.

Assessment of Collaborative and Cooperative Learning

Collaborative and cooperative learning by students also is assessed. Chapter 4 discussed behaviors in group settings that can be assessed. Assessment occurs in all parts of the lesson and in all parts of the unit. Types of assessment used to evaluate collaborative and cooperative learning by students include observation, interviews, group work samples, portfolios, diaries/logs, and group discussion. As an example, one teacher checked work samples

FIGURE 5.1   **An Example of a Unit Pre-Assessment Using a K-W-L and Interviews**

Pre-Assessment for an Integrated Thematic Unit
Unit Topic: India
Grade Level: 6

What Do You Know About India?

I don't know anything about India.

Some movies have been made there.

India is in Asia.

They have palaces.

They wear jewels on their foreheads.

They wear veils.

They wear sandals.

They talk different.

They have a lot of animals and jungles.

They get married around 9 years old.

They have camels.

They have a dot on their foreheads.

They make pottery.

They have cobras.

They build temples.

They have a king and a queen.

They have rain forest.

There is a lot of sand there.

They worship many gods.

What Do You Want to Learn About India?

Do they have schools?

What kind of flag do they have?

What kind of religion do they have?

What kind of food do they eat?

What kind of transportation do they have?

Why do they have dots on their heads?

Where is the biggest castle?

Why do they worship many gods?

Where is India?

What do they look like?

What are their hairstyles?

Do they have malls?

Student Interviews:

Student A

"I don't know much about India. But, I really want to learn more. I think it will be interesting. I really want to know why they have that dot on their forehead. Also, why is their religion different from ours? Do they have lots of gods? Why do they have them? How are their temples different from our churches? What do they do there? Why?"

Student B

"I am really interested in the animals of India. I am especially interested in the cobras. How do they charm snakes, especially cobras? I want to know more about the land of India. I mean, like, the rain forests. I want to know what the wildlife is like. Is there a lot of it? Is it dangerous? Do they hunt? Are there still tigers running around? Could I go on a tiger hunt? Do they do that? Or, was that just long ago? I saw a tiger hunt in the movies. It was an old movie. It was black and white. Does India still look like that? Or, maybe was the movie made someplace else and so India really doesn't look like that. Do they drive cars or do they ride elephants? How do you train an elephant so you can ride it? Do some people have cars and still have an elephant? Is India modern?"

from a group's map of the world's major rivers to determine whether each member had contributed his or her share. The groups had divided the world into regions and assigned each member a region to research. Then, the member drew the rivers in the assigned region on to the map and taught the rest of the group about that region's rivers using an outline of major points to be covered that had been developed by the class. So, the teacher could determine whether each member had completed his or her individual task and thereby contributed to the group's work by examining the group's map and the items each student had filled in on the outline.

Assessment of Higher-Order Thinking

Authentic assessment involves using memory and lower-order thought processes but emphasizes higher-order thinking. Students are provided with challenges created by the instruction that has just taken place. Challenges are presented by the ideas and the context in which they were learned. During the expansion phase of a lesson, students use the ideas or process skills they invented in new and different contexts. Assessments include written formats such as multiple-choice tests, short essays, and papers; and using observational formats such as interviews, group discussion, portfolios, and performance testing.

Affects are important to depth of understanding and ability to transfer knowledge to the real world (Sunal & Haas, 1993). Teachers need to be aware of students' attitudes and dispositions in relation to the theme. Affects are assessed in the exploration and expansion phases of the lesson and of the unit in order to identify progress over time. For example, students may be studying conflict and its resolution. Government sometimes has a role in conflict resolution. Students might debate whether government should censor music that might suggest or endorse conflict. Students have some attitudes toward government's role in controlling various aspects of our lives such as airline regulation and food labeling. Does this view transfer to their views on government's possible role in regulating music? If their view on music regulation differs why does it differ? Should it differ? These are questions that can be discussed in class and will give the teacher an indication of attitudes and dispositions the students may have.

Depth of understanding is assessed by narratives constructed by the students describing their understanding of the experiences they have and how they use their understanding in solving problems. The students also can be assessed through products using the idea in different contexts. The student should be able to transfer what was learned in a meaningful way to the real world. Dance is another means of assessing depth of understanding. For example, small groups of students can create a dance that demonstrates the role of different factions in a conflict. Such a dance requires deep understanding of the causes of the conflict, the factions involved in the conflict, and how each faction is pursuing the conflict.

Assessment of memory best occurs during the expansion phase of the lesson or unit. This involves memorizing accepted spellings, the name of the

President of the United States, and other items deemed to be basic factual knowledge. Assessment can occur through the use of multiple choice, matching, true/false, fill-in-the-blank, short essay, labeling drawings, and role-play.

Students need specific feedback. Overly broad or general feedback is difficult to act upon. Students need to know which behavior to improve and how they might improve it. For example, if they have been working on the skill of decision making, students can use feedback on whether they are able to identify the important characteristics of the situation about which they are making a decision, whether they can rank order those characteristics, whether they can determine which characteristics apply, and whether they can reflect on and determine whether they need to reconsider the characteristics and the importance they have assigned them. Specific feedback gives students guidelines for comparing their progress against appropriate models of decision-making behavior. Students need to receive credit for making progress toward an appropriate model.

USING LESS TRADITIONAL ASSESSMENTS

Testing is the most common form of assessment of learning. Less traditional evaluation formats involve collecting information in a structured environment without direct testing. These assessments are trying to identify authentic student achievement. Authentic achievement distinguishes between achievement that is significant and meaningful and that which is trivial and useless (Newmann & Wehlage, 1993). Three criteria define authentic achievement: 1) students construct meaning and produce knowledge, 2) students use disciplined inquiry to construct meaning, and 3) students aim their work toward production of discourse, products, and performances that have value or meaning beyond success in school (Archbald & Newmann, 1988). Authentic achievement is assessed in many ways. The method of assessment must be appropriate to the type of achievement expected. Direct testing often does not assess authentic achievement. There are several types of less traditional evaluation formats including observation, interviews, portfolios, discussions, group evaluation, and performance testing.

Observation

Teachers continuously make observations of their students, watching them work, plan, discuss ideas, express frustration, etc. (Boehm & Weinberg, 1987). These observations usually are informal and quick. They are used to adjusting the pace and content of a lesson. Occasionally, more structured observations are used to find out how a student or a group of students are progressing. For example, the teacher observes the interactions occurring in a cooperative learning group every five minutes to determine whether the students are encouraging each other to participate. Or, a teacher observes an individual during the beginning of lessons over several days to decide whether the student is able to adjust quickly to a new activity. These observations are integrated into the lesson and unit taught. Observations of everything that is occurring are not possible. Deciding which behaviors contribute to meaningful learning and making observations of those behaviors is important. Anecdotal records and checklists are two major types of observation instruments.

Anecdotal Records

The anecdotal record lists the student's name, the date, the time of day a behavior occurred, and a description of the behavior observed (Figure 5.2). In describing the observed behavior, the teacher tries to be objective and avoids drawing any conclusions. For example, the teacher uses an anecdotal record to determine whether a student is having difficulty in keeping records of decisions made in her cooperative group. The teacher observes the student at the beginning of cooperative group work for three days. Anecdotal records report observations of the same behavior over a period of time. In this instance, the teacher may note the student has more difficulty in the morning than in the afternoon. These observations may lead the

---

Sample Anecdotal Record   **FIGURE 5.2**

Student's Name: _Susanne_ Date: _12/18/98_
Time of Day: _10:05–10:20_

Description of the Behavior Observed: *Susanne was in her three person group beginning to work on their reading and critique of the book Diego Rivera by Jan Gleiter and Kathleen Thompson. Susanne told the other two children she was really excited about this book because she thought art was "so interesting, I love it." Susanne went to get the book from the materials station. She looked at the cover picture of Diego Rivera as she walked back to her group's table. She told her group "he is funny-looking, his hair is curly and his skin is a little brownish." Wayne took the book and opened it saying he wanted to read it aloud to the others. He read the first paragraph in English and then started on the second paragraph and realized it was not in English. Gayle said, "I know, it's Spanish, cool, huh?" Susanne said nothing but closed her eyes so they were slits. Wayne wondered if the Spanish text said the same thing as the English text and came up to ask me about it. I told him it was the same material. Wayne went back to the group and told them this information. Gayle said "that is cool" and then asked Susanne to read the next page after they had all looked at the picture accompanying the first page. Susanne read the two paragraphs on the next page. She passed the book to Gayle and told her to read it. Gayle said, "we didn't get a chance to look at the picture, let's do it." Susanne said she was not interested in looking at it, and that Gayle should go ahead and read the next page. Gayle and Wayne both looked at the picture and commented on it. They laughed because Diego Rivera's parents set aside a room for him in which he could draw on the walls. They said their parents would never let them get away with that. Susanne took no part in the conversation. Gayle read next and Wayne followed her. Susanne did not look at the pictures with them. When her turn came, Susanne refused her turn. Wayne asked what was the matter with her, she liked art so much, now she wasn't interested any more. Susanne did not respond. So, Gayle read again. Wayne then said, "Hey, Susanne it's your turn, stop being weird." Susanne said she did not want to read. Wayne and Gayle finished reading the book.*

teacher to keep another set of anecdotal records describing observations of the student's demeanor and physical appearance. The teacher may note the student appears tired in the morning but looks much more alert a half hour or so after lunch. A discussion with the student might find that she is skipping breakfast and so has little energy in the morning.

Figure 5.2 is one of several records kept by a teacher documenting what appears to be an attitude held by a student. It documents behavior over a rather lengthy time period of 15 minutes. Usually it is difficult for a teacher to find such a long time period during which to observe a student. This teacher was assisted by an aide, who was able to work with the rest of the class while the teacher focused on one student and her group. The teacher had noted what appeared to be a serious problem and decided that a series of anecdotal records of observations needed to be kept in order to determine whether concern was warranted.

Anecdotal records often are best used with students about whom the teacher has concerns. However, every student deserves observational attention from the teacher. Observations give the teacher information that otherwise is missed about a student. Sometimes, surprising things are revealed when carefully noting a student's behavior. One method for making sure each students gets some of the teacher's attention through observation is to randomly choose a child each day to observe and to keep selecting a student a day until the pool of students has been used up. Then, the teacher starts over randomly selecting a student a day from the class so that each has a second observation period. This process continues throughout the school year. Systematic use of anecdotal records with all students during a lesson is time-consuming and not practical. Anecdotal records enable the teacher to get a picture of the behavior of a single student or of a few students when several systematic observations of behavior are made.

Checklists

Checklists are lists of behaviors of interest to the teacher. They can be constructed after patterns of behavior among several students are noted in anecdotal records. They guide the observation because the teacher collects specific pieces of information about many students. A teacher may begin systematic observation by using a checklist and later follow-up behaviors of interest or of concern with anecdotal records. An example of a checklist appears in Figure 5.3.

In a typical class of 20 or more students, it often is difficult for a teacher to systematically use checklists and anecdotal records. When a teacher is actively involved with students, it is not always possible to stop and make a careful observation of a student. With planning, a teacher can identify times when it is likely that systematic observation can be carried

A Checklist Assessing Decision-Making Skills in a Unit on Communication   FIGURE 5.3

Examples of a Skills Checklist for a Unit

Level of Skill	Characteristics
1	Cannot identify characteristics of a situation that requires a decision to be made even when they are pointed out to him.

The lowest level of this skill.

2	Occasionally identifies a situation as unsettled or confused. Asks the teacher or someone else to decide what to do.
3	Often identifies a situation as unsettled or confused. Can identify some characteristics that lead to the need for a decision.
4	Can identify one or more criteria that could be used to make a decision about a situation. Sometimes mixes statements of criteria for making the decision and characteristics of the situation about which the decision is being made.

An intermediate level of this skill.

5	Can order criteria in terms of their importance to the decision to be made. Provides a limited set of relevant criteria. Identifies a limited set of characteristics of the situation.
6	Can make detailed decisions. Can select those criteria relevant to the decision in the particular context under consideration. Identifies an adequate amount of relevant characteristics in the situation under consideration.
7	Can make detailed wide-ranging decisions using all available evidence. Can select criteria relevant to the decision that are independent of the context in which the decision is made. Can order criteria in terms of their importance to the decision to be made. Can identify relevant characteristics of the situation in which the decision is to be made. Can reorder criteria if the decision made does not appear to be tenable, practical, or realistic.

The highest level of this skill.

---

out. One such time is during individual study or practice sessions when a teacher moves freely among students. Such observations are designed to require little time. Checklists also are useful with small groups of students as they are working. If used immediately following work with a group, they are accurate and completed rapidly.

The type of observation procedure used can introduce bias. A checklist may not match the purpose of the observation. Or, the observation procedure may be too complicated, introducing error into the observation. When the behavior observed is global and not defined specifically enough to be easily observed, errors result. If the checklist mixes a number of skills together, the teacher is unable to identify the cause of poor performance. Finally, using a checklist just once provides an incomplete and, therefore, inaccurate view of a student's ability.

Creating a checklist involves the following steps:

1. Determine the purpose of the assessment to be conducted using a checklist.

2. Identify the objective students are expected to meet.

3. Identify the behavior that is related to the accomplishment of the objective.

4. Identify the variety of levels at which students will be performing the behavior.

5. Construct the observational checklist on which student performance will be recorded.

In constructing a checklist, the teacher begins by identifying what is considered a low level of behavior, an intermediate level of behavior, and a high level of behavior. The checklist in Figure 5.3 uses a scale with seven points. The scale began with three points. Level one was identified as the lowest level of behavior, level four was identified as an intermediate level of behavior, and level seven was identified as the highest level of behavior. Then some additional levels were added in. It is possible to construct a checklist with three levels of behavior, five levels, or seven levels. An odd number of levels is best because the midpoint is obvious.

The checklist provides the teacher with an easily used assessment. Such an assessment has specific observable behaviors. These are described clearly so there is little misunderstanding about the level on which the students are performing. If the same checklist is used over several lessons, a unit, or throughout the year, a student's progress over time is documented.

Feedback provides students with a target level of behavior to be achieved and potentially builds self-confidence and willingness to take charge of their own learning. Members of a cooperative group can use some checklists to assess each other. If necessary, the teacher assigns points or a grade to the checklist. The teacher might use the same checklist several times during a grading period. The points received on each checklist can be averaged. Or, the points received on the final checklist can be used to establish a grade.

Checklists often are used to measure areas that are hard to measure. These include hands-on, minds-on learning and cooperative learning.

Interviews

Interviews provide an opportunity to explore students' ideas, discuss their planning, and talk about how they evaluate their own work. Interviews may be highly structured or relatively informal. In a highly structured interview, the student responds to a set of questions asked in a specific order. In a more informal interview, the student responds to a few leading questions but can go off into unplanned avenues.

Interviews often explore students' alternative conceptions about a topic. They also are used to assess students' attainment of learning outcomes near the end and after the lesson. These intended learning outcomes are conceptual and skill-oriented. Interviews generally are not used to assess memorization of facts.

Different techniques are used during interviews. Students can generate their own questions about a concept or a skill. The interviewer follows up by asking for the thinking behind the students' comments. A student might, for example, ask a question about the impact of new technologies on communication, "What can we do to help poor people who can't afford to buy a computer and have e-mail, so their children don't know so much about how you can use computers to communicate?" The interviewer reflects on the thinking involved in forming this question. The student is aware of the cost of technology and that many people cannot afford it. The student also is aware that children who have less access to technology will not understand its use in communication as well as will others. Finally, the student is asking for a solution to the problem identified in the question. Can the student generate some realistic solutions? The interviewer can follow up the student's question by asking the student to explain and provide evidence for the ideas expressed in the question. The interviewer also can ask the student to generate a possible solution, evaluating the student's ability to use existing knowledge in problem solving.

Most often an interview involves one student talking with one adult. But, an interviewer can talk with a cooperative learning group or some other grouping of students. The interviewer has a list of prepared questions or topics to guide the interview. If the interviewer follows the list, needed information is collected. In all interviews, the interviewer is a listener. The interviewer does not comment nor offer information unless it is necessary to restate or otherwise clarify a question. An example of an interview guide is given in Figure 5.4.

An interview allows the teacher to obtain different information to a greater depth than students produce on written tasks or during an activity. The teacher is prepared to ask an additional question or two as the need arises in order to determine the student's understanding of the idea or skill taught.

Interview Guide on Conflict Resolution   FIGURE 5.4

Parts of an Interview Guide Examining Conflict Resolution Abilities

For this interview the students will be presented with a narrative describing a situation in which there is a scarcity of materials and conflict erupts between students.

1. Identify the parts of this situation for me.

2. Describe the part of the situation you think is most important for the conflict to be solved.

3. How is this part related to the other parts of the situation? *(Make sure the student relates the functions of all parts of the situation to each other.)*

4. In what ways are the parts of the situation related to what might have come before?

5. Give me one question that you have about the conflict in this situation.

Student responses often are recorded in writing, on a tape recording, or on a checklist. Interviews can provide a lot of information, so it is easy to forget some of it if it isn't recorded quickly. A tape-recorded interview is played back to the student a couple of times during the interview. Because interviews often provide lots of information, the adult reviews notes of the interview organizing and summarizing them soon after they are completed (Sunal & Haas, 1993).

Portfolios

A portfolio contains a variety of work demonstrating a student's range of knowledge and skills. Its materials are produced by a student over a period of time. The materials demonstrate the amount and quality of the student's activities. The portfolio is used to evaluate the assessments completed by the student.

The portfolio also serves as an assessment process. For this purpose, the portfolio includes some student-selected productions along with performance tests, other tests, and quizzes. These items form the basis upon which the evaluation is made. The portfolio organizes qualitative and narrative types of assessment items that are otherwise hard to handle and score. Such items can include student logs, student reflections on work, group evaluations of performance, and videotapes of student performances.

The implementation of portfolios is a slow and evolving process. There are three roles to consider in using portfolio assessment:

1. the person who is responsible for setting up the portfolio,
2. the person constructing the portfolio, and
3. the person evaluating the portfolio.

Each of these roles varies. Three questions also need to be asked:

- What does the portfolio contain (see Figure 5.5)?
- What will count as evidence?
- How should the evidence be weighed and the final evaluation made?

The three roles and three questions need to be considered together in order to develop an effective plan for using portfolios in a classroom. The person(s) responsible for setting up the portfolio can be the teacher, the teaching team, the student, or a student group.

The portfolio must identify its purpose. This may be the assessment of hands-on performance, depth of understanding, or any of the other purposes of assessment. The teacher may ask students to include materials in the portfolio that identify their early thinking related to the theme and their most recent ideas. It may ask students to demonstrate the evolution of their

Sample Portfolio Contents	**FIGURE 5.5**

Drawings
Maps, Charts, and Graphs
Narratives
Writing Samples
Interview Responses
Lists of Favorite Books
Audiotape Recordings of Reports or Demonstrations
Copies of Letters Written to the Editor or Public Officials
Videotape of Presentations
Games Developed
Computer Disks of Word Processed Reports
Lists of References Used
Cartoons
Peer Assessment Sheets
Self-Assessment Checklists
Personal Goal Statements
Descriptions of Main Themes of Lessons
Parent Comments on Portfolios

ability at a particular process skill. Teachers can suggest the number of items to be included in the portfolio. For example, students may be asked to submit their five best items. An individualized approach can be taken so that specific groups or individual students address different skills or ideas and submit different types of evidence.

Types of Evidence in a Portfolio

The types of evidence in a portfolio can reflect each of the three categories of assessment: prior knowledge, monitoring, and summative assessment. Each category determines a particular approach to selecting materials for the portfolio.

Assessing Prior Knowledge

When the teacher wishes to assess prior knowledge, examining specific work samples from previous units and first activities in a unit provides valuable information about students' background experiences, alternative conceptions, and work patterns. Typically, students select samples of what they believe to be their best work. Younger students are provided with opportunities to select products from some of their assignments. Or, young students are given a list of required types of assignments to be included in the portfolio. An example of such an assignment is the chart in Figure 5.6. A student has identified and recorded characteristics of a set of five rocks.

Samples of work can include products from a variety of assignments (see Figure 5.5). Very young students often do not want the teacher to keep their work; they want to take it home. When this happens, the teacher may make photocopies. Or, a teacher might ask students to place work samples in a student-decorated special folder given to parents periodically.

Before evaluating the portfolio, it is important to focus the evaluation by listing specific items of interest. A teacher might be interested, for example, in focusing on a student's classification skills or in identifying the attitudes a student seems to hold in regard to an issue.

A portfolio can be constructed to monitor a student's development over a period of time. Evidence from both early and late unit activities provides student and teacher with information about consistency, growth, and level of attainment at a particular time. An example is given in Figure 5.7 in

FIGURE 5.6   Sample of Assignment Required as Part of a Portfolio

NAME _____

SENECA STONE READING

SHAPE	COLOR	TEXTURE	WEIGHT	FIGURE
oval	black	ruff	heavy	fish
square	brown	smooth	light	Face
sircle	brown	smooth	light	bird
Diamond	red brown	rough	light	bug
sircle	red brown	ruff	light	Man with hat

FAVORITE ROCK:

SHAPE: _oval_

COLOR: _Brown Red_

TEXTURE/WEIGHT: _Rough   /Rough - Heavy_

FIGURE: _fish_

SYMBOL: _____

A Student's Work Sample Used to Monitor the Understanding of the Concept of a Pulley   FIGURE 5.7

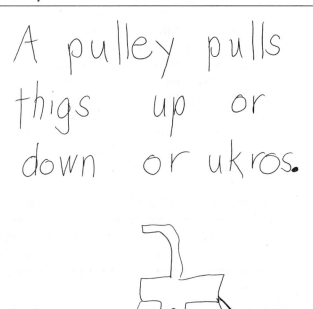

which a first-grade student describes her concept of a pulley. Using such information the teacher monitors the student's understanding of the concept of one simple machine, the pulley. The portfolio can contain first and later drafts of reports, charts, and diagrams; data collected before it is put on a formal table; or a tape of conversations in a collaborative group.

This portfolio does not represent a final or end product or the student's highest level of achievement. It provides a structured view of student performance across a wide variety of areas.

Summative Evaluation

Summative evaluation uses evidence demonstrating that the goals of the lesson or unit are being met. It includes quizzes and tests, library reports, language experience stories, webs, Venn diagrams, laboratory worksheets, and laboratory reports. An example of a laboratory report in which a fourth-grade student has drawn the electrical circuits she worked with during a laboratory is shown in Figure 5.8. In Figure 5.9 a student's prediction of the growth of a corn plant over a four-week period is shown. It also shows the student's record of observations of the plant made every three days. An example of a post-unit web is given in Figure 5.10. This is a student's web following a unit on the American Revolution. The students were asked to produce several webs. One web was to describe the life and accomplishments of one individual associated with the American Revolution. The students chose the individual. The evidence also can include documents produced by others in the setting, such as letters and newspaper reports of student involvement in the community, and notes included in the portfolio documenting student participation in the final materials, such as typing or artwork.

Student reflection on the portfolio includes how it demonstrates what was learned. Such reflection is used for summative evaluation. The student tells why the portfolio is evidence for her own growth. Notes may be attached to the front of specific documents or the student might write an overall paper explaining the portfolio contents and how the pieces and the whole relate to her own learning.

The organization and format of the summative portfolio is important. It can be evaluated by a diverse group of evaluators. The portfolio can be used by one teacher or by a teaching team to grade the student and plan future work. The student can use the portfolio for self-reflection and

FIGURE 5.8   **A Fourth-Grade Student's Portfolio Laboratory Report on Work Done With Electric Circuits**

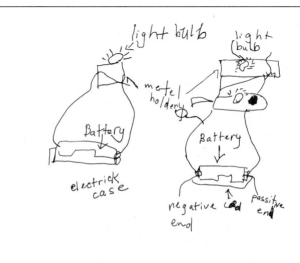

A Student's Prediction of the Growth of a Corn Plant   FIGURE 5.9

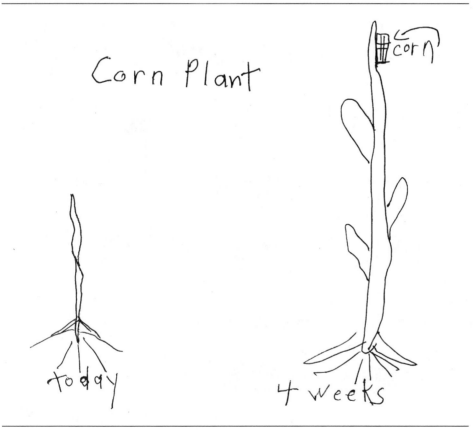

feedback. Parents can examine the portfolio to gain information regarding the progress of their child and about what is being done in the school.

Students should feel ownership of the work presented in the portfolio. They need some control over decisions made about the portfolio process. The teacher initially may determine the format and the content of the portfolio while giving students some choice as to which experiment or journal item they might include. Over time students are given more control by allowing them to determine the number of documents in a category, the number of categories, or the entire format of the portfolio. The teacher identifies the purpose of the portfolio but allows the students to reflect and make important decisions regarding which evidence provides the best information to demonstrate their experience and growth. Students are encouraged to think about how each document provides evidence of a type of growth that otherwise would not be known to the evaluator. This helps

FIGURE 5.10   Student's Post-Web

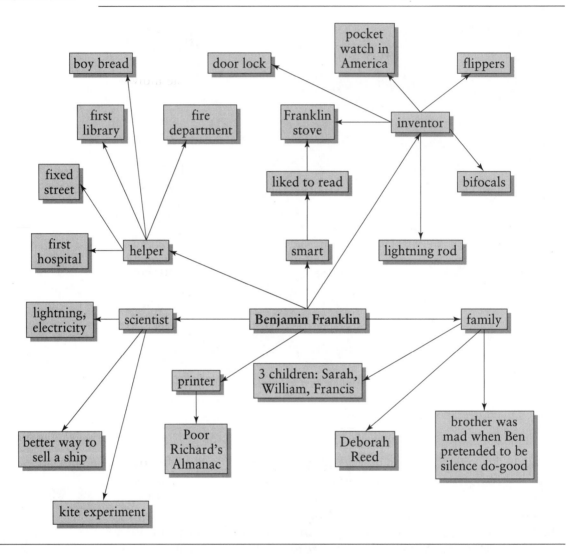

them understand the problem of redundancy and trivial materials. Students develop higher-level thinking skills in planning, monitoring, and reflecting on their own behavior. An alternative allows cooperative decisions to be made by small groups regarding the evidence necessary to demonstrate the group's learning. Peer evaluation of documents or of evidence submitted by others in the class is one part of the evaluation process. Simplified evaluation keys are provided to students to help in this process (Collins, 1991; Hein, 1991; Meng & Doran, 1990; Wolf, 1989).

Students must maintain the portfolio on a regular basis. The portfolio and its contents are reviewed and organized each one to two weeks. The teacher helps the students at the beginning of the year in this process but later, providing instructions for them to do it is sufficient for most students. All items entered into the portfolio are dated and indicate student's name and group. Each item indicates whether it was completed by the individual, with a peer, or with a group. A regular schedule for evaluation of the portfolio is given to the students to indicate when peers, the teacher(s), or family members will be reviewing the materials. In general, family members have regular access to the portfolio. It is available at family-teacher and family-teacher-student conferences, open houses, and schoolwide family-teacher meetings. It is available at any time when family members come in to visit. In this case, the family member is told that the portfolio may not be complete nor well organized. It is in the process of construction. An interested family member expects to learn much about the student by viewing the portfolio at different times of the year and seeing it at various stages of development. The student's growth throughout the year is represented by the changes seen in the portfolio over the course of the year. The family member is given a place in the classroom in which the portfolio is examined. Depending on the activity in the classroom at that time, the family member can be encouraged to discuss the portfolio with the student and/or the teacher.

Discussions, Diaries and Logs, Presentations, and Dances

The social dimension of learning is important and centers on students' interactions with each other (Piaget, 1950; Vygotsky, 1962). These include conversations or informal discussions and formal discussions. The social dimension of learning is fostered when ideas and materials are brought into the classroom to be shared, examined, and reconsidered in various ways. Diaries and logs often report the social dimension of learning.

Social interactions can be formal or informal and spontaneous. Informal discussion is evaluated by listening to students' conversation and focusing on whether key words are used. These words provide the teacher with cues about student thinking. Specific ideas or questions that persistently come to the surface enable the teacher to evaluate students' prior knowledge, growth, and understanding of a concept. Teachers also note whether all group members contribute to an informal discussion.

Formal discussions occur in more structured whole-class sessions. Students are asked to talk about their experiences and observations related to the unit. Discussions that are evaluated involve a conversation sustained by student-initiated questions and ideas. The students control direction of the discussion. Teachers' open-ended questions in their role as a guide brings out evidence that is used in assessing students. Group discussions that are assessed:

1. begin with open-ended questions such as "What can you tell me about successful ways to reduce conflict?" or "Where do you experience 'high-tech' communication in your daily lives?"
2. welcome students' comments when they are made without correcting or modifying them,
3. involve all of the students in the discussion, and
4. involve keeping records of students' comments and participation.

Evaluating students' comments to determine prior knowledge helps teachers identify appropriate points to emphasize during a unit. A coding scheme can be used with both informal and formal discussions to determine the extent of students' prior knowledge (Chittenden, 1990). Five categories of statements can be examined across all discussions. These are:

announcements—statements of a fact or bits of information such as "We have 10 post offices in town,"

reported observations—personal or second-hand observations stated by the student such as "When you send an e-mail you don't have to use a stamp but the address is really important and it's long,"

explanations—statements relating events and objects together in attempting to deal with cause and effect such as "the more time you spend making sure you get your spelling right, the easier it is for somebody else to make sense out of what you write,"

questions—statements inquiring into problems facing students such as "Why doesn't someone come up with an easy way to organize the Internet because it is so hard to find things you want on it?" and

references—statements identifying sources of information such as books, television, "I used the Internet at school," or "My mother told me about her job at the post office." Some statements may be classified using more than one of these categories. Noting the level of student statements in each of the categories, however, will make possible better inferences as to the extent of students' prior knowledge.

Discussions can be thought of as "staged" observations involving a part of classroom life that ordinarily remains undocumented student talk. Teachers often get the feeling that conversation is "just talk" because no evidence of learning is produced—such as drawings or graphs. This is particularly common with primary-grade students (Chittenden, 1990). The assessment of student conversations validates the idea of cooperative and interactive learning.

Diaries and logs are another way in which students record their ideas and social interactions. Many students have kept diaries and logs. An example of a sixth-grade student's diary entry appears in Figure 5.11. The student has been participating in the first day of an integrated thematic unit on India. Individual diaries can be used to have students write about the integrated thematic unit using leading questions such as:

- What was the main idea today (or, this week)?
- What questions do you have about what you learned today?
- What did you do today?
- What did you like best today?
- What did you like least today?
- What do you think was the most important thing you learned?
- What confused or bored you?
- What else do you want to mention?

Students are encouraged, but not required, to respond to all the questions depending on their level of development.

A log is similar to a diary but usually is a form that students fill out (see Figure 5.12 for an example). It is an effective way for students to sum up what they liked or did not like about a lesson or a unit, and what they learned and did not learn (Sunal & Haas, 1993).

Groups use both diaries and logs to keep track of their work. They help group members evaluate how well their planning process went, how well their plans worked out, and what they will do next. Diaries and logs serve as the basis for discussion in class when students use them as notes for evaluating their own work and the unit and its lessons.

Students often use diaries, and sometimes logs, to express very private feelings. When encouraging students to use diaries and logs to evaluate work in a group or in other ways in which the content of the writing becomes public, it is important to use caution because students should not be

Sample of a Student Diary Entry   FIGURE 5.11

November 18

I think the slide show on the airplane was pretty cool. I really like learning about the women wearing their saris, and about how they ate rice and wheat mostly.

While we were on the airplane, I learned about the story behind the Taj Mahal. And about the prince loving his wife so much, that when she died, he built a palace out of white marble that took them 20 years to build, and over 21,000 people to build it!

I really like the refreshments and how it really looked like a airplane, and how Mr. Matthews got on the intercom and acted like a pilot! I'm really looking forward to learning all about India!

FIGURE 5.12   **A Log**

Name: _____   Date: _____

Log

What was the main idea of the lesson?

_____

_____

What questions do you have about the lesson now?

_____

What else would you like to know about the main idea of the lesson?

_____

_____

What else would you like to say?

_____

_____

_____

put in a position where they feel their privacy is violated. If the diary or log is going to be read by the teacher or shared in any other way, students must aware of this before they are encouraged to write in it.

Presentations and dances are concrete types of assessment allowing students to see the results of the work they did leading up to the presentation. Other students in the class use the presentation as a means of peer evaluation. It creates social interaction at a high level of thought.

Group Evaluation

Group assessment is an important part of cooperative group learning. Students become more active members of a group when involved in interdependent tasks and provided feedback through assessment of group experiences. Providing feedback for students in cooperative settings increases the value they place on working in such settings.

Students always are involved in some part of the assessment process. Self-evaluation enables students to develop an awareness of their own performance and behavior. It also is a necessary element for the successful functioning of cooperative learning groups (see chapter 4). Self-evaluation involves students in assessing their planning, monitoring their behavior, and evaluating the results of their actions. Students can use a checklist and group discussion to evaluate work periods, group cooperation, data sources, study skills, and information gathering activities as well as the progress of their plan.

Peer evaluation can be part of a student's grade on cooperative tasks. Peers can examine the:

- ideas contributed,
- information or data collected,
- organization of the data, and
- reporting of the results.

The ideas contributed can be assessed by the number of times comments were made and by the relevance of the ideas to the problem at hand. The data collected can be assessed by examining each student's involvement in obtaining or setting up the materials needed, the number of measurements made, the drawings made, the models constructed, and the number of pieces of information recorded. The organization of the data collected can be assessed through the construction of a table of the information, rewriting the data in a more usable form, the number of points plotted on graphs, or the suggestions made about patterns discovered in the information. Reporting of results can be assessed by the number of sentences written by the group secretary, the number of sentences suggested for the secretary to write down, offering a plan for completing the report, word processing the report, making graphs and artwork that are part of the report, and the level of participation in the presentation of the report. Students should be asked to rate each other on the extent of their participation in each of these basic areas.

An average score for each student in the group is calculated from the individual ratings. The groups can be asked to do peer evaluation on just one of these four areas during a particular task. Or, they can assess each student's contribution to all of the tasks. Each student can independently rate the other students' contributions in the specific area. The average of each student's scores adds up to 100% (see Figure 5.13). Over time, each student's contribution is a record of the amount of effort expended. This assessment data can be used as part of a group discussion on how well their group is performing. It can be used as part of individual student grades. A

Peer Self-Evaluation Scheme for a Group of Four Students   FIGURE 5.13

Student Names/Scores	Billy	Keisha	Juanita	Ahmed	Total
Contributing Ideas	2	3	3	2	10
Collecting Data	1	4	2	3	10
Organizing Data	2	2	3	4	10
Reporting Data	2	3	2	3	10
Total	8	12	10	11	40

discussion about individual participation helps group members realize that it is not necessary for everyone to do tasks equally well. It may be that some members contribute more to one phase of a project or activity than to others. It points out to them that different tasks require different types of skills. All members do not have to contribute equally in each area.

Learning in cooperative groups requires students to develop and use social skills necessary in everyday life. Interpersonal and group skills are taught and face-to-face positive interaction and accountability is fostered (see chapter 4). With appropriate information and feedback students become self-correcting in their social behaviors. Students are told that the teacher will be watching their performance of the skill and will provide information on how well they did during the lesson. Assessment of the skill is accomplished in two different ways. To provide feedback for older students, a five-point scale can be developed. A score of "5" indicates that every time the group was observed their target social skill was appropriate. A "4" indicates that at least one time, the target social skill was not appropriate during the lesson. The same pattern occurs for a rating of "1," "2," or "3." It is important to set a lower limit whereby some action from outside the group occurs. This may be at "2" or "1." For very young students this process is made more concrete by placing a chip on a group's table when they are monitored and found to be demonstrating appropriate behavior. A maximum of five chips and five observations might be set. A preset level of chips at the end of the week is used to determine a reward such as free reading or computer time in the classroom or school library.

One strategy for involving the students in group evaluation is providing the class with a series of questions that are generalizations related to the unit to be studied. Small and Petrek (1992) described this strategy with a unit, "Experimenting With Matter." Students worked in groups of five. Each group constructed a question it would investigate. Next, they developed a hypothesis to answer the question and a way of testing the hypothesis. After testing the hypothesis, a written report and an oral presentation were developed. Guidelines were given to the groups for the hands-on activities. These included skillful use of laboratory equipment, the condition of the laboratory station and equipment, attention to safety rules, honesty in reporting data gathered, and use of project time. Each section of the written project report was assessed and given equal weight. The sections were identified as introduction, hypothesis, procedure, results, conclusions, and further questions. Each was assessed on completeness of information, organization, clarity of language, clear representation of the data, and accuracy. The oral presentation was assessed using seven criteria: 1) appropriate length of the report, 2) interest generated in the audience, 3) creativity, 4) quality of visual aids and props, 5) completeness, 6) honesty in reporting the data, 7) use of voice and body expression, and 8) participation by all members of the group. Each group member received a grade for carrying out the activities, involvement in the written report, and involvement in the oral report.

Each of these assessments could carry different weights. For instance, the written report might be worth 50% of the project grade while the activity guidelines could be 20%, and the oral presentation 30%.

Performance Testing

Integrated thematic teaching is activity-based, oriented toward problem solving, and involves interactions between students. Students apply intellectual and practical skills in order to use and develop a body of knowledge. They develop and use their understanding across a range of content and with a variety of everyday tasks. Because of this, integrated thematic units often are not assessed well using paper-and-pencil tests. Performance assessment is a better tool for evaluation. Students are asked to perform a skill they have learned or to apply a concept in a new situation (Rivera, Kuehne, & Banbury, 1995). In a unit on communication, for example, a performance test occurs when a student successfully sends an electronic mail message to someone or uses a telephone directory to locate an individual's phone number. Student performance assessment can involve written tests, learning stations, role-plays, a dance, individual practical work at desks, or practical work in cooperative groups. An example of one performance assessment is found in Figure 5.14. This second-grade student has been working with types of photographic devices. He is comparing two cameras and identifying similarities and differences between them.

There are six categories of performance.

First is the use of graphic and symbolic representation such as reading information from, or constructing information as, graphs and tables or charts.

Second is the use of apparatus and measuring instruments involving estimating, measuring, following instructions, and solving problems.

Third are the categories of observation involving making, interpreting, and using observations to solve problems.

Fourth is interpretation and application involving data already gathered and applying that information in various contexts.

Fifth is planning investigations with a focus on sequencing elements.

Sixth is performing investigations where some or all of the preceding categories are implemented (Sunal & Sunal, in press).

FIGURE 5.14   A Performance Assessment

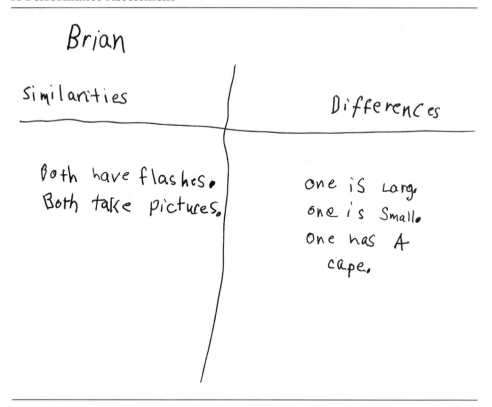

Assessment of student problem solving involves a variety of practical actions. These are assessed individually or in combination with each other. They include problem perception, problem reformulation, planning and carrying out, recording and interpreting, and evaluation by the student.

There are some guidelines for developing performance assessment items for written tests and tasks for practical work. Performance items are direct and simple, and easily performed by the whole class. All assessments are short, no longer than five minutes in length. Diagrams and clear instructions that students follow with little guidance are provided. Students use familiar materials. Written items must assess the skills and content areas developed in the lesson or unit. Preferably, written items are similar to those found in the expansion phase of the lesson or unit just completed. Once a task is determined, scoring procedures for the range of acceptable answers are developed. Performance, not content, is the focus of the task and is reflected in the scoring.

Among the types of tasks and projects used for performance assessment are role-playing, writing assignments, simulations, displays, projects, drawings, and models. Students can be given a set of questions that ask them to describe the skills and steps they used in completing the performance assessment. For example: How did they decide on the content of the role-play? What characteristics were important? How did they construct the role-play and assign roles?

There are barriers to the effective use of performance assessment in the classroom. A lack of time and poorly defined content and performance standards hinder teachers' efforts to adopt performance assessment (Khattri, Kane, & Reeve, 1995). Time is important for the planning and development of performance-based tasks and for scoring and interpreting the information gained from such assessments. When a team of teachers is developing performance assessments, agreement is reached on what constitutes acceptable performance. For example, what is acceptable performance on an outcome such as "effective communication in mathematics?" Teachers need access to adequate professional development and support to develop and implement performance assessment.

ASSESSMENT WITH TESTS AND QUIZZES

Multiple-choice, matching, true-and-false, fill-in-the-blanks, and short essay are assessment formats used in tests and quizzes. With very young students, a version of short essay test is given by asking students to dictate language experience stories related to activities with which they have been involved. Primary-grade students can write and illustrate short essays related to the unit's content. The other types of items are carefully constructed if used with very young students.

All test items determine whether students have met the objectives of the unit and its lessons. The match between objective and test item is critically important. Test items are used to assess factual knowledge related to those objectives that specify a factual knowledge learning outcome. Questions for knowledge objectives are the easiest to construct. Testing process skill objectives requires providing new data for students to use in answering the question. It is possible to measure attitudes, but giving grades for attitudes in a nation that supports freedom of thought is not appropriate.

Before writing test items, teachers consider unit objectives and make decisions about which objectives have a priority in assessment. Those objectives most heavily focused on in the unit are assessed. Then teachers decide what type or combination of types of questions will be used in the test and write the test items. Guidelines for writing appropriate essay and objective test items follow.

Essay Questions

- Decide what process skills students should use before writing any questions,

- Write essay questions with clear tasks (for example: Are students to describe steps in completing an activity?),
- Write essay questions that require more than repeating information,
- Use only a few questions, and make sure they require short answers,
- Make sure the questions vary in difficulty, and
- Give clear directions. (Students should know whether an answer should be in outline form or paragraphs, its point value on the test, and what criteria will be used to evaluate answers.) (Sunal & Haas, 1993; Good & Brophy, 1986)

Objective Test Questions

Objective test questions in multiple-choice, true and false, and fill-in-the-blanks formats should ask students to respond to important content. Guidelines for objective questions are:

- the question must present a problem,
- the question should be as short as possible,
- answer choices should be short,
- the question should use the negative infrequently and make it noticeable by underlining the *not* when it is used,
- there should be only one correct or clearly best answer,
- all answer choices should be plausible, and
- a particular response should not be longer than the others because this suggests it is the answer (Sunal & Haas, 1993; Good & Brophy, 1986).

MULTIPLE ASSESSMENT: TYING THINGS TOGETHER

Whenever student learning is assessed in an integrated thematic unit, teachers need to include those abilities and products they think are essential in the types of situations where they were learned and are used. Teachers ask themselves, "What are the performances in which our students should do well?" and "What are the challenges our students should be able to meet?" This type of assessment is authentic assessment. It establishes a global approach for assessing learning. In a global approach multiple assessment is used. Teachers do not view assessment as tests or as an after-the-event way of finding out what students learned. Instead, they view assessment as instructional. It is a way of determining students' prior knowledge, monitoring student learning, and determining summative or learning outcomes. Multiple, authentic assessment is a way of clarifying, providing feedback, and setting goals toward which to direct student activity.

Multiple assessment has four parts (Anthony, Johnson, Mickelson, & Preece, 1991). As Figure 5.15 indicates, assessment involves observation of

Multiple Assessment   FIGURE 5.15

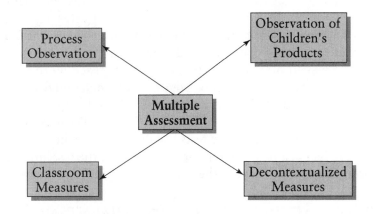

process, observation of children's products, classroom measures, and de-contextualized measures. Observation of process includes:

- anecdotal comments from both classroom observation and reflection,
- interviews and conferences with students, parents, and other professionals such as a special educator, and
- student responses and comments such as retelling a story or reconstruction of the process of manipulating items in constructing a solution to a mathematics problem.

The observation of children's products involves the analysis any items produced by the students. These include logs, journals, audio and videotapes, *hyper card* stacks, interest inventories, electronic mail communications, and student self-assessments. Classroom measures include teacher-made assessments of content and process skill knowledge and assessments imbedded in unit activities and textbook readings. Decontextualized measures involve the use of criterion-referenced tests and required standardized testing programs.

Individual teachers and teaching teams typically give heavier emphasis to one or two of these sources of data and reduced emphasis to the others. The choice depends on the purpose of the integrated unit, teaching styles, the students' learning styles, and requirements for standardized testing in the school.

PLANNING FOR REQUIRED STANDARDIZED TESTING

Standardized testing often is required for all students by school systems and states. Standardized tests are not developed specifically to measure learning from integrated units. These tests do not fit well into classrooms that heavily use authentic and alternative assessments.

Students must be prepared for standardized tests if they are to take them. They may need a few activities where they "bubble in" answers. They need to have experience with the multiple-choice format and other formats used in standardized testing. Students must learn to work in a rigid time frame. Teachers ensure that the type of content tested is addressed in the integrated units.

In providing such preparation teachers are not teaching the test but are helping students construct their knowledge of the format and restrictions such tests impose. Tests and the testing formats used should match how and what students have learned if they are to be of real value. Because the choice of whether or not to use standardized tests usually is not the individual teacher's decision, students must be prepared for the format of the test and for the type of content it will test. Otherwise, the results have reduced validity.

REPORTING STUDENT ACCOMPLISHMENTS TO FAMILIES

Families are involved in the student assessment and evaluation process through receiving the reports of its results and by contributing to it. The information reported to families should be analyzed using the following questions (Anthony et al., 1991, p. 149):

1. Does the information represent an appropriate balance of process and product observations, contextualized and decontextualized measures?

2. Are enough anecdotal comments provided? Do those that have been gathered offer sufficient support for the comments made on the report families will receive?

3. Are any of the data contradictory? If so, is there sufficient evidence provided by other sources of information to permit interpretation or resolution of the discrepancies?

Family-teacher conferences are an important part of the evaluation process. The family member and teacher discuss a summary evaluation of the student including illustrative relevant anecdotes. An example is:

> Maria is able to use coordinates such as A-1 and C-7 to identify locations on a map. She is able to use the map scale to identify distances. She is working on learning to use latitude and longitude coordinates to identify locations. Maria has talked about how she would like to be able to tell a friend where a town is by describing its latitude and longitude coordinates. She has said it is nice to know just where a town is because then you always know where you are going.

To enhance family involvement, family members can be asked to identify two to three areas of interest and/or concern prior to the conference. They are

Family members continually evaluate children's development and must be a part of the school's evaluation of children's progress.

given a form listing parts of an integrated unit, disciplines incorporated into the unit, process skills, or the names of all the integrated units taught during the reporting period. There is a space for other interests and concerns. The teacher provides additional anecdotes illustrating the student's progress in the areas identified. Family members need to be introduced to this aspect of the family-teacher conference. A meeting with students' families is the most productive means of doing so. However, a note describing the process can be sent home or it can be described in the class or school newsletter.

During the conference the teacher also provides an interpretation of the student's growth and development and suggestions for strategies that will initiate, maintain, or improve progress. Finally, the teacher predicts the student's future progress. As these areas are discussed, the teacher shows the parent material from the four categories of multiple assessment that support the evaluation of the area.

Student-led conferences are another option that works well with integrated unit teaching. Student participation in the discussion of evaluation encourages reflective self-assessment. Student participation requires long-range planning. Students need to brainstorm, then discuss a list of the work samples they wish to discuss with their parents. These samples demonstrate the range of participation as well as its depth. Family members need to know that the process helps students develop increased responsibility for reporting their progress, helps them evaluate their work fairly, become accountable for their work and behavior, and learn organizational skills (Anthony et al., 1991, p. 149).

Students write a letter to their families inviting them to the 30- to 45-minute conference. The letter gives several alternate meeting times and days. Family members reply indicating which time is convenient for them. Several conferences are scheduled at the same time at tables. The teacher circulates between the tables during the conferences, thus giving major responsibility for the conference to the student. The teacher is not the focus of the conference, but can step in to change the direction of the meeting if a family member is being too critical.

In preparation for the conference, students write another letter to their family and put it in their file of work samples. This letter asks the family member to notice special things about the file. For example, it may tell the family member to notice how well organized the file is, the nice comments on the student's group work by cooperative group members, and the clear directions the student is able to give for accomplishing science activities. The student can inform the family member of those things he or she does very well. The student can comment on things needing improvement. Finally, the letter asks the family member to write a note back to the student about the file and provides a space for these comments.

Before the conferences, students practice presenting their information to a student from another class or another cooperative group. The partner asks the type of questions family members are expected to ask. The student has an opportunity to learn to explain the file clearly and comfortably.

After the conference family members sign a guest book with a space for a few general comments. This gives the teacher feedback regarding attendance and family members' views. Light refreshments are provided to convey an informal atmosphere. The students and teacher(s) debrief after the conferences are concluded. The debriefing discusses what went well and how the various steps in the process of preparing for and conducting the conference might be adjusted prior to the next conference. Student-led conferences take a lot of preparation and initially may occur once or twice during the school year. They may be expanded to three or four conferences a year depending on the teacher, family member, and student time available for them.

SUMMARY

Assessing and evaluating integrated thematic units is an ongoing process. It uses the strategies found in single-discipline units but focuses on multiple forms of assessment. A single means of assessment yields an evaluation that is too limited to represent the range and depth of learning occurring in an integrated thematic unit. Authentic assessment is a part of the integrated thematic unit. Many people are involved in the evaluation process including students, teachers, family members, and other professionals. Reporting to families is important and takes many forms. Integrated thematic units lend themselves well to student-led family conferences as one means of reporting the evaluation of a student.

REFERENCES

Anthony, R., Johnson, T., Mickelson, N., & Preece, A. (1991). *Evaluating literacy: A perspective for change*. Portsmouth, NH: Heinemann.

Ary, D., Jacobs, L., & Razavieh, A. (1990). *Introduction to research in education* (4th ed.). Ft. Worth, TX: Holt, Rinehart and Winston.

Boehm, A., & Weinberg, R. (1987). *The classroom observer* (2nd ed.). New York: Teachers College Press.

Borko, H., Flory, M., & Cumbo, K. (1993, October). Teachers' ideas and practices about assessment and instruction. A case study of the effects of alternative assessment in instruction, student learning, and accountability practice. CSE Technical Report 366. Los Angeles, CA: Center for Research on Evaluation, Standards, and Student Testing.

Champagne, A. B. (1990). Assessment and teaching of thinking skills. In G. E. Hein (Ed.), *The assessment of hands-on elementary science programs* (pp. 68–82). Grand Forks, ND: University of North Dakota, Center for Teaching and Learning.

Chittenden, E. (1990). Young children's discussions of science topics. In G. E. Hein (Ed.), *The assessment of hands-on elementary science programs* (pp. 220–247). Grand Forks, ND: University of North Dakota, Center for Teaching and Learning.

Collins, A. (1991). Portfolios for assessing student learning in science: A new name for a familiar idea? In. G. Kulm & S. M. Malcolm (Eds.), *Assessment in the service of reform* (pp. 291–300). Washington, DC: American Association for the Advancement of Science.

Driver, R. (1990). Assessing the progress of children's understanding in science: A developmental perspective. In G. E. Hein (Ed.), *The assessment of hands-on elementary science programs* (pp. 204–216). Grand Forks, ND: University of North Dakota, Center for Teaching and Learning.

Dyasi, H. M. (1990). Children's investigations of natural phenomena: A source of data for assessment in elementary school science. In G. E. Hein (Ed.), *The assessment of hands-on elementary science programs* (pp. 248–262). Grand Forks, ND: University of North Dakota, Center for Teaching and Learning.

Harmon, M., & Mokros, J. (1990). Assessment in the new NSF elementary science curricula: An emerging role. In G. E. Hein (Ed.), *The assessment of hands-on elementary science programs* (pp. 184–203). Grand Forks, ND: University of North Dakota, Center for Teaching and Learning.

Hein, G. E. (1990a). Assessing assessment. In G. E. Hein (Ed.), *The assessment of hands-on elementary science programs* (pp. 1–17). Grand Forks, ND: University of North Dakota, Center for Teaching and Learning.

Hein, G. E. (1990b). Conclusion. In G. E. Hein (Ed.), *The assessment of hands-on elementary science programs* (pp. 264–279). Grand Forks, ND: University of North Dakota, Center for Teaching and Learning.

Hein, G. E. (1991). Active assessment for active science. In V. Perrone (Ed.), *Expanding student assessment* (p. 106). Washington, DC: Association for Supervision and Curriculum Development.

Herman, J., Aschbacher, P., & Winters, L. (1992). *A practical guide to alternative assessment*. Alexandria, VA: Association for Supervision and Curriculum Development.

Khattri, N., Kane, M., & Reeve, A. (1995, November). How performance assessments affect teaching and learning. *Educational Leadership, 53*(3), 80–83.

Meng, E., & Doran, R. (1990). What research says . . . about appropriate methods of assessment. *Science and Children, 56*(1), 42–45.

Murphy, P. (1990). What has been learned about assessment form the work of the APU science project? In G. E. Hein (Ed.), *The assessment of hands-on elementary science programs* (pp. 148–179). Grand Forks, ND: University of North Dakota, Center for Teaching and Learning.

Piaget, J. (1950). *The psychology of intelligence*. London: Routledge and Kagan Paul.

Rivera, D., Kuehne, C., & Banbury, M. (1995, September/October). Performance-based assessment: A tool for authentic learning and instructional decision making. *Gifted Child Today, 15*(5), 34–40.

Small, L., & Petrek, J. (1992). Teamwork testing. *Science Scope, 15*(6), 29–30.

Sunal, C., & Haas, M. (1993). *Social studies for the elementary/middle school student*. Ft. Worth, TX: Harcourt Brace.

Sunal, D., & Sunal, C. (in press). *Elementary and middle school science*. Ft. Worth, TX: Harcourt Brace.

Wolf, D. (1989). Portfolio assessment: Sampling student work. *Educational Leadership, 46*(7), 35–39.

Vygotsky, L. S. (1962). *Thought and language*. Cambridge, MA: MIT Press.

C H A P T E R 6

INTEGRATING SOCIAL STUDIES COMPONENTS

Social studies lends itself well to integration in thematic units. It has been called "the great connection" by Goodman and Adler (1985), who see it as the core to which all parts of the elementary and middle school curriculum can be tied. Social studies as it exists today already is an interdisciplinary approach striving to integrate numerous disciplines and approaches. It relies heavily on the content of history and the social sciences including anthropology, archaeology, economics, geography, political science, philosophy, psychology, and sociology. Material from mathematics and the natural sciences also is incorporated.

The vitality of a democracy depends on the education and participation of its citizens. Hence, the primary purpose of social studies is to help young people develop the ability to make informed and reasoned decisions for the public good as citizens of a culturally diverse, democratic society in an interdependent world. This purpose can be accomplished through deep and continuing social studies in the elementary schools (National Council for the Social Studies, 1994). It is best accomplished when social studies is integrated with other disciplines resulting in a curriculum that represents the interdependent world in which we live.

CURRICULUM STANDARDS FOR SOCIAL STUDIES

The *Curriculum Standards for Social Studies* serve as a framework for social studies program design (National Council for the Social Studies, 1994). The standards are a guide for curriculum decisions. They can be used to consider the role of social studies in an integrated thematic unit. Ten themes create the framework of the standards. They are:

1. culture;
2. time, continuity, and change;
3. people, places, and environments;
4. individual development and identity;
5. individuals, groups, and institutions;
6. power, authority, and governance;
7. production, distribution, and consumption;
8. science, technology, and society;
9. global connections; and
10. civic ideals and practices.

Each theme incorporates more than one contributing discipline. For example, theme three (people, places, and environments) derives much of its content from geography but also addresses physical science, political science, sociology, and history. Some themes, such as number eight (science, technology, and society), do not derive much of their content from a single discipline but cross several contributing disciplines. Each theme is addressed at each grade level, although some grade levels may give greater attention to some themes and less to others. The Standards include examples of implementation of the themes in the early, middle, and high school grades.

THE NATURE OF THE SOCIAL STUDIES

Social studies involves a search for patterns in our lives. A pattern is a regular activity that occurred in the past and can be expected to occur again in the future (Sunal & Haas, 1993, p. 9). Examples of such patterns are:

- Climate has an effect on traditional house design.
- People in the past were more like us than different from us.
- People join with others who are similar to them.
- There are not enough resources to satisfy everybody's wants.
- Arguments and controversy arise when there is a scarcity of resources.

All people process large amounts of information about their social world. This information comes from family, friends, acquaintances, strangers, and the media. People try to make sense out of this information, for example, figuring out why housing design differs from one region of the nation to another and noticing that people argue more often when they are stressed by the scarcity of commodities they need. Finding patterns in the events of the social world enables people to predict what will happen next and to explain the cause of an event. When this occurs, the individual has a feeling of control. Life is a little less chaotic since it is more possible to solve the problems with which one is faced. More appropriate and accurate decisions are made because patterns suggest causes and effects. Once a pattern is identified, it can be reconstructed as new information is obtained (Osborne & Freyberg, 1985). These patterns are labeled as concepts, generalizations, and values.

Social studies involves both content and the process skills through which we learn content. Process skills involve "doing." Students might observe someone speaking to a group of people, noting how the inflection of her voice changes at various points in the speech. They might infer that she wants the audience to become excited about those points she is making in a rising inflection. Then they might hypothesize that the speaker is a political candidate who is trying to convince the audience to vote for her in the next election. Later, they interview the speaker and find that she is a political candidate trying to woo voters. They also interview members of the audience and determine that many of them now intend to vote for the speaker. The students are using several process skills including observing, inferring, hypothesizing, and interviewing to acquire content. The content involves political candidacy and political speeches.

Social studies involves the processing of information into concepts and generalizations that are more usable than the isolated pieces themselves (Dworetzky, 1990). Students learn to process information by using the process skills. Rote memorization does not help them learn to process information (Sunal & Haas, 1993, p. 11).

Once information is processed it is used to solve problems and make decisions. Successful problem solving involves waiting until enough information is available to make an adequate decision and processing the information so that different solutions are examined and thoughtfully considered. Decision making results from problem solving. Appropriate decisions can be made when adequate information is available and processed appropriately. Social studies focuses on the decisions people make and have made and on the impact of those decisions.

Throughout problem solving and decision making, social studies involves the development and analysis of values and the application of values in social action. It helps students exert some control over their lives as they define and clarify their values (Sunal & Haas, 1993, p. 12). When students consider the implications of their values and then act on them, they further extend the control they have over their lives (Banks & Clegg, 1985). Students analyze their values, become consciously aware of them, and recognize alternative values. The teacher models some values and helps students think about their own values. Personal and public policy decisions are based on criteria requiring reflection on facts, generalizations, consequences, and feelings toward people. Value decisions translate into social action that demands reflective and careful decision making from individuals and from society's leaders.

Students have definite ideas about their social world. These ideas come from past experience, from adult comments and the behaviors that adults display, from the media, and from their educational experiences. Many of their conceptions are different from those accepted by social science researchers (Osborne & Cosgrove, 1985). Lessons including an exploration, an invention, and an expansion help students construct an understanding of important social studies concepts, generalizations, values, and process skills.

UTILIZING MANY VIEWPOINTS, ORIGINAL MATERIALS, AND DATA GATHERING

The social world often is intangible yet people are always aware of it and of their struggle to understand it and make a satisfactory place for themselves in it. Many materials are used in studying the social world (see Figure 6.1). These include artifacts such as a bead from grandmother's necklace, to a 1927 Model-T Ford, to a 1983 postage stamp, to an historically preserved community such as Williamsburg, Virginia, to the Great Wall of China. Obviously some artifacts are more likely to find their way into the classroom than others. Some are available only through a field trip and some will never be experienced first-hand but through video or photographs.

Documents also are used in social studies. These range widely and include:

the Declaration of Independence,

the treaty ending World War II in the Pacific,

John C. Fremont's map of the Oregon Trail,

a photograph of Rosa Parks taken on her 75th birthday by a newspaper photographer,

a copy of a page from a city code at the turn of the century that declared public checker-playing an activity disturbing the public peace,

a photograph of one's grandfather as a young man standing by his first car,

an editorial cartoon in today's edition of the local newspaper,

a letter from an Alabama girl named "Amy" to a girl named "Amy Carter" living in the White House with her parents,

Sources of Social Studies Information
FIGURE 6.1

Artifacts

Some examples are:

A pencil box from five years ago, a coin with a 1951 date, a picture of Uncle Billy as a child, a computer keypunch card

Documents

Some examples are:

A reproduction of a World War I recruiting poster, a copy of a letter to a legislator written by students about an issue last year, a song sheet from the 1930s, a map of the community

Diaries, Novels, and Other Lengthy Written Documents

Some examples are:

A diary kept by a farm girl in Iowa in the 1920s, a story about Helen Keller, a description of events in the late 1960s by a high school student in Selma, Alabama

People

Some examples are:

A parent, the local volunteer firefighters chief, the operator of a corner grocery, the director of the Humane Society shelter

Natural Places

Some examples are:

Lake Michigan, Chesapeake Bay, a ridgetop in Tennessee, a mountain trail just west of Los Angeles, a piece of original prairieland in Kansas, a bit of swampland near Tampa, Florida

Human-Built Places

Some examples are:

The Golden Gate Bridge, the French Market in New Orleans, Mt. Rushmore, a footbridge over a stream in West Virginia, a bowling alley in Scranton, Pennsylvania, a mall in Denver

Computer Resources

Some examples are:

Web sites such as those for the Birmingham Zoo, Tennessee Aquarium, Vietnam War Memorial, and National Postal Museum, and CD-ROM disks of landmark documents in American history and an encyclopedia of images of Native American leaders

a birthday card from an aunt in Glendale, California,

a message left on the answering machine by a friend from school, and

an e-mail message received yesterday from someone at a pulley manufacturing company describing the company's best-selling pulley in response to a query from a third-grade class.

Diaries, novels, and other written materials, both fiction and nonfiction, that are lengthier than documents are yet another set of sources for social studies (Levstik, 1986). Diaries, letters, and other written materials often are interesting to students. The older the document, the more translation by the teacher is needed. Both writing style and vocabulary change over time making written materials progressively more difficult to read. Sometimes students may be unfamiliar with the activities or events described and may need to have them explained. Such difficulties present learning opportunities that many students enjoy. An example is one of a set of letters written in pencil on school tablet paper between a group of eighth-grade students living near the top of the lower peninsula of Michigan in 1897.

> Dear Letty,
> Please come to a hay ride and picnic in Martin's Meadow on Saturday next. Jonathon's father and older brother will drive the mules and we will all have a ride on the hay wagon to Martin's Meadow and home again. We can fish if we want to and play games. The mill will be work-ing too. Mary Anna will come for you as she can ride the horse to Jonathon's farm and you can ride with her.
>   We will have ham and piccalilli, and will roast corn. Peter will bring watermelon and muskmelon because they will be ready. Jonathon will bring berry pies. There will be a lot to eat.
>   All the children who will be in grade eight in school are invited. I hope all seven of us can come. Please send a note with your father to the feed store telling me if you can come.
> Your friend,
> Constance

This letter can be a doorway to a study of U.S. rural life near the beginning of the 20th century. Students can talk about hay rides and picnics, hay wagons and mules, piccalilli and muskmelon and berry pies. They can talk about the small number of eighth graders and consider questions such as: What is a mill? What might have been milled in this area? What is a feed store? Why didn't Letty just phone and say whether she could come?

Students enjoy historical fiction as well as diaries and other nonfiction materials. There is evidence that students become deeply engaged with the stories and diaries they read. Students enjoy such an approach more than textbook reading, finding it livelier and richer in detail. However, all materials—including historical fiction and diaries—should be chosen care-fully. It is difficult to obtain enough such materials to cover all the impor-tant aspects of a topic in a valid and appropriate manner. Levstik (1986) suggests children choose their own book from a set of books, have a read-ing time each day, and discuss their reading in small and large groups. Their reading should be part of a larger project involving data gathering and ma-nipulation, high standards for class behavior and work, and critical exami-nation of stories for fact, opinion, fiction, and causal relationships. The U.S. National Archives is putting its collections of documents including treaties, letters to Presidents, maps, posters, newspaper editorials, and much more on its Web site. This is one source of authentic materials students find both interesting and challenging.

People are not materials but serve a similar purpose in social studies. They are a first-hand source of information. They can be guest speakers in the classroom, interviewees in the neighborhood, or participants in a city council meeting visited by a group of students. Places also are not materials but serve as a source of information that often contains materials. They can be natural places, such as the delta area formed by the end of a rivulet running across the school playground after a rain or a geyser at Yellowstone National Park. Or they can be made by humans, such as the Empire State Building or the Lincoln Memorial.

There are many sources of information for social studies experiences. Even in communities that seem to be limited in resources such as rural, isolated areas there are many sources of information available. These include natural places but also the people that live there. The home economics agent, fisheries supervisor, banker, catalog store clerk: All these people offer rich opportunities for learning social studies. Many of them provide or lend materials that deal with their workplace ranging from catalogs to fish-feeding devices. Their personal interests and hobbies also serve as a source of information for investigation by students.

Many materials are available today on CD-ROM disks for use in social studies. These include copies of issues of *Cobblestone* magazine, a wonderful history magazine for children. Other CD-ROMs offer pictures of individuals and places with important roles in the American Revolution, copies of *Time* magazine's "Man of the Year" issues, a gallery of pictures of children, chronicles of 20th-century events, pictures enabling students to explore castles from the 14th century, and maps of regions large and small. The World Wide Web is a huge reservoir of all sorts of materials for social studies. One can take a walk through the White House, clicking on a piece of furniture and receiving a detailed description of it, including close-up views of its carving. Or, a tourist map of Veracruz, Mexico, can be printed. Directions to King's College at the University of London from the local subway metro station are available. Recordings of songs from the Union Army and the Confederate Army can be found. A recipe for "Hoppin John," a concoction of black-eyed peas and onions eaten in the southern United States can be obtained. The U.S. Census Bureau's "pop clock" is on the Web and gives a continuous updating of the U.S. and world population. A joint project can be carried out on local weather patterns between two towns in the same county. The Web is a tremendously varied resource, but a difficult one to use. It also has much material to which children should not have access. There are a number of methods of screening material and limiting access to sites. A teacher needs to surf the Web for a while to discover its potential and its problems. Then, steps are taken to help students use the Web efficiently and appropriately.

Data Gathering

Data collection is a foundation of social studies. Without appropriate and adequate data causes of events and human actions cannot be inferred, sequences of events cannot be established, and predictions for the future cannot be made. Often data gathering in social studies is viewed as library research. This is an important source of data. But this is data that has been gathered and interpreted by someone else. If a lot of information is available the author may have to select:

- which information to present,
- which to highlight, and
- which to put in a central role.

If little data is available, the author may make much of very little information. Students need to recognize that encyclopedias and other nonfiction resources are the result of data gathering by the author and the interpretation of that data. The interpretation of data is necessary and occurs even when the decision is made regarding where and when to gather data. Students understand the role of data interpretation by reading library sources, gathering data from them, and interpreting them in a paper they write or a presentation they make. However, students often view the written words they read as better constructed than anything they can write and copy portions directly. Data interpretation is not clearly recognized by students when they mostly read and copy information.

Gathering Original Data

Data gathering in social studies should involve as much direct experience with raw and undigested data as possible. Such data is collected when:

students conduct interviews with family members,

stand on a street corner to count cars in order to determine peak traffic hours during the day,

graph the numbers of products in their home by country of origin,

compare an old mail order catalog with a recent catalog to decide whether a set of specific products has changed in design,

compare an old map of the community or of a portion of it with a recent map produced by the U.S. Geological Survey, and

examine a copy of a letter written to President Eisenhower by girls in Montana begging him not to make Elvis Presley get a "G.I." haircut after drafting him into the army (National Archives, 1989).

Data with little or no previous interpretation challenges students. They must collect it, analyze it, and find a way to communicate their interpretation of it to others. Sometimes, students find others in their group or class may interpret the same information differently. The process involves many thinking skills and helps students understand the role of interpretation and the necessity for having as much information as possible and for using information gathered from a variety of sources.

Textbooks as a Source of Data

The social studies textbook serves as the primary information source for most students in the United States (Sunal & Haas, 1993). Many students have difficulty reading textbooks (Anderson & Armbruster, 1984). These difficulties arise from a lack of experiential background and the complex content presented (Hoge, 1986). Students with little experience outside their neighborhood or community may find it hard to be interested in learning about faraway places. Students with little sense of personal or family history may find it hard to relate to historical settings (Hoge, 1986).

Social studies textbooks have a heavy technical load of concepts and generalizations. These are specialized ideas in social studies such as "delta," "interdependence," "economy," "revolution," and "constitution." These concepts are related in some way to form generalizations such as "The *economies* of countries in today's world are *interdependent* upon each other" (Sunal & Haas, 1993, p. 140). Many students have a weak understanding of the concepts of *economies* and *interdependent*. As a result, they have trouble relating them to form this generalization. Textbooks often pile too many concepts and generalizations into a few paragraphs without enough supporting examples and discussion. They often refer to long periods of time and huge distances. Hoge (1986, p. 1) wonders what expressions such as "far to the north" or "over a thousand miles to the east" mean to students who are not sure which direction is which and have never traveled further than across the state.

The Textbook Teaching Plan

With all their problems, textbooks are a resource for teaching which most teachers can access and use. With planning, they are useful in an integrated teaching unit as a resource or as required reading for all students. Developing a teaching plan for using a social studies textbook begins with a content analysis of the textbook's material. If the unit is part of the course of study, the textbook's material is compared to that identified in the course of study. Notes are made by checking off which topics are covered and whether the coverage is adequate (see Figure 6.2). If several textbooks from different

FIGURE 6.2   ## Planning Instruction With a Textbook

Teaching With a Textbook

Step One: Check off textbook topics that are part of the state or local, course of study.

Step Two: Identify whether textbook coverage of course of study topics is adequate or needs expansion.

Step Three: Identify in the textbook the *most important*
         facts,
         concepts,
         generalizations,
         attitudes,
         values, and
         process skills.

Step Four: Select from step three those ideas and skills most appropriate to this group of students.

Step Five: Develop and teach lessons for those ideas and skills selected in step four.

Step Six: Have students read less important material from textbook.

publishers are used as resources, a table is developed indicating which textbook covers each topic and the adequacy of the coverage (see Figure 6.3). Whether or not a course of study specifies content to be taught, the teacher identifies the *most important* facts, concepts, generalizations, attitudes, values, and process skills found in the textbook material. These are considered

FIGURE 6.3   ## Comparing Topics Across Multiple Textbook Sources

Using Multiple Textbooks as Resources

When multiple textbooks are used as resources a table can be created indicating which textbook covers each topic and the adequacy of the coverage as in the example below.

Publisher	Topic	Coverage	
		Inadequate	Adequate
1 = Harcourt			
2 = Macmillan			
	exploration/settlement (North America)		
1.		X	
2.		X	
	conflict/cooperation		
1.			X
2.		X	
	change: culture and technology		
1.		X	
2.			X
	developing democracy		
1.			X
2.		X	

and sifted until a set appropriate to the needs and experiences of the students are identified. Next, the teacher develops lessons for the important material identified. Material identified as less important is read from the textbook. Because of the heavy technical load of concepts and generalizations in a social studies textbook, it is not possible to develop thorough lessons to teach all of them. Instead, the important ideas and skills are identified and taught. With this foundation, students read the textbook(s) to learn additional, related material. The textbook is best used as part of the invention portion of the lesson where students are constructing their idea of the material to be learned. The wide range of materials used in social studies enables students to construct the important facts, concepts, generalizations, attitudes, values, and process skills to be learned in the unit. Textbook readings support the construction initiated by materials that directly involve student in inquiry learning through data collection and interpretation.

DEVELOPING SKILLS OF MAKING INFERENCES AND INTERPRETATIONS

The holistic nature of integrated thematic units assists students in developing skills of making inferences and interpretations, important elements in social studies and in all other disciplines. This is fostered when teachers:

1. listen empathetically;
2. model thinking;
3. collaborate with students;
4. design learning as problem solving and experimentation;
5. plan, monitor, and evaluate progress; and
6. empower students toward self-direction (Barell, 1991).

In an example suggested by Barell, Ms. Mulcahy talks with her first- and second-graders about how she thinks through problems. Her students decide that a good problem-solver does four things:

1. discards the parts of the problem that are not needed and gets to the main problem,
2. looks at the problem from different angles,
3. adds onto someone else's thinking, and
4. works the problem out on paper.

This teacher is helping students design experiences enabling them to pose a variety of "what if" questions throughout their lives. Developing skills in making inferences and interpretations involves constructing and using "what if" questions.

Processing new and unfamiliar information is made easier when resource materials are available (Ginsburg & Opper, 1988). Children have limited space in their sensory memories (Sylvester, 1985). They can address just a few items coming in through their senses. When all the sensory memory space is used items additional items are not addressed. Having concrete examples in front of students allows them to work with greater amounts of new information. The items enable students to refer to them and make it possible for them to work with a greater variety of information at the same time.

As students work with a specific item they go through a process of first trying to identify a pattern in it. Once they have identified a pattern, they disregard some of the specifics and write it in a generalized form. For example, they may be examining a photograph from the 1920s. They note that the car in the picture "looks old." It doesn't look like the cars they see on the streets today. Then, they notice the people in the picture are wearing one-piece clothing with legs that end just above the knee and short sleeves. Finally, they see what looks like water in the background. They decide they are looking at a picture of a seashore and people visiting it. Then, they examine a second picture and determine whether it fits the same general pattern. They look at the second picture of the same people and the car taken from farther away. In this picture they notice sand dunes and decide both pictures fit the pattern they have identified of people visiting a seashore a long time ago. As another example, students have conducted a survey of students' views regarding a proposed redesign of the school playground. They see a pattern in the survey the students in their class filled out. Next, they give the survey to a group of older students. They find the same patterns.

Evaluation is a component of this process. The evidence available is evaluated to determine whether or not the pattern identified is substantiated by the evidence available. The pattern is considered to decide whether it is unusual. Does it go beyond what you know or consider to be common knowledge? Then it is examined to determine whether it is reasonable given the context. If the pattern isn't reasonable, can it be supported in this instance? If it can be supported, how reliable is it? If it is reliable then the pattern is substantiated. Generally patterns that are not substantiated are vague, ambiguous, or have little meaning. Patterns are not found to have support when they overgeneralize, oversimplify a causal relationship, lack a credible source, include slanted information, or appeal to emotions. The stereotyping found in statements such as "she has red hair so she has a fiery temper and you better watch out if you put her in the school play" or "Ah Soong won't have any trouble with that because she is Asian and math is easy for them" are examples of patterns that are not credible, overgeneralize, oversimplify, include slanted information, and appeal to emotions.

Identifying the Value Given to a Concept or Statement   FIGURE 6.4

Examining Values

First: Decide whether a concept or a statement is

       Positive   Negative   Neutral

       (Consider your emotional response to the concept or statement to identify its value to you.)

       Example: "Cats are the best family pet." I rate this as a positive statement.

Second: Identify the assumptions or knowledge that support your value rating.

       Example: I have had two cats and a dog as a pet. The cats did not bark, did not bite, and did not slobber. They were affectionate. But, people might be allergic to a cat.

Third: Decide how accurate your assumptions or knowledge are?

       Example: I think all my assumptions and knowledge are correct. But, cats scratch and declawing them leaves them defenseless and the surgery is rough on cats.

Fourth: Decide whether you still give the concept or statement the same value rating.

       Example: Yes, I still give "Cats are the best family pet" a positive value rating.

Values are examined in social studies (see Figure 6.4) by identifying whether you consider a concept or statement to be positive, negative, or neutral. Usually your emotional response to the concept or statement helps identify the value you give it. Then the assumptions or knowledge base from which the value rating was assigned are identified. Why do you think this is positive, negative, or neutral? Next the accuracy of the knowledge base for the assumptions is considered. Where have you seen this happen? Who told you about this? Who has written about it? Finally, a set of assumptions are identified that might give you a different value weight for the statement or concept (Marzano & Arredondo, 1986). For example, after thinking through all of this, it seems that this is true, and this is true, but that isn't true. So, when I think about this statement I now am more positive toward it than previously.

SAMPLE SOCIAL STUDIES IDEAS AND ACTIVITIES RELATED TO THE SIX DIFFERENT TYPES OF INTEGRATED UNITS

Social studies can be a part of any of the six types of integrated units if it is incorporated in a relevant and important way. Table 6.1 gives an overview of the six different types of integrated units and a social studies example of each.

Concept-Focused Units

The concept-focused integrated unit is commonly found in social studies curricula. The themes identified in the national standards are concept-focused:

TABLE 6.1   **Overview of Types of Integrated Units with Social Studies Examples**

Type of Unit	Description	Social Studies Example
Concept-focused	Unit designed around teaching one or a few major concepts	Studying characteristics of clothing of different time periods
Process Skills–focused	Unit designed around teaching one or a few major process skills with less emphasis on content	Studying informal communication skills by acting as an observer during small group conversations
Content and Process Skills focused	Unit designed around teaching nearly equal amounts of content and process skills	Developing interviewing skill to obtain information on people's views about stereotyping
Issue-focused	Unit designed around investigating an issue through research and data collection	Investigating how to resolve conflicts through surveys and research on media reports
Project-focused	Unit designed around solving a problem or exploring an alternative	Researching issue of air quality, determining local air quality, and considering means to improve local air quality
Case Study–focused	Unit designed around doing something on a local level based on a topic investigated	Developing a plan and cost breakdown for adding scrubbers to smokestacks at a local factory

culture, governance, time, and so on. An example of an integrated concept-focused thematic unit with important social studies content is the unit on "constancy and change" found in chapter 1. There are many social studies ideas and activities in this unit, including: examining human constructions such as harbors and dams; sequencing clothing children have worn by size and talking about the characteristics of clothing for children of different ages; and examining the children's feelings about the rearrangement of furniture in the classroom space or of the daily schedule.

Process Skills–Focused Units

The process skills-focused integrated unit is not as common as is the concept-focused unit in social studies. However, teachers often create units in social studies with a heavy process skills focus. An integrated thematic unit built around "communication skills" has many components important to social studies. Communication skills are important in social studies since our social world is built on communication between individuals and between groups of individuals. In social studies both formal and informal verbal communication are important. Written communication and communication through graphics also are common in social studies. Less often communication in social studies occurs through music, art, and dance although these are powerful means of communication.

Informal communication skills are basic to social studies as they are to all human communication. Such communication is critical in the functioning

An Informal Discussion Checklist

FIGURE 6.5

Topic: Giving examples in which science and technology have changed the lives of people, such as in homemaking, work, and transportation.

Behavior	Group Member Tally Marks			
	Ted	Tamela	Christy	Keith
Tell the others whether you do or do not like something, but do it in a nice way.	111	11	11111	11
Talk about each person's idea and why it might not work but don't criticize the person.	11	1111	1111	111

of a democratic society. People must know their comments are welcome and expected during informal conversation. They also must know that others are due the opportunity to make comments. There are responsibilities associated with informal discussion. In a democratic society speakers are not disparaged nor do they use informal discussion to disparage others. Everyone gets an equal chance to speak and his comments are considered fairly. These characteristics identify a democratic society.

In a communication skills unit, informal discussion skills can be developed through having a student sit out a discussion and act as an observer. The student records each instance during which a group member displays a supportive informal discussion behavior (see Figure 6.5). Informal discussion skills can be modeled through a role-play situation prepared by the teacher or the students.

Formal communication occurs often in class discussions and in debate. Argument or debate of ideas and of the evidence supporting those ideas is fundamental to social studies. Students learn to put the evidence together, interpret its meaning, and then debate other interpretations made by fellow students. It is important to establish causality if possible and to weave in a chronological sequence (Leinhardt, Stainton, Virji, & Odoroff, 1992). Formal discussion is modeled by the teacher and steps are identified for the students (see Figure 6.6).

Students can watch a portion of a video tape of a debate between presidential candidates or of a local debating team. Or, they might watch a video tape of a class discussion in which they participated. They can check off appropriate behaviors they see on a prepared checklist. Students rate the presentations made by other groups of their work. A formal discussion has many of the same characteristics as an informal discussion. Everyone has an equal chance to participate, respect is demonstrated for all comments, and mean comments are not to be tolerated. In a formal discussion, however,

FIGURE 6.6   **Structuring a Formal Discussion**

Steps to Take in Formal Discussion

1. Open discussion by stating the topic or problem. Write it on the board or overhead if possible.
2. Invite discussion.
3. Offer ideas in a predetermined order (example: starting at the left of a semicircle of discussants) or have the moderator call on individuals who signal they wish to speak.
4. Do not call on one person a second time before everyone who wishes to has a chance to speak.
5. All speakers should address the moderator.
6. Speakers should not get into a two-way discussion or argument with each other, they should address the moderator.
7. When there are no new ideas to contribute, the moderator states the consensus of the group or takes a vote.

the teacher is present and often actively participates or mediates and fewer off-hand comments are made. Because many more people are involved, the rules of discussion are stricter, for example, the students may have to raise their hand before speaking.

Content and Process Skills–Focused Units

Some units mix concepts and skills almost evenly. A unit on "diversity" is likely to have such a mixture. Among the major concepts that can be addressed are gender, race, ethnic heritage, stereotyping, conformity, culture, and conflict. (See Figure 6.7 for a concept web for this unit.) If the unit on diversity focuses on differences in ethnic heritage many activities require the use of one or more process skills. (See Figure 6.8 for an activity web.) Some lessons focus on further development of a process skill. For example, the students work with interviewing, a process skill. Then, they develop and conduct interviews with family members focusing on: traditions in family first names, childhood games passed on through family members, and favorite foods in the family. This is the content of the interviews. The information gathered is brought to class and recorded on charts. While the students are carrying out the interviews after school, during the school day they are learning more about how to make charts. Next, the students research the origins and history of their traditional family first names, demonstrate a traditional family childhood game, and share the recipe for a favorite food. They further develop their reporting skills. They classify the games into categories. Classification is possible because they have played the games and are now familiar with them. They examine their charts and try to determine whether there are any patterns in the information. The focus of their activities shifts back and forth between concepts and process skills.

Diversity Unit Concept Web   FIGURE 6.7

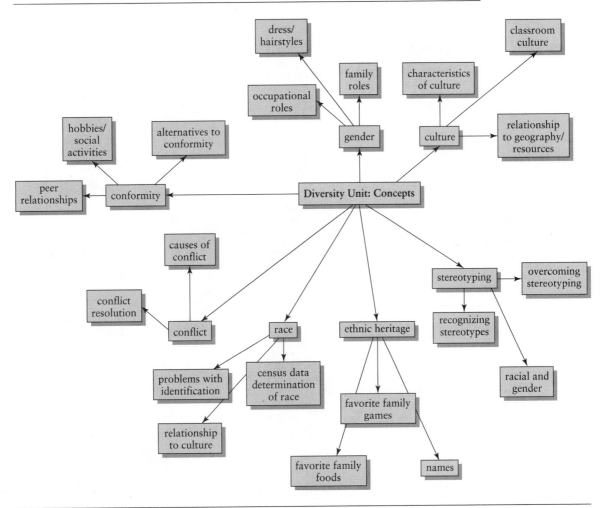

Issue-Focused Units

Issue-focused integrated units impartially investigate an issue through research and data collection. Students might work on the issue of conflict resolution and peace. For example, there has been an increase in fights at school, on the school bus, and in their neighborhoods. They wonder whether students at other schools and in other states are experiencing the same problems. What is happening? What can be done to reduce the conflicts? Figure 6.9 displays the goal setting worksheet the students develop to organize their issue-focused unit activities. They develop a survey and

FIGURE 6.8   Activity Web for a Concept-Focused Unit

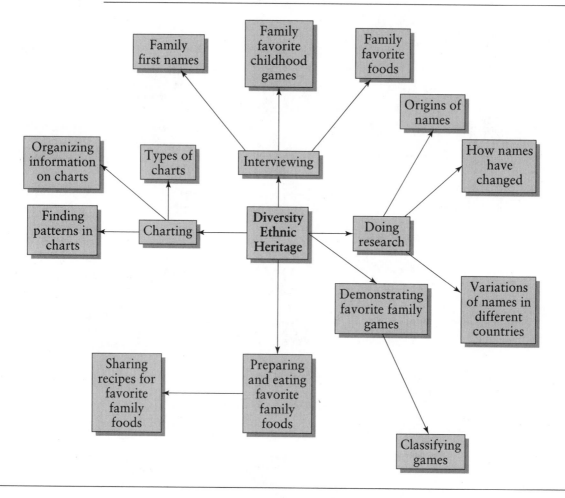

arrange for students at other schools in their school system to fill it out. Then, they make contact with some schools in other states through the Internet and transmit their survey instrument to them. After they put their survey data together, they decide that there is evidence of a problem with fighting in some other local schools and in other states.

The students decide to split into two groups. One group researches conflicts in elementary schools as reported in the media. Members of this group contact local newspapers and television and radio stations to find out whether they have reported elementary school conflicts in the past year. They also search issues of some of the national magazines and newspapers such as *USA Today* and *Newsweek*. The second group focuses on conflict

Planning Chart for an Issue-Focused Unit   FIGURE 6.9

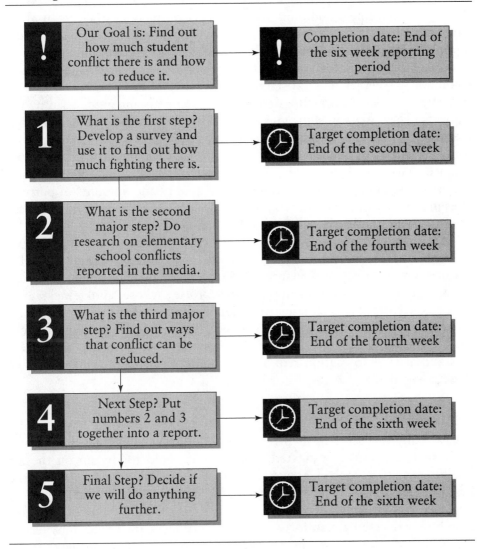

resolution, how to stop or reduce elementary school conflicts. They use many of the same sources being used by the first group. They also talk to a middle school teacher who has been training her students in conflict resolution.

Both groups organize their findings. Their reports are combined to produce a document describing what seems to be happening in regard to conflicts between elementary school students and ways in which those conflicts might be reduced and resolved.

Project-Focused Units

Project-focused integrated units try to solve a problem or explore an alternative solution to a problem. Air quality is a problem facing much of the world's population. Students have been studying the issue of air quality and have researched it. Now they want to determine the air quality in their community, whether it is satisfactory, and what routes might be taken to improve it if necessary. Figure 6.10 displays the planning guide used by the students. They invite in some guest speakers. These include a local environmental engineer, community college science instructor, a physician specializing in asthma, a student who is an asthma sufferer, and an industrial engineer. The visits by the guest speakers are followed up by obtaining their help in constructing devices to monitor air quality and amounts of particulates in the air. Students also write to city government officials and state legislators about pending legislation addressing air quality standards.

After testing for particulates, the students find high percentages of two particulates. They wonder where these come from. They examine the literature about these particulates. Their original guest speakers are contacted again. They are told about two factories whose smokestacks emit heavy concentrations of these particulates. They contact these companies requesting that they find a way to reduce their emission of these particulates so local air quality can improve. They also write their state legislators and ask for legislation requiring companies to reduce the emission of these particulates.

Case Study–Focused Units

A case study-focused unit involves students in doing something based on a topic that has been investigated. Such a unit could follow up on the air quality project described above. Students investigate ways in which the heavy concentrations of two particulates they have identified might be scrubbed from the air so they do not leave the smokestacks. After doing research they develop a plan for smokestack scrubbers, including drawings of the scrubbers and a cost breakdown for the work that would have to be done, and present it to company officials.

An example of another quite different case study involves students in developing a job description for the manager of a nearby national forest, the Talladega National Forest in Alabama. These students have been studying environmental issues and national forests. They have completed a project in which they mapped all the national forest land in their state. They have found that national forests regularly sell off rights to do logging on some forest land. They also note that the national forests in their state are trying to bring back the longleaf pine, the climax forest tree. Finally, they have found that lots of people work for the national forest and that the

What Is the Quality of the Air in Our Community?   FIGURE 6.10

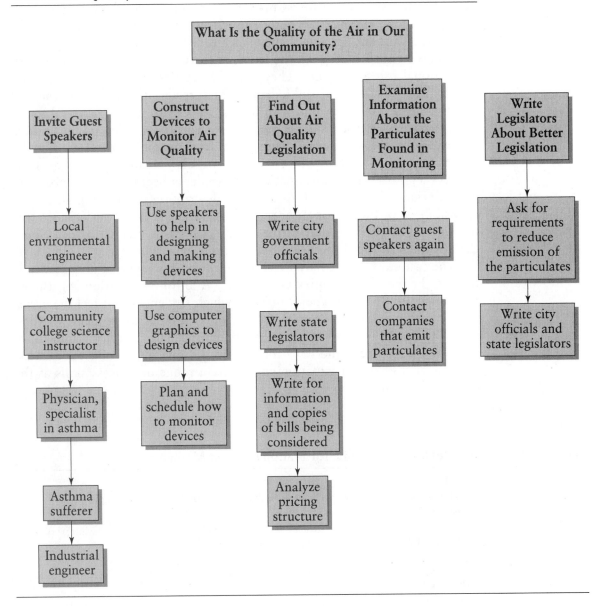

proceeds from the logging of some of the national forest lands pay the salaries of those workers.

The students have become interested in the role of the national forest's manager. They recognize that this individual must enforce national laws and also find ways to hire and pay the workers who keep the national forest functioning. They have decided this is an interesting and complicated job. To better understand the forest manager's role, they decide to create a job description for the job. Their outline for the job description is shown in Figure 6.11. It contains questions they want to ask.

To accomplish their goal, the students carry out several interviews with the national forest manager. They research legislation relating to national forests. They talk to local and federal legislators about their view of the role of national forests. They talk with people who work in this national forest from biologists to trash haulers. They talk with people who live on the borders of the national forest. They talk with hunters and people who like to fish in the forest's streams. They talk with environmental club members and loggers.

As they gather their information, the students begin to sort it into categories. Gradually they build up their job description, identifying all the responsibilities of the national forest manager and the types of decisions this individual makes. Each part of the job description is verified by describing the evidence they have gathered in relation to it.

The case study is the narrowest and most focused type of unit. It also is likely to be the most complex type of unit. A lot of information is gathered and processed. It is the type of unit for which students often feel the greatest ownership. All types of units provide opportunities for students to "do" social studies rather than to be reservoirs of information pumped into them. Case study–, project–, and issue-focused units, however, involve the greatest amount of student participation and utilize a range of process skills as the content of the unit is investigated.

FIGURE 6.11   **Job Description Outline for National Forest Manager**

Major Responsibilities

Provide information about ? Works on projects about ? Supervise ? (how many) people.

Business and Technical

Is responsible for the business and technical aspects of the national forest. These are ? Must work well with the different departments and specialists and understand their needs. These are ?

Supervision of Projects

Must provide supervision on projects in the forest. These are ? Has responsibility for staff and costs. These are ?

Evaluation Criteria

Forest Project Responsibilities:

Relationship with People who use the Forest:

Supervisory Duties:

Administrative Duties:

Technical Duties:

Social studies and science are being integrated by this student as he finds a delta on a map.

SUMMARY

Social studies is a vital part of most integrated thematic units. The themes around which national standards in social studies are focused are used to integrate social studies into units. Social studies takes its content from many disciplines yet it also incorporates process skills. Social studies is an active, not a passive, part of learning. Throughout social studies, data collection and interpretation always are important. Materials, people, natural places, and places made by human beings all are sources from which data is obtained and used by students to "do social studies."

REFERENCES

Anderson, T., & Armbruster, B. (1984). Content area textbooks. In R. Anderson (Ed.), *Learning to read in American schools* (pp. 87–123). Hillsdale, NJ: Lawrence Erlbaum Associates Publishers.

Banks, J., & Clegg, A. (1985). *Teaching strategies for the social studies: Inquiry, valuing, and decision making* (3rd. ed.). White Plains, NY: Longman.

Barell, J. (1991). Reflecting teaching for thoughtfulness. In A. Costa (Ed.), *Developing minds: A resource book for teaching thinking* (Rev. ed., Vol. 1, pp. 207–210). Alexandria, VA: Association for Supervision and Curriculum Development.

Dworetzky, K. (1990). *Introduction to child development* (4th ed.). St. Paul, MN: West Publishing Co.

Ginsburg, H., & Opper, S. (1988). *Piaget's theory of intellectual development.* Englewood Cliffs, NJ: Prentice-Hall.

Goodman, J., & Adler, S. (1985). Becoming an elementary social studies teacher: A study of perspectives. *Theory and Research in Social Education, 13*(2), 1–20.

Hoge, J. (1986). *Improving the use of elementary social studies textbooks.* ERIC Digest No. 33. Bloomington, IN: Clearinghouse for Social Studies/Social Science Education.

Leinhardt, G., Stainton, C., Virji, S., & Odoroff, E. (1992). *Learning to reason in history: Mindlessness to mindfulness.* Pittsburgh, PA: University of Pittsburgh, Learning Research and Development Center.

Levstik, L. (1986). The relationship between historical and response and narrative in a sixth-grade classroom. *Theory and Research in Social Education, 15*(1), 1–17.

Marzano, R., & Arredondo, D. (1986). *Tactics for thinking.* Alexandria, VA.: Association for Supervision and Curriculum Development.

National Archives and Records Administration. (1989). *Teaching with documents: Using primary sources from the National Archives.* Washington, DC: National Archives and Records Administration.

National Council for the Social Studies. (1994). *Curriculum standards for social studies.* Washington, DC: The Council.

Osborne, R., & Cosgrove, M. (1985). Children's conceptions of changes of state of water. *Journal of Research in Science Teaching, 20,* 825–838.

Osborne, R., & Freyberg, P. (1985). *Learning in science* (pp. 91–111). London: Heinemann.

Piaget, J. (1960). *The child's conception of physical causality.* Totowa, NJ: Littlefield, Adams & Co.

Radford, D. (1977). *Changes: Stages 1 and 2 and background.* Milwaukee, WI: Raintree.

Sunal, C. (1981). The child and the concept of change. *Social Education, 45*(8), 438–441.

Sunal, C., & Haas, M. (1993). *Social studies and the elementary/middle school learner.* Ft. Worth, TX: Harcourt Brace.

Sylvester, R. (1985, April). Research on memory: Major discoveries, major educational challenges. *Educational Leadership, 42*(7), 69–75.

Toffler, A. (1970). *Future shock.* New York: Random House.

Walsh, H. (1980). *Introducing the young child to the social world.* New York: Macmillan.

CHAPTER 7

INTEGRATING SCIENCE

hat image do students have of science and scientists? What image do you have of science and scientists? Draw a quick sketch of a "scientist" at work. When asked to draw such a sketch, many people draw a picture of a Caucasian male scientist, wearing a white lab coat with a pocket full of pens and pencils, working in a laboratory, performing dangerous experiments. He is middle-aged, wearing glasses, and partially bald. He is surrounded by flasks, test tubes, filing cabinets, and books (Mead & Metraux, 1957; Chambers, 1983; Mason, Kahle, & Gardner, 1991). When people talk about their picture, their comments suggest he is antisocial, poorly adjusted, or an eccentric male, but very busy with his experiments (Kahle, 1988; Mason, Kahle, & Gardner, 1991). If you are similar to most people, your sketch will have many of those characteristics.

There is a popular image of scientists—and by extension, of science—that is inaccurate, negative, and likely to discourage students from considering a career in science as either interesting or welcome. The masculine image of both science and scientists probably detracts from a girl's interest and self-confidence in science. Kahle, Mason, and Gardner (1991) found that these stereotypes could be reduced with a consistent effort to change them. It is important that teachers recognize the stereotypes they may hold. Once they are recognized, action can be taken to reduce and limit the perpetuation of these stereotypes with our students. Because many hold a stereotyped view of science, it is important to find out what science really is.

Watching young children in a park can be enlightening. They sense, play, and explore; all without being "taught." They ask, "What do birds do at night?" "Where do animals get their fur?" "When do trees eat?" "How are rocks made?" "If birds fly, and ducks are birds, then why don't I see all birds swimming?" This natural exploration begins at birth and continues as the "tools" of language, reading, and mathematics are learned and used. The exploration involves understanding oneself and interpreting what happens in the environment. The investigation of the physical environment, how aspects of the environment are related, and the relationship of the environment to the cultural, social, and inner worlds of the child constitute science for children. Science happens every time a child steps purposely into a puddle, asks a question about why the moons move up and down at night, or sticks a finger into the icing of their birthday cake.

Science is an active process occurring in the student and influenced as much by the student as by the teacher. Science learning depends on how the student perceives events, what information is encountered, and the student's prior knowledge. It is the student's construction of meaning (Saunders, 1992). In this view, science is *a construction of knowledge from sensed information that is interpreted in terms of a student's prior knowledge.*

Constructivism, the view that students construct their own knowledge, has implications for science in the classroom. Students must have experiences in which they have interaction. They must have evidence developed through their own experience that can be related to the idea or skill to be taught. Students collect this evidence using all their senses as they make observations of materials with which they work and experiences they have. They need to work with this perceived data in their minds, relating it to prior experiences and knowledge, and to their ways of thinking. Predictions are made and discrepancies are encountered. Students describe their experiences, then attempt to organize their information so that they can group, classify and ultimately create new knowledge based on their prior knowledge. These higher-order thought processes are natural, but often students are not always good at doing them. It is only after time is provided for activities that challenge them and make them think that students are ready to see patterns in the world around them and draw conclusions about those patterns.

Elementary school science is a construction process that goes on in students' minds but begins and ends in their hands-on actions. If a classroom lesson involves essential hands-on components, it is defined as science teaching.

Science Is a Verb

TABLE 7.1

Elementary School Science:

begins with observations that *gather* information about objects and events, or *utilize* information reported by other sources.

involves processing observations and information in a variety of ways including:
classification,
prediction,
inferring, and
other process skills.

continues through construction of patterns, as a result of the processing that occurred earlier.

results in the students' construction of *new meaning* involving *content* and the associated *process skills* used in development of the constructed meaning.

The *context* in which the student constructs meaning influences the result. Thus, the characteristics of the classroom and the teacher that influence student attitudes are a part of meaning that is constructed.

Leaving out any single component creates learning based on rote memory rather than understanding through meaningful learning (Sunal & Sunal, 1991a). Science in the elementary classroom is a *verb* not a *noun* (Table 7.1).

SCIENTIFIC LITERACY

Scientific literacy is a general goal for schools. Scientifically literate students have a basic understanding of key principles of science, the ability to use available technology, and an interest in and appreciation for science (National Science Teachers Association, 1992). The American science education program is viewed as having failed to create meaningful science learning in students (Carnegie Commission, 1991). A national study reported that a majority of the nation's students already are turned off to science by the time they reach seventh grade, with the greatest losses occurring among women and minority groups (U.S. Department of Education, 1986). These are serious problems in a complex society where citizens are expected to make informed technological decisions.

Science plays a critical role in education. In science, students make meaningful use of basic tools they bring from mathematics, reading, and writing. Science provides experiences through which students can develop the thinking skills that are the foundation of reading, writing, and mathematics. When confronted with an interesting problem related to their environment, it is natural for students to first, observe, then to ask questions, seek aid in books, draw what they see, make measurements, and write about the event. This is what science is about and what reading, writing, and mathematics strive to do. When students "do" science they use thinking skills and knowledge from the entire school curriculum as they construct an understanding of their environment.

There are many skills involved in teaching meaningful science. These are key skills. The science key skills include observation, gathering and communicating evidence, inquiry, and using hands-on science. Science education reform movements incorporate these skills and identify critical elements of meaningful science curricula. The integration of meaningful science key skills can be viewed throughout the development of the reform movements for science education.

REFORM EFFORTS IN SCIENCE EDUCATION

National and state science standards promote an interdisciplinary and integrated development of knowledge (American Association for the Advancement of Science, 1993a; National Research Council, 1995). National standards identify a framework for science curricula. The American Association for the Advancement of Science (AAAS) describes science literacy as knowledge organized around themes that interconnect the natural sciences, social sciences, mathematics, and technology. In addition, the National Committee on Science Education Standards and Assessment (NCSESA) defines science literacy as a unifying process of content standards. To ensure scientific literacy among all students, the AAAS states that curricula must be changed to reduce the sheer amount of material covered; rigid subject-matter boundaries must be reduced or eliminated; and more attention must be paid to the connections among science, mathematics, and technology (AAAS, 1993b). In addition, the NCSESA (1996) promotes science for all students, regardless of gender, culture or ethnic background, physical or learning disabilities, future aspirations, or interest or motivation in science, and that science is an active process not the isolation of memorization of facts.

Project 2061 by the American Association for the Advancement of Science

In 1985, the American Association for the Advancement of Science (AAAS) began a long-term reform effort for science education. This project is known as Project 2061. The name, Project 2061, represented the year of 2061 in which the reform movement recommendations would be universally accepted as well as the next time Halley's Comet would be close to Earth.

There were three phases for this reform effort. The first phase defined science literacy for graduating students in a K–12 program. It was concerned with the necessary concepts, skills, and attitudes the students should acquire. These concepts, skills, and attitudes were articulated though broadly based goal statements involving science, mathematics, technology, behavioral, and social sciences. The first phase resulted in the publication of *Science for All Americans* (AAAS, 1993b). In *Science for All Americans* the broadly based goals for science literacy are organized into 12 chapters. The broad extent of the goals is evident in the chapter's titles. Those titles are:

1. The Nature of Science
2. The Nature of Mathematics
3. The Nature of Technology
4. The Physical Setting
5. The Living Environment
6. The Human Organism
7. Human Society
8. The Designed World
9. The Mathematical World
10. Historical Perspectives
11. Common Themes
12. Habits of the Mind

The second phase of Project 2061 involved using the broad based themes to design curricula reflecting those goals. Six teams composed of 5 elementary teachers, 5 middle-school teachers, 10 high school teachers, 1 principal from each level, and 2 curriculum specialists from six diverse sites across the country were asked to design a curriculum model for K–12. The models they created represented the integration of typical separate subject content areas into broad-based integrated science themes. The themes were interdisciplinary as well as cross-grade applicable. The efforts of the teams resulted in the publications of *Benchmarks for Science Literacy.* (AAAS, 1993a) and *Designs for Science Literacy* (AAAS, 1997).

Benchmarks for Science Literacy (1993a) identifies what K–12 grade students should know and be able to do in natural and social sciences, mathematics, and technology. The science literacy topics relate to the earlier published report, *Science for All Americans* (AAAS, 1993b), in which the broad based interdisciplinary nature of science literacy was determined. *Benchmarks for Science Literacy* (AAAS, 1993a) specifies thresholds, or levels of understanding, for all students. Specifically, the recommended learning thresholds are described in terms of what students in grades 2, 5, 8, and 12 should know and be able to do within the context of science literacy.

Designs for Science Literacy (AAAS, 1997) is a handbook for educators assisting them to develop a systemic, goal-oriented approach for science curriculum development. It contains descriptions of curriculum blocks and models so educators can assemble interdisciplinary curricula based upon their students' needs, local and state policies, resources, and their educational preferences.

The third phase of Project 2061 is implementation of science reform within K–12 schools. This implementation is ongoing throughout the nation. The implementation is based upon the components of science interdisciplinary literacy developed in the first two phases.

National Committee on Science Education Standards and Assessment

The first nationally developed standards appeared in 1989 with two publications: *Curriculum And Evaluations Standards For School Mathematics* by the National Council of Teachers of Mathematics (NCTM, 1989) and *Everybody Counts: A Report To The Nation On The Future Of Mathematics Education* by the National Research Council (NRC, 1989). These two publications provided the basis for development of other national standards, in particular the *National Science Education Standards* (1995). An interdisciplinary committee provided a broad base of content experts to make recommendations for the standards.

The four goals for school science contained in the *National Science Education Standards* are to educate students who are able to:

1. experience the richness and excitement of knowing about and understanding the natural world;
2. use appropriate scientific processes and principles in making personal decisions;
3. engage intelligently in public discourse and debate about matters of scientific and technological concern; and
4. increase their economic productivity through the use of the knowledge, understanding, and skills of the scientifically literate person in their careers.

These goals define a scientifically literate person in society. They are addressed in the *National Science Education Standards* in the form of recommendations for science teaching standards, standards for professional development for teachers of science, assessment in science education, science content standards, science education program standards, and science education system standards. The science content standards provide recommendations for what students should know, understand, and be able to do in the natural sciences over the course of K–12 education. They are divided into eight categories with the suggested grade levels of K–4, 5–8, and 9–12 for student competency. The categories are:

1. Unifying concepts and processes in science
2. Science as inquiry
3. Physical science
4. Life science
5. Earth and space science
6. Science and technology
7. Science in personal and social perspectives
8. History and nature of science

The first broad content standard of unifying concepts and processes for all grade levels states: "As a result of activities in grades K–12, all students should develop understanding and abilities aligned with the following concepts and processes: systems, order, and organization; evidence, models, and explanation; constancy, change, and measurement; evolution and equilibrium; and form and function" (NCSESA, p. 115). This standard presents broad unifying concepts and processes that compliment interdisciplinary teaching. The concepts and processes provide the connections between and among traditional science disciplines with other content areas. The multidisciplinary perspectives provide many opportunities for integrated approaches for teaching science.

The goals of Project 2061 (AAAS, 1985) and recommendations from the National Committee on Science Education Standards and Assessment support blending of the traditional lines of content-based science into integrated learning, teaching, and assessment models. This integrated learning and teaching of science is valuable to students, teachers and scientifically literate citizens of the future. However, for this to occur in a truly integrated situation, there are key science process to be included throughout the process.

KEY SCIENCE TEACHING PROCESSES

Several key processes are inherent in effective science teaching. These are observation, classification, measurement, gathering and communicating evidence, inquiry, and hands-on science.

Observation

Observation is the fundamental process. It starts with using the five senses to gather information from the environment. As students gain experience their observation skills become more complex involving: distinguishing inferences from observations; using both qualitative and quantitative descriptions in observations; observing change as well as the beginning and ending states of an event; ordering observations; using measuring devices to extend the range of observations; and recording information using drawings, tables, narratives, and other communication tools.

People observe the real world using what they already know, their prior knowledge. The existing ideas students bring to an activity are the ways by which they are able to make sense of new ideas. It is only through student discussion relating the new information to their prior knowledge that meaning becomes possible.

Classification

Classification begins when a student views various objects, using his or her five senses. The students begin this process skill by seeing, smelling, touching, hearing, or even tasting the objects. Classification occurs when students sort or group objects from a large group into subgroups with common attributes. Younger students use this skill by classifying objects by a single characteristic. For example, when asked to classify or group seashells, the younger student may classify or group the shells by color or size, but not by both attributes. However, older students with more experience in classifying, may classify the shells into several groups: those that have smooth surfaces, those that are large, those that are medium size, those that are small, those that have a spiral shape, those that have a rounded shape, or those that could be a home for a hermit crab.

It is important to provide many experiences in classification because this skill does not spontaneously happen to children. They need exposure to this skill in many situations to learn to organize facts, using the observations they have made. Classification skills are vital because they are widely used in real-life as well as being used throughout scientific investigations.

Measurement

Measurement is a skill developed by using observations and then making those observations into meaningful abstract representations. Young students need not be concerned with the conventional measurement systems, such as centimeters, liters, or grams, but should be concerned with determining relationships of objects. For example, they could use the length of their pencils to measure a piece of paper in order to determine how many pencils long the paper is. For older students, measurement has five basic components: length, volume, mass or weight, temperature, and time. Measurement skills are important, so students can translate observation skills into quantitative representations in order to construct meaningful knowledge.

Gathering and Communicating Evidence

Knowledge comes from students' use of evidence to construct it. Evidence is developed from information gathered through observation. It is also the result of inferences made from the information gathered. Many thinking skills are used to form a body of evidence from which students construct knowledge. They do not construct knowledge from hearing an authority tell them some information. The more the teacher presents information or the textbook is used to teach a topic, the less opportunity students have to construct knowledge so that they understand it. Students should not be presented with "ready-made" knowledge—concepts or generalizations to be memorized. They will not understand the meaning of these concepts and generalizations because someone else constructed them. It is important to provide students with experiences and materials through which they can construct knowledge.

Diverse evidence should be gathered through making observations. The evidence gathered will vary depending on the developmental level of the student. For example, drawing and other forms of artwork are natural ways in which very young students record observations. Observations of a leaf or a sound relate to the students' perception of texture, color variations, and loudness. Comparisons can be made of the relative strengths of the observations made by different students. Thus, both qualitative and quantitative information can be a part of young students' observations. Older students continue to use art, but also can use narratives involving poems, journals, and short stories to communicate evidence discovered through their observations. Technology can help students quickly record their observations on tables, bar graphs, and charts.

Inquiry

Inquiry has been a popular term in science teaching with many interpretations. These include an approach to teaching through discovery and use of the scientific method. The total inquiry process is the method by which students construct meaning as they learn science. New meaning is constructed only by asking questions about events that don't fit with the students' present thinking, making predictions about events related to these questions, testing the predictions, and checking to see if the results of these tests answer the original questions better than the students prior knowledge answered them.

Hands-on Science

Hands-on science has come to mean a method for teaching science using materials to manipulate. However, asking students to work with materials relating to a science topic is not sufficient for meaningful learning to take place. For example, asking students to complete a task using step-by-step directions such as putting a magnet to paper clips and counting how many paper clips are picked up or observing seeds germinate over a two-week period is not enough. Minds-on science also is needed. Activities should be structured so students interactively experience them. Students should not only have an effect on the materials but they also should be affected by them. The activities should pose problems and create conditions that change the students' approach to the activity. It is only through interactive experience, which at times produces conflict, confrontation, or confusion, that students are challenged to create meaning from an activity.

EFFECTIVE SCIENCE LESSONS

Effective science lessons match three elements: the needs of the student, the science content or skill to be taught, and the instructional approach to be used (Figure 7.1). The learning cycle is an excellent approach to teaching science. It involves students in a sequence of activities beginning with exploration of an idea or skill, leading to a more guided explanation and invention of the idea or skill, and culminating in expansion of the idea or skill through additional practice and trials in new settings. Because of what occurs in each phase, the three parts of the learning cycle are called: exploration, invention, and expansion. A teacher has a large number of choices in deciding how to provide instruction for students. The selection of strategies to use in teaching

FIGURE 7.1   Effective Teaching Requires a Match

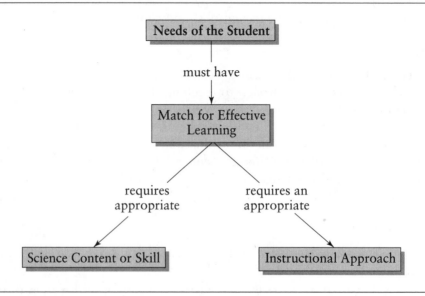

(e.g., lecture, inquiry, a hands-on approach, film, cooperative learning, etc.) should be determined by the 1) type of idea(s) or skill(s) to be taught, 2) developmental level and specific learning needs of the student, and 3) part of the learning cycle with which the teacher is involved.

INTERCONNECTIONS BETWEEN SCIENCE AND OTHER DISCIPLINES

Science educators are not alone in recognizing the need to integrate material originating in various subject matter areas. Whole language advocates involve students in writing and reading activities that are integrated with their subject matter studies. Mathematics educators have described the goals of mathematics as processes involved with themes in all subject areas. In many classrooms, interconnections between the disciplines in the elementary school curriculum subjects are being identified and incorporated into units. Integration is seen as an important goal for education. It can be accomplished through each of the six types of units described in earlier chapters.

APPROPRIATE TOPICS FOR UNITS INCORPORATING SCIENCE

There are three criteria for the construction of integrated units with valid and important science content. The first is *significance*. The content taught should not be trivial to the scientific discipline nor to the student's need for scientific literacy. The unit teaches the nature of scientific knowledge not the products of science. Less is more in the unit. Fewer concepts are taught but these are the most critical concepts related to the topic and they are taught in depth.

The second criterion is *coherence*. There is consistency with the nature of scientific inquiry, reflecting scientific values, giving students direct experience with the kinds of thought and action that are typical of work in the scientific disciplines. Memorization is not the focus since science is a discipline characterized by intellectual discovery. Instead, the emphasis is on critical and creative thinking skills in science. There is an emphasis on conceptual understanding, application, and transfer of scientific knowledge to the student's own world.

The third criterion is *relevance*. The content impacts the individual's thinking and personal actions, social interactions, societal, and career decisions. There is an emphasis on portraying science as human, as impacting human decisions, and as impacting the quality of life.

TYPES OF INTEGRATED UNITS

Earlier chapters have discussed several ways in which to focus and organize an integrated unit including concept-focused, skills-focused, content-and-skills-focused, issue-focused, project-focused, and case study–focused. Each focus can incorporate significant, coherent, and relevant science content (see Figure 7.2).

Concept-Focused Units

Probably the most common units are those which have a descriptive and conceptual focus. Sample concept-focused topics include matter and energy, light, plants, weather, animal life, oceans, the solar system, sound, the rock cycle, the universe, and the water cycle. Content plays the major role. Skills typically are integrated into the concept-focused lessons but play an incidental role. Usually, there is no assessment of skill development.

The sources of such units most often are state and local courses of study and textbooks. Science content themes frequently are spiraled through the curriculum. They are introduced in the early grades and repeated at various points in higher-grade levels. Each time they are repeated, new information that is more abstract and complex is introduced. Generally, the breadth as well as the depth of the topic is expanded.

When these concepts are taught well, they build on the foundation the students bring from earlier grades. The concept's development can be matched

FIGURE 7.2   Types of Integrated Science Units

Type of Unit	Description	Science Examples
Concept-focused	Unit designed around teaching one or a few major concepts	Studying electricity, sound, or mammals
Process Skills–focused	Unit designed around teaching one or a few major process skills with less emphasis on content	Studying observation, or classifying, or experimenting
Content and Process Skills–Focused	Unit designed around teaching nearly equal amounts of content and process skills	Studying sinking and floating, observation, classifying relevant variables, or mass
Issue-focused	Unit designed around investigating an issue through research and data collection	Studying effects of pollution, endangered species, or flood control
Project-focused	Unit designed around solving a problem or exploring an alternative	Analysis of the impact of mining operations in the area, or on water quality in streams, or on strategies for earthquake survival
Case Study–focused	Unit designed around doing something on a local level based on a topic investigated	Management of household insects, urban forests or air quality or school noise

closely to student's own intellectual development gradually building a good understanding of the topic. Unfortunately, sometimes, earlier teachers may not have taught the topic or they may have taught it as a mass of facts neglecting the need for science instruction that focuses on conceptual development. As a result, students are unprepared for the more advanced exploration of the topic they find at a higher grade level. In such an instance, students need hands-on, minds-on experiences to construct the needed concepts.

Concepts are ideas that people form to help them better understand their physical world (Beyer & Penna, 1971). They are formed by finding similarities between many facts and temporarily emphasizing those similarities. For example, *tree* is a concept we form by focusing on its structure of bark, leaves, and branches, as well as its usefulness in wood products and in fires. We emphasize similarities between the structure and functions of the concept we call "tree" and ignore tree differences such as size, color variations, where we find them, and the fact that some have visible flowers or seeds. Another example is the concept of a *mammal*. A mammal is a concept we form by focusing on the characteristics of a mammal having hair, a four-chambered heart, giving live birth, and females providing milk for her young. We emphasize the similarities of the functions and ignore the differences concerning where the mammal lives, what it eats, what color it is, and the difference in the life spans of various species of mammals.

A concept can be defined as the set of characteristics common to any and all instances of a given type. It also can be defined as the characteristics that make certain items examples of a type of thing and distinguish any and all examples from nonexamples.

As concepts are formed, a number of examples and nonexamples of the concept are usually examined (Eggen, Kauchak, & Harder, 1979). If a class is working with the concept of *planet* for instance, a teacher might use examples such as Mars, Jupiter, and the Earth. Students look for planets in the real sky and in a planetarium. They use the naked eye, a telescope, and sky photographs. They also look for them in books, slides, and videotapes from telescopes and spacecraft. Another example is the concept of an *insect*. Students are provided with actual insects to observe such as ants, bees, and flies. The students discover similarities of body parts, number of legs, and the number of body parts.

Nonexamples are any and all individual items that have some but not all the characteristics that make items examples of a given concept (Seiger-Ehrenberg, 1991, p. 291). As part of the process of constructing the concept of *planet,* students examine nonexamples such as stars, asteroids, and moons. While these have some characteristics similar to those of a planet, they are not similar enough to be considered a planet. Stars look like planets in the sky to the naked eye. Asteroids and moons look like planets through a telescope.

While studying the concept of *insect,* the students would be provided with a picture of a spider (a nonexample). Based upon their prior observations of body parts, number of legs, and the number of body parts of previously determined insects, the students compare what they have discovered about insects to the newly presented spider. Their prior knowledge of insects should lead them to discover that the spider doesn't fit their definition of an insect. They should find out that a spider really isn't an insect, but something else. For example, a spider has eight legs, not six legs as an insect has. The spider represents a nonexample for the definition of an insect.

It is important to identify characteristics *essential* to the concept. For example, in learning the concept *magnet* young children may consider "stickiness" as an essential characteristic. Glue and tree sap have the same characteristic. With help students must learn about the other characteristics that are associated with magnets alone and not with other sticky examples such as tree sap or glue: 1) magnets attract and repel other objects, 2) only certain materials are attracted to and repelled by a magnet, 3) the "stickiness" action works at a distance, 4) different strengths of "stickiness" exist in different parts of the magnet. For older students, teachers will add characteristics such as the existence of magnet poles, the attraction of objects most often made of iron, and the existence and structure of the magnetic field around a magnet using iron filings.

Students of all ages have science concepts that are different from those accepted as accurate in scientific literature (Osborne, Bell, & Gilbert, 1983; Blosser, 1987). Other terms used for these alternative conceptions in the past have been "critical barriers to learning" and "misconceptions." The science standards identify many of the alternative conceptions researchers have found among students.

During the early part of the lesson, the exploration, each student must identify his own existing concept. An experience and discussions encourages students to think about and analyze their views. This leads to a confrontation between different conceptions, their alternative conception and the conception the experience is conveying. Students continue this process until they reconsider the validity of their original assumptions. Dissatisfaction with existing conceptions is critical. Only at this time will students realize that they must reorganize or replace their prior knowledge. Their existing concepts are inadequate to understand the experiences with which the students have just been involved. To be useful, retained, and transferred to a new setting, the concept just formed must be clear, understandable, plausible, and successful for the student (Posner, Strike, Hewson, & Gertzog, 1982; Berliner & Casanova, 1987).

Students' existing concepts may be inaccurate. A student may, for example, have an alternative concept of a magnet that says *magnets are attracted to all metals.* The student has formed the concept on the basis of the limited facts available to her. She may have available to her only various items of iron, for example, so she generalizes magnetic attraction to all metals. The very young student may not recognize that there are different kinds of metals. Since iron is so common and has magnetic attraction she concludes that all metals are attracted to a magnet. Another student may decide that magnets are attracted to all silver-colored metals and not to other-colored metals. Common examples of unpainted metals students have available to them usually include silvery iron objects and yellowish objects made of copper or brass. The individual may not have abstracted essential characteristics. It is only later, with more experience, that the student realizes the metal objects used may have been painted or coated so that the color of metals may not be a good indicator of attraction. Another student may decide that *magnets are attracted to all metals except soft or pure metals such as copper or gold.* A narrow range of facts can result in an alternative concept. The student may have tested only iron objects, which are hard, and a few copper or silver objects, which are soft metals.

Another example of an inaccurate concept among young children is that all rocks will sink in water. Many children have had the experience of throwing rocks into water and watching them sink beneath the surface. Undoubtedly, children have done this activity repeatedly with various sizes and types of rocks with the same results. However, when a child throws a rock composed of scoria into water, the rock floats. The child's observation that the rock floats doesn't fit into her previous observations. Up to this point, the child's knowledge of rocks included the concepts that rocks come in different sizes, shapes, colors, sizes and textures; but not that some rocks are less dense than water. Suddenly, the concept of density enters into the child's world.

Although a concept is inaccurate, it does represent an effort by the individual to abstract similarities. As more facts are acquired, or when the individual reviews the inventory of facts, the concept may be changed and become more accurate. Teachers provide opportunities for students to have experiences that add to their inventory of facts. They also provide opportunities to discuss the facts they have acquired and relate them to the concepts they have formed.

There are five ways through which teachers can influence students' concepts.

- First, to successfully influence students' concepts, teachers need to be aware of the ideas students are bringing to the lesson. What do they think this is? Why? What words do they use to describe or explain it?
- Second, teachers need to provide students with an opportunity to become familiar with the context in which the concept to be discussed

belongs. Whenever possible this involves students in first-hand experience. This encourages students to try out their ideas by investigating a situation or objects for themselves. The exploration phase of a learning cycle is an appropriate time to accomplish these activities.

- Third, communication is important, particularly during the invention phase of a learning cycle when students are guided to construct a new concept or reconstruct an existing one. Students present their ideas to others and learn to appreciate the ideas of other students and of the teacher. Often, small group discussion challenges students to find evidence for their ideas. Large group discussions brings a number of ideas together for consideration.
- Fourth, during the investigative and discussion process characterizing the invention phase of the learning cycle, students are offered the concept as constructed by the teacher and encouraged to explore it for themselves without the teacher's insistence that this is the only correct view of the concept. Don't present ready-made concepts and expect students to understand them without some time in which to construct their own meaning.
- Fifth, the value of the concept presented by the teacher is made evident through expansion, using it to solve new problems and applying it to make sense of the new experiences. Through reasoning, the consideration of observations and experiences, and communication, students may realize that there are different ideas and may decide that another idea is more usable and appropriate.

The "constancy and change" unit in chapter 1 teaches concepts important in science. Fundamentally, science examines the factors related to constancy and change. It considers the temporariness of both constancy and change. All of the activities described have a science component. Some are more directly related to science, however, than are others. For example, studying the water cycle and watching storm clouds building are both strongly science-related. Sculpting a tornado funnel is more of an art-related activity but is meaningful later in a lesson when it uses knowledge gained through studying tornadoes, watching them on a video, and looking at the sky on a day when the weather is appropriate for the formation of a tornado funnel. Without such prior activities, the art activity is not meaningful.

Process Skills–Focused Units

Science teaching involves helping students develop scientific skills (Presst, 1976). Almost all recent research indicates that elementary students typically are not ready to make abstractions without real experience (Renner & Marek, 1988). Instead, they are ready for experiences that give them a basis for understanding abstract ideas by building concrete foundations. These foundations are the thinking skills underlying the more key science skills described above. Which skills can we usefully encourage students to attempt, learn, and practice? For everyday classroom purposes, five groups of skills can be identified: 1) *early physical skills,* 2) *combined physical and thinking skills,* 3) *thinking skills,* 4) *combined thinking skills,* and 5) *social thinking skills.* These skills may be developed on three different levels, the generic, the topic, and the specific task. The topical and the task specific skills are closely related to the science content taught. A hands-on and minds-on approach is necessary. Assessments of the broad range of science skills places a higher value on them and develops meaningful learning in students.

Early Physical Skills

People have five senses that are used in investigating their environment. The skills associated with these senses are seeing, hearing, tasting, touching, and smelling. Very young children refine and apply these five skills to develop numerous physical skills as they play. Sand and dirt are favorite play materials of many children. When children play with sand or dirt the skills they develop are varied and include packing, molding, pouring, pounding, pressing, shaping, and flattening. These skills are gained much earlier than is the science content involved in the experiences. For example, young children pack, mold, and pour sand and dirt before they understand how sand is formed and what happens to sand in the formation of sedimentary rocks. Another example is when children play with a garden hose they discover that if the opening is left open the water comes out in a directed stream. However, when the opening is partially covered by the child's fingers, the water doesn't come out in a directed stream, but is a fine spray going in all directions. In addition, when children play with a garden hose and water they experiment with the water's directionality based on cause and effect of the size of the opening before they understand the concept of pressure. These skills are basic and are prerequisites for the understanding of such concepts. Early science experiences should focus on building early physical skills (see Table 7.2).

Early Science Physical Skills   TABLE 7.2

Activity	Sample Early Physical Skills
Water Play	Pouring, Wetting, Dropping, Splashing, Filling Containers, Emptying Containers, Spilling, Spreading, Stirring, Mixing
Motion Play	Pushing, Pulling, Sliding, Rolling, Jumping, Skipping, Running, Hopping, Lifting, Carrying, Throwing
Plant Play	Soaking, Tearing, Ripping, Opening, Digging, Watering, Supporting, Mashing, Squeezing, Pressing

Combined Physical and Thinking Process Skills

Physical and thinking skills are combined in much of the science program. Observing and thinking about what you have observed occurs in most experiences. This combination of physical and thinking skills leads to the development of an explanation for what has been observed. The explanation students develop is called an "idea" or "knowledge." The challenge for the teacher is to make experiences meaningful to each student so that she can create ideas or knowledge from them. During play with sand or dirt, for example, students work with physical skills such as pouring and flattening. They also work with thinking skills such as comparing and contrasting different samples of sand and the capacities of different containers (see Table 7.3).

Thinking Process Skills

Thinking skills are natural thought processes in all individuals (Glatthorn & Baron, 1991). Four groups of thinking skills can be defined by the role the thinking skill accomplishes. These are data gathering, data organizing, data processing, and communicating (see chapter 2). Transfer of a thinking skill is likely to occur automatically only after a student has had multiple opportunities to practice the skill (Costa, 1991). For example, a unit on plants involves a student in studying plants and classifying them in order to distinguish fungi from molds. A few weeks later the class is working on a unit on rocks. The classification skill a student developed in the earlier unit on plants will not automatically transfer when she tries to classify types of sedimentary rocks such as limestone and sandstone. The teacher should help the student use classification during this experience.

Each thinking skill (see chapter 2 and Table 7.4) has a number of aspects to be addressed. For instance, as younger students learn the skill of observing teachers must address their need to make many observations using all of the senses. Teachers also must encourage students to examine

TABLE 7.3	Sample Activities That Combine Physical Skills and Thinking Skills	
Activity	**Sample Combined Physical and Thinking Skills**	
Water Play	Mixing—Communicating, Classifying Filling Containers—Comparing, Ordering	
Motion Play	Pushing—Inferring, Ordering Throwing—Predicting, Communicating	
Plant Play	Watering—Inferring, Interpreting Data Squeezing—Comparing, Contrasting	

Thinking Skills in Learning Science   TABLE 7.4

Sample Thinking Skill	Student Behaviors Involved When Using the Skills
Observing	
	1. *Identify* and *name* properties of an object or situation by using at least four of your senses.
	2. *Construct* statements of observations in quantitative terms.
	3. *Construct* statements of observations that describe observable changes in properties of an object.
	4. *Distinguish* between observations and inferences.
Communicating	
	1. *Describe* the properties of an object in sufficient detail so that another person can identify it.
	2. *Describe* changes in the properties of an object.
	3. *Construct* a bar or point graph of number pairs obtained from measurements.
	4. *Describe* verbally the relationships and trends shown in a graph.
Classifying	
	1. *Identify* and *name* observable properties of objects which could be used to classify the objects.
	2. *Construct* a one-, two-, or multi-stage classification of a set of objects and name the observable characteristics on which the classification is based.
	3. *Construct* two or more different classification schemes for the same set of objects—each scheme serving a different purpose.
	4. *Construct* an operational definition based on a classification scheme.
Observing and Inferring	
	1. *Distinguish* between statements that are based on observations and those that are based on inference.
	2. *Identify* which observations support a given inference.
	3. *Describe* alternative inferences for same observations.
	4. *Construct* one or more inferences from a set of observations.
	5. *Describe* and demonstrate additional observations needed to test alternative inferences.
	6. *Identify* inferences that should be accepted, modified or rejected on the basis of additional observations.
Predicting	
	1. *Name* predictions by interpolating between observed events or by extrapolating beyond the range of observed events.
	2. *Construct* tests of a prediction.
	3. *Order* a set of predictions in terms of your confidence in them.
Measuring	
	1. *Demonstrate* the use of simple measuring instruments to measure length, mass, and time.
	2. *Apply* rules for calculating derived quantities from two or more measurements.
	3. *Distinguish* between accuracy and precision.
	4. *Construct* estimates of simple measurements of quantities such as length, area volume, and mass.

(continued)

TABLE 7.4   *(continued)*

Sample Thinking Skill	Student Behaviors Involved When Using the Skills

Organizing, Interpreting, and Drawing Conclusions From Data

1. *Describe* in a few sentences the information shown on a table of data or graph.
2. *Construct* one or more inferences or hypotheses from the information given in a table of data, graph, or picture.
3. *Describe* certain kinds of data, using the mean, median, and range; *construct* predictions, inferences, or hypotheses from this information.
4. *Distinguish* between linear and nonlinear relations.
5. *Describe* the information provided by the slope of a graph.
6. *Apply* a rule to find the slope of graphs of linear relations.
7. *Name* coordinates of points in three-dimensional graphs.
8. *Construct* a three-dimensional graph given number triples.

Isolating and Using Variables

1. *Identify* variables that may influence the behavior or the properties of a system or event.
2. *Identify* variables that are manipulated, responding, or held constant in an investigation or description of an experiment.
3. *Distinguish* between conditions that hold a given variable constant and conditions which do not hold a variable constant.
4. *Construct* a test to determine the effects of one or more variables on a responding variable.
5. *Identify* and name variables that were not held constant in the description of an investigation, although they varied in the same way in all treatments or were randomized.

Formulating Hypotheses

1. *Distinguish* between statements of inference and hypotheses.
2. *Construct* a hypothesis that is a generalization of observations or of inferences.
3. *Construct* and demonstrate a test of a hypothesis.
4. *Distinguish* between observations that support a hypothesis and those that do not.
5. *Construct* a revision of a hypothesis on the basis of observations that were made to test the hypothesis.

quantitative as well as qualitative characteristics. If an event involves change, students should be encouraged to make observations of the event during the change process as well as before and after the event. As an example, a student should continuously make observations of a sugar cube put in water throughout the entire dissolving process. The good observer also will want to describe the size of the sugar cube at various times by comparing it to the size of a unit of measurement (a quantitative aspect), using all senses including taste (a qualitative aspect), touch, smell, and hearing at various times. Another example occurs when a student observes the flame of a burning candle. Student observations, based upon using their senses, could include the flame's shape changes in length and width (quantitative), the flame has many colors including blue (quantitative), there is a smell (qualitative) and if the student closely listens, she may hear a slight popping noise (qualitative).

Combined Thinking Process Skills

Creating sequences or patterns of thinking skills leads to combined thinking skills. These skills involve an investigative or inquiry strategy. They are *critical thinking, reflective decision making, problem solving,* and *experimenting.* These thinking skills are more than tools; they have a purpose. Determining the best color of clothing to wear in the winter, the best design for a model airplane intended to fly a long distance, or the proportion of sand and mulch that will hold the most water around a tree when there hasn't been much rain for weeks are all reasons to use a combined set of thinking skills. Other combinations of thinking skills with purposes include determining whether to use a screwdriver or a pair of pliers to remove a rusted screw holding the chain from an old swing set so that a new chain can be installed, deciding the amount of sugar and water to add to a powdered soft drink mix so that the taste is palatable, and determining how many books a book bag can hold and still zip closed. The six categories described in Table 7.5 are the most common ways of grouping thinking skills for specific purposes.

Combined Thinking Skills in Learning Science	**TABLE 7.5**

Combined	Student Behaviors Involved When Using the Combined Thinking Skills

Critical Thinking—*Understanding new knowledge*
1. Being open minded.
2. Asking questions.
3. Focusing on a question.
4. Distinguishing relevant and irrelevant knowledge statements, value statements, and reasoning.
5. Willingness to analyze arguments and knowledge statements in terms of strength.
6. Desiring to use credible sources.
7. Judging credibility of an argument or source.
8. Tolerating ambiguity.
9. Respecting evidence.
10. Preferring for considerable evidence before judging.
11. Being willing to search for more evidence.
12. Being willing to revise in light of new evidence.

(continued)

TABLE 7.5   *(continued)*

Combined	Student Behaviors Involved When Using the Combined Thinking Skills

Decision Making—*Choosing a best alternative*

    1. Become aware that a decision is needed in the current situation.

    2. Identify purpose or goal.

    3. Identify elements of the current situation.

    4. Identify differences between the current state and the desired state.

    5. Identify obstacles in moving to the desired state.

    6. Brainstorm alternative paths to the desired state.

    7. Relate the current situation to similar past experiences or cases.

    8. Determine for each alternative path the end goal, side effects and risks, resources needed, and efficiency.

    9. Compare the highest ranked alternative paths in terms of purpose, side effects, resources, and efficiency.

  10. Select the best decision path.

Problem Solving—*Resolving a difficulty*

    1. Sensing a problem.

    2. Identifying important components of the problem: variables, relations between variables, and goal.

    3. Identifying known and unknown variables and conditions.

    4. Putting elements of the problem into own words by representing the problem in imagination, writing, or graphically.

    5. Constructing or identifying a problem statement.

    6. Defining terms and conditions.

    7. Identifying alternative solution plans.

    8. Selecting a plan appropriate to the type of problem identified.

    9. Anticipating and planning for obstacles.

  10. Trying out the solution plan.

  11. Monitoring the solution plan process.

  12. Adapting procedures as obstacles are encountered.

  13. Describe the solution resulting from the procedure.

  14. Validate the findings in terms of procedure and goal.

  15. Determine efficiency and effectiveness of the overall process.

Conducting an Experiment—*Generating new ideas or explanations*

    1. Acquiring a background.

    2. Establish initial questions.

    3. Design focus of study.

    4. Collect and analyze data.

    5. Formulate tentative explanations.

    6. Test against new data.

    7. Reexamine and reformulate explanations into hypotheses.

Conducting an Experiment—*Testing an idea or explanation*

    1. Identify the variables.

    2. Identify variables to be controlled.

    3. Write operational definitions as needed.

(continued)

Combined	Student Behaviors Involved When Using the Combined Thinking Skills

4. Construct a question to be answered.

5. Write a testable hypothesis which answers the research question.

6. Plan a test that will provide data to answer the question.

7. Carry out a test.

8. Collect and interpret data related to the hypothesis.

9. Write a report of the experiment, including a statement about whether the data support the hypothesis.

10. Develop and carry out additional tests for other contexts or conditions to become confident about hypothesis.

Creative Thinking—*Creating novel ideas or products*

1. Interest in exploring the novel and the unexpected.

2. Willingness to try to create innovative or original thoughts, patterns, products, and solutions.

3. Willing to take risks in creating and exploring new ideas and different viewpoints.

4. Aware of the potential of generating alternatives.

5. Aware of the potential of applying ideas, analogies, and models in new contexts.

6. Ready to change ideas or approaches as the situation evolves.

7. Willingness to work at the edge of one's competence and to accept confusion and uncertainty.

8. Learn to view failure as normal, interesting, and challenging.

9. Willingness to set products or ideas aside and come back later to evaluate from a distance.

10. Feel comfortable with and be motivated from intrinsic rather than extrinsic rewards.

Critical Thinking Process Skills.   Critical thinking is having good reasons for what you believe (Ennis, 1991). It involves careful, precise, persistent, and objective analysis of any knowledge claim or belief in order to judge its validity and/or worth (O'Reilly, 1991; Beyer, 1985). Both before and after arriving at a conclusion, students need to be willing to consider the *process* they followed in reaching the conclusion. Are their methods logical? Are they making unwarranted assumptions? Are they skipping a necessary step? *Wanting to improve* on the ideas they have and on the processes they use to come to conclusions is an important attitude in students. A desire to improve leads to a willingness to consider the processes followed in reaching conclusions. It makes students more willing to identify problems and seek alternatives.

Reflective Decision Making Using Process Skills.   Reflective decision making evaluates how well a decision matched the evidence used in making it. Schon (1987) describes reflection as knowledge-in-action where the knowledge is inherent in the action. During reflective thinking a person uses and processes data to test the answers that have been posed to problems. Dewey (1933) described the process as:

- suggestion,
- formation of a problem,
- hypothesis,
- reasoning, and
- testing of the hypothesis.

The individual creates new knowledge as ideas are formulated and tested out, resulting in the knowledge-in-action described by Schon (1987).

Reflective Problem Solving Using Process Skills.   As students create meaning from data by processing and applying it, there is an increased chance that the meaning will enter their long-term memory and become lasting, durable, and applicable to new situations (Costa, 1991). As they work, students reflect on their thinking process to decide what a "good problem-solver" does (Barell, 1991). Since reflective problem solving incorporates critical thinking, decision making, and knowledge-in-action, it is not well developed in elementary students. As students master the earlier processes identified in this chapter and in chapter 2, they are working toward developing reflective thinking. Teachers have a multifaceted role in helping students become reflective problem-solvers. They:

1. listen to students' ideas;
2. model thinking;
3. collaborate with students;
4. design learning as problem solving and experimentation;
5. plan, monitor, and evaluate progress; and
6. empower students toward self-direction (Barell, 1991).

Experimenting Using Process Skills.   When teaching the skill of experimenting, the teacher is assisting students in becoming able to design experiences that will help them pose a wide variety of "what if" questions throughout their life. These experiences are called experiments. Human life involves continual experimentation, acting "in order to see what follows" (Schon, 1987). Two types of experimenting are needed for students to develop an understanding of the nature of science and the creation of meaningful learning outcomes.

The *first* is the discovery of knowledge or idea generation. This involves generating a number of alternative explanations in situations where explanations are needed.

The *second* experimenting activity involves testing explanations to determine whether they provide a reasonable alternative or idea testing. This involves construction and testing of a hypothesis. The test, if successful, provides evidence to support the hypothesis. If not successful, the idea must be changed to incorporate the new information or dropped from consideration as a fruitful explanation.

Creative Thinking Using Process Skills.   Creative thinking uses the basic thought processes to develop constructive, novel or aesthetic ideas or products (chapter 10 discusses creative thinking in depth). Emphasis is on the use of prior knowledge to generate other possibilities in the same context, similar possibilities in other contexts, or to extend ideas in new directions.

Social Thinking Skills: Development of Attitudes That Promote Meaningful Learning

Attitudes are affective responses that reflect our feelings and personal likes and dislikes. The development of attitudes that promote meaningful learning is a fundamental goal of the science curriculum (Table 7.6).

Curiosity.   A curious student wants to know, try a new experience, explore, and find out about things around her. This is an attitude that promotes learning. Curiosity often is shown through questioning. Inviting students to ask questions is one way of showing curiosity is valued. Questioning brings satisfaction if it helps students share their pleasure and excitement with others. Teachers promote curiosity by welcoming and

Science Attitudes	**TABLE 7.6**

1. **Curiosity**
   questioning
   wanting to know

2. **Respect for Evidence**
   open-mindedness
   perseverance
   desire to know the evidence behind statements
   willingness to consider conflicting evidence

3. **Flexibility**
   willingness to reconsider ideas
   recognition that ideas are tentative

4. **Critical Thinking**
   willingness to consider methods
   wanting to improve on past ideas and performance

5. **Responsibility to People and the Environment**

providing opportunities to ask questions. Satisfaction resulting from expressing curiosity helps students gradually sustain interest for longer periods and ask more thoughtful questions relating what the student knows to the new experience.

Curiosity is a *wanting to know* rather than a flow of questions. Wanting to know stimulates efforts to find out, perhaps by investigations such as putting a diverse set of objects into groups, making paper airplanes with different wing shapes, mixing different colors to make new ones, finding the missing piece to a puzzle, or matching a baby animal to its mother. One of the goals of the exploration phase of the learning cycle is to create curiosity.

Respect for Evidence. To examine the physical world and make decisions about it, evidence must be gathered and used to develop and test ideas. An explanation or theory is not useful until it has been shown to fit evidence or make sense of what is known.

Open-Mindedness. Students show they know an unsupported statement is not necessarily to be believed when they ask, "How do you know that's true?" or say "Prove it." Adults often expect students to accept statements because of the authority behind them. This may reduce the students' desire to ask for evidence. If a teacher appears to accept statements without evidence, or offers no evidence for a statement, the attitude that evidence is not necessary is transmitted. Asking for evidence and reasons is essential in science teaching. It conveys the true nature of science as an effective process society has invented to solve specific types of problems.

Perseverance. Obtaining convincing evidence often takes perseverance. Sometimes it seems impossible to gather evidence for something, yet when the student keeps on trying, it becomes possible. Perseverance doesn't mean keeping on trying if something is not working. It does mean waiting for new evidence to be reported, being willing to try again, learning from earlier difficulties, and changing your ideas as a result of what has been learned. Teachers should provide students with some assignments that require seeking out information rather than just accepting the most easily available evidence at hand.

Willingness to Consider Conflicting Evidence. It is not easy to respect evidence in situations that may conflict with what you think you already know. A respect for evidence involves the willingness to do so. Students are more likely to be willing to consider conflicting evidence if their teacher models this behavior, accepts mistakes, and rewards the student's effort even if it led to a mistake.

Flexibility.   Mental flexibility relates to the *products* of science activities in a manner similar to how respect for evidence relates to the *processes* occurring in science activity. The concepts and generalizations we form when trying to understand the physical world change as experience adds more evidence to develop or contradict them. Such changes are most rapid in student's early years since their limited experience means their first ideas are often quite different from what they need to understand. Unless there is flexibility, each experience that conflicts with existing ideas causes confusion and creates a rival idea instead of modifying and developing an existing one.

Flexibility and the recognition that conclusions are always tentative are important in science. We never have all the evidence so there is no certainty that our ideas can be absolutely correct. Elementary students may not be able to understand the tentativeness of ideas, but teachers need to promote attitudes that will enable them to eventually develop this understanding. One way of doing this is to preface conclusions with statements like "As far as we can see . . ." or "According to what we know now . . ." or "From what we observed, it appears that." It also helps to occasionally talk with students at times about how their ideas have changed, and about how they used to think.

Responsibility to Others and to the Environment.   In science, students are encouraged to investigate and explore their environment in order to understand it and to develop skills for further understanding. Such investigation and exploration should involve an attitude of respect for others and the environment and a willingness to care appropriately for the people and things in the environment. Growth in inquiry skills should be accompanied by a development of sensitivity and responsibility toward the physical and social environment.

A sense of responsibility towards someone or some thing is more likely to occur when a person has had experience with that person or thing or knows something about them. For example, students who have picked up litter in their classroom or from the school grounds understand the effort that goes into this task. These students are likely to take more care of their school or community than someone who has not been so involved. Knowledge and experience help although they are not enough to create the attitude. Many of the concepts relating to responsibility for and sensitivity to people and the environment are complex (interdependence, for example) and sometimes controversial (the use of nuclear power, the cutting of forests, strip pit mining for minerals, synthetic food additives, or cloning), but it is still possible to begin the development of respectful attitudes toward the environment and people by example and rules of conduct. Rules that teachers and students form together help to establish a pattern of response, but only when students begin to act responsibly (e.g., remembering to feed the class hamster every day, or not destroying another's property). The way to accomplish this is to gradually hand over to the students the responsibility for making decisions about how they should behave.

Aesthetics of Nature. Appreciation of the beauty of nature is a worthwhile goal in elementary science. It is only through development of an appreciation of natural events and of the beauty in nature that one begins to value it. With these attitudes, students can begin to perceive science as a search for knowledge and understanding (Sunal & Sunal, 1991a, 1991b).

Values and Morals. Values are decisions about the worth or importance of something based on a standard we have set. When we value something, we believe it is important or that it has worth. The standards used to make value decisions are morals, judgments of right and wrong. Elementary students are developing values and the moral standards used in determining what to value. As they learn to recognize others' values, they also begin to notice how their own are similar to, or differ from, the values expressed by other students. During the middle school years many students begin to question why specific values are held. With their increased cognitive skills, they begin to examine the moral standards which people use to make value decisions. The examination and questioning in which they are involved can be used as a basis for understanding how people and societies can most effectively use science knowledge and its applications in technology.

CREATING CONDITIONS FOR STUDENT THINKING IN TEACHING SCIENCE

Teaching for thinking requires planning and classroom conditions that facilitate student interaction. Teachers must pose problems, dilemmas, and discrepancies and raise questions to involve students in using a variety of thought processes related to the science content to be taught. Addressing three basic categories in planning lessons will provide a proactive approach in creating conditions for thinking in science lessons. These categories are verbal interaction, classroom structure, and teacher modeling (Costa, 1991).

Planned verbal interaction should help students connect prior knowledge, gather and process information into meaningful relationships, apply those relationships in new situations, and be aware of their own thinking during this process. Teaching for thinking starts with students' prior knowledge of an idea and leads to current experiences with the idea. Teachers follow up on student thinking with questions such as:

> "What can you tell me about you past experience with events such as this?"
>
> "What is your evidence for that statement?" and
>
> "What can you now do to become more comfortable with your answer?"

Teachers help students to question more. To accomplish more effective questioning, teachers plan for higher thought level questions, questions that ask for evidence to support responses, and questions that require students to become aware of their own thinking; plan time for students to ask students questions; and the use of wait time (3 to 5 seconds) after the question is asked and before the teacher takes any action to the student response.

Classroom structure relates to arrangement for effective interaction between a student and the environment and other students. This involves planning for effective time, positive interaction, space, and resources to create and facilitate thinking. The classroom and outside school environment can be structured so students have real objects and experiences with which to interact. Students should be involved in at least some risk taking in the learning process. A safe environment must be created to allow students to put their energy into exploration rather than being self-conscious and defensive. This requires a positive and creative atmosphere with students listening to each other's ideas, and working with each other in effective cooperative learning groups. Collaborative thinking should be encouraged regularly. Students need to look at problems from multiple perspectives. They also need opportunities for acting on their thinking.

Modeling intellectual behaviors should be planned in advance until they become a natural event for classroom use. The teacher should regularly model the behaviors of thinking that are desired in students as they experience a science lesson. Posing a problem and thinking out loud while demonstrating a solution using materials to provide concrete cues are effective strategies.

Teaching Skills-Focused Units

In skills-focused units the specific science content learned is less important than are the skills developed. A skill such as classification can be taught with almost any content. Students can classify rocks and minerals, clouds in the sky, plant leaves, or the colors of stars. The teacher recognizes that the students will learn content, but remains focused on the development of the skill. Hence, the unit is organized around a significant critical or creative science thinking skill. This skill is developed and practiced within a set of content. Assessment of this type of unit can include assessing if the student performed the designated skill, without assessing specific science content. The process is assessed within the science content.

A skills-focused unit allows the teacher to provide students with development of new skills or can remedial help for students who have difficulty in science. It is the lack of thinking skills, not a student's prior knowledge of science that often creates learning problems in science. The skills-focused unit also enables students to develop new skills or further develop a skill so that they may work with ideas in greater depth. Assessment of a skills-focused unit can include assessments in the various content areas as well as assessment of the specific skills within the content areas.

Examples of Skills-Focused Activities

A skills-focused unit using the topic of communication could include the following process skill activities. By using the skill of observation the students could compose a list of the ways they have observed people communicating with each other. This list could include talking, electronic communication using a computer, sign language, writing letters or notes, talking on a phone, using signs or symbols to relay information and nonverbal communication in the form of a smile, frown, or even a wink. Then, using the skill of classifying, students could take the class-composed list of observed communications and classify each method into two groups. One group would include communication methods that the student has used today and the other group would include communication methods that the student has not used today. Other classifying activities might involve using the class list of communication methods to determine if the communication method was used by their grandparents when they were in school or when their parents were in school; classifying places that the communication could take place or not take place; classifying implements or devices that the communication methods use; or classifying the communication methods as individual or group centered activities.

Using the same list of communication methods, the students could watch a short (3 to 5 minute) prerecorded videotape of their daily classroom activities to determine the number of times each communication method was used. After determining the number of times each communication method was used, the students could communicate the findings in graphic or pictorial forms by creating graphs, charts, or tables.

The science processes used in the communication unit activities include observation, classifying, measuring, and communication. Although the unit topic is "methods of communication," the process skills are the focal points, not the scientific components of communication.

Content and Skills-Focused Units

Some units combine content and skills in approximately equal amounts. This type of unit works best with an inquiry or investigative strategy. The students learn a coherent set of content and the skills necessary to systematically study and construct an understanding of that content. For example, an investigation of why objects sink or float involves students in making predictions of which objects would sink or float, testing these predictions, classifying objects based on their sinking or floating properties, and selecting those relevant properties (variables) that appear to be related. The concepts involved with sinking and floating leading to the abstract concept of buoyancy are the content goals of the unit.

Another example of a content and skill unit is an investigation of pendulums. In this unit, the students would make observations, predictions about the conditions that change the rate at which the pendulum swings. A pendulum is a weight that swings suspended from a string. The variables are 1) the amount of the weight, 2) the size of the drop, and 3) the length of the string. The necessary skills involved are observing, measuring, inferring, predicting, and controlling variables. After observing the variables and measuring them, the student should control each of them and measure again to infer that some of the variables do not make a difference in the rate at which the pendulum swings, but that maybe one does make a difference. At this point, the student should predict which of the variables does make the difference in the rate. After predicting which one of the variables makes a difference, the students should experiment with the one variable to confirm their prediction. The overall concept of this unit is that the length of a string of a pendulum, not the amount of weight or size of the drop, makes a difference in the rate of the pendulum swing. The skills of observing, measuring, inferring, predicting, and controlling variables are necessary, but not the focal point of the content unit.

Students develop skills enabling them to use the content they are learning in meaningful ways. A weakness of these units can be that not all content lends itself to investigation in a concrete fashion. This type of teaching requires significantly more time than does the traditional approach. Fewer concepts can be covered during the school year.

An example that illustrates a content and skill-focused unit, in which concrete investigations are problematic, or impossible, is a unit concerned with discovering that the diversity of living organisms exists due to heredity. Observing, classifying, gathering and communicating evidence, inferring, and predicting arethe skills used throughout the unit. The content emphasis is "diversity among living organisms is a result of heredity."

In this unit, the students could begin by observing the eye colors of a predetermined family over several generations. Keep in mind that a predetermined "manufactured" family of several generations is preferable to using the students' families due to possible adoptions or other family situations. Using the "manufactured" eye colors of the generations, the students classify the eye colors, then gather the evidence and communicate their findings with graphs, charts, or tables, followed by predicting what the outcomes of future generations could be.

Other activities within the unit could focus on the abilities of the "manufactured generations" to "roll their tongues," the appearance of attached or detached ear lobes, the appearance of hair growing in a so-called "widow's peak" or even the ability to separate one's fingers between the middle and fourth finger, forming a V-shape that resembles the famous Spock gesture of "Live long and prosper" from the "Star Trek" television series or the movies. Using the data collected from the "manufactured" generations, the students classify, then gather the evidence and communicate their findings with graphs, charts, or tables, followed by predicting what the outcomes of future generations could be.

This unit, focusing on diversity based on heredity, is extremely time consuming and possibly impossible using actual student gathered data from their families due to adoptions, blended families, or single parent situations. However, using "manufactured" data and examples the students should conclude, "diversity of living organisms is a result of heredity."

Issue-Focused Units

An issue-focused unit can be considered as the attempt to answer a question that is relevant to somebody—an individual, a group of individuals, or society as a whole. An issue does not always have an answer. Many issues are complex and not easily resolved. Students can explore such issues, identify possible solutions, examine the arguments for and against each solution, and predict which solution(s) might be best implemented.

The strength of an issue-focused unit is that students can be highly motivated to investigate the issue if they perceive it as relevant. All students can be involved in the investigation at some level. The unit requires an understanding of the problem or issue from a variety of viewpoints. In addition to a scientific context, an issue generally will have social, political, economic, and technological contexts. This type of unit is best when interspersed with other units in a well-sequenced curriculum based on a course of study. The issue-focused unit might follow up a previous unit enabling students to investigate in some depth an issue discovered in the earlier unit.

In this type of unit, students often are pursuing different aspects of an investigation. The teacher must make sure there is an underlying organization, that all information is sequenced and communicated to all participants, and that information is analyzed and shared in relevant and clearly understood formats. Graphs, maps, charts, computer databases, and other means of organizing and communicating information are used. A reliance on library research papers that are then read to the class often produces boredom among the students and does not allow them to recognize which information is relevant.

An issue-focused unit centering on conflict resolution and peace must be relevant to the students. If the issues do not relate to the students' lives, then it is meaningless. One suggestion for a science activity for an issues-focused unit is to construct questionnaires to survey students, faculty, or community members concerning student-determined issues. Then the gathered data from the surveys is used to communicate the findings through graphs, charts or tables. Using the organized information, the students could communicate the results in the form of suggestions for possible resolution.

Another science activity could identify a conflict that has occurred during school time and list possible solutions to the problem. Then, taking those possible solutions, students can construct a concept map showing possible outcomes. Next, the possible outcomes can be classified as "will solve the conflict," "will not solve the conflict" or "will add to the conflict." Finally, each of the outcomes can be ranked ordered to determine the possible best and worst solutions to the conflict.

Project-Focused Units

In a unit, first graders might explore the issue of "Why don't we have more kinds of birds around our school?" This unit would have a project focus. One solution to the issue is the establishment of a bird feeder outside the classroom window and the planting of bushes and wildflowers around the school. The students record the different species visiting the bird feeder, bushes, and wildflowers and compare the findings with their records of birds around the school before the bird feeder and plantings. As part of their unit, the students also might use electronic mail to find out what birds first-graders at other schools find around their school. They might visit a store and a plant nursery to see what types of wild bird food are found and to find out what types of birds are attracted to different types of food.

In upper elementary grades, a project-focused unit could relate to air quality, in particular "What is in the air?" The best time for students to experience this unit is in the spring when pollen is abundant. The students collect small amounts of pollen from nearby trees, grasses, weeds, and flowers.

However, before collecting pollen or anything from the environment, safety and health precautions are mandatory. Especially when dealing with pollen, the teacher must be aware of any student's possible allergies. An alternative to gathering pollen is to identify the local plants and then purchase the corresponding pollen from a biological company.

After either gathering the pollen from the environment or purchasing it, the next step is for the students to view the pollen under a microscope to determine similarities and differences among the specimens. The students draw what each of the pollens looks like and make comparisons. Some of the comparisons could be that some have many circular spikes while others may have only a few spikes. The goal is for the students to discover similarities and differences among the pollens.

The next activity involves the students determining what pollen is found in their environment. To do this, have the students prepare a "pollen catcher" by spreading a thin layer of petroleum jelly on a piece of black construction paper that is approximately 12 × 18 inches. Have the students place their "pollen catchers" in various undisturbed locations in the outside environment for the next day. The next day the students count the pollen grains on the paper and attempt to match the pollen grains to the known pollen grains from the previous lesson. Then, the students classify the pollen grains according to the amounts found on their "pollen catchers." As part of the unit, students compare their results with pollen counts from other sources. Sources that take pollen counts include hospitals, weather stations, universities, and weather channels on television. Accurate information for pollen counts in all parts of the world can be located on the Internet. Currently, there are over 500,000 sites that have this information. Some of the Internet sites include the following:

http://www.redestb.es/csim/interp2.htm

http://www.wcvb.com/wcvb/webmate/wcvb/page/wcvb/5ol_pollen/other/pollen

http://members.aol.com/SurfTulsa/Allergy/ACTcount.html

http://www.unl.edu/pollen/

http://www.dep.state.pa.us/dep/deputate/airwaste/aq/pollen/sites/Monaca.htm

http://www.dep.state.pa.us/dep/deputate/airwaste/aq/pollen/sites/Lebanon.htm

http://www.dep.state.pa.us/dep/deputate/airwaste/aq/pollen/sites/Swiftwater.htm

http://www.dep.state.pa.us/dep/deputate/airwaste/aq/pollen/sites/State_college.htm

http://www.dep.state.pa.us/dep/deputate/airwaste/aq/pollen/sites/
Pittsburgh.htm

http://kxas.com/poltoday.htm

With over 500,000 Internet sites with current information, the students can compare pollen counts by local areas or by country to determine air quality. In addition, many of the Internet sites have e-mail capabilities so students can share their data with others.

Case Study–Focused Units

A case study–focused unit usually deals in some depth with a problem. It might, for example, involve fifth-grade students in studying the Endangered Species Act and its implications for the environment, for people's jobs, and for landowners. This probably would be best approached as a case study. Students will soon find that an endangered species is part of an ecosystem that is endangered. The particular species no longer lives in an ecosystem that can support it. People are faced with the loss of this ecosystem. Protecting the species means protecting the ecosystem in which it lives. Protecting the ecosystem means that some people may lose their jobs or that landowners may not be able to do what they wish with their land. It also means that future generations will have access to that ecosystem. This is a complex issue with no easy solution.

Another example of using a case study could be for the students to develop a job description for the manager of the Talladega National Forest located in Alabama with a science focus. In order for a person to be a forest manager there are be many science competencies. Have the students develop a list of those science-based competencies. After creating the list of science competencies, have the students determine how those science competencies could be developed. For example, a person who would be a forest manager must know about the life cycles of trees and animals in order to manage the forest. The questions that the students attempt to answer could be "How would this person gain this knowledge?" "How do we determine if this person has this knowledge?" and "What is the long term impact on the forest from a manager who has these skills?" This is a complicated scientific endeavor based on inferring, predicting and communicating evidence.

PLANNING FOR SCIENCE IN THEMATIC UNITS

Researching the topic that is going to be taught is critically important. It enables a teacher to assess her or his prior knowledge, add to the knowledge base, identify alternative conceptions that may be held, and eliminate those alternative conceptions. Teacher's journals, encyclopedias, science texts, and trade books traditionally have been used in planning units. However, creating a search on the Internet, using the American Association for the Advancement of Science, *Benchmarks for Science Literacy* and other national and state courses of study, and sending e-mail queries to other teachers and scientists on Internet can provide structured ideas already linked to diverse concepts for planning the science content in integrated units.

Focus questions help students make a link with their prior knowledge and establish a rationale for studying the unit. Some examples of science-related focus questions are:

How can knowledge about the elements and compounds affect my choice of foods?

How should people interact with the environment?

What can families do to prepare themselves for natural disasters such as tornadoes, floods, hurricanes, and earthquakes?

What are the major forces involved in designing efficient transportation vehicles?

How has science helped change transportation in this century?

What is the difference between static electricity and current electricity?

How have science advancements changed communication?

In what ways have advanced communications technologies affected the learning environment?

How have the current views of suggested nutrition changed the ways that people choose food?

In what ways have farmers changed their production methods to accommodate the changing population's needs?

Intended learning outcomes (objectives) are statements of what the teacher wants the students to learn. The following is a list of ideas for a unit on habitats:

The students will observe and classify components of a habitat.

The students will demonstrate the interconnectivity of a food chain.

The students will measure the amount of water that is necessary for a plant to grow.

The students will infer that energy for life originates with the sun.

The students will gather data and communicate evidence of effects of pollution on habitats.

THE WEB

The technique of webbing, or concept mapping, is used to analyze the important ideas and skills that students will learn in the unit. To develop a web, or concept map, the ideas and skills identified in earlier planning are used. An example of a hierarchical web is given in Figure 7.3. An example of a schematic components web is given in Figure 7.4. In the sample schematic components web the unit topic is located in the center of the web.

Both webs connect the main ideas and skills with interlinking and process skill terms such as "has," "composed of," "depends on," "as measured in," or "as inferred in." These terms define the processes used in learning this

Our Environment   **FIGURE 7.3**

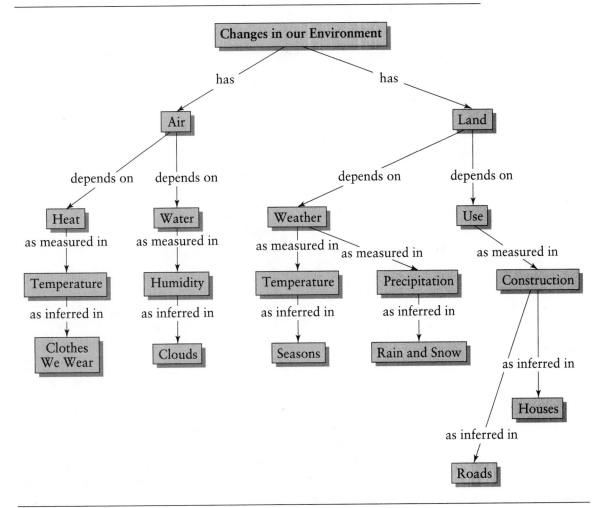

FIGURE 7.4   Oceans

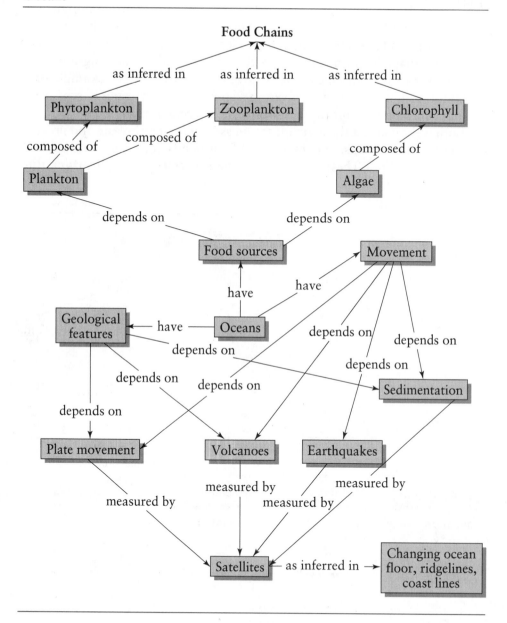

content—inferring, measuring, etc. If a textbook serves as the source for a unit, the teacher can make a list of the important ideas and skills from the book and from this list create the web. Using national and state courses of study the teacher will find it necessary to modify the web by changing or adding concrete ideas or process skills missing from the textbook's approach to the topic. The teacher also may have to de-emphasize and eliminate some concepts. For example, a second-grade textbook chapter on materials may be modified by deleting discussions and diagrams on atoms. At the same time, activities could be added where students investigate the properties of a variety of materials through experiences such as melting, evaporating, identifying odors, identifying colors, and determining hardness.

Now that some time has been spent thinking about the initial ideas of the unit, categorizing them as ideas and skills, and analyzing them by making a web, it is important to consider why the unit will be taught and how the rationale for the unit will be communicated to the students. A rationale statement will be affected by the values that influence the teacher's perception and conception of students (learners), society (learning's relationship to society), and science as a discipline. Current trends and directions in science teaching and education also can influence unit rationales. For example, since the 1970s there has been a shift toward a more student-centered (hands-on) science approach to the learner. In the 1990s the necessity for more reflective inquiry in effective settings for all students has added to the previous trend to create a hands-on, minds-on approach.

The rationale includes a statement of goals. These are broad statements of intent reflecting the integration of ideas concerning students, society, and the nature of science. For example, a rationale for a unit on Our Environment might contain a goal statement such as, "Our environment is a result of many connections."

A complete rationale contains a goal statement, as well as how the unit attends to conceptions of the student, society, and the nature of science. Added to the goal statement above, "Our environment is a result of many connections," a rationale for the unit could end with "throughout our lives and the lives of other living organisms."

The unit will conclude by investigating the necessary components of our environment, with the similarities of those components relating to the students' daily lives. In addition, the students would relate those necessary components to other areas by addressing questions such as:

How do farming techniques affect obtaining fresh and safe food?

How does pollution affect our leisure time activities?

How can I contribute to our environment?

In what positive ways can our environment change for our society?

The K-W-L

The K-W-L is a three-step procedure giving the teacher some indication of what prior knowledge the students have and what they would like to learn about the science unit topic. First, a teacher asks students "What do you *know* about the topic of _____?" Second, the teacher asks students "What *would* you like to learn about this topic?" Third, after the unit has been taught, the teacher asks students "What did you *learn* about this topic?" Students' comments are recorded on a chart with three columns labeled "K" (know), "W" (would like to learn), and "L" (what was learned).

In this step, the initial learning outcomes are revised, written as objectives, and categorized into practical categories for teaching. There are many ways to write learning objectives. All objectives, whatever the specific format, focus on what the student will learn and how success can be achieved.

Objectives can identify many types of potential learning. Ideas include concepts and generalizations. Process skills are another area in which objectives are written. A third area deals with affect—attitudes and values. With some topics psychomotor skills may be taught, particularly in measurement, in science laboratory experiences, in handling materials safely, and in recording events.

Examples of science objectives indicating *ideas* (a concept or a generalization) students will construct are:

Students will identify plants used as food sources.

Students will identify animals used as food sources.

Students will recognize the Northern Hemisphere circumpolar constellations.

Students will infer that rocks are composed of minerals.

Students will conclude that magnets attract some objects and not others.

Students will infer that compounds are made of elements.

Students will identify vitamins and minerals found in foods.

Students will conclude that friction opposes motion.

Students will identify the three states of matter.

Students will identify the positive and negative effects of drugs on the human body.

Science objectives indicating *process skills* with which students will work are:

Students will observe the similarities of leaves.

Students will classify animals according to their environments.

Students will communicate gathered data from fossils to provide evidence of living organisms from the past.

Students will measure the effects of exercise on the human body.

Students will predict the outcome of mixing red and blue water.

Students will infer the identity of an unknown substance.

Students will identify the variables of a pendulum (mass, string length, height of drop).

Students will control the variables of a pendulum.

Students will formulate a hypothesis addressing the needed components of growing plants.

Students will test the hypothesis concerning the needed components of growing plants.

Students will interpret data gathered from the testing of the hypothesis addressing the needed components of growing plants.

Students will define operationally what a growing plant represents.

Students will experiment with the variables of a pendulum.

Students will construct a model of the Earth's landforms.

These children are exploring some of the many connections making up our environment.

Science objectives indicating *attitudes or values* with which students will work are:

Students will state that science is fun.

Students will conclude that scientists' contributions help make life comfortable.

Students will infer that science is creative and changing.

Students will conclude that science means to discover.

Students will relate science to their daily life.

Potential activities should emerge from the list of learning outcomes. One way to look at the activities is to consider the resources available and resource strategies possible. These might include textbooks, field trips, games, guest speakers, Internet, computer software, laboratory equipment, commercial videos, video cameras, tape recorders, manipulatives, case studies, debates, and simulations. Each of these can serve as a focal point for a type of experience designed to facilitate the accomplishment of an objective. For example, in a science unit on "constancy and change" several objectives might be:

Students will infer that although changes take place in an environment, some things may remain constant.

Students will predict that some changes are steady trends.

Students will infer that some changes occur in cycles.

Possible resources and resource strategies for these objectives are:

Students describing the visual changes that take place when mixing red and blue colored water.

Students stating that the physical composition of the water does not change, but the red and blue colorings mix to form a new color: purple.

Students observing, gathering data, and communicating the population equilibrium of an ecosystem.

Students observing, measuring, and graphing the vibration of a guitar string.

Students observing, gathering data, and communicating the daily temperature of the classroom and the outside environment's temperature.

Each of these resources and resource strategies has an integrity of its own. Each can be used to achieve one or more different outcomes. However, the overall goals for the unit are accomplished in various ways.

Lesson plans are drafted using the list of resources and resource strategies (activities) for the intended learning outcomes. They also are based on the rationale and learning objectives. As the science lesson plans are written, the teacher considers how each lesson can be adapted to the special needs identified among the students. Additional accommodations must be made for all students. Teachers ask themselves questions about how learning can be enhanced or what activities require special attention for safety. How can technology enhance learning in this setting? If concrete materials are available for the concepts and skills involved, can technology help create more meaningful learning? If concrete materials are not available, can technology provide the bridge or a ladder to help students learn the concepts meaningfully? Are there objects, chemicals, or events in the lesson where special care is needed?

Students must learn how to deal with these problems. Effective teachers do not address a problem by telling students that there is a problem. They help students learn how to handle each situation. First, teachers find out what students already know about the problem. What attitudes do the students have about the personal harm that can result? Then, teachers decide on an action and develop instructional activities to train students in this setting to deal effectively with the problem. If the science activity is too dangerous for students to do in the classroom, the teacher decides whether to provide a demonstration or use simulations combined with electronic media in an interactive way to foster student learning of the concept involved. Sometimes technology provides additional practice or transfer experiences that are not possible in the real life situation.

ASSESSMENT OF INTEGRATED SCIENCE

Assessment of integrated science occurs in many ways. However, it is important to remember that the science assessment must reflect the science objectives. Those objectives include content knowledge, process skills, and attitudes or values. The process skills and attitudes or values assessments are easily integrated into science content areas, as well as other content areas. However, sometimes the science content is not easily integrated. When this occurs, an individual assessment of that science content is valuable.

Connections among the integrated content areas allow for science assessments of science content, processes, and attitudes and values in integrated modes. For example, the integrated connections between science and language arts can be viewed in a science assessment that could include holistic assessments of the unit, including student journals, student report writings, portfolios, student interviews, student-created poetry, or student-constructed concept maps. Mathematical connections can be assessed by using charts, graphs, tables, sorting and classifying activities. Art activities, such as drawings, painting, or construction of models can serve as science assessments. The performing arts allow for science assessment using student created songs, dance, or plays. In addition, a teacher's anecdotal records and student self-assessments can provide science assessments.

SUMMARY

Science can be a valid and important part of many integrated thematic units. Any of the types of units can incorporate science. Once a clear focus for the incorporation of science into an integrated thematic unit is established, careful planning occurs if the unit is to be meaningful to students. There are many steps involved in such planning. Throughout planning, implementation, and assessment of the unit, teachers work to insure it has significance, coherence, and relevance for their students.

REFERENCES

American Association for the Advancement of Science. (1993a). *Benchmarks for scientific literacy.* New York: Oxford University Press.

American Association for the Advancement of Science. (1993b). *Science for all Americans.* New York: Oxford University Press.

Barell, J. (1991). Reflective teaching for thoughtfulness. In A. Costa (Ed.), *Developing minds: A resource book for teaching* (Rev. ed., Vol. 1, pp. 207–210). Alexandria, VA: Association for Supervision and Curriculum Development.

Berliner, D., & Casanova, U. (1987). How do we tackle kids' science misconceptions? *Instructor, 97,* 14–15.

Beyer, B., & Penna, A. (Eds.). (1971). *Concepts in the social studies.* (Bulletin 45). Washington, DC: National Council for the Social Studies.

Beyer, B. (1985). Critical thinking: What is it? *Social Education, 49,* 270–276.

Blosser, P. E. (1987). Secondary school students' comprehension of science concepts: Some findings from misconceptions research. *ERIC/SMEAC Science Education Digest,* (2), 1–2.

Carnegie Commission on Science, Technology, and Government. (1991). *In the national interest: The federal government in the reform of K-12 math and science education.*

Chambers, D. W. (1983). Stereotypic images of the scientist: The draw-a-scientist test. *Science Education 67*(2), 255–265.

Costa, A. (1991). Teacher behaviors that enable student thinking. In A. Costa (Ed.), *Developing minds: A resource book for teaching* (Rev. ed., Vol. 1, pp. 194–206). Alexandria, VA: Association for Supervision and Curriculum Development.

Ennis, R. (1991). Goals for a critical thinking curriculum. In A. Costa (Ed.), *Developing minds: A resource book for teaching* (Rev. ed., Vol. 1, pp. 68–71). Alexandria, VA: Association for Supervision and Curriculum Development.

Glatthorn, A., & Baron, J. (1991). The good thinker. In A. Costa (Ed.), *Developing minds: A resource book for teaching* (Rev. ed., Vol. 1, pp. 63–67). Alexandria, VA: Association for Supervision and Curriculum Development.

Internet. (1997). http://kxas.com/poltoday.htm

Internet. (1997). http://members.aol.com/SurfTulsa/Allergy/ACTcount.html

Internet. (1997). http://www.dep.state.pa.us/dep/deputate/airwaste/aq/pollen/sites/Lebanon.htm

Internet. (1997). http://www.dep.state.pa.us/dep/deputate/airwaste/aq/pollen/sites/Pittsburgh.htm

Internet. (1997). http://www.dep.state.pa.us/dep/deputate/airwaste/aq/pollen/sites/State_college.htm

Internet. (1997). http://www.dep.state.pa.us/dep/deputate/airwaste/aq/pollen/sites/Swiftwater.htm

Internet. (1997). http://www.redestb.es/csim/interp2.htm

Internet. (1997). http://www.unl.edu/pollen/

Internet. (1997). http://www.wcvb.com/wcvb/webmate/wcvb/page/wcvb/5ol_pollen/other/pollen

Internet. (1997). http://www.dep.state.pa.us/dep/deputate/airwaste/aq/pollen/sites/Monaca.htm

Kahle, J. B. (1988). Gender and science education II. In P. Fensham (Ed.), *Development and dilemmas in science education* (pp. 249–265). Philadelphia, PA: Falmer Press.

Mason, C., Kahle, J., & Gardner, A. (1991). Draw-a-scientist test: Future implications. *School Science and Mathematics, 91*(5), 193–198.

National Research Council. (1995). *National science education standards.* Washington, DC: National Science Academy Press.

National Science Teachers Association. (1992). Position paper. Washington, DC: National Science Teachers Association.

O'Reilly, K. (1991). Infusing critical thinking into United States history courses. In A. Costa (Ed.), *Developing minds: A resource book for teaching* (Rev. ed., Vol. 1, pp. 164–168). Alexandria, VA: Association for Supervision and Curriculum Development.

Osborne, R. J., Bell, B. J., & Gilbert, J. K. (1983). Science teaching and children's views of the world. *European Journal of Science Education, 5*(2) 1–14.

Posner, G., Strike, K., Hewson, P., & Gertzog, W. (1982). Accommodation of a scientific conception: Toward a theory of conceptual change. *Science Education, 66*(2), 211–227.

Presst, B. (1976). Science education—A reappraisal, Part 1. *School Science Review, 57* (201), 628–634.

Saunders, W. L. (1992). The constructivist perspective: Implications for teaching strategies for science. *School Science and Mathematics, 92*(3), 138.

Schon, D. (1987). *The reflective practitioner.* New York: Basic Books.

Seiger-Ehrenberg, S. (1991). Concept development. In A. Costa (Ed.), *Developing minds: A resource book for teaching* (Rev. ed., Vol. 1, pp. 290–294). Alexandria, VA: Association for Supervision and Curriculum Development.

Sunal, D. W., & Sunal C. S. (1991a). Woodland aesthetics. *Science Scope, 15*(1).

Sunal, D. W., & Sunal C. S. (1991b). Young children learn to restructure personal ideas about growth in trees. *School Science and Mathematics, 91*(7).

Third International Study of Mathematics and Science. (1998). Internet, http:wwwcteep.bc.edu/timss

U.S. Department of Education. (1986). *What works.* Washington, DC: U.S. Department of Education.

C H A P T E R 8

INTEGRATING MATHEMATICS COMPONENTS

Mathematics is difficult to think about in a context other than computational skills. As a result, it is overlooked as being a viable part of an integrated thematic unit. The mathematics included in an integrated unit should teach an idea or concept about the topic and make use of a mathematical skill. When planning an integrated unit, the classroom teacher must identify possible situations in which mathematics applies. Mathematics is not to be forced or contrived into an integrated unit just for the sake of having included the subject. Examples of forced integration are found in the unit sometimes implemented during Thanksgiving: students count feathers to be placed on paper turkeys, create men from geometric shapes and call them Pilgrims, or sort food supposedly eaten by our first settlers.

There should be a natural upsurge of mathematics from the material being taught. For example, the Thanksgiving unit may emphasize the amount of supplies needed for survival during an ocean voyage, the length of travel time, weather conditions for the area and time of year, ocean currents, the size of ships and crowded conditions, or planning and purchasing food for a large Thanksgiving dinner. The students utilize the skills needed

For their study of plants, second-grade students use measurement, graphing, labeling, and recording skills to document the growth of their tomato plants.

for counting, sorting, graphing, mapping, measurement, fractions, and problem solving. To develop such an integrated thematic unit takes time, planning, and insight as to what relevant knowledge is needed for individual topics based on the level of development of the students. Students find mathematics "naturally." Very young children are interested in "how many" objects are in the environment, "when" something will happen, and "why" something looks small from far away but becomes larger as you get nearer to it. These are all mathematical concerns. Integrated units are structured to include relevant mathematics, interesting mathematics, and mathematics that answers important questions.

Not all topics relevant to science or social studies lend themselves to the integration of mathematics. The studies of insects, fish, reptiles, individual animals, plant identifications, or leaders in world history often are difficult topics to integrate with mathematics. Limiting a study to only one subject often makes it difficult to use mathematical data or concepts to reinforce the study. Mathematics should be naturally forth coming from within the topic.

FIGURE 8.1   **Student Plant Log**

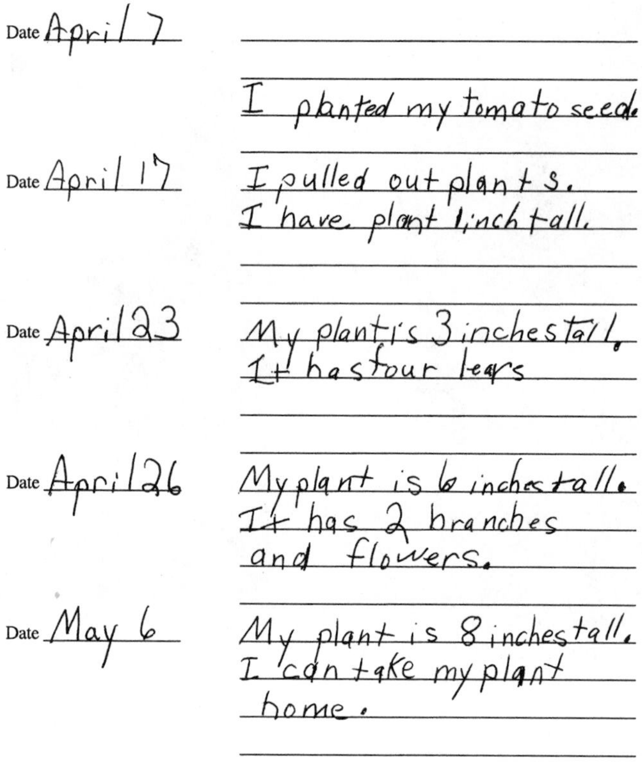

Date April 7

I planted my tomato seed.

Date April 17   I pulled out plants.
I have. plant 1 inch tall.

Date April 23   My plant is 3 inches tall.
It has four leaves

Date April 26   My plant is 6 inches tall.
It has 2 branches
and flowers.

Date May 6   My plant is 8 inches tall.
I can take my plant
home.

CURRICULUM STANDARDS FOR MATHEMATICS

In 1989, the National Council of Teachers of Mathematics (NCTM) published the *Curriculum and Evaluation Standards for School Mathematics (Standards)*. The *Standards* list five goals that stress the importance of mathematical literacy for all students. The *Standards* state that all students:

1. learn to value mathematics,
2. become confident in their ability to do mathematics,
3. become a mathematical problem solver,
4. learn to communicate mathematically, and
5. learn to reason mathematically.

According to the *Standards,* students who learn to value mathematics are able to "appreciate the role of mathematics in the development of our contemporary society and explore relationships among mathematics and the disciplines it serves: the physical and life sciences, the social sciences, and the humanities (p 5)." When students become confident in their ability to do mathematics and be problem solvers they see mathematics not as a separate entity from other subjects but as a tool to use in learning concepts within those subjects.

The *Standards* list 13 standards for grades K–4, 13 standards for grades 5–8, and 14 standards for grades 9–12. The first four standards are common for each of the grade levels:

1. mathematics as problem solving,
2. mathematics as communication,
3. mathematics as reasoning, and
4. mathematical connections.

Problem Solving

Learning to solve problems is the principal reason for studying mathematics (National Council of Supervisors of Mathematics, 1989). To most individuals problem solving means answering an algorithm such as "4 × 2." The *Standards* (NCTM, 1989) state:

> Problem solving is not a distinct topic but a process that should permeate the program and provide the context in which concepts and skills can be learned. (p 23)

In an integrated unit consistent with the NCTM *Standards,* students are presented with a variety of problem situations for which they develop and use mathematical skills and problem solving strategies. In the past, textbook word problems were the only exposure students had to problem solving. A typical example of such a problem is "On Tuesday, Tommy checked out five library books. Then on Wednesday, he checked out two more books. How many books in all does Tommy have checked out from the library?" This type of word problem does not challenge the students to think. The students read the clue words "how many in all" and they know addition is needed to solve the problem. A valid word problem needs to incorporate several mathematical steps, be relevant to everyday situations, and avoid the use of clue words.

Today, students need to be exposed not only to textbook problems but also to everyday situations involving mathematical problem solving. In developing problem solving skills students learn to observe, investigate, verify, and interpret results. When students observe and investigate, they note details that help them look for and identify patterns. For example, a teacher has students take one shoelace out of their shoes. These are laid on a table and compared. All shoelaces are long, have a hard material at the ends and a soft material in the rest of the shoelace. However, the lengths differ somewhat so the students order them by length. Someone suggests "the bigger shoes have longer laces." The class chooses the three biggest and three smallest shoes and the three longest and shortest laces. Do they match up? Now the students are trying to verify their idea. They find two short laces and two long laces match the smallest and biggest shoes but two long laces do not match. How can we interpret these results? As this activity demonstrates, mathematics is problem solving that is relevant and interesting to students.

As students mature in their problem-solving skills they transfer these skills to situations within and outside mathematics. Students acquire confidence in using mathematics in other areas. By using examples of troop movement during the Civil War, for example, a fifth-grade social studies class is challenged to verify the adage "an army travels on its stomach." In science a third-grade class may be asked to predict the weather for the next day based on weather fronts, their speeds, and their paths moving across the United States.

A variety of problem-solving strategies are taught in mathematics. Students should be faced with problems in which the solution is not readily apparent (Suydam, 1982) or problems that involve a multistep approach. The following is a list of 10-problem solving strategies (Reys, Suydam, Lindquist, 1995) taught in mathematics that may be applicable to other disciplines.

1. *Act it out*—In kindergarten and first grade students often are acting out addition or subtraction problems such as "There were five blue birds on the wire and one blue bird flew away. What is the remaining number of blue birds on the wire?" In social studies, students may be asked to act out an event of the American Revolution, such as the signing of the Declaration of Independence, or an event of the Civil War, such as Lincoln's Gettysburg Address. In language arts, students may write, read, and act out stories from literature or from their own creative imaginations. Students will retain the facts of an event or story if they have active participation.

2. *Make a drawing or diagram*—In mathematics students often draw and label a triangle or rectangle in order to find perimeter or area. In science, students may use a grid to draw and label a flower or vegetable garden to be planted on the school grounds. In social studies the students may make a map or a drawing of troop movement during the Civil War or World War II. In physical education, students may draw plans for strategic plays to be used in football, basketball, or soccer.

3. *Look for a pattern*—Students easily recognize and continue the diagonal pattern created on a hundreds board by coloring the multiples of three. Students remember the numerical pattern of the multiples of nine. They create patterns using pattern blocks, Tangrams, and tiles. In science students recognize the layers of soil and rock in land formations or the pattern of temperatures in a weather front across the nation. They see a pattern created in a Native American necklace or the weave of a blanket or quilt in social studies. In music, students carefully listen to the pattern of a favorite melody then reproduce it by clapping or tapping their feet. By learning to look for patterns in mathematics, students begin to see patterns in other areas.

4. *Construct a table*—Second-grade students have a difficult time separating events in time. Some seem to think Columbus landed with the Pilgrims and Abraham Lincoln fought with George Washington in the American Revolution. A time line is one example of a table that helps students visualize the progression of events. A simple time line with dates and spacing forms a table separating the events.

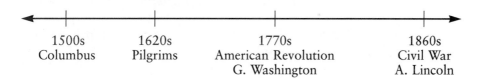

1500s	1620s	1770s	1860s
Columbus	Pilgrims	American Revolution	Civil War
		G. Washington	A. Lincoln

Students construct tables in all subject areas. Fifth graders may construct a table of the batting averages of favorite baseball players throughout the century. Fourth graders might construct a table showing the favorite song of each student and how many other students also named a song as their first choice. Kindergartners may build a table by arranging their milk cartons from lunch in two rows, one for white milk and one for chocolate milk.

5. *Account systematically for all possibilities*—Second- and third-grade students can explore the possibilities of establishing and locating stores, schools, churches, homes, and public buildings in a community. Which would be the best type of business for a location in a community? An ice cream shop; a pet shop; or a hardware store. Students work through the pros and cons of owning and operating each type of store with all the possible outcomes for creating a sound business venture.

In reading, students predict events that may occur in the last half of a story. Their predictions are written in a list on the board and as they read the story, they check their predictions. As a predicted event occurs it is crossed off the list. Afterwards the students examine the remaining predictions and talk about what would have to happen in the story in order for the predicted event to occur.

6. *Guess and check*—In mathematics, estimation is an educated guess or approximation of an amount that can be verified. Long division is solved by making a reasonable guess of the digits in the quotient and multiplying to determine which digit is correct. In science the areas of chemistry and physics have problems for which the students need to use a guess and check procedure. In scientific or historical research students form hypotheses that have to be validated in order to be correct assumptions.

7. *Work backwards*—When a student looks in the back of an algebra book for the answer to the odd number problem and then uses that answer to work the problem, then that student has worked backwards from the answer. A student asked the effects of the Civil Rights Movement must backtrack to find the reasons for the time of unrest in the country. For the student, history is the looking back at the causes and effects of situations in time. In reading, students often trace back events in a story.

8. *Identify wanted, given, and needed information*—Students are given simple one step problems to solve through out their daily lives. They may need to decide whether or not to buy dessert at lunch. In order to make this decision they need to know how much lunch will cost, how much more money will they need to buy dessert, whether they have enough money to buy both lunch and dessert, and whether they will have any money left over to buy an after school treat. This decision requires having the information needed for adding, subtracting, knowing the value of money, and being able to count the money. Based on information available, individuals must make rational decisions that effect their lives. In conducting research in science or social studies students consult many possible sources and then decide the information needed from each source to complete and validate the study or project. To construct a dance about an event as a thunderstorm, students listen to news reports, watch storms in progress, and study the water cycle. They decide whether more information is needed about the frequency of storms in their region and about people's reactions to the loud sound of thunder at night and in the daytime. The dance is the product of all this information.

9. *Write an open statement*—A statement can be made in such a way as to question its validity. Students then are challenged to prove or disprove the statement. In mathematics the statement, "The length of your bare foot equals the length between your elbow joint and your wrist," challenges students to measure their foot and inside arm. The point is

not whether the statement is true but if the students have an opportunity to use a ruler to measure and prove the statement true or false. In social studies and science, statements are made in an open manner that encourages students to think and possibly research a topic to find facts and data to validate an opinion. Examples of such statements are: "The cheetah is the fastest animal on Earth." "Columbus was not the first to discover the new world." "All clouds contain water." "It can be too cold to snow." Students are challenged to prove or disprove these statements using research skills.

10. *Solve a simpler or similar problem*—In mathematics students who have difficulty doing a two-digit addition problem with regrouping may need to take a step backwards and work on one-digit addition or two-digit addition with no regrouping. If there is a problem doing multiplication or division then students may need to do easier problems to reinforce skills needed for the next level of difficulty. In science students may be shown a scale replica of the solar system which is a simple way to illustrate the relative size of the sun in comparison to the planets. Students may use a ruler as a lever to lift a small object as a simple demonstration of a similar machine. When students create a volcano or a topographical salt map they are making simple but similar representations of the real subject.

Communication

Students often say they solved a problem "in my head," but they cannot communicate how they solved that problem. *Representing, discussing, talking, listening, writing,* and *reading* are key communication skills (*Standards,* 1989). The awareness of different learning styles among students has made it evident that all forms of communication are necessary for a total instructional program. Students on the elementary level are developing all their communication skills. In mathematics they need to experience a variety of ways to communicate their knowledge. Students clarify their thinking by using representations in the forms of graphs, drawings, and symbols. Hearing a student explain a problem or procedure during a discussion enables the teacher to have a better understanding of the students' conceptions or misconceptions. Students need to share their thought processes with others, talking through the steps they are taking to solve a problem. Listening to others share their thoughts gives students new ideas and challenges old ideas. Writing down your ideas, the steps you took, and what worked or did not work is a way by which a student thinks through an activity. Having others respond to your written ideas after reading them brings about further communication. They are given the opportunity to communicate their ideas to themselves, their teacher, their classmates, and all interested individuals.

Communication is a major part of an integrated thematic unit. Students have the opportunity to express their views, ideas, feelings, and thoughts through writing, drawing, discussing, and acting. An understanding of symmetry is seen in a student's drawing of a butterfly for science or art. In science the student's ideas of the effects of air pressure can be expressed through journal writing and scale modeling can create a representation of the solar system or London Bridge. Mathematics can be communicated in art, music, science, social studies, and literature.

Reasoning

Students have a natural curiosity about why or how things work. They are always seeking answers to questions. Teachers need to constantly ask students to justify or give reasons for their answers. When asked to explain a solution, students may think they have the wrong answer because often that is the only time a teacher asks them to explain. This learned behavior needs to be changed because one student's explanation may be the key to understanding for another student or may lead to an overall higher understanding of the concept.

Mathematical reasoning involves being able to draw logical conclusions, justify answers and solutions, use patterns and relationships to analyze situations, and use models, facts, properties, and relationships to explain thinking (*Standards,* 1989). The skills necessary for reasoning in mathematics also are necessary in science, social studies, literature, and other disciplines. The following are sample questions that engage students in mathematical reasoning.

- What happened first, second, third, and last in the story read for literature?
- From what you have read, what do you think will happen next in the story?
- The character in the story has a problem. How do you think the character will resolve this problem?
- What repeated pattern do you hear in this song? Can you create your own pattern?
- How much water is wasted daily by one individual? What are some ways we might stop this wastefulness?
- What conclusions can we draw from the two bar graphs that show destruction of the rain forest and extinction of the animals who live in the rain forest? What part might we play in stopping this destruction?
- What is your daily calorie intake or how many fat grams have you eaten today? What is considered a healthful diet? Why?

- How is your pulse rate measured? What is your pulse rate? What can we do to reduce the risk of heart problems?
- How many animal pelts are used in a full-length mink coat? How many minks are raised yearly for furriers? Do you think animals should have rights? Besides minks, what are some other animals that might need protective rights and why?

As they use reasoning skills, students become independent investigators and thinkers. They seek answers to questions they ask themselves. Students learn what is logical and what is illogical to accept not only in mathematics but also in everyday life. The use of logical reasoning provides a sound base for students to analyze claims critically (Heddens & Speer, 1995). Students also learn to respect other people's opinions. When they can see or hear justification for ideas or problems, then they more readily accept what has been proven to be true or valid.

Connections

Traditionally, mathematics is taught as a separate subject isolated into periods of 1 hour or 90 minutes. Through this process, students perceive mathematics as being unrelated to other subject matter or to everyday existence.

According to the *Standards* (1989) making mathematical connections involves:

1. linking conceptual and procedural knowledge;
2. relating representations to one another;
3. recognizing relationships among topics in mathematics;
4. using mathematics in other curriculum areas; and
5. using mathematics in daily life.

Mathematical connections have to be taught and used daily in order for mathematics to be valued by the students. When asked, "What is mathematics?" Students almost always answer with a computational problem. When asked, "Is math needed in the grocery store?" "to pump gasoline in the car?" "to get a cola from a machine?" or "to wake up in the morning?" students often show a blank look because they have not made the mathematical connection to everyday experiences. When asked, "How is addition related to multiplication?" "How is geometry related to measurement?" and "How are fractions related to decimals or percents?" again students show a blank look. Only through extended exposure to integrated topics do children have a better chance of retaining the concepts and skills they are taught (NCTM *Standards,* 1989, p 33).

CONSIDERING THE NATURE OF MATHEMATICS

As in social studies, science, and all other subject areas the mathematics curriculum involves the study of patterns and relationships. In mathematics students have opportunities to examine various patterns in shapes, sets of numbers, letters, events, and designs. Beginning in the earliest of grades, students are exposed to patterns within their environment. The ability to discern repeating and continuing patterns enables students to look beyond the present and predict what comes next in the sequence. Students begin to see patterns in heirloom quilts, in Native American jewelry and weaving, in the pattern of highways running through mountain valleys, in antique wallpaper, and in clothing during times of prosperity or recession. They see patterns in butterflies, large cats, the music and dance of their ancestors, and the study of art. Students see patterns and relationships in the weather and temperature of a region, animals indigenous to an area, layers of soil and rock, the use of simple machines, and the stars and planets.

The question of "What comes next?" is brought from the mathematics curriculum into the realms of social studies, science, language arts, music, dance, art, and physical education. Students no longer wait to see what will happen next but they begin to make their own events and happenings. They develop the confidence to create their own patterns and relationships in all disciplines. Students realize they have the imagination and know how to be productive, experimental, and creative. They look for and extend patterns and relationships in their everyday environment. A classroom of second graders extends a pattern of letters, numbers, or shapes every day during their morning board work. These students are now looking for patterns within stories during reading, finding patterns in the veins of leaves, estimating the number of sunny days in a month based on the weather graph, and creating their own designs using pattern blocks.

The process skills developed in science and social studies also are developed in mathematics. Toddlers have begun developing the process skills of observing, inferring, sorting, classifying, comparing, ordering, and sequencing. Young children want to bring order to their worlds. They know that "daddy" is a man so, therefore, all men are named "daddy." They have made a "daddy" category into which men are placed. In mathematics students are taught to describe what is observed and make inferences both orally and pictorially. From an array of colored tiles, students may infer multiplication, area, and perimeter. Students make comparisons of likenesses and differences between number values, shapes, designs, angles, and, patterns. Students bring order to number values and measurement. They sort and classify objects, shapes, and pictures by one or more attributes. Students sequence numbers, letters, objects, and shapes based on a set of given characteristics (Sheffield &

Cruikshank, 1996). The process skills in mathematics of observing, inferring, comparing, ordering, sorting, classifying, and sequencing also are found in science, social studies, and language arts.

The classrooms of today are no longer passive environments. Students develop process skills that take them through everyday situations. It is the responsibility of the classroom teacher to provide various opportunities for the students to use their process skills. Often students are not included in the planning of a class party or field trip. The classroom teacher sends home a note telling the parents the times and the cost of an event. Why not include the students in the planning? If a field trip is planned, then the students can determine length of travel time in order to set time of departure and time of return. Students can calculate the amount of money needed for admission to a park, lunch and snacks, and souvenirs. Then the students should be included in the process of writing the note to be sent home to the parents.

A class party offers an opportunity for students to use their mathematical skills in planning the amount of food, drink, money for supplies, and time needed for their class celebration. A real situation often is the most ideal because students see the results of their work, since these situations are few for some students, more experience should be provided in school. Integrated units offer various opportunities to develop and use process skills in many contexts. Students do not automatically transfer a higher level of classification skill they developed in a mathematics activity to a social studies related activity. An integrated unit allows students more opportunities to use the skill in a variety of contexts and fine the skill useful in many contexts.

TIME MANAGEMENT AND PLANNING

Developing an integrated unit requires time and planning. The classroom teacher is limited to planning time during the normal school day; therefore it is often necessary to plan such units outside daily school time. Collaborating with grade level teachers reduces time spent on such projects.

Chapter 3 discusses the planning for a school year focusing on required topics for a grade level course of study. Once a topic or theme is determined, the teacher correlates the various subject areas around the topic. Brainstorming and the use of a web provide visual realization of what may be taught in each area. Examples of webs for science, social studies, and mathematics for teaching plants in kindergarten, the rainforest in third grade, and Japan in the second grade are given in Figure 8.2a–d. Language arts, music, physical education, and art also should be added to the web. The teacher needs to consult courses of study, textbooks, and curriculum guides to determine the necessary content and skills to be taught.

FIGURE 8.2a   Japan Web, Part 1

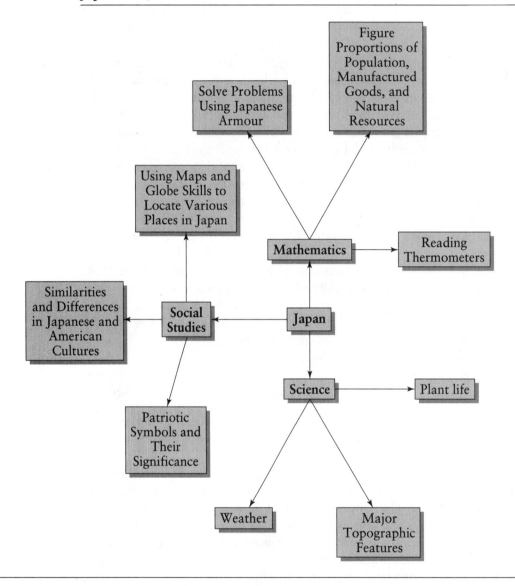

Japan Web, Part 2

FIGURE 8.2b

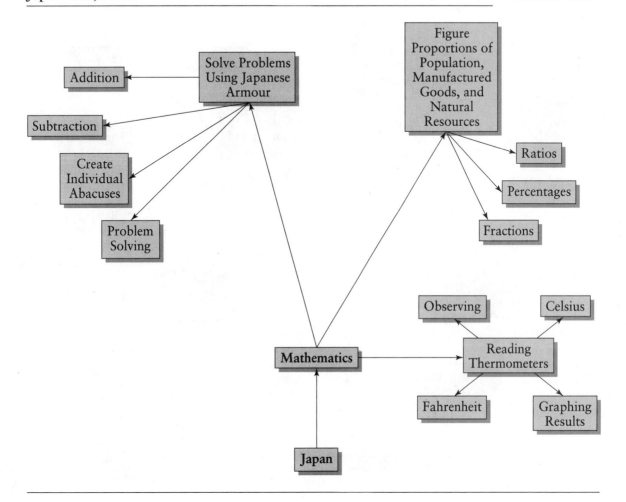

FIGURE 8.2c   Japan Web, Part 3

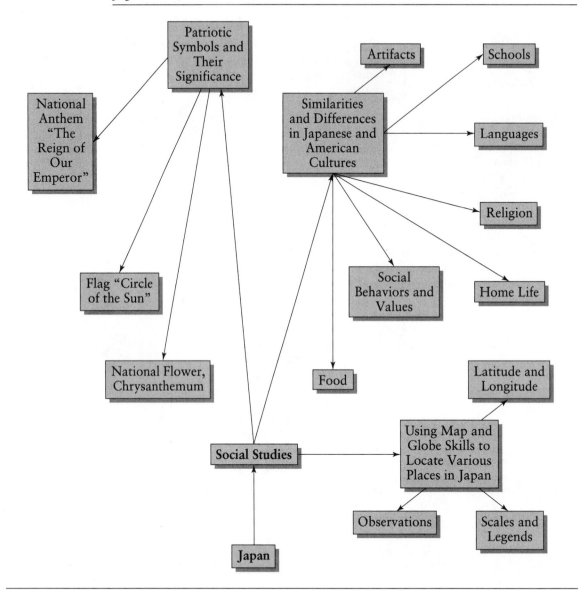

Japan Web, Part 4   **FIGURE 8.2d**

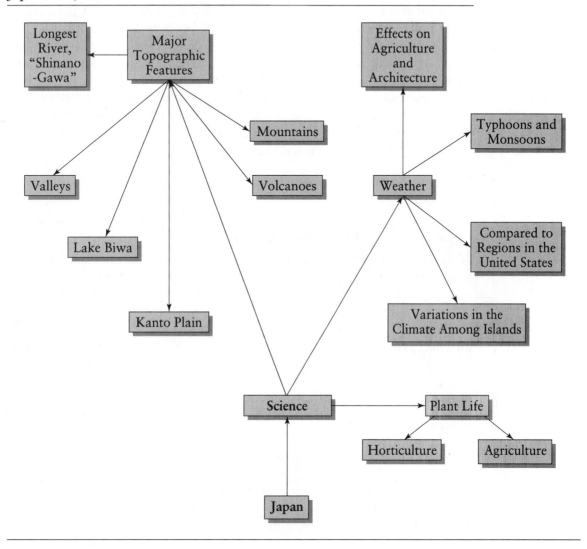

When brainstorming, too many ideas and activities often are formed. It becomes necessary for the teacher to decide exactly what can be accomplished in the daily lessons. Each teacher has his or her own format for teaching a topic. One teacher may teach each subject (science, math, social studies, language arts, music, art, and physical education) in an independent time frame. Another teacher may start the morning with a theme and teach a subject area as the opportunity arises throughout the day. In such a situation, the students may not realize they are doing math and another subject at the same time.

Regardless of how a teacher implements the subjects, planning still is needed for what can be taught in a day:

1. decide the sequence of teaching the concepts or objectives for the topic or theme;

2. write an outline for each day integrating the subject areas around the concepts or objectives (see Figure 8.3a–d for examples);

3. decide what materials are needed for teaching in each subject area; and

4. write the lesson plans.

A question often asked by teachers is "How can I teach what is required by the course of study and teach using integrated units?" Teachers are to teach the concepts, skills, and content required by each subject's course of study. A

FIGURE 8.3a   **Japan Alive! Three-Day Outline**

JAPAN ALIVE!

Three Day Outline

Grade 2

DAY 1

Science: Topographic and geographic features of Japan

Social Studies: Map and globe skills for locating islands of Japan and place names

Mathematics: Coordinate graphing for introducing latitude and longitude

DAY 2

Science: Weather and climate conditions in Japan (emphasis on monsoons and typhoons)

Social Studies: Japanese culture (schools, religion, languages, home life, artifacts, social behaviors, values, and foods)

Mathematics: Introduce the Japanese abacus. Solve related word problems with Japanese theme using the abacus

DAY 3

Science: Plant life variations among the islands of Japan

Social Studies: Historical aspects of Japan

Mathematics: Research information on Japan that is stated in the form of percentages, fractions, ratios, and proportions. Create individual word problems.

Save Our Rain Forests. Three-Day Outline

FIGURE 8.3b

SAVE OUR RAIN FORESTS

Three Day Outline

Grade 3

DAY 1

Science: Listen to a tape recording of the sounds of the rain forests (identify sounds)

Social Studies: Geography and location of the rain forests (continents and countries)

Mathematics: Coordinate graphing to introduce latitude and longitude for map reading skills

DAY 2

Science: Types of trees and plants found in the rain forests and how they help the earth

Social Studies: How the rain forests are threatened and reasons for saving them

Mathematics: Measurement—inches to measure the amount of rainfall during a period of time and feet to measure the amount of destruction over a period of time

DAY 3

Science: Types of animals in the four layers of the rain forests

Social Studies: What we can do to save the rain forests

Mathematics: Group and graph pictures of animals belonging to the four layers of the rain forest

school district also may require the complete use of a textbook purchased at a great expense. Especially in mathematics, teachers are faced with the tasks of teaching certain skills (addition, subtraction, multiplication, division, fractions, decimals, etc.). How can these skills be integrated into a unit if they have not been taught yet? It takes time and planning. In planning the

Plants. Three-Day Outline

FIGURE 8.3c

PLANTS

Three Day Outline

Grade: Kindergarten

DAY 1

Science: Identify different types of seeds (fruits, trees, flowers, and shrubs)

Social Studies: Identify different occupations associated with plants (farmer, forester, nursery worker)

Mathematics: Examine and sort different types of seeds. Match seeds to fruits (cucumber, apple, kiwi, grapefruit) and create a class graph of favorite tasting fruit

DAY 2

Science: Identify different parts of a plant

Social Studies: Identify how different cultures use plants

Mathematics: Measure and record plant growth of individual plants grown in the classroom

DAY 3

Science: Identify types of plants (fruit, trees, flowers, and shrubs)

Social Studies: Identify the uses of plants in our everyday lives

Mathematics: Weigh and measure vegetables for the making of soup in the classroom

FIGURE 8.3d   Weather. Three-Day Outline

WEATHER

Three Day Outline

Grade 4

DAY 1

Science: Aspects of weather (wind, precipitation, temperature, severe weather, and the water cycle)

Social Studies: Weather in different regions of the United States (use of weather maps)

Mathematics: Coordinate graphing and map skills (latitude and longitude)

DAY 2

Science: Identify the three basic types of clouds. Associate the weather with each cloud type

Social Studies: Identify how weather affects the environment

Mathematics: Daily precipitation data. Work with percentages and averages of precipitation

Language Arts: Read *The Cloud Book* by Tommie de Paolo

DAY 3

Science: Identify weather instruments and the significance of their uses

Social Studies: Identify weather symbols used by forecasters (view television weather reports) and create individual weather maps and weather reports

Mathematics: Reading thermometers and barometers. Graphing temperature and barometric pressure

Language Arts: Have students role play being a weather forecaster. Read *Weather Forecasting* by G. Gibbons

---

unit the teacher may decide: 1. not to use a skill that has not been taught; 2. teach a separate math lesson on the skill and then use it in the unit; or 3. teach the skill using the content of the unit. Many factors determine which option to use including the type of skill to be taught, the level of difficulty of the skill, the mathematical abilities of the students, and the time available.

The grade-level mathematics textbook is a good source for determining skills and scope and sequence for teaching mathematics concepts. Since the publication of the NCTM *Standards* in 1989, most school mathematics texts adhere to the proposed recommendations of the *Standards*. Using the textbook as a resource and guide, the teacher can incorporate mathematical skills into an integrated unit.

MATERIALS

Mathematics and other subject areas have taken a hands-on approach to learning. According to the NCTM *Standards* (1989, p. 17 and p. 67) grades K–8 should have a wide variety and an ample supply of physical materials and supplies. Such materials might include interlocking links; attribute shapes; pattern blocks; tiles; rulers; geometric models; colored rods; geoboards; balances; cubes; compasses; protractors; scissors; fraction pieces; and graph, grid, and dot paper. Upon looking at the list of materials one may only see

Mathematics Manipulatives   FIGURE 8.4

Art	Science
Pattern Blocks	Attribute Shapes (sorting)
Tangrams	Weather Instruments
Geoboards	Measuring apparatus (liquids)
Mirrors (symmetry)	Charts and Graphs
Geometric Solids	Weights and Scales
Rulers	Balances (simple machines)
	Rulers
	Maps

Social Studies	Language Arts
Pattern Blocks (flags, quilts, and jewelry)	Pattern Blocks
Maps and Grid Paper (coordinates)	Time Lines
Clocks (time zones)	Time Schedules (train, bus, plane, and tides)
Money (U.S. and foreign currency)	Newspapers
Calendars and Time Lines (historical events)	Telephone Books
Recipes (measurement and fractions)	Charts and Graphs
Sewing Patterns (measurement)	
Craft Sticks (scale construction and measurement)	
Newspapers (economics, dates, stock market reports, sales)	
Telephone Books (local information)	
Charts and Graphs	

For their study of plants, second grade students use measurement, graphing, labeling, and recording skills to document the growth of their tomato plants.

mathematics manipulatives or supplies, and may not see the use of these in other subject areas. However, these materials are used in other subject areas. In planning the integrated unit, the teacher also must plan the integration of manipulatives, materials, and activities with other subjects (see Figure 8.4).

SAMPLE MATHEMATICS IDEAS AND ACTIVITIES RELATED TO THE SIX DIFFERENT TYPES OF INTEGRATED UNITS

Mathematics has a role in each type of integrated unit. Figure 8.5 gives examples of mathematics as a part of each of the six types of integrated units.

Concept-Focused Units

Concept-focused units often are integrated with mathematics skills and concepts. As an example, consider the social studies concept-focused unit on constancy and change as described in chapter one. For the construction of

FIGURE 8.5   Overview of Types of Integrated Units With Mathematics Examples

Type of Unit	Description	Mathematics Example
Concept-focused	Unit designed around teaching one or a few major concepts	Measurement; Elapsed time; Money; Geometry
Process Skills–focused	Unit designed around teaching one or a few major process skills with less emphasis on content	Mathematical Statistics; Surveying; Graphs, Tables and charts
Content and Process Skills–focused	Unit designed around teaching nearly equal amounts of content and process skills	Mathematical facts and figures; Number sense
Issue-focused	Unit designed around investigating an issue through research and data collection	Collection, Organization, and Analysis of data
Project-focused	Unit designed around solving a problem or exploring an alternative	Measurement; Map skills; Fractions; Percentages;
Case Study–focused	Unit designed around doing something on a local level based on a topic investigated	Computational skills; Money; Scheduling

buildings, bridges, and cities students use measurement, geometric shapes and models, grids, and land plots. Students determine elapsed time for daily schedules and routines. Time lines show changes during the Ice Age, the Industrial Age, the Space Age, and the Technological Age. Graphs are used to visualize area, population, and economic growth of a city, state, country or nation. Climate conditions such as rainfall and temperature variations are measured to justify a change in animal habitation or plant growth in an area. Simple measurement of the daily growth of their bean plant helps early elementary students become aware of constancy and change in their environment.

An integrated unit can be built around a mathematics concept such as measurement. Students study measurement of length and weight. They think about whether equal amounts of water and milk weigh the same then they measure to prove the point. They weigh two students who are the same height. They interview older family members about measurements in the past and find out Great-Grandpa used to go to buy cloth with his mother because he had the largest feet in the family and his mother could always talk the cloth seller into measuring off the cloth she was buying by using Great-Grandpa's feet. Students talk to a high school physics teacher about modern devices for making very fine measurements. Throughout the unit they read stories that talk about far places and try to measure the distance from their town to those places.

Process Skills–Focused Units

An integrated process skills–focused unit for communications skills would seem to be more language arts oriented than mathematics oriented. What part does mathematics play in a unit based on communication skills? Consider the question, "Where would a politician be without charts and graphs to illustrate ideas and plans?" A good debate often needs facts and figures to back up a viewpoint. Advertising agencies depend upon sales numbers to promote their product. Newspapers and television both use marketing skills to survey or poll readers and audiences for public opinion. Newspapers have sport statistics, grocery and department store sales, want-ads, weather forecasts, and almost every article contains a date, time, and mathematical statistic. Mathematics skills integrated with a unit on communication skills add a dimension that clarifies, justifies, or validates necessary facts.

Mathematics itself is a processing of information. To do so, students make inferences, classify, and carry out many forms of thinking. When an integrated unit focuses on a process skill, such as making an inference based on available information, mathematics has a role. For example, in a unit helping students construct higher levels of the skill of making an inference students compare line graphs to solve a problem by making an inference from the information provided in the graphs. Then they talk about whether the information they are using is limited and whether collecting more information might lead to a more accurate inference.

Content and Process Skills–Focused Units

The content and process-skill unit is most adaptable to mathematics. A unit on "diversity" or "conflict" has facts to substantiate the information. An important issue at this time is the United States collaboration in the space station. Should the United States continue to support this space venture? Students can discover the cost of building, operating, and maintaining the United States' involvement in the space station and the space program. The Internet is helpful as a source of information that students use. For example, information on the space program is available at a Web site maintained by the National Aeronautics and Space Administration (NASA) at http://www.nasa.gov.

Other topics which are sources of conflict or diverse opinions include: deforestation of the rainforest versus global warming; lumber companies versus environmentalists; medical testing versus animal rights; and religious conflicts in the Middle East. These issues all contain numerical facts giving information about each conflict and the different sides to it. Using the factual information, students have the opportunity to make mature judgments and decisions regarding the cause they support in this changing world. Mathematical facts have little meaning by themselves. In a content and process skill focused integrated unit, students use those facts to construct higher levels of the process skills targeted in the unit. In turn, with higher levels of process skills, students create more meaning out of the information with which they work. Using information gives it meaning.

Issue-Focused Units

Research and data collection are major supports for an issue-focused unit. As in the "diversity" or "conflict" unit facts and figures substantiate the issue. The issue may be fighting in the schools; the growth of gangs in a community; land development of a neighborhood park; the closing of a local school; prayer in the schools; or the use of air bags in cars. Students research the topic. They develop a survey to identify public opinion, collect and organize data to support the topic, display the findings in the form of graphs and charts, and deliver their report. Numerical facts, addition, subtraction, multiplication, division, fractions, decimals, percentages, statistics, and graphing all may be required to complete the data collection and analysis for an issue-focused thematic unit. Students learn the value of public support for an issue that may have an impact upon their lives.

Issue-focused units typically include mathematics. Gathering information leads to having sets of numbers. For example, in a unit on conflict and conflict resolution, students gather information on the number of fights in the school and on the playground. They keep a record for three weeks. Using the recorded information, students create bar graphs for each hour of each school day. The information is analyzed using the graphs. Students notice more fighting in the hour before lunch as indicated by the height of the bars of the graphs at this time of day. They decide one graph with information from all the days is needed. The teacher helps them learn how to synthesize their information and display it on one graph. The new graph confirms their inference that fighting increases before the lunch hour. Mathematics is an important part of the unit. Students learn more about mathematics and how to use it to investigate the issue under consideration.

Project-Focused Units

A project-focused unit usually tries to resolve a problem. Air quality in a city, traffic control, flooding, school overcrowding, animal migration or extinction, crop failure, and logging of a national forest are possible topics presenting a problem for students to investigate. Mathematics is required in the form of measurement, instrument reading, map skills, percentages, graphing, and statistics. Students read, interpret, and understand the facts and figures created by the problem in order to know its extent.

The Internet is a good source of current information for many projects such as: human population growth and how it effects air quality; animal migration; and school overcrowding. The U.S. Census Bureau's Web site at http://www.census.gov/ftp/pub/population/www/ is a source of current population statistics that may be helpful. Students doing projects on air quality or flooding may need current and recent weather information. This is available on Internet sites such as: the National Weather Service at http://www.nws.noaa.gov/ or the Weather Channel at http://www.weather.com/twc/homepage.two. If a solution to a problem is found, then facts and figures again are used to measure the validity of that solution. A project-focused unit has a variety of opportunities for the use of mathematics.

In the example given above where students investigated conflict and conflict resolution, they found fighting occurred at their school and increased before lunch. This finding gives them a new problem to solve, why is there an increase in student fights before lunch? This question leads to a project-focused unit. Certainly, social studies is involved as is reading and language arts. Science is part of the unit as students find out that body chemistry has an effect on behavior. As students become hungry they grow more irritable and more likely to fight. Mathematics has an important role. Students use mathematics in this project-focused unit to continue to keep track of fighting, to survey others about possible solutions, and to investigate the role sugar and carbohydrates have in our body chemistry.

Case Study–Focused Units

The case study–focused unit may be a continuation of the project-focused unit as students continue to keep a watchful eye on the solution to the problem to verify the results. This continuation generates more data to be analyzed and interpreted. Students doing an environmental study of national forests can integrate mathematics into the unit in multiple ways. In studying the land, students discover the amount of acreage in a national forest, the number of trees per square foot or acre, the growth rate of the trees, the number and kinds of animals which inhabit the forest, the amount of land or vegetation needed to support the animals, and the amount of destruction that may be caused by human interference in the forest. Logging of lumber in a national forest offers a means to use various mathematical skills. Students can calculate the amount of trees cut per square acre, the length of time to replant and produce new growth, the amount of lumber needed to build a home or to produce a newspaper, the amount of money made by the government and how much of that money goes back to the national forest. In studying the position of the national forest manager the students discover the responsibilities associated with the job. Students can determine the amount of money needed to maintain the forest for visitation, to hire workers, to restore plant and animal life, and to pay the salary of the manager. Information on national forests can be obtained from the Internet site for the U.S. Department of Agriculture's Forest Service at http://forest.moscowfsl.wsu.edu/contacts.html. Studying the national forests, students can integrate mathematics into a unit that is generally considered to be social studies or science.

In the example discussed above, students investigated the problem of fighting among students in their school as part of a large study of conflict and conflict resolution. Having found fighting increased before lunch, and having analyzed why this occurred, they proposed solutions. The case study unit involves them in trying out one or more solutions and analyzing effects. For example, a mid-morning snack might enable students to make it to lunchtime with less conflict. After surveying students, faculty, and families, a mid-morning snack is arranged. The school provides the snack and charges the families for it. Students work with the school to determine the lowest fair price and the type of snacks available. Provisions are made for students who cannot afford the cost. A new study is conducted and new bar graphs are created to show the numbers of school fights occurring after the snack time is implemented. Mathematics has a major role in this case study unit.

SUMMARY

Integrating mathematics with other subject areas in a unit takes time and planning. The classroom teacher considers all situations within the topic of the unit that make use of mathematical skills. In planning the integrated unit the teacher sequences the objectives to be taught, outlines the daily integration of subject matter, collects needed materials, and writes lesson plans for teaching. Today's mathematics stresses the use of a variety of problem-solving skills, mathematical reasoning, subject area connections, and communications with reading, writing, representing, discussing, talking and listening. Students take an active role in all disciplines developing the skills of observing, inferring, sorting, classifying, comparing, ordering, and sequencing. Using various manipulatives and materials, a well-planned unit contains integrated activities that prepare students for real-life experiences. Learning to make the connections within an integrated unit teaches students to approach learning with an open mind in order to examine every aspect of a situation.

REFERENCES

Heddens, J. W., & Speer, W. R. (1995). *Today's mathematics* (8th ed.). Englewood Cliffs, NJ: Prentice-Hall.

Kellough, R. D., Carin, A. A., Seefeldt, C., Barbour, N., & Souviney, R. J. (1996). *Integrating mathematics and science.* Englewood Cliffs, NJ: Prentice-Hall.

National Council of Supervisors of Mathematics. (1989, September). Essential mathematics for the 21st century. *Arithmetic Teacher, 37,* 44–46.

National Council of Teachers of Mathematics. (1989). *Curriculum and evaluation standards for school mathematics.* Reston, VA: NCTM.

Reys, R. E., Suydam, M. N., & Lindquist, M. M. (1995). *Helping children learn mathematics* (4th ed.). Boston: Allyn and Bacon.

Sheffield, L. J., & Cruikshank, D. E. (1996). *Teaching and learning elementary and middle school mathematics* (3rd ed.). Englewood Cliffs, NJ: Prentice-Hall.

Suydam, M. N. (1982, February). Update on research on problem solving: Implications for classroom teaching. *Arithmetic Teacher, 29,* 56–60.

C H A P T E R 9

INTEGRATING THE LANGUAGE ARTS

Many people would place literacy—the ability to read and write—as the preeminent goal of education. Listening, reading, speaking, and writing have long been considered the foundation for the elementary school program. Further, the language arts have been viewed as the vehicle for learning in science, social studies, mathematics, physical education, and the arts. Evidence for the relative status of the language arts can be found in educational history books (remember the 3 Rs—readin', 'ritin', and 'rithmetic) as well as in states' and local school systems' curriculum guides that allocate a considerable block of time to these subjects and skills.

But just as the sacred cow of sequenced, decontextualized skills teaching is being called into question, so too is the idea that first we must teach children how to read, count, and cipher, then move on to writing, and then finally to learning scientific and social studies concepts and methods of inquiry. The four traditionally taught language arts: reading, writing, listening, and speaking, and two recent additions, viewing and visually representing, are now being taught simultaneously in early childhood classrooms because trying to separate the learning and teaching of these closely related skills is an absurd endeavor (Smith, 1977, 1983). Teachers now understand that children do not need to know all the letter names and sounds before they caption their drawings or write a shopping list. Their invented spellings are seen for what they are—a systematic approximation of standard English spelling (Beers & Henderson, 1977; Gentry, 1978).

Whole language advocates use the familiar example of how relatively effortlessly children learn to speak and understand their mother tongues to advocate for authentic teaching and learning in elementary literacy programs. This same metaphor can be used to make a case for teaching children how to read and write *as* we teach the content areas. With this philosophy, the concepts of science and social science become as much the meat and potatoes of our students' literacy diets as stories, nursery rhymes, and riddles once were. In other words, educators now acknowledge that young children want to learn about the natural world and the customs and ways of peoples living both near and far just as keenly as they want to hear *The Tale of Peter Rabbit* and compose their own story about last week's camping trip. Early childhood and elementary teachers also recognize that their students want to learn how to read and write all kinds of texts—not just stories. Happily, there is a plethora of engaging and accurate expository texts about scientific and social studies topics that can be read to or by our youngest schoolchildren. Eric Carle, Joanna Cole, and Dorothy Hinshaw Patent teach scientific concepts through their written texts and their colorful illustrations. Richard Ammon's *Growing Up Amish,* Roxie Munro's *The Inside-Outside Book of Washington, D.C.,* and Nick Merriman's *Early Humans* make social studies content more accessible and interesting to students of all ages.

If language arts instruction is to be authentic, then students must learn to read, write, listen, speak, view, and represent visually by reading, writing, learning, speaking, viewing, and representing visually in meaningful ways. Another important facet of the authenticity that is sought is achieved when children acquire language skills in an integrated way—their mastery of language skills for expression, communication, and understanding print and other media is seamless. For example, the principles of authenticity, responsibility, and independence are achieved when students in a fourth grade classroom read and discuss Christopher Paul Curtis' *The Watsons Go To Birmingham—1963;* write a simulated journal entry about the church bombing from Kenny's, Momma's, or Joetta's point of view; and compare the version in the novel to historical accounts of the bombing of the Sixteenth Avenue Baptist Church on September 15, 1963.

It is important to note that just as writing has taken its rightful place alongside the other language arts, our revised literacy pedagogy considers spelling, grammar, phonics, handwriting, decoding, diction, etc., as means to an end—powerful language use—not as superordinate ends in and of themselves. The language user's tools enable him or her to communicate and it is important to hone these skills in authentic daily use, not through meaningless drills and exercises that are far removed from the ways that people really use language. Thus, fill-in-the-blank verb practice sheets are supplanted by writer's workshop mini-lessons. Spelling list word searches are replaced by pedagogy that encourages students to develop a spelling conscience, the desire to spell correctly, because they are writers who share their work with many different audiences. Reading comprehension inquests are abandoned and literature response groups take their place.

A final vital change in language arts teaching that has taken place in the past 20 years has to do with the texts students read and author. Readers with controlled vocabularies written by reading specialists have been replaced by "real literature" written by trade book authors and poets. Language arts teachers also place a premium on developing their students' appreciation of the literature of various cultures, eras, and genres. The writing and reading of both fiction and nonfiction by even the youngest students are emphasized and children's individual and group choices often determine what is read, written, and viewed.

STANDARDS FOR THE ENGLISH LANGUAGE ARTS

In 1996, The National Council of Teachers of English and the International Reading Association jointly published a set of standards for the language arts. This was a four-year project that sought a great deal of input "from the field"—from K-12 teachers, parents, administrators, researchers, and policymakers. These content standards establish "what students should know and be able to do in the English language arts" (p. 2).

The *Standards* document outlines three core beliefs about the need for standards in the language arts:

- First, we believe that standards are needed to prepare students for the literacy requirements of the future as well as the present. Changes in technology and society have altered and will continue to alter the ways in which we use language to communicate and to think. Students must be prepared to meet these demands.
- Second, we believe that standards can articulate a shared vision of what the nation's teachers, literacy researchers, teacher educators, parents, and others expect students to attain in the English language arts, and what we can do to ensure that this vision is realized.
- Third, we believe that standards are necessary to promote high educational expectations of all students and to bridge the documented disparities that exist in educational opportunities. Standards can help us ensure that all students become informed citizens and participate fully in society. (p. 2, 4)

Before reviewing the 12 standards for the English language arts, the reader should note that three terms have been defined broadly to reflect the importance of technology in today's culture. A *text* refers to printed texts, but also to spoken language, graphics, and technological communications. *Language* embraces written, spoken and visual communication. *Reading* includes three receptive processes: print-reading, listening, and viewing. The 12 standards for language arts are reprinted in Table 9.1.

Standards for the English Language Arts   TABLE 9.1

IRA/NCTE

The vision guiding these standards is that all students must have the opportunities and resources to develop the language skills they need to pursue life's goals and to participate fully as informed, productive members of society. These standards assume that literacy growth begins before children enter school as they experience and experiment with literacy activities—reading and writing, and associating spoken words with their graphic representations. Recognizing this fact, these standards encourage the development of curriculum and instruction that make productive use of the emerging literacy abilities that children bring to school. Furthermore, the standards provide ample room for the innovation and creativity essential to teaching and learning. They are not prescriptions for particular curriculum or instruction.

Although we present these standards as a list, we want to emphasize that they are not distinct and separable; they are, in fact, interrelated and should be considered as a whole.

1. Students read a wide range of print and nonprint texts to build an understanding of texts, of themselves, and of the cultures of the United States and the world; to acquire new information; to respond to the needs and demands of society and the workplace; and for personal fulfillment. Among these texts are fiction and nonfiction, classic and contemporary works.

2. Students read a wide range of literature from many periods in many genres to build an understanding of the many dimensions (e.g., philosophical, ethical, aesthetic) of human experience.

3. Students apply a wide range of strategies to comprehend, interpret, evaluate, and appreciate texts. They draw on their prior experience, their interactions with other readers and writers, their knowledge of word meaning and of other texts, their word identification strategies, and their understanding of textual features (e.g., sound-letter correspondence, sentence structure, context, graphics).

4. Students adjust their use of spoken, written, and visual language (e.g., conventions, style, and vocabulary) to communicate effectively with a variety of audiences and for different purposes.

5. Students employ a wide range of strategies as they write and use different writing process elements appropriately to communicate with different audiences for a variety of purposes.

6. Students apply knowledge of language structure, language conventions (e.g., spelling and punctuation), media techniques, figurative language, and genre to create, critique, and discuss print and nonprint texts.

7. Students conduct research on issues and interests by generating ideas and questions, and by posing problems. They gather, evaluate, and synthesize data from a variety of sources (e.g., print and nonprint texts, artifacts, and people) to communicate their discoveries in ways that suit their purpose and audience.

8. Students use a variety of technological and informational resources (e.g., libraries, databases, computer networks, video) to gather and synthesize information and to create and communicate knowledge.

9. Students develop an understanding of and respect for diversity in language use, patterns, and dialects across cultures, ethnic groups, geographic regions, and social roles.

10. Students whose first language is not English make use of their first language to develop competency in the English language arts and to develop understanding of content across the curriculum.

11. Students participate as knowledgeable, reflective, creative, and critical members of a variety of literacy communities.

12. Students use spoken, written, and visual language to accomplish their own purposes (e.g., for learning, enjoyment, persuasion, and the exchange of information).

LITERATURE'S PLACE IN THE INTEGRATED UNIT

A primary way that students gain information during their integrated unit study is by listening to and reading both informational and fictional texts. As stated earlier, this is a boom time for children's literature. Thousands of titles are in print and most meet high standards of quality for both their illustrations and their written texts. Because a great number of books are available in both hardbound and paperback editions, children's books are not as expensive as they once were. Most elementary teachers are able to stock their classroom libraries with texts purchased with school monies, with book club points, with titles on loan from public or university libraries, and with books they have purchased with their own income or received as gifts. In addition, many teachers procure books from yard sales, book swaps with other teachers, or public library giveaways. During the holidays, some literature-loving teachers ask that parents donate books to the classroom in lieu of personal Yuletide gifts to the teacher. Some parents also routinely order books for their children through school book clubs and order an additional title for the classroom with each order.

One way to maximize instructional time in the elementary classroom is to select the trade books for small group, whole group, and teacher read-alouds carefully. While not every title being used in the classroom at any given time need be related to an integrated unit topic, teaching language arts skills through tradebooks that also relate to unit focus questions, objectives, ideas, and skills makes sense. A teacher might have selected several titles to be used with the Constancy and Change unit and be planning to teach a stand-alone genre study of biographies at the same time. Students also may be reading self-selected texts for their independent reading. Some examples of how to use both fiction and nonfiction with a concept-based unit on Constancy and Change follow.

Using Fiction

Noted children's author Eve Bunting has collaborated with illustrator David Diaz on a book that is a good fit with the Constancy and Change Unit. *Going Home* is a picture book about a farmworker family who takes a car trip to visit their relatives in La Perla, Mexico. The three children were born there but have no memories of the town; they consider the United States to be their home. Carlos, the middle child between two sisters aged 10 and 5, is the narrator. Through his eyes, readers note many changes and also what stays the same. When the family crosses the border into Mexico Carlos says, "I see no difference, but Mama does. Mama exclaims, 'Mexico! Mexico!' and blows kisses at the sun-filled winter sky."

The four days and nights traveling and sleeping in the car seem interchangeable to the children, just as the towns they pass appear to be carbon copies of each other. During their visit with Grandfather and Aunt Ana in La Perla, the children realize that their parents' town has not changed much since they left, but their family has changed. The two older children, Dolores and Carlo, also come to understand why their parents initiated such a big change in their lives by immigrating to the United States. Though the family must work hard as farmworkers in the United States, just as they labored in their home country of Mexico, the United States provides opportunities. As Papa says in answer to the question "Why did you ever leave?"—"There is not work in La Perla. We are here for the opportunities."

During the literature study that is a vital part of the Constancy and Change unit, the five focus questions guide the students' understanding of the texts. The five questions are:

1. Is something different?
2. What is changing or has changed?
3. What caused the change?
4. How much does the change cost? (This question can be answered in emotional, social, physical, financial, or environmental terms.)
5. Is the change worth what it costs?

Several prereading activities that emphasize readers' making their own unique responses to literature lend themselves to the reading of *Going Home*. The Directed Reading-Thinking Activity (Stauffer, 1969), a guided reading method that encourages students to make predictions about the text; to read to confirm, disprove, or revise these predictions; and to repeat this process as the text is read and discussed with other readers, can be used with this book. Another strategy that jump-starts students' thinking about the issues raised in a piece of literature is the Contrast Chart (Yopp & Yopp, 1996). Figure 9.1 shows a contrast chart that could be used with *Going Home*. The Contrast Chart can be completed by the whole group, small groups, or individuals *before* the text is read, with whole group sharing and discussion following the small group or individual completion of the chart. After the students read the text, they revisit their charts, commenting on what they could add now that they have read *Going Home*. Points of agreement and disagreement between the story characters' views and the class members' opinions also can be noted.

Anticipation Guides (Readence, Bean, & Baldwin, 1981; Wiesendanger, 1985) also are useful tools for getting students to explore their attitudes, opinions, and beliefs. The guide is filled out before the reading and

FIGURE 9.1   **Contrast Chart**

Contrast Chart for *Going Home*

Good Things About Moving	Bad Things About Moving
1.	1.
2.	2.
3.	3.
4.	4.
5.	5.

reexamined after the reading. Students should be encouraged to tell why they made the response that they did during the initial discussion. Does their response come from direct experience, what they have read or seen, or what they have heard others say? The teacher writes the anticipation guide, selecting three to five declarative statements that will spark discussion about differences of opinion. Yopp and Yopp (1996) outline five steps for designing an anticipation guide:

1. Identify themes in the written work.
2. Write three to five declarative statements that relate to the piece and are likely to provoke discussion.
3. Present the statements via the chalkboard, the overhead projector, or a handout.
4. Give students time to record their agreement or disagreement with the statement.
5. Lead a discussion of how the students responded and why. Stress that differences of opinion are to be expected.

Figure 9.2 shows an Anticipation Guide for *Going Home*. After the reading of the text, students often revise their answers. The text itself and the varying views of their fellow readers have informed the individual's understanding of the issues addressed by the text.

Journaling has become a familiar tool for teachers when they seek a reader's response. The double-entry journal (Berthoff, 1981; Barone, 1990)

Anticipation Guide FIGURE 9.2

Anticipation Guide for *Going Home*

Agree	Disagree	
_____	_____	1. Most people who leave Mexico to live in the United States do this to make more money.
_____	_____	2. Once people leave their home towns in another country, they usually don't return to live there.
_____	_____	3. Farmworkers have a hard life.
_____	_____	4. People who live in the United States should be made to speak English.

allows readers to select particularly meaningful or memorable quotes from the text they are reading that they would like to address in writing. The student transcribes the quote in a column on the left-hand side of the page. Directly across from the quote the reader writes her reaction to what the author has written. Figure 9.3 illustrates a double-entry journal response completed by a fourth grader after reading *Going Home*. The students were encouraged to select passages that demonstrated constancy or change in the story.

Venn diagrams and book charts are just two of several ways that students can compare two different texts. Figure 9.4 shows a book chart comparing two books that deal with moving to a new country and the conflicting feelings that arise. Allen Say's book, *Grandfather's Journey,* tells of the Japanese American narrator's grandfather and his move to the United States from Japan. Both *Grandfather's Journey* and *Going Home* are excellent texts for the Constancy and Change Unit or a social studies oriented unit that deals with immigration.

Double-Entry Journal FIGURE 9.3

Double-Entry Journal for *Going Home*

Quote	Response
"Mama looks so young and beautiful. And Papa . . . so handsome. She has forgotten about her sore shoulders," I say. "And he's forgotten about his bad knees," Dolores adds.	Mama and Papa seem like they were young again. Like when they met before they were married. It's like they are going back in time.
"Imagine Consuelo! Your son—and all your children—speaking English. So smart!"	This is a way the family has changed. The children are speaking English even though Mama and Papa can't. The kids speak Spanish, too, so they know two languages.

FIGURE 9.4   **Book Chart**

Title	Author	Narrator	Lessons
Going Home	Eve Bunting	Carlos	The U.S. is a land of opportunities for many people from other countries.
			People miss the land they were born in.
			Sometimes you have to sacrifice to make a better life.
			Moving can be both good and bad.
			Some people and places change more quickly than others.
Grandfather's Journey	Allen Say	grandson	People miss the land they were born in.
			Moving can be both good and bad.
			War creates big changes.
			Young men and women often leave home for adventure.
			Some people and places change more quickly than others.

Using Nonfiction

Just as there are many different social studies and science topics that can be explored in the Constancy and Change unit, there are scores of nonfiction reading materials that can inform the study of these topics. Magazines such as *Ranger Rick, World, National Geographic, The Weekly Reader,* and others provide information about natural changes, changes created by people, and current events. There are also scores of informational books available to children that contain accurate factual content in the form of illustrations, charts, graphs, diagrams, maps, and of course, texts.

One such text is written by Malcolm Penny and illustrated by Vanda Baginska. Part of The Animal Kingdom series published by Bookwright Press, *Animal Migration,* is a very attractive text with detailed illustrations of animals and their habitats, maps showing migratory routes, a glossary, a list of other books about migration, and the names and addresses of several wildlife foundations. Reading the one- and two-page chapters provides the following answers to the unit's focus questions when applied to animal migration.

1. Is something different?
   Yes.

2. What is changing or has changed?
   Insects, birds, fish and mammals have migrated or moved as a group from one place to another because of changing conditions in their environments. Most migrations are seasonal, but some are daily.

3. What caused the change?

There are five major reasons for migration in the animal world:

Movement in response to dry or wet conditions.

(zebras, gazelles)

Movement in response to changing air and/or water temperatures.

(whales, Arctic tern)

Movement toward and away from breeding grounds.

(salmon, eels, seals)

Movement to find food.

(tuna, wildebeest)

Movement toward or away from sunlight.

(small ocean animals living in plankton)

4. How much does the change cost? (This question can be answered in emotional, social, physical, financial, or environmental terms.)

   Some animals die during migration. They might be separated from their group and lose their way, they might become prey, they might die from disease, they might starve, or they may be caught and killed by humans. Migration is the costliest for the least-fit animals that make the trip.

5. Is the change worth what it costs?

   Yes. The animals that migrate do so in order to survive. They move to find food, to perpetuate the species through breeding, to escape predators, and to experience more tolerable living conditions.

As with the fiction that was discussed above, there are many prereading, during-reading, and postreading strategies that the teacher can use with her students when reading and responding to nonfiction literature. Some of the strategies that work well with nonfiction are listed below:

Prereading, During-Reading, Postreading

anticipation guide	double-entry journal	Venn diagram
contrast chart	DRTA (Directed Reading Thinking Activity)	book chart
K-W-L	note-taking	summarizing
questionnaire	webbing of information	response journal
semantic maps	DRA (Directed Reading Activity)	story map
word wonder	RRL (Reconciled Reading Lesson)	story frames/grids
semantic feature analysis	Gipe's cluing technique	predict-o-gram

THE WRITING PROCESS

The area of writing represents the language art that has probably been most changed by current views of language learning and teaching. That is, the teaching of writing in today's elementary classrooms is very different from the approach to writing that most students experienced 20 years ago. Much of this change has come about as a result of the work of the National Writing Project, which was established in the early 1970s in Berkeley, California. The research of Donald Graves, whose influential book, *Writing: Teachers and Children at Work,* was first published in 1983, made "The Writing Process" a schoolroom word, if not a household one. Lucy Calkins, Nancie Atwell, Ken and Yetta Goodman, Regie Routman, and many others have published books and articles that helped classroom teachers become teachers of writing—a difficult undertaking when most of the nation's teachers had been victims of very questionable writing pedagogy themselves.

The following paragraphs describe how the teaching of writing can be easily integrated with the teaching of the concepts, generalizations, process skills, and values in the Constancy and Change Unit described in chapter 1. The first writing assignment asks fourth grade students to think about the ways they have changed in the past three to four years.

Writing an "I Used to Be . . . , But Now" Poem

One of the generalizations in the Constancy and Change Unit is that our viewpoints change over time. Children can understand this better by taking a look backward at their own lives and the way they used to be. In his classic book about teaching poetry to elementary students, *Wishes, Lies, and Dreams* (1970), Kenneth Koch describes the "I Used to Be . . . , But Now" poems he wrote with New York City students. This idea forms the nucleus of the writing process lesson plan below.

Prewriting Activities

The teacher might begin this extended lesson with a homework assignment: bring in pictures of yourself when you were three, four, five, or six years old. Students also might be asked to bring in an artifact linked to their pasts—a baby blanket, a favorite stuffed animal, or the first book a child read independently. The students then gather around to share their pictures and objects and to talk about their memories of being younger. To close the sharing session, the teacher asks, "How have you changed since you were little? How have you stayed the same?" Students answer these questions one at a time to a partner and then with the whole group.

A second prewriting activity is the completion of the Then/Now Chart. (Figure 9.5 shows one that was completed by a fourth-grade student.) After reminding students of the sharing session and discussion that took place earlier, the teacher cites examples of some of the ways that they said they had changed over the past few years. She emphasizes that some of their ideas and beliefs have changed. Marty thought that if one person was taller

Now/Then Chart

FIGURE 9.5

	Then	Now
Emotions/Fears	afraid of the dark—light in hall and night light	just hallway light while falling to sleep
	afraid to ride the bus	bus is OK but too noisy
	looked up to older brother	hate older brother
Ideas/Beliefs	thought you picked out new baby at the hospital	know where babies come from
	thought you could write as many checks as you want without having money in the bank	know how checks work
Behaviors	sucked my thumb	don't suck thumb—braces
	never ate vegetables except corn	eat beans, broccoli, salads

than another was, that always meant that they were older too. Some of their feelings have shifted also. Some students used to be afraid of the water or heights. Their behaviors have been transformed too. Several students used to suck their thumbs. Some used to be terrible soccer players but now they are good at this sport. The students then are directed to the Then/Now Chart and the teacher models how to fill in each of the six boxes. This chart becomes a text that will help them get started on their poems.

Drafting

The drafting stage of the writing process begins with the students' being introduced to the form they will write—the "I Used to . . . , But Then" poem. The teacher selects a few of the poems written by Koch's students to read aloud and welcomes the students' open-ended comments. The teacher also might share her completed Then/Now Chart and the first few lines of her "I Used to . . ." poem. The students then begin drafting their poems, referring to their charts. They are encouraged to add ideas that might come to them during the process of writing that are not on the charts because putting words on paper often triggers fresh memories. In *Turning Memories into Memoirs: A Handbook for Writing Lifestories,* Denis Ledoux attests, "Like water pouring from a hand pump that has been primed, memories will begin to flow once you prime them with writing. As you write, from somewhere in your mind you may have thought you had no access to, memories will come to you. The more you write, the more you will remember" (p. 44).

Revising

Students may make some minor revisions during their first drafting session, but it is wise to put these pieces away for a day or two before the first serious attempt at revision. The writing needs to get cold before the writer can get a fresh look at it. This new view will help the writer know what sounds good and what doesn't, what is clear or unclear, what needs to be added and what should be deleted. Reading the poems aloud to themselves is encouraged so that the students can hear the word choice and rhythms of the poem. This is an unrhymed form, but during this revision session, students can be persuaded to add other tricks of the poet's trade: alliteration, assonance, internal rhyme, metaphor, simile, etc.

Often as students revise their pieces, they also edit glaring errors—missing words, repeated words, omitted punctuation, misspellings, and the like. Students and teachers need to be reminded that writing is a recursive process; the writer moves forward from stage to stage but also leaps ahead and steps backward according to his desires and needs (Smith, 1981). After the first revision by the writer, students may share the piece with a peer and get comments regarding revision. A peer can let the writer know what he understood from the piece and what questions he has. The questions may come from unclear phrases or what was not said. The piece may then move on to a teacher revision conference where the teacher conveys what he understood the poem to say and what he wonders about.

Throughout the revision stage, the writer may or may not be making the changes that peer and teacher comments suggest; the writer is in charge and decides what to change and what to keep the same. Students who are motivated to polish a piece will revise their poems more than once and may seek more than one round of feedback from peers and the teacher. An advantage of poetry writing is that because the form is brief, revision is not a laborious task. Well-timed and well-chosen mini lessons given by the teacher on using vivid verbs, similes, and internal rhyme should help motivate even the most reluctant poets to "resee" their first drafts. The teacher also might share some revisions she has made to her poem. For example, the line "I used to interrupt people all of the time, but now I try hard to wait my turn to speak" might have been replaced with "I used to explode with questions in the middle of someone's story, but now I patiently wait my turn to speak—like a customer at the Wendy's drive-through."

Even though some students appear to make only minimal, superficial revisions to their texts, they may be storing the constructive feedback they received from peers, teachers, and parents to be used in subsequent drafting and revising sessions. As student writers mature and log more hours in the writer's workshop, they will revise more during the drafting and revision stages. Teachers need to be aware of the fact that some of their students' revisions will be invisible because they occur in the writers' heads as they write.

Editing

Editing is the stage of the writing process when the writer turns to issues of form and tries to correct grammar, spelling, and punctuation. Some fourth-grade students possess the language and reference skills to make their "I Used to . . . , But Now" poems letter-perfect. Other students should be asked to correct the errors that they can detect and make right, with the piece going to a final edit by the teacher. Students are overwhelmed when they are asked to correct *every* error, even though they cannot find every error. A second-year foreign language student would not be expected to write a composition in that language and revise and edit it until it is 100% correct. Likewise, it is too great a task for some emerging writers to edit and correct their pieces completely. Students can be paired with more able students for a buddy edit and then the piece can go to the teacher who can sit with each student and go over the errors that remain. Thus each student receives valuable skills instruction that is individualized to her needs.

Sharing/Publishing

A preliminary sharing of the poem has taken place already during the revision and editing stages. A sharing of the finished product takes many forms with this particular piece. Within the fourth-grade classroom, students share their poems in a read-around from the Author's Chair. The polished poems also are collected in a class book, that is subsequently shared with several kindergarten and first grade classrooms. Pairs of fourth-grade students sign up to take the collected "I Used to Be . . . , But Now" poems to classrooms where they take turns reading the poems aloud to younger students who can identify with the older students' fears, beliefs, and actions.

Writing a Lab Report

One of the science experiments in the Constancy and Change Unit focuses on cooling. The completion of this experiment requires students to use several process skills to come to the conclusion that cooling represents a common way that things change. Through this experiment, students also should recognize another example of the value that both constancy and change are to be expected because they are an integral part of life.

The writing process can and should be integrated into the writing of a laboratory report. The ability to accurately state a hypothesis, report a procedure, record the data collected, communicate the results, and form and convey the conclusions that can be drawn from the results are important skills for elementary students to master. The following is an illustration of how the scientific method and the writing process go hand-in-hand during the completion of the cooling experiment from the Constancy and Change Unit.

Prewriting

When the writing task is a lab report, the prewriting activities are completed with a lab partner. Together the students form a hypothesis, conduct the experiment, discuss the procedures and findings, and record the data. Thus the experience of conducting the experiment, the discussion of it throughout the sequence of procedures, and the accurate recording of the hypothesis and the data constitute the prewriting phase of the writing process. It is no less true in the area of scientific writing than in narrative writing that writers should write from experience. In this instance, "doing science" readies the students for communicating as scientists through the lab report. From this experience and many others, they learn that the better they are at observing, classifying, interpreting, finding patterns and relationships, predicting, questioning, and critical thinking, the more able writers they will become.

Drafting

When students draft their lab reports about this particular experiment, they use the partially completed form shown in Figure 9.6. As with the poem they wrote about the way that they have changed as they have grown, the first draft is one that will be reworked before it is recopied and handed in for a grade. Each lab pair is responsible for writing their hypothesis, procedures, results, and conclusions and for also turning in their Data Sheet (Figure 9.7) on which the results and conclusions sections are based. Before they conduct the experiment, the teacher presents models of other lab reports so students know what scientific writing sounds and looks like. The teacher also might show some examples of poorly written hypotheses, procedures, results, and conclusions—ones that confuse because they are vague, incomplete, or tainted by unscientific terms, opinions, and/or unfounded conclusions. Because the students will be writing in pairs, one person might act as recorder, but both should help decide what is put on paper.

FIGURE 9.6   **Lab Report of Cooling Experiment**

HYPOTHESIS: The best insulator will be cotton, then paper, then polyester.

PROCEDURE: We microwaved a one-quart container of water for 60 seconds. We then stirred the water and poured one cup of water into each of three identical glasses. One glass was wrapped with paper towel, one with cotton batting, and one with polyester cloth. We recorded the temperature of the water right after we poured it, one hour later, two hours later, three hours later, and four hours later. We took our measurements with the same thermometer.

RESULTS:

CONCLUSIONS:

Data Sheet for Cooling Experiment

FIGURE 9.7

Times	Paper	Cotton	Polyester
9:44 A.M.			
10:45 A.M.			
11:50 A.M.			
12:45 P.M.			
1:43 P.M.			

Revising

Again, revision should be delayed for a day or more after the drafting. The teacher might conduct a mini-lesson on this second day that demonstrates common mistakes students make in writing lab reports. This mini-lesson will be more relevant now that the students have drafted a lab report on their own. After the mini-lesson, one partner might read the lab report aloud to the other, asking for input about how it sounds. Attention is focused on order of information, completeness of information, clarity, a match between the data and the results and conclusions sections, and so on. The teacher might prepare a checklist (Figure 9.8) that the students can use in their revision conference to be sure that their draft is complete and conforms to the expectations for the assignment.

Cooling Experiment Checklist

FIGURE 9.8

Names _____ Date _____

Students' Check Teacher's Check

1. Filled out Data Sheet accurately and neatly. _____ _____
2. Hypothesis clearly states what the scientists predict will occur—how the materials will perform as insulators. _____ _____
3. The Procedure section clearly explains what the scientists did to conduct the experiment. _____ _____
4. The scientists' efforts to control the variables can be seen in the Procedure section. _____ _____
5. The Results section explains in paragraph form the *same* results found on the data sheet. _____ _____
6. The Results section is factual, clearly stated, and brief. _____ _____
7. The Conclusions section begins with a statement about whether the hypothesis was confirmed or not confirmed. _____ _____
8. The Conclusions section gives possible explanations of **why** the results are what they are. _____ _____
9. The Conclusions section tells ways the experiment could be improved or suggests further research. _____ _____

Editing

As explained earlier in describing the poetry lesson, students edit their own pieces, trade with someone else and edit each other's pieces, and then forward their writing to the teacher for a teacher edit. Because students worked in pairs on the lab report, two pairs of eyes have already checked each part of the lab report.

One editing technique that many teachers use, which also helps their students to develop their spelling and dictionary skills, involves asking students to underline words that they think are misspelled in their own piece or a peer's piece. The teacher also underlines words that are misspelled when she completes the teacher edit. Then it is the writer's job to go to the dictionary or to an alphabetized word list to check the correct spellings of the underlined words. The student makes the corrections and also may write these words down in an individual, self-made spelling dictionary. This method replaces a widely used and quicker method—the peer or the teacher writes the correct spelling on the writer's piece. But this quick-and-dirty way of editing for spelling does not challenge writers to become better spellers. The opposite occurs when young writers quickly learn that they need not work at approximating the correct spellings as best they can; the teacher or another student will spell for them.

Sharing/Publishing

Most lab reports are handed to the teacher with only the writer's having seen it. Often, the reports are graded and returned to the students who jam it into their notebooks or folders. The lab report never sees the light of day again. It makes more sense for emerging scientists to share their reports in small or large groups. Routinely sharing writing with someone other than the teacher makes students take more pride and care in their writing as they compose, revise, and edit. When they hear what their peers have written in response to the same or a similar assignment, students' exposure to all levels, types, and topics of writing is expanded (Britton, Burgess, Martin, McLeod, & Rosen, 1975). Many authors suggest that the writing of peers, rather than the writing of adults, shows students both where they have been, developmentally, in their writing and where they will go. The Cooling Experiment Lab Reports also might be displayed in the classroom, the science room, the library, or some other area where parents, teachers, volunteers, and other students may examine the results. The reports might appear on a bulletin board with the caption, "Which is the best insulator: cotton, paper, or polyester?" Photographs of the lab-in-progress could be displayed.

THE LANGUAGE ARTS AND THE SIX TYPES OF INTEGRATED UNITS

The skills and content taught in the language arts curriculum can be readily taught via integrated units, as Figure 9.9 and the following text illustrate.

Concept-Focused Units

Many of the examples of language arts lessons and activities cited in this chapter relate to a concept-focused unit on constancy and change. Integrated units of this type also may concentrate on language arts curriculum—a genre, an author, or a specific piece of literature may be at the center of a concept-focused unit. The content areas of social studies, science, math and the arts can be integrated as appropriate with these core topics. For example, a genre study of myths may include a study of the myth-creators whether they are Native Americans, Greeks, or Nordic peoples. Jane Yolen's novel, *The Devil's Arithmetic,* may lead to a study of World War II, Adolf Hitler, the Holocaust, Jewish culture (customs, holidays, arts, language), German language, or related literature.

Overview of Types of Integrated Units With Language Arts Examples   FIGURE 9.9

Type of Unit	Description	Language Arts Example
Concept-focused	Unit designed around teaching one or a few major concepts	Studying Native American myths
Process Skills–focused	Unit designed around teaching one or a few major process skills with less emphasis on content	Developing surveys to learn about peers' fiction preferences so that students may have input into new book acquisitions
Content and Process Skills–focused	Unit designed around teaching nearly equal amounts of content and process skills	Developing interviewing skills to obtain information for a persuasive essay about immigration policies in the United States
Issue-focused	Unit designed around investigating an issue though research and data collection	Composing a photo essay about the prevalence of eating disorders
Project-focused	Unit designed around solving a problem or exploring an alternative	Authoring poetry anthologies to help younger students refine their reading skills and their understanding of insects
Case Study–focused	Unit designed around doing something on a local level based on a topic investigated	Writing a teachers' guide to avoiding sexism in the classroom to be piloted in local schools

Process Skills–Focused Units

Since thinking and language skills are so closely intertwined, there is considerable overlap between the process skills listed in Table 2.1 and the skills areas of the language arts curriculum. A process skills–focused unit that features communication skills would be a good integrated unit to initiate at the beginning of the school year. The teacher emphasizes that the students will be developing and refining their communications skills all year long as they study and learn together. In order to cultivate a classroom environment that will nurture this community of learners, the teacher needs to teach the proper way for students to communicate with each other, whether it be about their writing, their science survey instruments, their oral reports about the Constitutional Convention, or their original numeric systems.

One objective in this process skill-focused unit might be to compare and contrast communications today with communications at the turn of this century. Researching and observational skills come into play as students record the various types of written and spoken communications used in the past and currently. Figure 9.10 shows one student's first efforts at completing a contrast

FIGURE 9.10   **Student Compare and Contrast Chart**

	Communications Today	Communications 100 Years Ago
WRITTEN	letters	letters
	books	books
	newspapers	newspapers
	magazines	
	word processed texts	
WRITTEN AND SENT A DISTANCE	fax machine	telegraph
	regular mail (truck, car, train)	pony express
	air mail	
	electronic mail	
	Internet	
	U.S. Postal Service, UPS, Federal Express	
SPOKEN	human voice	human voice
	tape recordings	
	compact discs	
SPOKEN AND SENT A DISTANCE	telephone	
	cellular phone	
	radio	
	television	

chart that highlights different types of communications as well as how they have changed in this century.

A process skills–focused unit might concentrate on a single process skill such as surveying a population about their knowledge, opinions, or behaviors. This data gathering skill could be taught and applied to many language arts projects. Second-grade students might develop a questionnaire to learn about their classmates' favorite authors. Fifth-grade students might probe their peers and their parents' opinions about censorship of young adult fiction. Another survey might be aimed at seeing if the average amount of weekly television viewing affects the amount of time students read at home.

Content and Process Skills–Focused Units

This type of integrated unit is a hybrid—a review of this type of unit's objectives reveals that content and process skills are equally important. Chapter 6 presented a unit on diversity as a good example of a content and process skills–focused unit. In the area of language arts, an integrated unit on diversity could tap a wealth of fiction and nonfiction in picture books, historical fiction, biography, and young adult fiction. The concepts webbed in Chapter 6, on social studies: conflict, conformity, culture, ethnic heritage, gender, race, and stereotyping, also make excellent discussion points in a literature-based study of diversity. Communication skills (writing, discussing), data processing skills (finding patterns, predicting, finding relationships), and thinking skills (critical thinking, reflective thinking) are the key process skills to be developed in such an integrated unit.

Violent conflict, racism, and stereotyping are three concepts addressed in *Smoky Night,* a Caldecott Award–winning book by Eve Bunting and illustrator, David Diaz. This picture book deals with one boy's experience of the Los Angeles riots that took place in the aftermath of the Rodney King trial. While Daniel and his mother are victims of the mayhem that occurs in their neighborhood, Daniel's mother comes to see that she has stereotyped Mrs. Kim, a Korean neighbor and owner of a local market. Mrs. Kim is equally guilty of intolerance that gives way to mutual understanding when the two women get to know each other. An in-depth discussion of the characters, plot, points of conflict, themes, and the thought provoking painting and collages could lead to several different types of writing.

Issue-Focused Units

Issue-focused units investigate a relevant issue through both research and data collection. One long-term project that could be a central vehicle for meeting the goals of an issues-focused unit is the photo essay. This activity—which teaches question raising, researching, reporting, critical and reflective thinking, as well as surveying skills—was developed by a sixth grade teacher and reported in *Writing Teacher* (McClelland & Mason, 1995). The goals of the photo essay are to identify a problem or issue of interest, to research both the problem and some possible solutions to it, and to compose a photo essay—photographs and text that illuminate the issue that was selected. Figure 9.11 displays the steps students take to complete this research project that captures their interest and engages them in a way that more traditional assignments do not.

Project-Focused and Case Study–Focused Units

These two types of units might be a natural outgrowth of the photo essay research/writing project described above. The student who explores the dangers of smoking by pregnant mothers might develop an education program for teenaged mothers in the community. The student whose photo essay dealt with censorship of books in middle and high school libraries might work on establishing a local committee that would then develop guidelines for inclusion or exclusion of books from school libraries. The

FIGURE 9.11   Photo Essay Questions

Beginning draft of student's contrast chart on communication might spawn these questions:

How do children get money? How do they spend money? How much allowance do most sixth graders get?

1. Choose one topic by using the criteria questions:
   Can I find information on this topic?
   Can I locate people to interview about this topic?
   Will I be able to take pictures that illustrate this topic?
   Am I interested enough in this topic to study it for the next nine weeks?
   Will my parents approve of this topic?

2. Develop guidance questions (questions beginning with the words what, where, who, how when, and why).

3. Conduct research using packaged information (periodicals, books, reference books, videos, etc.), people (students interview "experts"), and the world (students conduct experiments, administer surveys, gather information, and take photographs).

4. Learn how to take notes, use library, make bibliography cards, create endnotes, develop survey and interview questions from teacher mini-lessons.

5. Organize notes according to guidance questions.

6. Order notes and develop outline.

7. Draft the text.

8. Develop the photo list and take photographs.

9. Revise.

10. Edit.

11. Write the final draft.

12. Prepare oral presentation including a product (game, refrigerator magnet, video, model, poster, graph, etc.).

individual who investigated sexism might design a teachers' guide to avoiding sexism in the classroom that would then be piloted in several schools.

The value of student-centered inquiry and action need not be belabored. When students become part of a community of questioners, researchers, data gatherers, writers, problem solvers, and communicators they are empowered to not only excel in school, but in life. Issue-focused units, project-focused units, and case study–focused units can help teachers provide instruction that will set their students on this path.

SUMMARY

Students of all ages develop and refine their abilities in the language arts *in action*—as they use these skills both inside and outside of school. Current pedagogy, which includes integrated unit teaching, facilitates students' mastery of the language arts *as* they learn in the content areas of math, science, and social studies. Children's natural curiosity about the world of nature and people is acknowledged when teachers conduct integrated studies that expose students to all kinds of texts, teach them to write everything from lists to biographies to lab reports to poems, and help them master the tools of language arts learning—spelling, grammar, phonics, handwriting—in meaningful, applied contexts. If all students are to be prepared to meet the literacy requirements of today's world and the future, language arts instruction must conform to the consensus among researchers, teachers, policy makers, and administrators about what students should know and be able to do in the area of literacy. Integrated unit teaching can both help teachers to maximize their teaching time and to take advantage of the way students learn best—in an integrated, hands-on, minds-on fashion.

REFERENCES

Barone, D. (1990). The written responses of young children: Beyond comprehension to story understanding. *The New Advocate, 3,* 49–56.

Beers, J. W., & Henderson, E. H. (1977). A study of developing orthographic concepts among first graders. *Research in the Teaching of English, 11,* 133–148.

Britton, J., Burgess, T., Martin, N., McLeod, A., & Rosen, H. (1975). *The development of writing ability* (pp.11–18). London: Schools Council Publications.

Gentry, J. R. (1978). Early spelling strategies. *Elementary School Journal, 79,* 88–92.

Koch, K. (1970). *Wishes, lies, and dreams.* New York: Random House.

Kuzmeskus, J. (Ed.). *We teach them all: Teachers writing about diversity.* York, ME: Stenhouse.

Ledoux, D. (1993). *Turning memories into memoirs: A handbook for writing lifestories.* Lisbon Falls, ME: Soleil Press.

McClelland, S. M., & Mason, D. (1995). The photo essay. *Writing Teacher, 8,* 14–17.

National Council of Teachers of English & International Reading Association. (1996). *Standards for the English language arts.* Urbana, IL: Author.

New Zealand Ministry of Education. (1992). *Dancing with the pen: The learner as a writer.* Wellington, New Zealand: Learning Media Limited.

Readence, J., Bean, T., & Baldwin, R. (1981). *Content area reading: An integrated approach.* Dubuque, IA: Kendall/Hunt.

Smith, F. (1983). *Essays into literacy.* Portsmouth, NH: Heinemann.

Smith, F. (1981). Myths of writing. *Language Arts, 58,* 792–798.

Smith, F. (1977). The uses of language. *Language Arts, 54,* 638–644.

Stauffer, R. G. (1969). *Teaching reading as a thinking process.* New York: Harper & Row.

Tompkins, G., & Hoskisson, K. (1995). *Language arts: Content and teaching strategies* (3rd ed.). Englewood Cliffs, NJ: Merrill.

Wiesendanger, K. D. (1985). Comprehension: Using anticipation guides. *The Reading Teacher, 39,* 241–242.

Yopp, H. Y., & Yopp, R. H. (1996). *Literature-based reading activities* (2nd ed.). Boston: Allyn & Bacon.

CHILDREN'S BOOKS

Ammon, Richard. (1989). *Growing up Amish.* : Atheneum.

Bunting, Eve. (1996). *Going home.* New York: Harper Collins.

Bunting, Eve. (1994). *Smoky Night.* San Diego: Harcourt Brace and Company.

Curtis, Christopher Paul. (1995). *The Watsons go to Birmingham—1963.* New York: Bantam Doubleday Dell.

Merriman, Nick. (1989). *Early humans.* : Knopf.

Munro, Roxie. (1987). *The inside-outside book of Washington, DC:* Dutton.

Penny, Malcolm. (1987). *Animal Migration.* New York: Bookwright Press.

Say, Allen. (1993). *Grandfather's Journey.* Boston: Houghton Mifflin.

CHAPTER

INTEGRATING ART AND CREATIVITY INTO A THEMATIC UNIT

THE CHANGING PURPOSE OF ART EDUCATION

Historically, art education became a part of the American curriculum in response to four main strands of cultural influences that have their roots in the industrial revolution (Freedman, 1987). Drafting and art design skills first were taught to satisfy the labor needs of the 1870s industrial market. Students were trained to reproduce traditional design patterns and pleasing decorative motifs for mass-produced manufactured goods. Secondly, art was considered to be a means of transmitting cultural heritage and an appropriate leisure time activity for the middle class. Middle-class parents wanted their children to attain the upper class's "good life." Good living involved the acquisition of culture—refinement, aesthetic sensibility, and higher learning evidenced by the study and collection of art objects. Infusion of moral standards and character education through the study of religious, uplifting, or morally instructive works of art was conceived as a third purpose of art education. This occurred in response to the large urban population of immigrant children who were to be taught to adopt the new values of industrial labor: loyalty, thrift, obedience, punctuality, and family responsibility. A final strand viewed art as healthful and creative self-expression. This movement toward individualism and autonomy was a response to mechanistic production's threat of anonymity. The psychological benefits for children in creative art production were recognized. Art education was to provide a release from the pressures of contemporary society through creative self-expression. These four strands have interacted to produce each generation's concept of the purpose of art education.

More recently, two other aspects of art education have been emphasized: higher-level thinking skills and multicultural appreciation. The increasing level of cultural diversity in America has precipitated another movement in education reform that began in the early 1980s and continues today. Old educational tenets are being re-examined and replaced by new and expanded definitions of cognition. The trend is away from teaching facts and toward higher order thinking skills such as analysis, synthesis, and critical thinking. Thinking and knowing is now viewed as being much broader than verbal and mathematical skills. Howard Gardner's (1983) model of multiple human intelligences outlines seven different ways of knowing and thinking: linguistic, musical, logical-mathematical, spatial, bodily kinesthetic, intrapersonal, and interpersonal. This broader idea of what comprises the human intellect calls for a redesign of the curriculum and of teaching methods. The existing general educational curriculum is compartmentalized and fragmented without significant bridges from one subject area to another. An integration of subject areas with student experiences that foster higher order thinking skills and make learning relevant is crucial. The type of thinking and problem solving that occurs when people have in-depth experiences with the arts can provide linkages between different areas of the curriculum. By including aesthetics, art criticism and art history, art education personalizes and reinforces social studies, literature, science, and mathematics, making these subjects significantly more relevant to students. Analysis, synthesis, evaluation, response, appreciation, and production of art tap higher level thinking skills that are important for all students, not just those gifted in the arts. These critical thinking skills allow students to sift through the numerous alternatives of contemporary society and become responsible decision-making citizens (Dunn, 1995).

Art education can provide a way of learning about cultural values and beliefs that will help dispel cultural misconceptions and foster cross-cultural acceptance and understanding. America consists of a highly complex array of ethnic groups, each with its own cultural universe of moral, aesthetic, intellectual, attitudinal, and behavioral characteristics. These ethnic children need to acquire the knowledge, attitudes, and skills to function effectively in the mainstream culture. At the same time, the values, perspectives, and cultures of these ethnic groups can enrich the national culture. A school environment that validates their cultures and a curriculum that reflects the heritage, perspectives and histories of ethnic groups will result in higher levels of achievement for these students (National Arts Education Research Center, 1989).

ART EDUCATION GOALS

The goals of art education have evolved in reaction to the changing needs of society. In response to *Goals 2000: Educate America,* which states what all students are expected to achieve in basic subjects including the arts, many state and national groups have re-examined the curriculum and set up new goals for art education. Table 10.1 shows a list of thirteen themes that appear again and again in the goals of various authors and educational curriculum reform groups (Carey and others, 1995; Dunn, 1995; Maryland State Department Education, 1990; National Arts Education Research Center, 1989; Chapman, 1985).

Art Education Goals	**TABLE 10.1**

Beauty Appreciation—develop an understanding of the aesthetic qualities that exist in both natural and human-made environments.

Communication—develop an understanding of how visual art is created in response to images, forms, and experiences.

Human History—develop knowledge of art in the past and present, recognizing art as a basic aspect of human experience.

Cultural Expression—develop an understanding of the relationships among works of art, individuals, and the societies in which they were created.

Artistic Processes—develop concepts necessary for understanding and producing art: basic elements, design principles.

Techniques—develop skills and techniques (including safety awareness) necessary to producing art in different media: drawing, painting, printmaking, sculpture, folk crafts.

Motor Skills—development of fine and gross motor skills, and the coordination skills for manipulating art tools and materials.

Visual Skills—develop visual perception skills and spatial ability.

Critical Thinking—develop higher-level thinking skills for appreciating, evaluating, communicating about art.

Creativity—develop creative thinking skills such as fluency, flexibility, originality, elaboration, and analogy while producing and analyzing art.

Connections—develop an understanding of art linkages between curriculum areas and everyday life.

Personal Expression—Develop positive attitudes about self, others, and art.

Career Development—Develop awareness of art as an avocation and a profession.

THE NATIONAL STANDARDS FOR VISUAL ARTS EDUCATION

The *Goals 2000: Educate America Act* acknowledged that the arts are a core subject as important to education as mathematics, science, history, English, or geography. Title II of the Act establishes a National Education Standards

TABLE 10.2 **Visual Arts Standards for Grades K–4 and 5–8 (NAEA, 1994)**

1. Content Standard: Understanding and applying media, techniques, and processes

Achievement Standard:

K–4 students

    a. know the differences between materials, techniques, and processes

    b. describe how different materials, techniques, and processes cause different responses

    c. use different media, techniques, and processes to communicate ideas, experiences and stories

    d. use art materials and tools in a safe and responsible manner

5–8 students

    a. select media, techniques, and processes; analyze what makes them effective or not effective in communicating ideas; and reflect upon the effectiveness of their choices

    b. intentionally take advantage of the qualities and characteristics of art media, techniques, and processes to enhance communication of their experiences and ideas

2. Content Standard: Using knowledge of structures and functions

Achievement Standard:

K–4 students

    a. know the differences among visual characteristics and purposes of art in order to convey ideas

    b. describe how different expressive features and organizational principles cause different responses

    c. use visual structures and functions of art to communicate ideas

5–8 students

    a. generalize about the effects of visual structures and functions and reflect upon these effects in their own work

    b. employ organizational structures and analyze what makes them effective or not effective in the communication of ideas

    c. select and use the qualities of structures and functions of art to improve communication of their ideas

3. Content Standard: Choosing and evaluating a range of subject matter, symbols, ideas

Achievement Standard:

K–4 students

    a. explore and understand prospective content for works of art

    b. select and use subject matter, symbols, and ideas to communicate meaning

5–8 students

    a. integrate visual, spatial, and temporal concepts with content to communicate intended meaning in their artworks

    b. use subjects, themes, and symbols that demonstrate knowledge of contexts, values, and aesthetics that communicate intended meaning in artworks

(continued)

Improvement Council to work with the appropriate organizations in each content area to establish voluntary content standards. In 1991, the National Art Education Association began work on the Visual Arts Standards (Table 10.2). These visual art standards focus on student learning results, not on how art should be taught. The standards provide art education goals—not a national curriculum. The job of devising a curriculum is left to state and local school systems.

(continued)   **TABLE 10.2**

4. *Content Standard: Understanding the visual arts in relation to history and cultures*

Achievement Standard:

K–4 students

  a. know that the visual arts have both a history and specific relationship to various cultures

  b. identify specific works of art as belonging to particular cultures, times, and places

  c. demonstrate how history, culture, and the visual arts can influence each other in making and studying works of art

5–8 students

  a. know and compare the characteristics of artworks in various eras and cultures

  b. describe and place a variety of art objects in historical and cultural contexts

  c. analyze, describe, and demonstrate how factors of time and place (such as climate, resources, ideas, technology) influence visual characteristics that give meaning and value to a work of art

5. *Content Standard: Reflecting upon and assessing the characteristics and merits of their work and the work of others*

Achievement Standard:

K–4 students

  a. understand there are various purposes for creating works of visual art

  b. describe how people's experiences influence the development of specific artworks

  c. understand there are different responses to specific artworks

5–8 students

  a. compare multiple purposes for creating works of art

  b. analyze contemporary and historic meanings in specific artworks through cultural and aesthetic inquiry

  c. describe and compare a variety of individual responses to their own artworks and to artworks from various eras and cultures

6. *Content Standard Making connections between visual arts and other disciplines*

Achievement Standard:

K–4 students

  a. understand and use similarities and differences between characteristics of the visual arts and other arts disciplines

  b. identify connections between the visual arts and other disciplines in the curriculum

5–8 students

  a. compare the characteristics of works in two or more art forms that share similar subject matter, historical periods, or cultural context

  b. describe ways in which the principles and subject matter of other disciplines taught in the school are interrelated with the visual arts

The Standards ensure quality and accountability in art education by requiring study to be disciplined and focused and by providing a reference point for assessment. The Standards insist that art education is sequenced and comprehensive, centers around hands-on learning, reveals the globally focused diverse cultural and historical heritage of art, involves interdisciplinary study, incorporates technology, develops problem-solving and higher-order thinking skills, and provides student assessment on an individual basis.

There are six content standards for art education. Each is broken down into achievement standards to be accomplished by K–4 or by 5–8 students. These achievement standards are developmental in nature with the 5–8 standards building on earlier learning (Table 10.2).

INTEGRATING ART AND CREATIVITY INTO A SCIENCE OR SOCIAL STUDIES THEME

The actual incorporation of art lessons that support and expand a theme is more difficult that it may first appear. One cannot "just draw a picture of it" and satisfy art education goals or visual arts standards. However, with a little practice, teachers can invent meaningful art lessons that support other curricular areas while still fulfilling art education standards. See Tables 10.3, 10.4, 10.5, and 10.6 for examples of lessons that fulfill art goals and interface with other subject areas. Detailed below are some suggestions for developing art activities that mesh with a science or social studies theme. Each suggestion is then applied to the physical changes in the environment lessons of the Constancy and Change unit detailed in chapter 1. Figure 10.1 shows a web of these suggestions.

1. Discuss the aesthetic aspects of the environment, earth materials or features, organisms, costumes, cultural artifacts, architecture, etc. Involve students in discussions of how different colors, forms, lines, and textures produce different human responses.

   Ask students to tell what they find beautiful about the stream and sand fan environment. They may mention the swirls of sand, the form of the undercut bank, the shiny pebbles, the graceful curves of the stream or the twigs aligned with the current. Ask what effect these shapes and textures produce. "How do you feel when you look at them?" Another part of the stream or ditch may elicit different responses: chopped grass clippings mixed with dirty froth, a dented soda can bobbing in an oil slick, a stained tennis shoe wedged into the mud. Discuss reactions to what is found. These may vary as one child notices the beautiful pink and green spectrum of the oil slick rainbow while another focuses on the ugly yellow-gray foam. A discussion of responses allows children to notice

Overview of Ways to Incorporate Art Into a Unit on Constancy and Change

FIGURE 10.1

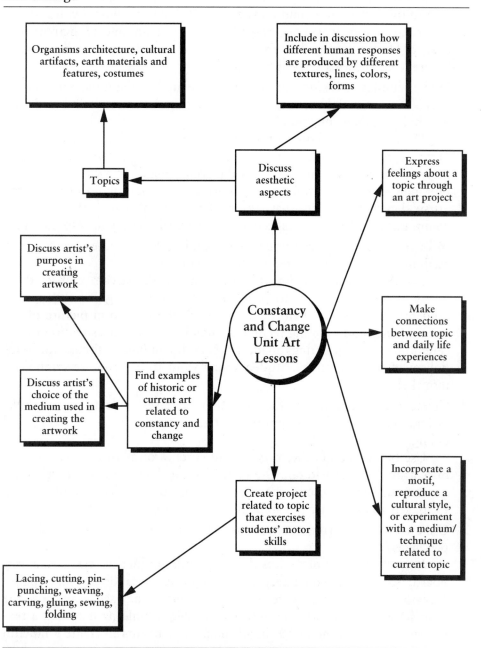

Organisms architecture, cultural artifacts, earth materials and features, costumes

Include in discussion how different human responses are produced by different textures, lines, colors, forms

Topics

Discuss aesthetic aspects

Express feelings about a topic through an art project

Discuss artist's purpose in creating artwork

Constancy and Change Unit Art Lessons

Make connections between topic and daily life experiences

Discuss artist's choice of the medium used in creating the artwork

Find examples of historic or current art related to constancy and change

Create project related to topic that exercises students' motor skills

Incorporate a motif, reproduce a cultural style, or experiment with a medium/ technique related to current topic

Lacing, cutting, pin-punching, weaving, carving, gluing, sewing, folding how colors, forms, textures and arrangements influence our perception of the mood of a setting. Ask students, "If you were going to photograph a part of this stream to communicate peace, which part would you choose? What part shows waste or decay? What part communicates activity and energy? How and why does the perceived 'mood' of the stream change?" Figure 10.2 shows a web of this discussion.

2. Find examples of historic or current art related to the topic and analyze these. Discuss each artist's purpose in creating the artwork and in choosing that particular medium.

The teacher can show a photograph of an Egyptian tomb painting depicting a river teaming with fish and waterfowl, a pastoral scene with a meandering river, a painting of flood torrents engulfing a village, and current magazine photographs of the aftermath of a flash flood. Why did the artists depict the streams these ways? What messages were they trying to communicate? To which aspects of the artwork were you responding?

3. Incorporate a motif, reproduce a cultural style, or experiment with a medium or technique related to the current topic.

Collect sand and sediment samples along the stream and let them dry. Glue these to paper to produce a "sand painting" of the stream. Students can make a "before" and "after" the rainstorm picture of the stream. The sand painting technique may lead to an investigation of the ceremonial sand paintings made by Navaho Indians. Discuss the symbolism of sand paintings. Students may want to incorporate symbolism into their work also.

4. Create a project related to the topic that exercises students' motor skills: lacing, weaving, sewing, pin-punching, cutting, carving, folding, and gluing.

Use bargello and other needlepoint stitches on plastic canvas to produce a small hand-held fan. Use light blue for the stream and earth tones for the sediments. Discuss the symmetry and design elements of the fan. Compare and contrast the students' fans with oriental fans.

5. Use creativity to make connections between the topic and daily life experiences.

Brainstorm a list of devices that use sand: sandblaster, cleanser, emery board, sandpaper, concrete, mortar, aquarium, sandbox, sand paint, Navajo sand paintings, water treatment center. Analyze the purpose the sand serves in each case: an abrasive, a filler, a building material, a texturizer, an art medium, or a filter. Then, ask students to create a fanciful or practical invention that uses sand. Draw a picture of this invention and label or explain its parts.

6. Allow students to express their feelings about a topic or theme issue through an art project. Guide students in selecting media, techniques

Art Lessons on "What Is Beautiful About a Stream and Sand Fan Environment?"

FIGURE 10.2

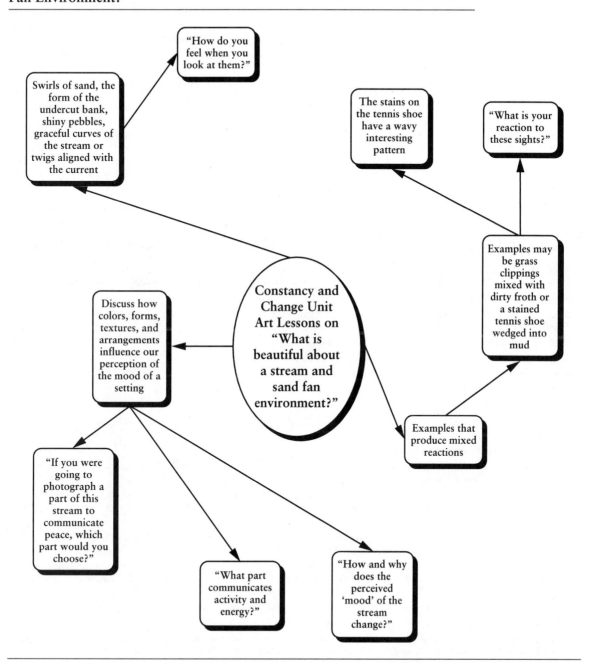

TABLE 10.2 Overview of Types of Integrated Units With Art Examples

Type of Unit	Description	Art Example
Concept-focused	Unit designed around teaching one or a few major concepts	Studying the period of impressionism in art history
Process Skills–focused	Unit designed around teaching one or a few major process skills with less emphasis on content	Using creative thinking skills to transform junk into art
Content and Process Skills–focused	Unit designed around teaching nearly equal amounts of content and process skills	Producing political cartoons that relate to current events and incorporate puns
Issue-focused	Unit designed around investigating an issue through research and data collection	Investigating issues of beauty related to endangered bats and the public's perception
Project focused	Unit designed around solving a problem or exploring an alternative	Launching an advertising campaign to boost the image of an endangered species
Case Study–focused	Unit designed around doing something on a local level based on a topic investigated	Beautify the school grounds by designing a wall to screen off the dumpsters

TABLE 10.3 Examples of Activities That Fulfill Art Goals and Interface With Science

Activities that support themes detailed in this book are followed by the pertinent theme in parentheses (themes: *Constancy and Change, Communication Skills, Diversity, Conflict Resolution and Peace, Air Quality, The Talladega National Forest Manager*).

Beauty Appreciation:

- Discuss the qualities that make the rhinoceros, saguaro, Mississippi delta, a chair, a vase, a thunderstorm, or a tree in the Talladega National Forest beautiful *(The Talladega National Forest Manager)*.
- Keep a pencil sketch diary of aesthetic aspects of the natural outdoor school environment.
- Make a mosaic trivet of collected stream pebbles *(Constancy and Change)*.

Communication:

- Make a booklet of paintings of the mushroom's life cycle.
- Create a poster persuading people to provide homes for bats.
- Assemble a collage of elements of the Arctic environment. Identify elements that remain constant and those that change *(Constancy and Change)*.
- Use photography to record urban backyard wildlife.
- Produce editorial cartoons related to nuclear waste disposal or current issues impacting the Talladega National Forest *(The Talladega National Forest Manager)*.
- Create a mosaic tile sundial after recording shadows of a nail every daylight hour for various days over the course of several weeks. What remains constant and what changes about the shadows' positions? *(Constancy and Change)*.

Human History:

- Compare and contrast art relating to horses in many different media from different time periods and different cultures. Examine how different groups of people use horses. Investigate breeds and genetic traits of horses *(Diversity)*.
- Experiment with making primitive art materials from rocks, clay, sticks, fibers, and oils. Apply concepts of constancy and change to a time line of art material technology. Discuss innovations in art media through time. What contemporary artists use "primitive" materials and techniques? *(Constancy and Change)*.
- Make natural fabric dyes from onion skins, beets, walnut hulls, and berries.

Cultural Expression:

- Make a scrapbook of photocopied pictures of artifacts related to whales. Discuss the importance of this animal to humans. Research the natural history and ecology of whales. Explore the points of view of conservationists and current day whalers. Examine laws related to whaling. Discuss how conflicts might be resolved *(Conflict Resolution and Peace)*.
- List items found in local stores that advertise endangered species. Invent a similar but new item that you believe would be popular.

(continued)

(continued)   **TABLE 10.3**

Artistic Process:

- Classify designs according to symmetry.
- Find magazine pictures of dogs that express different moods. Discuss inferences and responses. List examples of other animals that communicate different moods. Name specific elements in a work of art that would help express the mood of an animal subject *(Communication Skills)*.
- Create a balanced design of crayon rubbings of identified tree leaves from the Talladega National Forest.

Techniques:

- Make a lift-the-flap book showing sources of air quality problems and the pollutants they produce on one page and solutions on the following page *(Air Quality)*.
- Use crayon-resist and watercolors to make a mural of cave life.
- Use levers and simple machines to make mechanical puppets.
- Mix colors to produce a color wheel.
- Experiment with various techniques to make paper from recycled rags and paper products.

Motor Skills:

- Trace, cut, and mount silhouettes of objects rotated to different positions. Make a matching game with actual objects.
- Make textural rubbings of leaves, tree bark, and surfaces of trees from the Talladega National Forest.

Visual Skills:

- Locate shadows and light sources in paintings / drawings.
- Make observations of the pine bark beetle with magnifying lens and record with detailed sketches. Discuss the devastation this insect has caused in the Talladega National Forest *(The Talladega National Forest Manager)*.
- Find differences between two nearly identical pictures.
- Use clay to make a scale diorama of a coral reef.
- Construct decorated three-dimensional crystal shapes with plastic canvas stitched together with yarn.

Critical Thinking:

- Host an anti-drug art show.
- Discuss beauty qualities and how these are involved in people helping some endangered species more than others are.
- Analyze cigarette advertisements for facts and persuasive methods *(Air Quality)*.

Creativity:

- Create jewelry fashions from recycled materials.
- Produce a shadow puppet play expressing points of view about Talladega National Forest land use. Have the puppets participate in a formal discussion of the issues *(The Talladega National Forest Manager)*.
- Invent new art media using available materials.
- Make a board game of the solar system.
- Design a symmetrical butterfly wing pattern that mimics another organism.

Connections:

- Collect products that are aerodynamically designed. Describe how their forms are appealing.
- Assemble a book of magazine pictures related to air pollution *(Air Quality)*.
- Make an illustrated web of energy interactions in a meadow.

Personal Expression:

- Design a miniature Japanese garden with living plants.
- Keep a dated portfolio of self-portraits showing physical changes.

Career Development:

- Write a report on artist Roger Tory Peterson who initiated the illustrated pocket guide to wildlife.
- Watch a video of a pottery/ceramic factory

TABLE 10.4   Examples of Activities That Fulfill Art Goals and Interface With Social Studies

Activities that support themes detailed in this book are followed by the pertinent theme in parentheses (themes: *Constancy and Change, Communication Skills, Diversity, Conflict Resolution and Peace, Air Quality, The Talladega National Forest Manager*).

Beauty Appreciation:

- Make an illustrated timeline of hairstyle "beauty" for different *(Diversity)*.
- Draw and color beautiful photographs of the country or environment being studied.

Communication:

- Carve an Egyptian hieroglyphic name cartouche in relief in plaster. Explore other forms of writing *(Communication Skills)*.
- Design a coat of arms for your family *(Diversity)*.

Human History:

- Create a paper mosaic featuring gods and characters from a Roman myth.
- Use sticks, charcoal, clay, soot, natural earth pigments, and handmade tools to create a cave drawing on a brown paper bag.

Cultural Expression:

- Research the life and times of Mexican mural artist Diego Rivera. Many of his murals record historic events. Discuss how depicted conflicts were resolved *(Conflict Resolution and Peace)*.
- Make a papier-mâché mask of a Northwest Coast Indians mythic character.

Artistic Process:

- Enhance a driftwood shape with glued-on cardboard pieces, paint, and feathers to model a Hopi Indian Kachina doll.
- Analyze historic and modern wallpaper designs for symmetry and balance. How have wallpaper designs changed through time? What aspects remain the same? *(Constancy and Change)*.

Techniques:

- Make a pop-up card of a mountain and label the mountain's parts.
- Make holiday greeting cards featuring block-printed African designs.

Motor Skills:

- Hand-sew felt and buttons to fabric to create a button blanket like those used by the Northwest Coast Indians.
- Use plastic knives to carve a polar bear or seal from a bar of soap in the Inuit soapstone tradition.

Visual Skills:

- Find, reproduce, or create landscape paintings that show different geographic features.
- Create a map game showing post-glacial land features or a map game of Earth's ozone layer *(Air Quality)*.

Critical Thinking:

- Critique current event photographs from a newsmagazine. Tell what is effective and not effective about the photographs.
- Analyze perfume ads in magazines. Discuss the persuasive methods used to attract customers. Discuss the increased use of scented products on indoor air quality *(Air Quality)*.

Creativity:

- Make valentine cards using geographic term word puns.
- Invent a "machine" that resolves conflicts. Such a device might include some sort of headgear, armor, "black box," wand, tape recording, or instrument. Explain how your machine works *(Conflict Resolution and Peace)*.

Connections:

- Find examples of animals used as symbols of strength, nobility, speed, or beauty on everyday items such as food products, clothing, dishes, and toys *(Communication Skills)*.
- Identify the pattern names of quilts brought in by classmates. Design and name a new quilt pattern.

Personal Expression:

- Create an illustrated family tree. List favorite games, activities, and foods of each member *(Diversity)*.
- Locate pictures of creatively decorated birthday cakes in cookbooks, magazines and cake decorating books. Design a beautiful cake of your own.

Career Development:

- Visit an art fair or art gallery reception with artists present. Choose one work of art and interview the artist to find out what message the artist intended to convey.
- Skim several issues of various art magazines including collectors' magazines and craft magazines. Discuss as a class the articles that interested students most. Encourage students to follow up their interests with projects.

Examples of Activities that Fulfill Art Goals and Interface with Mathematics.   TABLE 10.5

Beauty Appreciation:

Activities that support themes detailed in this book are followed by the pertinent theme in parentheses (themes: *Constancy and Change, Communication Skills, Diversity, Conflict Resolution and Peace, Air Quality, The Talladega National Forest Manager*).

- Find actual examples or magazine pictures of natural and manufactured items that show beautiful patterns.
- Make a design for the exterior of a National Forest building that has pleasing proportions *(The Talladega National Forest Manager)*.
- Research the Greek's idea of the "golden section" and how it was used in architecture.

Communication:

- Illustrate a book of counting numbers or fractional parts with fancy desserts.
- Make a mosaic mural that features ordinal numbers first through tenth.
- Use graphs to compare reactions of interviewed persons to a school art show.
- List and classify the ways numbers are used in an art museum: street address, catalog number, dates, floor numbers, identification numbers, numbers of works in a series, symbolic numbers appearing in art, Roman numerals, and so on.

Human History:

- Produce an illustrated timeline of breakthroughs in the history of mathematics. Include contributions of people from all continents *(Diversity)*.
- Compile a set of tracings of tessellation patterns from ancient cultures.

Cultural Expression:

- Study artist / scientist / mathematician Leonardo Da Vinci.
- Compare / contrast the Mayan system of numeration to ours. Produce a stele recording your date of birth and dates of important events in your life with hieroglyphs.

Artistic Process:

- Analyze the lines in a painting. Classify them as to parallel, oblique, perpendicular, curved, intersecting, etc.
- Use specified geometric shapes to create a balanced abstract pastel design.
- Observe the angles in an outdoor environment over a period of time. Determine which angles change (shadow angles, cloud forms, tree branches moving in the wind), and which angles remain constant. Draw two views of the same scene documenting this *(Constancy and Change)*.

Techniques:

- Alter and embellish a parallelogram to create a tessellation pattern.
- Make milleflori and cane type oven-hardening polymer clay beads. Write a plan for producing the beads with sequenced steps.
- Use straight lines to a vanishing point to construct three-dimensional shapes in a drawing.

Motor Skills:

- Trace a stencil of a geometric shape and carefully shade it in with a colored pencil.
- Sew beads onto plastic canvas to create a pattern.

Visual Skills:

- Draw a still life, reducing the forms to simple geometric shapes.
- Cut out magazine examples of different measured angles.

Critical Thinking:

- Interview a commercial artist to find out how that person uses mathematics.
- Calculate the cost of producing a monumental work of art.
- Make a statistical analysis of a specified element in a book of Impressionist paintings.
- Identify symmetry elements in a work of art.

(continued)

TABLE 10.5   *(continued)*

Creativity:
- Write and illustrate a story about a group of items being divided among several people.
- Transform the numerals 1, 2, 3, . . . into pictures that relate to each number by adding lines and details.

Connections:
- Research Salvador Dali's use of distorted clocks in his paintings. Find modern items that copy this idea.
- Illustrate common clichés and superstitions associated with numbers such as "three's a crowd," and "unlucky thirteen."

Personal Expression:
- Make a Cubist style self-portrait. Identify the geometric name of each form used.
- Make a collage of food pictures for a poster of three balanced daily meals. Include different ethnic foods. Calculate the nutrition and calories provided by the food *(Diversity)*.

Career Development:
- Research the life and works of artist M. C. Escher who produced many symmetry and tessellation drawings.
- Explore the ways a part-time artist can market his/her works. Calculate a budget.

TABLE 10.6   **Examples of Activities that Fulfill Art Goals and Interface with Language Arts**

Activities that support themes detailed in this book are followed by the pertinent theme in parentheses (themes: *Constancy and Change, Communication Skills, Diversity, Conflict Resolution and Peace, Air Quality, The Talladega National Forest Manager*).

Beauty Appreciation:
- Create a mobile that expresses the same feeling as a favorite poem.
- Write a haiku poem related to air quality to accompany a nature photograph produced by the student *(Air Quality)*.

Communication:
- Make a diorama of a story's climactic scene in which some conflict was resolved *(Conflict Resolution and Peace)*.
- Use drawing skills to produce a concrete poem on a piece of handmade paper, about winter in the Talladega National Forest.

Human History:
- Design a tombstone with period-appropriate epitaph and decorations for a historic book character.
- Make a paper doll—with period costumes—that represents a character in a historical novel or picture book.

Cultural Expression:
- Create stick puppets to tell different cultural versions of the Cinderella story *(Diversity)*.
- Rewrite a well-known American or European story to fit with animals, environment, and cultural traits of native African people.

Artistic Process:
- Make a scrapbook of reproductions of illustrations from children's books showing different line styles.
- Produce two works of art depicting conflict resolution in two different media. Write a paragraph telling which was more effective and *why (Conflict Resolution and Peace)*.

(continued)

(continued)   TABLE 10.6

Techniques:
- Make corn husk or yarn dolls to depict characters in a story.
- Dip cotton swabs in paint to produce a pointillistic picture to accompany a description of a story setting.
- Watch a video on craft-making. Write a step-by-step plan for making the craft.

Motor Skills:
- Punch holes in cardboard and weave yarn through to make a written message in a spider web as in E. B. White's *Charlotte's Web*.
- Design and produce a needlepoint bookmark.

Visual Skills:
- Plan and color a map of places mentioned in Kenneth Graham's *The Wind in the Willows*.
- Locate examples of foreshortening in illustrations in the basal reader.

Critical Thinking:
- Write a limerick that tells positive aspects of a work of art. For example:
  Mona Lisa's portrait on the wall,
  Has a smile I'll always recall.
  Her ease and her grace,
  The calm in her face,
  Bring serenity to us all.
- Produce a web of responses to a work of art.
- Make a poster with a human rights slogan *(Diversity)*.

Creativity:
- Construct a graham cracker - icing- candy haunted house to accompany student-written ghost stories.
- Make a crossword puzzle of spelling words with illustrations as clues.

Connections:
- Visit a card shop and select your favorite birthday card. Analyze the mood of the card and list factors that cause this response.
- Invent a cereal and design a cereal box with logo, slogan, and other information that a specific book character would enjoy.

Personal Expression:
- Create an abstract self-portrait. Write an explanation of the artwork.
- Create a slogan and draw the ad for your own election campaign based on air quality issues *(Air Quality)*.

Career Development:
- Research and report on an illustrator of children's books.
- Submit artwork with accompanying cover letter to a children's magazine for publication.

and processes, subject matter, symbols, and arrangements that will be effective in communicating their meaning.

Ask students to create a mural of the stream area that shows both constancy and change. Perhaps the lower half will show an unchanging rocky bed with crayfish, minnows, snails, and algae while the upper half shows seasonal changes in weather and vegetation on the banks. Another version may focus on changing water quality as sediment, pollutants, and debris enter and are removed from the stream. The channel and landmark rocks may remain constant in that mural.

OBTAINING ART MATERIALS

With a little effort and creativity, teachers can provide a large variety of low-cost art materials to fuel student projects. Producing art with primitive materials gives students firsthand experience in historical methods. Sculptures can be made from beeswax, cement, plaster, clays tempered with sand and grasses, driftwood, soft mudstones, or matted mosses. Paints can be made from berry juices, ground rocks, mud, charcoal with water, oil or egg yolk bases. Create mosaics with sycamore bark, birdseed, pine cones, pebbles, seashells, eggshells, and sand paintings with natural sands, coffee grounds, pollen, and soils. Pressed leaves, grasses, and flowers can be incorporated into collages and handmade paper. Cut vegetables make good printing stamps. Vines, willow stems, and grasses can be used for wreaths, weavings, and basketry. Experiment with spinning yarns of milkweed, coconut husk fiber, and dog hair as well as cotton and wool.

Recycled objects make great art materials not only because of price, but because their use teaches the important concept of reuse and conservation. Rubber from an old tire inner tube makes excellent rubber stamps for prints on paper or fabric. Figure 10.3 shows first- and second-grade students

These students have used recycled materials to create elaborate African clothing.

who stamp-printed African designs on caftans and hats they made as part of a unit on African culture. Some of the beads on their collars are made of rolled paper strips cut from magazine covers and wallpaper samples. 'Papier-mâché masks and sculptures can be made with torn magazine pages and white glue. Figure 10.4 shows three third-grade children who made masks of circus performers: a clown, a magician, and a magic rabbit.

Old magazines can provide a wealth of vivid photographs and artwork for collages, scrapbooks, and posters. Old wrapping paper, greeting card fronts, wallpaper sample book pages, and fancy package backgrounds provide deluxe materials for students to incorporate into their designs. Laundry lint from the clothes dryer mixed in with plaster or clays provides fiber reinforcement that prevents cracking and breakage when drying. Styrofoam meat and produce trays and cardboard cereal boxes can be the base of a three-dimensional diorama or scene. Figure 10.5 shows three kindergarten

Third grade students with paper mâché masks produced during a unit on the circus.

Kindergarten and first-grade students display dollhouses they made for characters from their favorite books. Cereal boxes and ice cream cartons were used to make the dioramas.

or first-grade children with dioramas they made from cereal boxes and ice cream cartons. Each house was made for characters from a favorite book.

A collection of plastic bottle caps, lids, knobs, spools, and discarded junk is useful in many projects. Picture framing stores will often give teachers free mat board scraps that are suitable for small projects and mosaic pieces.

INTERFACING TECHNOLOGY WITH ART

Computer technology offers a wide range of art capabilities. A variety of user-friendly drawing programs allow even young children to draw dressed characters and create backgrounds. Clip art resources provide numerous images that can be re-colored, re-sized, edited, and arranged with other clip art backgrounds or computer generated images. Drawings and photographs can be scanned for incorporation into artwork or for other alterations. Digital cameras allow photographs to be quickly inserted into computer work.

Several programs facilitate animation. Slides can be projected directly through the computer onto a screen for presentations. Text is easily added to drawings for book-making and classroom newsletters. Software CD-ROM collections of artwork also are available. Many art and cultural museums allow access to art images over the Internet.

Photographic technology opens up other possibilities. Instant film cameras and water-developing sunlight sensitive film provide rapid feedback to the photography student. Xerographic machines can provide all kinds of images at low-cost. Several copies of the same image can be produced and used to make interesting symmetry or repetitious arrangements. Photographs of famous people or places can be reproduced and then cut out and embellished for use in pop-ups or dioramas. Students can place small flat objects on the copier to experiment with balanced arrangements. Line drawings can be photocopied onto transparencies and then colored with markers for over-head projector presentations or cut out for shadow puppets.

TYPES OF UNITS SUITABLE FOR ART EDUCATION

Concept-Focused Units

The concept-focused unit is commonly utilized in art education. Units can be based upon specific media or techniques such as collage, clay, scrimshaw, basketry, egg-tempera, origami or pop-up paper constructions. These units would parallel visual arts content standard number one: understanding and applying media, technique, and processes (Table 10.2). Lessons from such units could easily interface with science or social studies topics. Other concept-focused units may revolve around periods or movements in art history, for example, cave art, Mexican mural art, Impressionism, Cubism, or Op Art. Art of a specific people or culture can form the basis of a unit: ancient Egyptian tomb art, Inuit sculpture, Navaho art symbolism in rugs and sand paintings, or masks of the Dan people of Africa. A unit also may be based on the life, times and works of a specific artist or illustrator: Beatrix Potter, Antoni Gaudi, Brian Wildsmith, Mary Cassatt, or Vincent Van Gogh. These latter three types of concept-focused units fit with Visual Arts Content Standard number four (understanding the visual arts in relation to history and cultures) and Standard number six (making connections between visual arts and other disciplines). In addition, concept-focused units may highlight visual arts careers and avocations such as advertising and design, book illustration, cartooning, folk art, art collecting, clubs, studios, galleries, and museums. Table 10.2 lists an overview of types of integrated units with art examples.

TABLE 10.8   Creative Comparison of Two Objects

How a gold gift package bow and a cardboard toilet paper tube are alike:
- They both are related to a paper of some sort: gift wrap and toilet paper.
- They both have circular shapes.
- They are both flammable.
- They are both inexpensive.
- They are both usually thrown away after being used.
- They are both related to spools or rolls: a spool of ribbon, a roll of bathroom tissue.
- Both can be undone to produce a long strip.
- The ribbon could be wrapped around the tube to make a party cracker.
- Both can be crushed to fit into a smaller space.
- Both are related to a shower of some sort: the bow appears on a shower gift, the tube is found in a bathroom near the shower.
- Both are found in a home.
- Both can be purchased at most grocery stores.
- Children like to play with both.

How a gold gift package bow and a cardboard toilet paper tube are different:
- Color and luster: One is metallic gold and the other is dull gray.
- Texture is different: one is smooth, the other is rougher.
- One is highly visible when used, the other is hidden when in use.
- One is a fancy decoration, the other is commonplace.
- One is seen on special occasions, while the other is seen daily.
- One comes in a rainbow of colors while the other is restricted to grays and neutrals.
- One rolls, the other does not.
- They start with different letters of the alphabet.

Process Skills–Based Units

The process skills–based unit is perhaps not as common, but can be very worthwhile. The process skills of art can range from cognitive to affective to motor. Viktor Lowenfeld (Michael, 1982) pioneered research into creative process skills necessary to art, finding that these were generally the same skills necessary for creativity in other areas. Carmen Armstrong (1994), in a guide to art assessment published by the National Art Education Association, defines seven visual art-related behaviors that should be considered when planning art experiences and instruction: *know, perceive, organize, inquire, value, interact/cooperate,* and *manipulate. Knowledge* involves comprehension of principles or rules of art production such as color mixing, perspective, line quality, and balance. *Perception* encompasses many things, including visual discrimination of similarities and differences (Lowenfeld's sensitivity to problems) and recognition of visual symbols. An early childhood unit focusing on the process skill of perception might include work with wooden puzzles, finding hidden pictures in *I Spy* books (Wick & Marzello, 1992), stringing beads according to a pattern, making a map of the classroom, matching pictures of different views of the same object, identifying the objects that make certain shadows, constructing pictures with tangrams, finding examples of camouflage in animals, examining optical illusions, viewing items through the microscope and telescope, and finding/classifying symbols on product packaging. *Organization* skills are similar to the classification, inferencing, and generalization skills of science, but are applied to art concepts. *Inquiry* involves creative process skills of problem finding, experimentation, and problem solving. The *Talents Unlimited* thinking skills (Schlichter & Palmer, 1993) of productive thinking, forecasting, communication, planning, and decision-making fit under the heading of inquiry as do Edward DeBono's thinking skill exercises of his CoRT (Cognitive Research Trust) Thinking Program. Lowenfeld's fluency (experimenting with alternatives), flexibility (avoidance of preconceptions and openness to changing possibilities), originality (uncommon or unique responses), redefinition, analysis, synthesis, and coherence of organization, are creative process skills of inquiry. *Valuing* skills start with personal preferences and move through informed choices to a set of consistent values that reflect a concern for society. Decision making and comparison skills are part of valuing. *Interaction and Cooperation* skills are important to students in the art classroom. Gardner's (1989) interpersonal intelligence construct addresses the behaviors and skills called for here: compliance, responsibility, and leadership. *Manipulation* involves fine and gross motor skills, which undergo refinement and sophistication as the student advances through the art curriculum.

A process skills unit based on the creative thinking skills of inquiry can benefit students greatly. Creativity is not just a characteristic one is either born with or not, but a complex assemblage of skills, traits, and abilities that can be improved upon and developed. A unit that concentrates on creative thinking gives students conscious techniques for reasoning, thinking, and dealing with problems both in art and other curricular areas. A unit that focuses on the use of analogies might include the following types of activities.

1. Choose two objects at random from a box of odd items and junk. Perhaps one item is a gold bow for a gift package and the other is cardboard cylinder from the inside of a roll of toilet paper. Ask students to think of as many ways as possible that these items are alike. Then ask students to think of ways these items are different. Table 10.7 shows some possible responses. Let students report all their ideas after they have had a few minutes to write them down. Record these ideas on the

board and place tally marks next to ideas that are repeated. Pointing out the ideas that are unique helps students begin to get a feel for what is an unusual or a common idea. Repeat this activity with different objects every day or two.

2. Choose another object and ask students to think of alternative uses for the object. Perhaps the chosen object is a blue plastic soup ladle. Figure 10.6 shows a web of possible ideas. Pointing out the properties of the item and generating other uses based on those properties is a teachable strategy for students to use. Figure 10.7 shows a set of different elephant trunks made by kindergarten and first-grade students. They were asked to find materials that could be used to make an elephant trunk. Students looked for materials that were long, tube-like, and flexible. A large variety of materials were found: a chicken-wire frame with colorful tissue paper "skin," plaster-saturated gauze for broken bone casts, clothes dryer vent pipe, paper, stuffed socks, papier-mâché over wire, plastic film canisters strung together, foam and painted aluminum piping, cotton-ball-stuffed nylon stocking, gathered and tied sheet material, taped paper bags, and sewn and stuffed fabric.

3. Provide examples of political cartoons for students to examine. Often the cartoon cover of a newsmagazine is based on a simple current event idea. Analyze the ways in which the cartoons were made: the outline of a country was transformed into the face of its leader; political figures are portrayed as engaged in a common activity or sport, but some of the items they use have been transformed to fit with the current issue; captions are added that contain homonyms or puns. Choose a current event and have students draw their own political cartoons.

4. Ask students to construct similes, encouraging them to use colorful, descriptive, unusual ideas. For example, ask students to generate many ideas that would complete this sentence: The stick was as pointed as _____. Some possible responses are:

   ■ The stick was as pointed as the Wicked Witch of the West's nose.
   ■ The stick was as pointed as an icicle during a spring thaw.
   ■ The stick was as pointed as shish kabob skewer.

5. Divide students into teams of four to six students each. Call one team at a time to sit in chairs at the front of the room. Give the team a problem to solve, such as: "Name things that contain holes." Students are allowed one minute to think of possible responses or ask questions about the problem or procedure. Then, students have two minutes to tell responses, rotating through the group again and again in the same order, allowing

Creativity Exercise on Alternative Uses for an Item

FIGURE 10.6

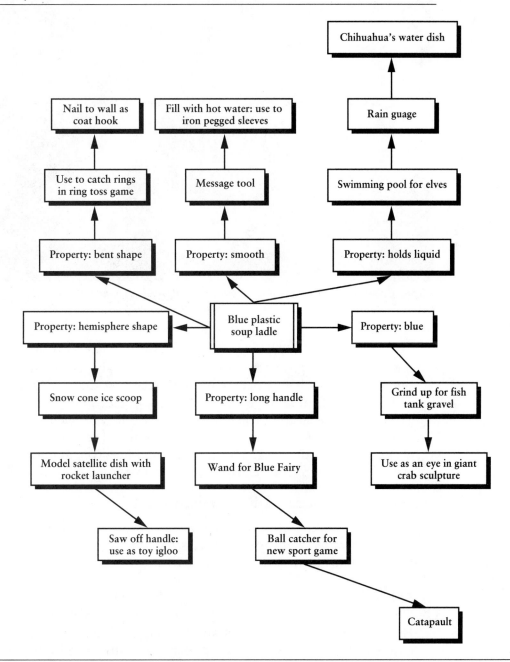

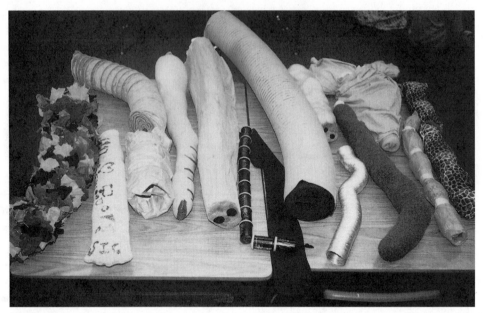

Elephant trunks constructed of a variety of materials made by kindergarten and first-grade students. Students searched for materials that were long, tube-like, or flexible.

each student to give one response. Answers may not be repeated: if the same response is given, the student must try again. Each student must supply a response before play moves on to the next student. At the end of two minutes, the total number of responses is added to the team's score. Then the next team comes up to the front and a new problem is presented. Figure 10.8 shows a web of possible problems and responses for this exercise in creative thinking. This game is a modified version of an activity used in the Odyssey of the Mind program (Micklus, 1985).

Content and Process Skills–Focused Units

Most art units feature a mix of concepts and process skills. A unit on the diversity of beauty in unexpected places focusing on a mixture of content and process skills might include these activities:

1. Examine art works by well-known artists. Discuss what makes the art-works beautiful. Produce a list of qualities and characteristics.

2. Have children search magazines for examples of unappealing, uninteresting, or ugly products that have been made attractive by the mode of presentation in an advertisement. List the ways of "beautifying" a product: connection with a glamorous person, placement in a gorgeous setting, beautiful wrapping or packaging, interesting photography or lighting, etc. Discuss the ways we value things in our society. Assign

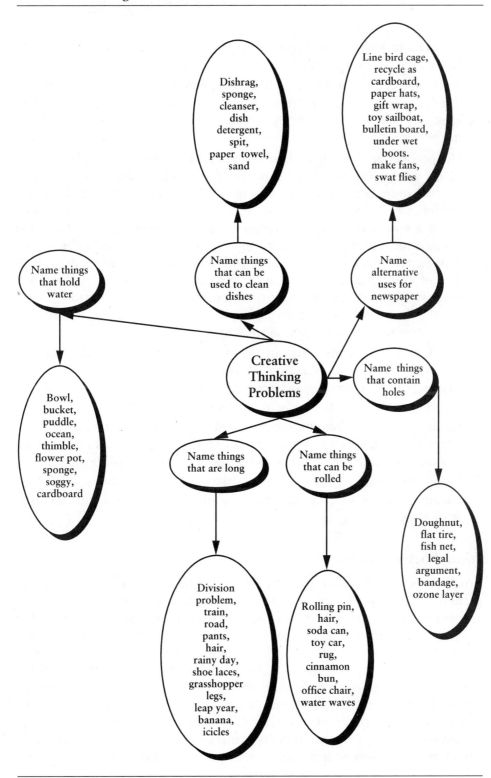

products to students and ask them to create an advertisement that enhances the product's beauty.

3. Examine the diverse ideas of beauty in hairstyle, jewelry, and dress in different societies. Create new hairstyles and fashions for an imaginary group of people from a strange place. Explain why this mode of dressing is beautiful.

4. Use productive thinking (Schlichter & Palmer, 1993) to generate a list of places where you would *not* expect to find beauty. Students might name the bathroom, a trash can or dumpster, dirt and soil, under a bed, a parking lot, a battle scene, a gas station, a junk drawer, on a scab, a puddle, inside a box of crackers, a graveyard, a street, a sewer, a vacant lot, and inside a rock. Prompt students to generate many ideas from different categories, to think of unusual ideas, and to add details to their ideas. Visit any of these places that are near the school (bathroom, parking lot, dumpster) and search for beauty. Interesting patterns or shadows, unusual colors, and pleasing arrangements of objects may be found. Students may want to use photography to record the images.

5. Conduct a search for illustrations of beauty in unexpected places by looking through reproductions of artwork in books. Books of art photography often contain good examples. Georgia O'Keeffe's paintings of skulls are examples of beauty in an unexpected place.

6. Create something beautiful out of trash or discarded/recycled items. Make a crown, jewelry, or centerpiece. This activity allows students practice in visualizing the design possibilities of different trash or junk items.

7. To practice small motor skills, make rolled paper beads by winding long triangular strips of magazine pages around a toothpick and securing with glue.

Issue-Focused Units

Students impartially investigate an art issue through research and data collection in an issue-focused unit. Students might work on the issue of how the beauty images of endangered species affect the sympathy and attention they get. Students would start out by researching endangered species and generating a list of local animals or creatures from a specific place of interest. Students can survey people to find out: awareness of the plight of the animal, liking and concern for the animal, willingness to donate funds or efforts to the animal's benefit, etc. Students also can have people rate the animals on a beauty scale from beautiful, to somewhat beautiful, to neutral, to somewhat ugly, to ugly. Students can then see how the beauty image of an animal correlates with the amount of positive action it receives.

Project-Focused Units

The survival problems of one of the endangered species investigated above can form the basis of a project-focused unit in which students try to help the animal by launching an advertising campaign to change its image. Similar campaigns have been held for the Florida manatee and for bats living around a small Texas town. Students can start by listing benefits of the animal and incorporating these into posters that enhance the beauty of the animals. Newspaper or television news coverage of this unit will motivate students and can turn an academic exercise into a real-life solution. Students may want to design, produce and market other products that advertise the endangered animal such as T-shirts, bookmarks, note cards, and key chains.

Case Study–Focused Units

A case study–focused unit in art allows students to work on a project based on a topic that has been investigated. There are many art-related case-study projects that students can become involved in around their schools and communities. Beautifying a part of the school can constitute a practical and esteem-building project. Students can incorporate their new skills in a particular art technique or medium into a mosaic sidewalk or sundial, a decorative screen in the school's lobby or entrance, a mural on the school walls, or flower/still life arrangements for the school office. Outdoors, landscaping skills and botany/ecology studies can culminate in a Japanese garden, herb garden, flower garden, nature path, or decorative pond. Search the school for problem areas that might be improved: unsightly dumpsters, a natural area that has become littered or damaged, a weathered school sign, the lifeless patio area, a dull lunchroom. Combine a current theme unit topic with art to remedy one of these problems. Perhaps the dumpsters can be hidden behind a trellis wall of climbing native plants designed and built by students. Student-made sculpture and poetry can enliven a patio area. Framed silk-screen prints can brighten up the lunchroom. Careful planning is required to make a project of this type effective.

SUMMARY

Art is an important core subject in the elementary curriculum as well as a medium for linking other curricular areas. The creative thinking and problem-solving skills required and practiced in art can be transferred and applied by students to other curricular areas. Art can provide a means for fostering cross-cultural acceptance, understanding, and self-discovery. Art instruction is best accomplished with active, hands-on learning. Art is easily related to other subject areas, providing meaningful and enjoyable experiences that bring topics to life. The National Standards for Visual Arts Education provide a framework for designing an effective art curriculum.

REFERENCES

Armstrong, C. L. (1994). *Designing assessment in art.* National Art Education Association, Reston, VA.

Carey, N. and others. (1995). *Arts education in public elementary and secondary schools. Statistical analysis report.* Westat, Inc. Rockville, MD. Sponsored by the National Center for Education Statistics. (ERIC # ED 388 607)

Chapman, B. H. (1985). *Arts education K–12; Teacher handbook.* North Carolina Competency-Based Curriculum Subject-by-Subject. (ERIC # ED 284 821)

DeBono, E. (1983). The direct teaching of thinking as a skill. *Phi Delta Kappan, 64,* 703–708.

DeBono, E. (1985). *DeBono's thinking course.* New York: Facts on File Publications.

Dunn, P. C. (1995). *Curriculum: Creating curriculum in art.* Point of view series. National Art Education Association, Reston, VA. (ERIC # ED 386 413)

Freedman, K. (1987). Art education as social production: Culture, society and politics in the formation of curriculum. In Thomas S. Popkewitz (Ed.), *The Formation of School Subjects: The Struggle for Creating an American Institution* (p. 63–84). Falmer Press, Bristol, PA. (ERIC # ED 341 607)

Gardner, H. (1983). *Frames of mind: The theory of multiple intelligences.* New York: Basic Books.

Maryland State Department of Education. (1990). Fine arts: A Maryland curricular framework. Annapolis, MD: Department of Education. (ERIC # ED 336 321)

Michael, J. A. (Ed.). (1982). *The Lowenfeld lectures: Viktor Lowenfeld on art education and therapy.* University Park, PA: The Pennsylvania University Press.

Micklus, S. (1985). *Odyssey of the mind program handbook.* Glassboro, NJ: Creative Competitions.

National Art Education Association. (1994). *The national visual arts standards.* Reston, VA: author.

National Arts Education Research Center. (1989). A framework for multicultural art education. (ERIC # ED 368 672)

Schlichter, C. L., & Palmer, W. R. (Eds.). (1993). *Thinking smart: A primer of the talents unlimited model.* Mansfield Center, CT: Creative Learning Press, Inc.

Wick, W., and Marzollo, J. (1992). *I spy Christmas: A book of picture riddles.* New York: Scholastic Inc.

Wick, W., and Marzollo, J. (1993). *I spy fun house: A book of picture riddles.* New York: Scholastic Inc.

C H A P T E R 11

INTEGRATING PHYSICAL EDUCATION AND DANCE COMPONENTS

The movement content of physical education can be integrated with subject matter or classroom content across the curriculum. Movement content comprises many movement concepts such as: fast, slow, curved, straight, high, low, over, under, around, through, run, kick, throw, catch, forceful, gentle, forward, backward, sideways, left, right, swing, swirl, shake, slither, slide, glide, rise, fall, tremble, tap, dab, bounce, balance, roll, strike, jump, and leap. These movement concepts and others form the movement vocabulary that elementary school children are taught in physical education and dance.

THE IMPORTANCE OF MOVEMENT FOR CHILDREN

Movement is central to children's lives. Children explore their world through movement. They run to feel the wind rushing in their ears. They roll down a hill to feel the effects of the speed of gravity. They jump into a lake to feel how water differs from air—how it cushions their fall, slows down their momentum, muffles sounds, causes buoyancy, and cools their bodies. They hike through the woods, jump into a pile of leaves, dig in the dirt, splash in a puddle. They try to push a heavy object, swing a stick, gently catch a falling feather, balance on a stump, or climb a tree. They move to learn about themselves and their world.

They move to play. Children's games and imaginative play are often skill-based: playing catch, playing tag, playing games, or playing ballerina. For children, movement is play. They experience great joy in running, skipping, leaping, and jumping. Through movement children express their emotions. They stomp off and slam the door in anger; they squirm with excitement and leap for joy; they shake with laughter and fidget with restlessness; they skip with happiness and slump with boredom.

Movement also is important for children's health and physical development. Through movement the body develops strength, flexibility, cardiorespiratory endurance, and muscular endurance. The ability to sustain vigorous exercise has been linked to a healthy heart and respiratory system and a decreased risk of heart disease.

Movement is natural for children. We often hear adults telling children to "sit still," "don't fidget," and "walk, don't run" in schools, places of worship, shops, restaurants, swimming pools, parks, parking lots, and a host of places where children's love of movement and their natural inclination to move takes over. Movement is important to and for children.

Children often move to music and other sounds in their environment. They sway, bounce, and leap. Children invent their own movement to music and environmental sounds and imitate the movements of others.

Movement Is a Way of Knowing and Learning

Beyond the importance of movement to and for children, movement is a way of knowing and learning. In the prenatal months and in the year after birth, the perceptual motor system is the primary means by which children learn about their world. Identified by Piaget, the sensorimotor stage lasts from birth to about two years old (Miller, 1983). During this stage, the child interacts with the environment through movement. Children learn that if they kick a teddy bear mobile, the teddy bears move in interesting ways. They drop food from their high chairs and learn that the dog comes running. Very young children learn to control their environment through intentional movement, such as learning to control their eating.

Throughout childhood, movement remains an important way of knowing for the child. Through bodily experiences we know such concepts as grasping and letting go, up and down, balanced and unstable, strong and gentle, push and pull, rise and fall, high and low, in and out, straight and curved. Such body-based concepts can later form the basis for understanding these concepts in more abstract ways (Johnson, 1987). For example, the following movement concepts, learned first through body experiences, are part of more abstract ideas: grasping an explanation, balancing a budget, winds sweeping across the prairie, national boundaries, two nations pulled into a conflict, temperatures rising, standing up for what you believe.

Not only do many abstract concepts have a bodily basis, but abstract concepts can have emotional content that is also bodily-based: she rose to the occasion, talks broke down, it was a shaky start, she fell to pieces, the sermon was uplifting, she gave a forceful argument, he deflected the criticism, they leaped for joy, he retreated into the shadows, the army advanced steadily, she twisted with anguish, he was wound tight, and she came dragging in.

In summary, movement can be an important mode of learning and knowing for a child. Children find movement meaningful. Through movement they come to know themselves and their world. Before their first science lesson on force, they experience force through their bodies. They learn about the relations among force, speed, and size of movement when they learn not to hit but to pat the dog gently by moving their arm slower with less muscle force and smaller movements.

How Movement Can Help Classroom Learning

Teachers have acknowledged the value of integrating movement and classroom content for many years. Movement can help facilitate learning many topics that are part of the elementary curriculum (Allen, 1996; Morley, 1994; Salz, 1980; Stevens, 1994; Werner, 1994a, 1994b). This is because movement offers a different mode of learning that can complement what children learn through other modes.

Howard Gardner (1983) in his theory of multiple intelligences proposed that humans are capable of at least seven distinctly different forms of information processing. He advocates a redesign of curriculum to encompass a more systematic and consistent use of all the different intelligences. One of the seven is bodily-kinesthetic, a strongly developed intelligence in some children and a weakness in others. Bodily-kinesthetic intelligence is part of the range of human capabilities that schools need to develop in all children. Through this mode of information processing, children acquire knowledge in ways unavailable through any other mode of learning. For example, in science class children can read, see, and hear about some aspects of prey and predators. However, they can learn about other aspects of the topic in dance by exploring the movement concept of bound flow. Bound flow means to travel so that the flow of the movement is stoppable, hesitant, and highly controlled. The movement feels bound as opposed to its opposite, "free" flow. (A prey and predator dance lesson is described in detail later in this chapter.) When children create a dance with a partner about prey and predators by exploring traveling on different pathways with bound flow, they acquire bodily, affective, and aesthetic knowledge of prey and predators that they could not acquire simply by hearing a story or reading the encyclopedia. In this sense, movement is a way of knowing that reinforces, expands, and elaborates on what children learn through other modes of knowledge acquisition. It is a way of experiencing the interaction between the self and the external world.

In schools the child's world is often divided into the cognitive, motor, affective, and aesthetic domains with separate classes for art, music, physical education, dance, technology, and classroom subjects. The child, however, acts on, and interacts with, the world as a whole. The child is a motor, cognitive, affective, emotional, social, and aesthetic whole. It is in touching the whole child that physical education and dance make critical contributions to children's learning of important concepts in integrated ways.

The Two Major Motor Goals of Physical Education

There are two broad motor goals for physical education. One is to help children acquire and master bodily skill. Childhood is an important time to master basic movement skills such as throwing; catching; kicking; striking with hands, arms, rackets, bats, and hockey sticks; dribbling with hands, feet, and hockey sticks; jumping, rolling, balancing, hopping, skipping, running, and cart wheeling movements. The challenge of mastering movement skills often captivates children. They willingly spend hours and hours perfecting their layup shot, overarm throw, back handspring, or split leap, for example. The elementary school years are an important time for children to develop their competence and confidence in a range of content areas, including movement.

The second goal is to acquire and maintain health-related fitness through vigorous physical activity. Fitness is an outcome of movement. It results from children's participation in activities that work on cardio-respiratory endurance, muscular endurance, muscular strength, and flexibility. Most adults are familiar with the adult forms of fitness including jogging, aerobics, weight training, exercises and calisthenics. These repetitive and often regimented forms of movement are adult-like and not particularly appropriate for children. Fitness experts recommend that the focus for maintaining children's fitness should be on keeping children physically active. The goal is to increase the amount of daily and weekly physical activity in activities such as sports and games, dance, highly active play, and skill practice that children enjoy.

Both skill and fitness goals are important, but it is not always feasible to work on acquiring bodily skill and participating in vigorous physical activity in the same lesson activities. Some activities, such as nature hikes and fitness walking, are aimed at improving children's health-related fitness, while other activities, such as striking a ball back and forth with small rackets, are more skill related. In monthly planning for instruction, teachers need to design some activities to ensure both goals are met.

NATIONAL STANDARDS FOR PHYSICAL EDUCATION

Like other subject areas, physical education has a set of national standards (National Association for Sport and Physical Education, 1995). These standards define what physically educated students should know and be able to do. The seven standards are:

1. Demonstrates competence in many movement forms and proficiency in a few movement forms. The goal for elementary physical education is for children to gain competence in a wide range of movement activities that form a strong foundation for later developing competence in adult movement forms. Regulation sports such as soccer and basketball and adult forms of fitness are not developmentally appropriate for children. Adult movement forms must be modified to meet elementary children's needs. The elementary school years are essential for developing the fundamental skills and strategies that will later become more specialized as children gain the ability to deal with more complex situations. Few children become elite performers. The goal for school physical education is to help all children develop the skills to be able to have satisfactory, enjoyable participation in physical activities as adults.

2. Applies movement concepts and principles to the learning and development of motor skills. This standard posits a cognitive understanding of the principles of movement and learning motor skills. With this understanding, children become increasingly independent learners. Being able to analyze and improve performance independently is important because participation in physical activities often occurs during leisure time.

3. Exhibits a physically active lifestyle. This standard addresses the need for regular participation in physical activities that contribute to a healthy lifestyle.

4. Achieves and maintains a health-enhancing level of physical fitness. There is a strong connection between physical fitness and good health. Students need to understand the components of fitness and how to develop exercise programs that will enhance their fitness levels.

5. Demonstrates responsible personal and social behavior in physical activity settings. This standard can be applied to any subject area. However,

in physical education, physical activities such as games and sports are group activities requiring both cooperative and competitive behavior, in addition to a focus on safety and caring for others.

6. Demonstrates understanding and respect for differences among people in physical activity settings. Because one goal of physical education is participation for all children, it is important that children learn to respect individual similarities and differences. Inclusion means working with differences in race, gender, ethnicity, body size, and physical abilities.

7. Understands that physical activity provides opportunities for enjoyment, challenge, self-expression, and social interaction. These affective and social goals can be valued aspects of participating in physical activities for both children and adults.

More detailed descriptions of the content standards for grades K–12 and guidelines for assessment are provided in *National Physical Education Standards: A Guide to Content and Assessment* developed by the National Association for Sport and Physical Education. These standards are meant to provide guidelines for teachers who are responsible for children's physical education.

National Standards for Music Education

Children's movement can be in response to music and supported by music. The national music education standards address the fundamental music processes of responding to music, creating music, and performing music (Music Educators National Conference, 1994). This chapter includes responding to music through integrated units. Many integrated units also include creating music and those that include a music teacher as part of the teaching team may include performing music.

Standards for students in grades K–8 include the following:

1. Singing, alone and with others, a varied repertoire of music.
2. Performing on instruments, alone and with others, a varied repertoire of music.
3. Improvising melodies, variations, and accompaniments.
4. Composing and arranging music within specified guidelines.
5. Reading and notating music.
6. Listening to, analyzing, and describing music.
7. Evaluating music and music performances.

8. Understanding relationships between music, the other arts, and disciplines outside the arts.

9. Understanding music in relation to history and culture.

Standard six is particularly appropriate for integrated units that incorporate children's movement. It addresses opportunities for children responding to music through purposeful movement such as swaying and skipping and through dramatic play. It also encourages children to demonstrate their perceptual skills by moving. Standard eight encourages children to use movement in dance, visual stimuli in visual arts, sound in music, and human interrelationships as found in drama to build relationships between music and other disciplines. At the upper grades, students might integrate music into their investigations as they explore the human hearing process, hazards to hearing, the muscles and bone structure allowing our bodies to move, frequency ratios of intervals in music, and the historical or social events chronicled and demonstrated in music and through movement and dance.

A CONCEPT-FOCUSED APPROACH TO PHYSICAL EDUCATION

There are three content areas of physical education:

1. dance
2. games (sports and sport-like activities)
3. functional movement activities (gymnastics, adult forms of fitness, swimming, track and field, and adventure activities).

Concept-focused units can be taught in all three content areas. A concept-focused approach to dance and games will be discussed in some depth in this chapter. In concept-focused approaches, physical education content is not divided into different sports, games, activities, and dances. Rather, lessons and units focus on movement concepts. A movement framework, based on the work of Rudolf Laban (1948), is often used in elementary school physical education to identify dance concepts (see Table 11.1) and game concepts (see Table 11.2). As shown in Tables 11.1 and 11.2, all movement has four aspects:

1. Body Aspect: What the body does
2. Space Aspect: Where in space the body moves
3. Effort Aspect: How the body moves
4. Relationships Aspect: The relationships of the individual to equipment, other individuals, and groups that occur in movement.

TABLE 11.1   Modified Laban Movement Concept Framework for Dance

Body Aspect: What the Body Does	Space Aspect: Where the Body Moves
Using Different Body Parts	General/Personal
Body Actions:	**Directions:** Forward, Back, Side, Up, Down
Curl, Stretch, Twist	**Pathways:** Straight, Curved, Angular
Walk, Run	**Extensions:** Near/Far, Small/Large
Skip, Gallop	**Levels:** High, Medium, Low
Hop, Jump, Leap, Sissone, Assemble	
Rise/Sink Collapse/Explode	
Open/Close	
Retreat/Advance	
Twist, Turn, Spin, Swirl	
Push, Pull, Sway	
Shake, Wiggle, Slither	
Body Parts:	
Lead, Support, Receive Weight	
Body Shapes:	
Round, Wide, Straight, Twisted, Angular	
Symmetrical, Asymmetrical	
Large, Small	

Effort Aspect: The Quality of How the Body Moves	Relationships
Force: Strong/Light, Firm/Fine, Rhythmic	Above, Below
Speed: Fast/Slow, Sudden/Sustained	On, Off
Flow: Bound/Free, Successive/Simultaneous	Along Side Of, On Top Of, Underneath
Use of Space: Direct/Flexible	Over, Under, Through, Around
	Behind, In Front Of
	Lead, Follow
	Call, Respond
	Match, Mirror, Contrast
	Complement, Similar
	Contrast, Same, Alike
	Meet/Part
	Cannon/Unison Alternating

Each of the four aspects has many components called movement concepts. These movement concepts can be integrated with classroom content. For example, in the younger grades, children can explore such concepts as over, under, around, through, narrow, wide, pause, grip, release, collapse, float, glide, near to, and far from in physical education while the meaning of these concepts is clarified and sharpened in language arts. Concepts of physical education such as force, pathways, directions, speed, and power

Modified Laban Movement Concept Framework for Games	TABLE 11.2

Body Aspect: What the Body Can Do

Throwing, passing with hands
Catching
Collecting (stopping with feet or sticks)
Kicking, passing with feet
Dribbling with feet
Dribbling with hands
Dribbling, passing, striking with hockey sticks
Striking with bats
Striking with hands
Striking with rackets

Effort Aspect: The Quality of How the Body Moves

Force: Strong, Light
Speed: Fast, Slow, Accelerate/Decelerate
Sense of Space: Flexible and Indirect/Direct
Flow: Bound, Free

Space Aspect: Where the Body Moves

Levels: High, Medium, Low
Directions: Traveling Forward, Back, Sideways
Pathways on Ground: Straight, Curved, Angular
Pathways in Air: Flat and direct, high curved
Body Parts and Rackets/Bats to Balls: Under, over, behind, along side of, in front of
Angle of Striking Surface to Balls: Straight, angled
Direction of Force: Up, down, forward, backward, sideways, angled
Basic Defensive Strategy Relationships:

covering space (zone)
covering individuals (person-to-person)
ball-side/goal-side (stand between player and goal and slightly closer to the ball)
"cat and mouse" guarding (stick close but not too close so the offense can dodge you, "pounce" on the ball when offense makes a mistake)

Guarding a Player Without the Ball: The closer you are to the goal, the closer to the player
Backing up a Defender: who is guarding player with the ball
Basic Offensive Strategy Relationships:

Cut into a space to get free for a pass
Dribble keeping your body between opponent and ball
Create space for self and teammates
Center the ball in front of the goal, follow up your shot
Back up teammates with the ball

Boundaries, Bases, Goals to Players: wide, narrow, near, far
Relationships

can be explored in science. Children learn about symmetry and asymmetry, patterns, and probability (prediction) in mathematics and physical education.

Integrating physical education and classroom concepts through concept-focused units enables children to come to a deep, elaborated understanding of those concepts. Moreover, concepts are important physical education content. Using concepts to integrate movement and classroom content makes it possible for the teacher to select worthwhile, authentic physical activities rather than activities that trivialize the physical education content. This trivialization is commonly seen when teachers turn classroom content into games that have little or no valuable movement content. Although games are part of physical education, the goal of physical education is not to play games, but to develop skillful movement. Playing fun, non-skill-based games is not physical education: it is recreation and recess. Learning skills and strategies of games and becoming skillful are goals of physical education.

SAMPLE PHYSICAL EDUCATION IDEAS AND ACTIVITIES RELATED TO THE SIX DIFFERENT TYPES OF INTEGRATED UNITS

Physical education content can be taught through the six different types of integrated units described in previous chapters. What follows is a description of teaching dance and games using the six types of integrated units. Each is followed by sample physical education activities that can be used as part of the units on communication, diversity, conflict resolution and peace, air quality, and the job of the manager of a national forest described in earlier chapters.

Concept-Focused Units in Dance

A concept-focused approach to dance has long been a part of physical education for children. There are two forms of dance that are developmentally and educationally appropriate for elementary school children: creative dance and folk dance. Creative dance is described first. Folk dance is described later in the sample unit on diversity.

Of all the content areas, integrating physical education content with classroom content is most easily done with dance. This is because integration can occur with the movement concepts that are the content of dance and also with the ideas, themes, and images that the dance choreography represents.

Overview of Types of Integrated Units With Physical Education Examples   TABLE 11.3

Type of Unit	Description	Physical Education Example
Concept-focused	Unit designed around teaching one or a few major concepts	Learning movement concepts such as push, pull, force, speed, symmetry, asymmetry, matching, contrasting, pathways, and directions in dance and games.
Process skill-focused	Unit designed around teaching one or a few major process skills will less emphasis on content	Learning to use dance movement to communicate emotions, ideas, and stories.
Content and process-Skill focused	Unit designed around teaching nearly-equal amounts of content and process skills.	Developing choreographic skills to represent cultural themes and diversity in dance.
Issue-focused	Unit designed around investigating an issue through research and date collection	Learning to resolve conflicts by designing, playing, and refereeing their own games.
Project-focused	Unit designed around solving a problem or exploring an alternative	Researching the issue of fitness, cardio-respiratory endurance, and the effects of air quality on exercising.
Case study–Focused	Unit designed around doing something on a local level based on a topic investigated	Experience hiking and orienteering, in a national forest.

Movement Concepts in Dance

Dance begins with movement. The movement concepts in Table 11.1 form the basic vocabulary of dance that children need to learn. To learn this vocabulary, children need to understand both the meaning of each concept and how the concept feels while moving.

Children need to learn concepts from all four aspects of movement (body, space, effort, relationships). From the body aspect, children need to explore different ways their body parts can move, different shapes the body can make (round, wide, narrow, twisted, and angular), different locomotor patterns (skip, leap, gallop, slide), different body actions (rise/fall, swing, turn, push/pull, shake, and sway), and the symmetry and asymmetry of their body and different body shapes. From the effort aspect children need to explore strong and gentle force, fast and slow speed, bound and free flow, and direct and flexible use of space. From the space aspect children need to explore moving at different levels (high, medium, low), in different directions (forward, backwards, sideways, diagonal, up, down), and on different pathways (curved, straight, angular). Finally, children need to explore different relationships such as matching a partner, contrasting a partner, and moving over, under, around, and through partners making different shapes.

Aesthetic Experience in Dance

Although movement concepts are the basic vocabulary of dance, dance is more than movement. Dance is an aesthetic experience. Children can have aesthetic experiences and movement can become dance when the children have a "heightened awareness" of the feeling and shape of the movement (Stinson, 1988). To help children gain this heightened awareness, teachers need to ask children how the movement feels while they are moving and how they feel inside their muscles and torsos. Teachers need to ask children to pay attention to the shape of their bodies, the shapes of different body parts, and the way body parts are moving in space. Teachers need to help children concentrate on how their total body feels and what they experience when they dance. In dance we try to touch children's spirits. We try to focus on their inner experience of their moving selves.

Themes in Dance

Dance choreographers create dances to express or represent an idea, image, or theme. From ballet stories such as "Swan Lake" or "Romeo and Juliet" to modern dance themes of "Prairie" and "When Push Comes to Shove," professional dance choreographers explore a wide range of topics through dance. Dance choreography aims to communicate the meaning and essence of an idea through movement. Movement is a unique mode for expressing aspects of the meaning of an idea, image, or theme that cannot be expressed through other modes of communication such as poetry, painting, music, drama, and literature.

Ideas, images, or themes for children's creative dance choreography can be drawn from topics the children are studying in their classroom. Many excellent suggestions are available (see citations at the end of this chapter) ranging from snow, baking bread (Stinson, 1988), instruments, rhythm (Joyce, 1994), bubbles, cats (Purcell, 1994), to butterflies (Clements & Oosten, 1995).

When selecting a topic for children's dance choreography teachers need to choose topics that are rich with potential movement content. Dance needs to focus on movement and how movement can enhance children's understanding of specified concepts. One danger is that dance lessons can easily slip from experiences of representing the essence of an idea through movement, to imitating and pretending. For example, having children stand with their arms circled around their heads pretending to be trees is imitation, but not dance, about trees. In a dance representing the essence of trees through movement, children explore different curved and angular shapes suggested by the shapes of branches as well as different round, pointy, narrow, and wide shapes suggested by the shapes of leaves. Children also explore different ways of swaying, with a variety of body parts and whole body, as well as different swirling and leaping movements suggested by branches swaying and leaves blowing in the wind. The goal of the dance lesson would be to feel and interpret the movement and shapes associated with trees but not to imitate or pretend to be trees.

The following is an example of an integrative dance lesson on the theme of prey and predator relationships. The idea was originally suggested by Dianna Bandhauer, a teacher at Lecanto Primary School in Lecanto, Florida. It is designed to accommodate the limited space of a classroom and is given here in script form.

Sample Integrative Dance Lesson

MOVEMENT CONCEPTS: Bound flow (movement that is hesitant, highly controlled, and can be stopped at any time), stretch and curl.

INTEGRATIVE THEME: *Prey and Predator*

OBJECTIVES

As a result of participating in this learning experience, children will improve their ability to

1. Understand, feel and show bound flow (especially those aspects of bound flow movement that are cautious, wary, frightened, calculating, and alert)
2. Stretch and curl in different ways
3. Lead with different body parts while traveling

INTRODUCTION

Our theme is prey and predator and the kinesthetic feeling, that is, the feeling inside your muscles, of prey and predator movement. The major movement concept we will work on today is bound flow. Bound flow is movement that can be stopped at any time. The flow of the movement is bound. Spread out around your desks and face me. Slowly and cautiously walk toward me. Stop. (Repeat.) Be ready to stop the instant I say stop. Feel the feeling inside you knowing that you must travel slowly and stop instantly. This is called "bound flow."

EXPLORING THE MOVEMENT CONCEPT AND THEME

This time watch me and stop the instant you see me start to move, pause, and then slowly start walking again. [As the children walk toward you, be very still and then suddenly move your arm. Repeat until some children have reached the front of the room.] Regroup. Let's try it again. Move slowly, cautiously, and control the flow of your movement so you can stop the instant you see me move. Concentrate on how it feels to move with bound flow.

This time travel on different pathways throughout the desks with bound flow. Don't move into anyone else's personal space. Stop each time you see me move.

This time pick what you think is a safe a spot in the room, a den. Plan a pathway to that spot that will get you there without anyone detecting where you are trying to go. Move with bound flow. Stop when you feel the need to be cautious, when you want to disguise your pathway, or when you think someone dangerous to you can see you move. When you get there stop and slowly, warily, scan the terrain as if you were prey watching for some unseen predator. Notice how you feel inside when you stop and scan. Repeat several times picking a new spot each time.

This time when you get to your safe spot, scan and then change your level by curling. Find a shape that represents hiding, fear.

Repeat several times changing the curled shape each time. [Where the chairs and desks are stable, children can curl on or under the furniture.] Repeat and each time you travel lead with a different body part; maintain the sense of being prey. Sometimes lead with your back, side, head, hands, feet. Each time you stop, slowly curl into a shape that shows you are prey. Try to do a different shape each time.

Now, beginning in your safe space, explore stretching slowly out of your den to see if it is safe, look around and curl back into your den. When you stretch, slowly extend your body parts and end as stretched as you can be. Feel the stretch in all of your muscles. Repeat several times. Now stretch out of your den, travel, and curl into a different den.

Still moving with bound flow and being cautious not to let anyone notice you moving, change your attitude to that of a predator. Imagine a prey somewhere in this room—decide on a pathway that will get you very close to the prey but one that you can move on undetected. Be calculating and patient. Notice how you feel inside as predator. When you reach the spot hold a position at a different level that will enable you to move on the prey when the time comes. Think about the tension in your muscles. Repeat several times.

This time as you travel try leading with different body parts such as your back, side, head, hands, and feet. Now explore stretching but capture the idea of a predator. Slowly stretch out of your hiding place to see if you can see your prey. Look around and if your prey is looking toward you, freeze and then, when you can move undetected, curl back into your hiding place. Repeat several times. Now stretch out of your den, really stretch your muscles, travel leading with different body parts, and curl into a different hiding place.

CULMINATING DANCE

With a partner create, refine, and practice a dance sequence using bound flow, stretching, curling, and traveling leading with different body parts. Represent the idea and feeling of prey and predator. Here is one possible dance structure, but you can modify this structure to represent the theme better. First, using bound flow, the prey moves and freezes, feels safe, then starts to explore. The predator then moves and freezes. The prey senses the predator but cannot see the predator and moves to a new spot and curls into hiding. The predator sees the prey and begins to stalk. The prey continues to move sensing the predator. The predator closes in. Make up your own ending.

In summary, a concept-focused approach to children's dance enables children to acquire the movement vocabulary of dance, to develop their aesthetic sensitivity in dance, and to create their own dances. It also enables children to learn about classroom topics through the bodily-kinesthetic mode of learning. Children then can develop a more elaborated understanding of the topic.

Concept-Focused Units in Games

In the games content area, as in dance, movement concepts are the basic vocabulary that children need to acquire in order to form a solid foundation for the later development of specialized sport skills. Table 11.2 lists these concepts. Under the body aspect are listed the fundamental skills of throwing, catching, kicking, dribbling, and striking. The concepts listed under the effort aspect are combined with the skills to help children learn to use skills in game-like situations. For example, children need to learn to dribble fast and slow; to throw with strong and light force, to kick with strong and light force, to dribble with bound and free flow, and to strike with rackets with strong and light force. The concepts under space also are combined with the skills to help children learn to perform in game-like situations. Children need to learn to catch balls at high, medium, and low levels; to dribble on different pathways; to dribble traveling forward, sideways, and backwards; and to strike balls at high, medium, and low levels. The relationship aspects help children understand basic mechanical principles such as how the direction of ball flight is caused by the angle of the hand or racket surface and the direction of force. Relationship aspects also include all of the basic offensive and defensive strategy concepts that children need to learn to have successful game experiences.

Game movement concepts, in particular those dealing with force, speed, and ball flight, can be integrated with science and mathematics lessons. Measuring distances of court boundaries and of classmates' performances of throwing, kicking, jumping, and striking skills can be integrated into mathematics lessons as can batting percentages (batting "averages"), scoring averages, win/loss percentages, and counting with younger children. Finally, the group interactions that occur in competitive game play with older children can be used to help children understand democratic principles taught in social studies (described later in this chapter).

Ideas for teaching a concept-focused approach to games will be discussed next. The first section focuses on skills and the second section on basic game strategy.

Section One: Teaching Skills and Concepts with Challenge Tasks

One technique for teaching skills using a concept-focused approach is to give children "challenge tasks." Challenge tasks are activities focused on a movement concept that challenge children to improve their ability to perform a skill. Challenge tasks also challenge children to apply their knowledge of a movement concept to either solve a problem or explore how the movement concept can be used in different ways. What follows are sample challenge tasks. Each task is completed in groups of 2–4. Tasks can include both movement and written components.

Sample Challenge Tasks

DRIBBLING WITH HANDS OR FEET
Possible concepts to use with dribbling with hands or feet:
1. pathways: straight/curved/angular
2. speed: fast/slow, accelerate/decelerate
3. directions: forward/backward/sideways
4. relationships: lead, follow
5. relationships: over, under, around

Sample challenge tasks:

Pathways. Using cones, jump ropes, and hoops design a dribbling course (like an obstacle course) that challenges your group to practice and improve dribbling with hands on different pathways. Make some straight, curved, and angular pathways using the equipment. Answer the following questions: What impact does the pathway have on the speed of dribbling? Why would you need to dribble on different pathways in games? Where outside of physical education do you travel on straight, curved, and angular pathways? Draw a picture using straight, curved, and angular lines.

Speed. Using cones, design a dribbling course that challenges your group to practice accelerating to a fast speed and decelerating to a slow speed while dribbling with your feet. Answer the following questions:

How far apart should you space cones when dribbling fast and slow? When in a soccer-type game, would you be able to dribble fast? When would you have to dribble slow? What is momentum? What do you need to do with your feet and center of gravity to slow down momentum? What slows down the momentum of a rolling ball? Which would be more difficult to dribble fast: a shoebox or a ball? Why?

Over, under, around. Using open (split) hoops stuck in tall cones to form arches, jump ropes, and short cones, design a dribbling course that challenges your group to practice going under, over, and around. Answer the following questions: Which part of your course is easier? More difficult? Why? What changes in force do you need to make when you dribble over and under an obstacle? How do you generate more and less force?

TOSSING, THROWING, KICKING, AND STRIKING FOR ACCURACY

Possible concepts to use with tossing, throwing, kicking, and striking for accuracy

1. levels: high/medium/low
2. force: strong/light, distance: near/far

Sample challenge tasks:

Levels. Using hoops, cones, different sized shapes cut out of paper (to tape to a wall), and tape, design several tasks to challenge your group to practice striking a plastic ball with your hand (or racket) to different targets at different levels. Answer the following questions: Where on the ball do you apply force strike to a high, medium, and low level? What is the relation between the angle of your hand (or racket) and the flight of the ball? What is the relation between the direction of your arm swing and the flight of the ball? When in a net game would you strike a ball to high and low levels?

Force/distance. Using hoops, cones, and different sized shapes cut out of paper (to tape to a wall), design several tasks to challenge your group to practice kicking to different targets from different distances. Answer the following questions: Which target and distance was more difficult and why? What did you need to do with your leg to kick with more force? What effect does the range of motion of the leg have on the force you can generate? What is the relation between the force you kick and the distance the ball travels? What principles of levers were involved?

CATCHING AND PASSING WITH THE HANDS AND RECEIVING AND PASSING WITH THE FEET

Possible concepts to use with catching, receiving, and passing:

1. directions: forward/backward/sideways
2. air pathways: high and loopy passes/medium level and straight passes

3. force: strong/light
4. levels: high/medium/low

Sample challenge tasks:

Directions. Design three tasks that challenge you and your partner to practice passing and moving to catch from different directions. Answer the following questions: What do you do with your hands, arms, and body to absorb force? What mechanical principles are involved with absorbing force? Which is more difficult: receiving from behind, the side, the front and why?

Force. Using cones, design a task that challenges you and your partner to pass with your feet four times, each time using different amounts of force. Answer the following questions: How do you absorb force with your feet? What is the difference between absorbing strong and light force? When in a soccer-type game would you kick with strong and with light force and why? What is the difference between generating strong and light force with a kick? What effect does the range of motion of the leg have on the force you can generate?

Levels. Design three tasks that challenge you and your partner to practice throwing and moving to catch at different levels. Answer the following questions: When would you need to throw and catch at different levels in basketball-type games? How would your throw change if your teammate was guarded or unguarded? What do you do to absorb force? Which level is most difficult and why? How would your movement change with different sized objects?

DRIBBLING AND SHOOTING WITH HANDS OR FEET

Possible concepts to use with dribbling and shooting with hands or feet

1. pathways: straight/curved/angular
2. speed: fast/slow, accelerate/decelerate
3. relationships: over, under, around
4. levels: shoot to high/medium/low levels

Sample challenge tasks:

Levels. Using cones, jump ropes, shapes cut out of paper, and tape, design a dribbling course that ends with a shot on goal (kick the ball to a target on the wall) to challenge your group to practice dribbling and shooting to different levels. Answer the following questions: Where and how do you apply force to a ball to change the level of the kick? When would you need to kick to high and low levels in a soccer-type game and why?

Pathways. Using cones, jump ropes, and hoops, design a dribbling course that ends with a shot on goal (kick the ball through a target) to challenge your group to practice dribbling on different pathways and shooting with feet. Include some straight, curved, and angular pathways.

What impact does the pathway have on the speed of dribbling? Why would you need to dribble on different pathways in games?

Speed. Using cones and a child-sized basketball hoop, design a dribbling course which challenges your group to practice accelerating to a fast speed and ends with a shot on goal. When in a basketball-type game would you be able to dribble fast? When would you have to dribble slow? What do you need to do with the ball and your body position when you change from fast to slow and from slow to fast?

Over, under, around. Using open (split) hoops stuck in tall cones to form arches, jump ropes, cones, and a child-sized basketball hoop, design a dribbling course which challenges your group to practice going under, over, and around and ends with a shot on goal. Which part of your course is easier and more difficult? Why?

Game Play and Basic Strategy Concepts

Developmentally appropriate games content for most children in grades K–2 are skills and movement concepts. Children in grades 3–5, however, are ready to learn modified games and the basic strategy concepts that are part of all games. There are two concept-focused approaches to teaching children game play. The first is to have children play or design their own simple games based on a skill and movement concept. After practicing the skills using a challenge course, the children can design a simple game of two versus two or three versus three that will enable them to practice their skills in a more complex game situation. Most children will design a game that will focus on the skill assigned. If they don't, the teacher will have to stop the game and get the children back on task.

SAMPLE CHILD-DESIGNED GAMES TASKS BASED ON SKILL/MOVEMENT CONCEPT:

Dribbling on different pathways. After practicing dribbling on different pathways, use cones and hoops to design a two-versus-two game during which you practice dribbling on different pathways. Be sure all members of your group are active.

Dribbling and shooting with feet. After practicing dribbling and shooting with feet, use cones for boundaries and goals and design a three-versus-three game during which you practice dribbling and shooting. Be sure all members of your group are active.

The second concept-focused approach is to have children play or design simple 2-versus-2 or 3-versus-3 games to practice a basic strategy concept (see list of strategies in Table 11.2). First, have children practice the strategy concept using a task that is not a game. Once children understand the strategy, have them design their own game to continue to practice using that concept in a game.

SAMPLE PRACTICES AND CHILD-DESIGNED GAMES TASKS BASED ON STRATEGY CONCEPTS:

Dribble keeping the body between the defender and the ball

Practice task: Scatter cones evenly throughout the gym or playground. Dribble about the space. When you come near a cone pretend that the cone is a defender and keep your body between the defender and the ball.

Child-designed game task: In groups of four, design a game (using hoops and ropes if needed) during which you practice dribbling keeping the body between the defender and the ball. Be sure all members of your group are active.

Cutting into a space, sending a lead pass

Practice task: In groups of three, have one person stand in a hoop with a ball and have a teammate receiver stand about five yards away guarded by a defender standing between the passer and receiver and about six inches from the receiver. The receiver quickly fakes and dodges the defender and then cuts to receive a lead pass from the passer. The passer must not pass unless the receiver gets free and must anticipate and send the pass ahead of the receiver so the receiver can catch it on the run.

Child-designed game task: In groups of four, design a game during which you practice cutting into a space and sending lead passes. You may choose to have scoring or no scoring.

Two offense versus one defense fast break

Practice task: In groups of three, have two offense players pass back and forth while traveling across the playground and send lead passes until one player shoots for a goal. Have one defender begin by standing ball side/goal side and then trying to intercept or steal the ball.

Child-designed game task: In groups of four, design a game with two targets for shooting to score during which you practice sending lead passes and attempting fast breaks.

Process Skill-Focused Unit: Communication

This section describes how dance can be used in conjunction with other subject areas for teaching a process skill unit. A communication skill unit has been discussed in previous chapters. Examples of activities from dance that can be included in that communication skill unit are presented.

Children's movement is expressed naturally through dance and physical education activities. Teachers support and build on these natural expressions as they help children construct broader and deeper means of expressing and controlling their movement. Teachers support children's movement experiences by creating a musically stimulating environment. Such an environment encourages children to extend their dance experiences by engaging with music-making materials. It also encourages children to consider through what music their physical activities such as stretching and curling or jumping can be expressed. For example, stretching and curling might be expressed in a slow, controlled melody while jumping might be expressed in a fast, explosive melody.

Movement Conversations

Movement conversation activities give children the chance to explore the meaning and structure of conversations through movement. Conversations, as means for communication, have a structure in which one person speaks, then the other responds. This structure and what it means to children can be explored through movement conversations. Activities include having children in partners have movement conversations (i.e., one person moves and the other responds with movement) first using only their fingers, then their hands and head, then their knees, then elbows, then whole body. Next, they take three different body parts and create a dance sequence showing movement conversations with three body parts.

A similar call and respond structure can be explored through rhythm. Children have a rhythm movement conversation first by clapping. One child "communicates" a rhythm by clapping and the other responds. Next the children create a rhythm conversation by clapping, stomping, and clapping on different body parts. Finally, the children can have a rhythm conversation using whole body movements.

Communicating Emotions in Dance

Children can express and communicate emotions through dance movement. One lesson on expressing emotions through dance movement could begin by having the children travel showing first joy and then sadness. The children then would discuss the differences in their movement when they showed joy and sadness. They then could create short sequences. Expressing either joy or sadness, they would select a starting shape, travel, and end in a shape. They would show their sequence to partners who guess which emotion was being expressed. They then could explore and create short dance sequences communicating the following emotions: worry, fear, nervousness, excitement, anger, and confusion. They would show one sequence to classmates who try to identify the emotion. They would discuss the different movements and the quality (the components of effort in Table 11.1) of movement associated with each emotion. For example, joy might include leaps, jumps, and skipping using light force, quick speed, and free flow.

Anger might include both quick and slow movements, strong force, bound flow, tension in the muscles, and movements at a medium level. Sadness might include slow, heavy movements at a low level.

It is important to help children understand that dance is different from drama in the same way that an expressionist painting is different from a photograph. To dance an anger dance means to represent that emotion through movement rather than act like an angry person. Dancers are free to do movements and make shapes that exaggerate aspects of the emotion and are more communicative and expressive. Dance is not imitation; it is representation.

Music is used to express emotion. As children's expression of emotion through dance is fostered, music is introduced after children have demonstrated some ability at using dance. Using both dance and music to express emotion is complex. So, music as a means of expressing emotion can be explored separately from dance initially and then added when children show some understanding of both. At this point children are encouraged to occasionally combine music with their dance, planning the use of both to express emotions. Because this is a complex process, it is best developed in the upper grades although younger children may occasionally combine both.

Communicating Abstract Ideas

For older grades, the idea of expressing an idea can be extended to abstract concepts being studied in a particular unit. The following ideas would be possible dance content: power, isolation, loneliness, community, togetherness, support, caring, confusion, unity, curiosity, individuality, justice, and freedom. The task for children would be for groups of 4–6 students to communicate the meaning of an idea by creating tableaus. A tableau is like a still picture of a group scene frozen in time, a group statue, or a group shape. This picture of a group scene represents the abstract idea. More than a photograph of a group scene, a tableau is like an expressionist painting representing the abstract concept. Children would be given either a set of ideas or asked to create 2–3 tableaus for each idea. Then the group would design some movement transitions to connect the three tableaus to become a dance sequence.

Communicating a Story

Dance can be used to communicate a story. This story might be one the children wrote themselves, a story from literature, or a historical story. Stories might be about Robin Hood, Frederick Douglass, Helen Keller, life on the prairie, or ancient Egyptian life along the Nile. Stories can also represent sequences of events in science such as the cycle of a storm, the human digestive system, the human circulatory system, the life cycle of butterflies, the growth of a flower, or the creation of a river delta (fans).

Dance stories, like all dance, aim to represent rather than imitate, pantomime, or act out the story or event. Children select the main ideas and time line that would most effectively capture the essence of the story they want to tell. They do not need to act out each part, rather, they select ideas that highlight or capture the essence of the story. They then explore different movements and group shapes that could represent their ideas, put ideas together, and then refine their dance story. They then can add a narrative introduction in which they explain their aesthetic intent, what they represented, and why.

For younger children the teacher will need to help develop the story line. For example, in a first grade dance about a storm, the main ideas could be about clouds, lightning, thunder, rain, and puddles. Children could first explore the curved shape of clouds by drawing different curved pathways with their hands at all levels all around their bodies, by exploring curved shapes of their bodies, by traveling gently on curved pathways while softly drawing curved pathways in the air and then ending in a curved shape. Next, for lightning, children could explore traveling quickly with strong force on angular pathways, jumping in the air making angular shapes, landing in an angular shape, and then making three sharp, quick, strong angular shapes. For thunder, children could explore running and making thrusting jumps and big jumps. For rain and puddles, children could explore quick and then slow gentle tapping movements as they slowly sink to the floor and end in a relaxed, flat shape.

The use of music and dance to express ideas as well as emotions is important as well. Again this is complex and requires students to have a meaningful understanding of the idea, of how it can be expressed in dance, and of how it can be expressed in music. An idea is expressed separately, at first, through dance and through music. It may be expressed eventually through a combination of both but only after children have a meaningful understanding of the ideas in dance and in music.

Content and Process Skill-Focused Unit: Diversity

A content and process skill-focused unit focuses on a topic as well as on process skills. Dance fits well into content and process skill-focused units because it includes both movement skills and choreographic skills while focusing on representing a theme or expressing a feeling or idea. The content and process skill-focused unit on diversity, described in previous chapters, would be greatly enhanced by including movement and choreographic skills from dance. Three types of dance activities can be easily incorporated in a unit on diversity: folk dance, child-designed folk dance, and creative dance.

Folk Dance and Festivals

Across cultures, dance is a form of cultural expression. As a formal performing art form, choreographers and dance companies around the world perform and interpret various cultural themes. More informally, dance has long been used in various cultural rites and rituals, celebrations, holidays, social gatherings, and festivals. Throughout history and around the world people have gathered together to dance. From American square dance, to break dancing, to the minuet, dance has been used to represent and celebrate parts of a culture. Often called "folk" dance, these dances are used in courtship, to demonstrate skill and prowess, and to celebrate and represent events, religious rituals, seasonal occasions, animals, features of the natural environment, war, trades, vocations, and myths.

Because it focuses on cultural themes, folk dance can make an important contribution to an integrated unit on diversity. In this unit, children can research and learn the dances from cultures they are studying. They can design costumes and props. They not only need to learn the steps of the dance but also to learn the stylistic differences that are part of the folk dance. They can research the stories behind the dances and the meaning of the dances within the culture they are studying.

Folk festivals are appropriate for a unit on diversity. Leah Creque-Harris (1994) describes in detail the tradition of the Caribbean Carnival and how it can be used as a basis for classroom work on cultural diversity. She suggests that the Caribbean Carnival is rich with opportunities to explore cultural diversity because of its roots in the indigenous, African, European, and Asian cultures that are part of the Caribbean. These Carnivals include drama, dance, music, and masquerade including elaborate masks and costumes. Drama and masquerade trace the history of the region as do the multiple cultural influences that are evident in various dances.

Child-Designed Folk Dance

Learning the precise dances, movement style, and modes of expression of the folk dances of different cultures can help children understand diversity. However, children also can design their own folk dances based on the cultures they are studying (Rovegno & Bandhauer, 1992). Child-designed folk dances can focus on aspects of the children's cultures or on different cultural and ethnic groups they are studying.

To begin a child-designed folk dance lesson, the children in groups of 4–6 discuss the cultural or ethnic group they have been studying. The aim of this discussion is to generate ideas for the focus of the folk dance. Ideas might include: stories, myths, legends, traditions, rituals, rites, seasonal events, holidays, festivals, land formations, foods, native plants, animals, agriculture, hunting, climate, clothing styles, tourist sites, architecture, types of housing, typical occupations, and recreational activities.

Once the children have selected ideas for their dance, they study the music and instruments of the culture or ethnic group. They choose music with an appropriate beat and style or compose or play their own music using available instruments. They then design the formations, locomotor steps, and simple gestures that make up their dance.

If the children are not already familiar with traditional folk dance formations and locomotor steps, the teacher may need to teach them. Formations from which children can select include: circles, double circles, lines, double lines, partner circles, partner lines, squares, and diamonds. Locomotor steps include: walk, skip, hop, step-hop, schottische (3 steps then 1 hop), slide, gallop, jump, step and kick, turn, leap, and grapevine (step to side, step and cross one leg behind, step to side, step and cross one leg in front).

To create their dance, the children combine locomotor steps with simple gestures or arm positions that represent the different ideas in the folk dance. They then plan different formations for each section of the dance, put the dance together and practice it. They also can make costumes and props to enhance their message.

Creative Dance on Diversity

Creative dance also can be part of a unit on diversity. One possible theme is a dance sequence entitled "Celebrating Diversity." In groups of three to six, each child creates a short, personal movement phrase (4–8 counts) demonstrating something unique or special about themselves and showing a personal movement style. Each child then teaches the other children in the group how to perform his or her personal movement phrase. The full dance begins by having each child, alone, perform her or his personal movement phrase. Then the group as a whole dances each child's personal phrase. Finally, the children create an ending section that combines or integrates their personal styles. Children also can select music for their dance that helps them express their personal style or an idea that represents them.

Issue-Focused Units: Conflict Resolution and Peace

For children working on an integrated unit on conflict resolution and peace as described in earlier chapters, competitive games and sports are excellent activities for learning about the processes and issues involved in conflict resolution. The formal system used in sport for conflict resolution includes standardized rules and paid referees to ensure that the rules are kept. Even with these formal systems, problems arise. Over time, as athletes and equipment improve, the rules are modified in order to maintain the character of the game and to keep an even balance between offense and defense.

Ideally, formal sport is not played in elementary physical education. The rules of formal sports should be modified to meet the developmental level of children. There are no paid referees. Instead, informal systems are used to keep the game fair and settle disputes. Children and teachers modify rules, equipment, and playing areas; often design their own games; and are responsible for self-refereeing. Although the teacher often decides what game to play and acts as a referee, these responsibilities can be given to children. When children design a game, develop and modify game rules, and are responsible for refereeing and settling disputes, they have the opportunity to learn valuable lessons about conflict resolution.

Having children design games is developmentally appropriate for grades three and older. There are two major types of games that can be used: net games (high net volleyball-type games and low net racket-type games) and "invasion" games such as tag, soccer, basketball, and hockey. When first teaching children about conflict resolution and peace in games, it is wise to begin with net games because the children will need only to negotiate with a partner.

Designing Net Games

Before children can design and play a net game, they must be skilled enough to keep a rally going. A rally occurs when partners successfully strike a ball back and forth across the net. It is important to use equipment appropriate for each child's developmental level. The easiest equipment for striking is a large, light plastic ball and striking with hands. A little more difficult to use are child-sized, lightweight rackets and soft, small balls with a slow bounce (not tennis balls which travel too quickly). Once children manage to sustain a cooperative rally, they can begin designing a net game.

The structure of child-designed games lessons is play-discuss-play. Children play the game, discuss the problems and successes and make needed modifications, then play again to see if they successfully improved the game.

To help children learn about conflict resolution, they need to be in situations where they have to negotiate. Part of successful negotiation in games means understanding the issues and problems involved in the game and what it means to have fair rules and regulations. To do this with net games, the children could begin to experiment with boundaries of different sizes.

Using ropes or cones, the children would set sideline boundaries that make a very narrow court (so narrow that keeping a rally going would be very difficult). After the children attempt a rally, they discuss the problems with the game. Then the children set sidelines that are very wide (so wide that a ball could be hit that would be in bounds but impossible for the receiver to get near). After the children attempt a rally, they discuss the problems with narrow and wide boundaries and decide on a principle of fairness to apply to decide how to set fair boundaries (e.g., fair boundaries are large enough that players can keep a rally going, but small enough so that the receiver has a chance to get to the ball). Then the children negotiate and experiment with different boundaries until each pair has agreed on sidelines that work for them. The above lesson activities could be repeated for end lines.

Next the children could decide on a system of scoring. This includes deciding on how points are scored (only by the server or by either player), the penalties for hitting a ball out of bounds, serving rotation, and the number of points in a game. The children play and negotiate any problems that arise.

Finally, if the children have not already recognized the need for a service box or a serving line, they could experiment with serving from different parts of the court and serving into boxes of different sizes. A class discussion could establish the kinds of rules needed to insure the receiver has a fair chance to return the ball.

Designing Tag and Other Invasion Games

Once the children have learned to negotiate with a partner in a less complex net game, they can begin to learn about resolving conflicts in team games. They need to begin with simple group tag games because adding the demands of kicking or throwing balls makes the lesson too complex. Once children have acquired the process skills and knowledge of how to design group tag games, they can easily design modified soccer-, basketball-, and hockey-type games to work on game strategy (Bandhauer & Rovegno, 1992).

The children can start by playing tag in groups of 4–6 with one tagger using very small boundaries. Cones and jump ropes can be used to set boundaries. Flag football flags can be used, if available. The children play tag and then discuss the problems with small boundaries. Then, the children could experiment playing tag with no boundaries and again discuss the problems. Next, the group can experiment with different sized boundaries until they agree on boundaries that make a good game. Once the children have worked on boundaries they need to develop rules (e.g., you can't run out of bounds, you can't push someone's hand away who is trying to take your flag), consequences (e.g., if you go out of bounds you lose your flag to the other team), and scoring systems.

To help children resolve conflicts, they need to understand the principles of fairness and the reasons behind rules that are relevant to the context and issue. After agreeing on good boundaries, the children can identify the principle of fairness for determining the size of boundaries. They also can discuss what makes a good tag game and a good invasion game. A good game is a game in which the opportunities for offense (runners) and the defense (taggers) are equal. In tag this means that the taggers have opportunities to tag and runners have opportunities to get free. In modified soccer-, basketball-, and hockey-type games a good game happens when it is not too difficult nor too easy to score and not too difficult nor too easy to stop a score. In other words, there is a balance between offense and defense. The next step can be to modify the tag game to be closer to games such as basketball and soccer. The children can make up a team tag game (2 versus 2 or 3 versus 3) with an offensive team beginning behind an end line trying to get to the opposite end line guarded by a defensive team. Using the same processes as before, they can set boundaries and determine rules for scoring and play. Problems will occur. When this happens children discuss problems with the rules, modify the rules, and set consequences for breaking rules. The children play again and "test" their modified rules and consequences. Problems and disputes occur because children will not initially design enough rules and consequences to deal with situations that arise. Don't referee. Have the children play, discuss problems, modify and add rules and consequences, and play again until they have designed a game that works and is fair for both teams. This process might take several lessons.

During these lessons periodically the children can discuss the process of negotiating disputes and deciding on rules and rule modifications. They can identify problems with their group discussions and group work—when it works well, when it works poorly, and why. They can develop norms for group work and principles for negotiating. Finally, they can discuss the issues of balancing the needs and rights of people on different sides of an issue, principles of fairness, and issues and problems with rules and consequences.

Once children have the knowledge of how to design basic tag games, they can use their knowledge and skill to design soccer-type, basketball-type, and hockey-type games. These games can be done in recess and physical education. In schools where children are taught how to design their games and resolve problems in physical education lessons, teachers notice there is transfer to recess. Children are more likely to engage in active game play (they don't need a teacher to get the game organized) and there are few arguments.

Project-Focused Units: Air Quality

With project-focused units, children try to solve a problem. An integrated air quality project unit was described in other chapters. To link physical education to this unit children could study cardio-respiratory endurance, an important component of fitness. Cardio-respiratory endurance is the ability of the circulatory and respiratory systems to work well while exercising. The ability of the lungs to take adequate oxygen from the air is related to the condition of the air including air quality, temperature, humidity, and wind speed.

Cardio-respiratory endurance is as important for children as it is for adults. Because children's physiologies and psychologies differ from adults, children need to participate in fitness activities that are appropriate for them. The major goal is for children to participate in enjoyable, vigorous physical activities. A brisk walking program is recommended here because it is safe for adults and children and offers an appropriate activity children can do with family members after school. If children do not like walking, they can substitute any vigorous activity that increases their heart rate.

As part of an integrated unit on air quality, children would study the importance of strong cardio-respiratory endurance for preventing heart disease. Also, they read about the effect of exercising in polluted air and the interactions between asthma and exercise and extreme temperatures. They then investigate how to design exercise programs that are safe and effective. They also need to learn to measure resting heart rate, exercising heart rate, and breathing rates. They then plan individual exercise programs of brisk walking. Each week they keep a record of the distance and time they walk. Successful integration of a walking program with classroom subjects can include math problems dealing with distances traveled per child per week and mapping the total class distance from city to city and state to state on a map (Francis, 1993). Each month children also can graph their resting heart rate, exercising heart rate and breathing rate. A decrease in resting heart rate indicates an improved level of fitness. Across several months they can keep journals describing differences in how they feel when they exercise when the temperature is hot and cold and when the humidity is high and low. Writing assignments involve them in describing how they feel about exercising, what they notice in the environment when they walk, and what they like and dislike about walking.

Case Study–Focused Unit: The Manager of a National Forest

In previous chapters a case study involving the development of a job description for the manager of a national forest was described. To get a realistic sense of the natural environment under the care of the forest manager, the children could take a field trip to the national forest and experience activities related to the Forest Manager's job. National forests provide a host of opportunities for physically active recreation. One of the most common is hiking the forest trails. Students also can learn about orienteering and how to read a compass. Learning about compasses can be related to learning about magnetism, compass points, topography maps, latitude, longitude, the earth's magnetic field, and magnetic and geographic poles. Children can work on short orienteering courses at school until they are proficient enough to do an orienteering course in the forest. As part of their field trip they also can experience climbing an observation tower or trees. They can write to the state agricultural extension office and ask for some tree seedlings to plant. To plant the seedlings they will need to prepare the soil and haul water to the site. They also can try other recreational activities in the forest such as fishing.

SUMMARY

Physical education provides a host of activities teachers can use in integrated units. Important physical education content can be taught through movement concepts, dance, games, fitness, and outdoor activities. Physical education is inherently "hands on" and gives children a unique mode for learning about concepts.

REFERENCES

Allen, V. L. (1996). A critical look at integration. *Teaching Elementary Physical Education*, 7 (3), 12–14.

Bandhauer, D., & Rovegno, I. (1992). Teaching game structure and strategy. *Teaching Elementary Physical Education*, 3 (6) 7–9.

Clements, R. L., & Oosten, M. (1995). Creating and implementing preschool movement narratives. *Journal of Physical Education, Recreation, and Dance*, 66 (3), 24–29.

Creque-Harris, L. (1994). Carnival: Expanding the classroom boundaries. *Journal of Physical Education, Recreation, and Dance*, 65 (5), 31–35, 47.

Francis, L. L. (1993). Integrating a school walk/jog program with other classroom subjects. *Journal of Physical Education, Recreation, and Dance*, 64 (6), 12–13.

Gardner, H. (1983). *Frames of mind*. New York: Basic Books.

Johnson, M. (1987). *The body in the mind: The bodily basis of meaning, imagination, and reason*. Chicago: University of Chicago Press.

Joyce, M. (1994). *First steps in teaching creative dance to children*. Mountain View, CA: Mayfield.

Laban, R. (1948). *Modern educational dance*. London: MacDonald and Evans.

Miller, P. H. (1983). *Theories of Developmental Psychology.* San Francisco: W. H. Freeman and Co.

Morley, V. (1994). Integrating movement and music with social studies. *Teaching Elementary Physical Education, 5* (6), 9–11.

Moving into the future national physical education standards: A guide to content and assessment. (1995). St. Louis, MO: Mosby.

Music Educators National Conference (1994). *The school music program: A new vision. The K–12 national standards, preK standards, and what they mean to music educators.* Reston, VA: Music Educators National Conference.

Purcell, T. (1994). *Teaching children dance: Becoming a master teacher.* Champaign, IL: Human Kinetics.

Rovegno, I., & Bandhauer, D. (1992). Child-designed folk dance: Seeking the deeper meaning. *Teaching Elementary Physical Education, 3* (5), 13–14.

Salz, A. E. (1980). Score a curriculum victory with sports. *Instructor, 89* (3), 62–64.

Stevens, D. A. (1994). Integrated learning: Collaboration among teachers. *Teaching Elementary Physical Education, 5* (6), 7–8.

Stinson, S. (1988). *Dance for young children: Finding the magic in movement.* Reston, VA: American Alliance for Health, Physical Education, Recreation, and Dance.

Werner, P. (1994a). Teaching reading in physical education. *Teaching Elementary Physical Education, 5* (6), 14–15.

Werner, P. (1994b). Whole physical education. *Journal of Physical Education, Recreation, and Dance, 65* (6), 40–44.

INDEX